THE ABBEY AND MINT OF BURY ST EDMUNDS TO 1279

THE BRITISH NUMISMATIC SOCIETY SPECIAL PUBLICATIONS SERIES

This Special Publication series was established in 1991, financed by the generous bequest of the late Mr Roy Osborne (1913–1990). The monographs that appear in it are peer reviewed, as are the contributions to the Society's *British Numismatic Journal*. This volume has been edited for the Society by Dr Martin Allen.

This work on the *Abbey and Mint of Bury St Edmunds to 1279* by Dr Robin Eaglen, FSA presents an account of the ecclesiastical mint of Bury St Edmunds from its origins in the mid-eleventh century down to to the recoinage 1279, set in its historical context. It draws on both documentary evidence and on a meticulous study of the surviving coinage.

Mark Blackburn
President, British Numismatic Society

1. *The English Coinage 1180–1247: Money, Mints and Exchanges*, by John D. Brand, 1994.
2. *The Soho Mint and the Industrialization of Money*, by Richard Doty, 1998.
3. *Tokens of the Industrial Revolution. Foreign Silver Coins Countermarked for use in Great Britain, c.1787–1828*, by Harrington E. Manville, 2001.
4. *The Durham Mint*, by Martin Allen, 2003.
5. *The Abbey and Mint of Bury St Edmunds to 1279*, by Robin J. Eaglen, 2006.

THE ABBEY AND MINT OF BURY ST EDMUNDS TO 1279

Robin J. Eaglen

Published for
THE BRITISH NUMISMATIC SOCIETY
Special Publication No. 5

SPINK
LONDON
2006

To Jenny

Published by Spink & Son Ltd,
69 Southampton Row, Bloomsbury,
London WC1B 4ET
for
The British Numismatic Society

ISBN 1 902040 75 9

British Library Cataloguing in Publication data
A CIP catalogue record is available from the British Library

Set by J&L Composition, Filey, North Yorkshire
Printed in Great Britain at The University Press, Cambridge

CONTENTS

FIGURES

TABLES

ABBREVIATIONS

Archives	*The Archives of the Abbey of Bury St Edmunds*, ed. R. M. Thompson (Woodbridge, 1980).
AS Charters	*Anglo-Saxon Charters. An annotated list and bibliography*, ed. P. H. Sawyer (London, 1968).
AS Chronicle	*The Anglo-Saxon Chronicle*, ed. and trans. G. N. Garmonsway, 2nd edn (London, 1955).
ASE	*Anglo-Saxon England*
AS Wills	*Anglo-Saxon Wills*, ed. D. Whitelock (Cambridge, 1930).
AS Writs	*Anglo-Saxon Writs*, ed. F. E. Harmer (Manchester, 1932).
BAR	*British Archeological Reports*
BL	British Library, London
BMC	*British Museum Catalogue* C. F. Keary, *Anglo-Saxon Series*, 2 vols (London, 1887). G. C. Brooke, *The Norman Kings*, 2 vols (London, 1916). D. F. Allen, *The Cross-and-Crosslets ('Tealby') Type of Henry II* (London, 1951).
BM	British Museum
BNJ	*British Numismatic Journal*
Bodley	Bodleian Library, University of Oxford
Cambridge UL	University Library, University of Cambridge
ChR	*Rotuli Chartarum in Turri Londonensi Asservati, 1199–1216*, ed. T. D. Hardy (London, 1837).
CLR	*Calendar of Liberate Rolls*
CPR	*Calendar of Patent Rolls*
CR	*Close Rolls of the Reign of Henry III Preserved in the Public Record Office*
DB	Domesday Book J. Morris, general editor: I. *Huntingdonshire* (Chichester, 1975), ed. J. Morris and S. Harvey. II. *Suffolk*, 2 vols (Chichester, 1986), ed. A. Rumble.
DNB	*Dictionary of National Bibliography* (compact edn, Oxford, 1975).
EcHR	*Economic History Review*
EHR	*English Historical Review*
EHD	*English Historical Documents* I. *c.500–1042*, ed. D. Whitelock, 2nd edn (London and New York, 1979). II. *1042–1189*, ed. D. C. Douglas and G. W. Greenaway, 2nd edn (London, 1981).

Feudal Documents	*Feudal Documents from the Abbey of Bury St. Edmunds*, ed. D. C. Douglas (London, 1932).
Hild.	B. E. Hildebrand, *Anglosachsiska mynt i Svenska Kongliga Myntkabinettet funna i Sveriges jord*, 2nd edn (Stockholm, 1881).
Inventory	J. D. A. Thompson, *Inventory of British Coin Hoards, A.D. 600–1500*, Royal Numismatic Society Special Publication 1 (London, 1956).
Jocelin	*The Chronicle of Jocelin of Brakelond*, ed. and trans. H. E. Butler (London, 1949).
KR	King's Remembrancer's Memoranda Roll
LTR	Lord Treasurer's Remembrancer's Memoranda Roll
Memorials	*Memorials of St. Edmund's Abbey*, ed. T. Arnold, 3 vols (RS, 1890–6).
Monasticon	W. Dugdale, *Monasticon Anglicanum*, ed. J. Caley, H. Ellis and B. Bandinel, 8 vols (London, 1817–30).
NC	*Numismatic Chronicle*
NCirc	*Spink Numismatic Circular*
Norman Kings	G. C. Brooke, *A Catalogue of English Coins in the British Museum. The Norman Kings*, 2 vols (London, 1916).
North	J. J. North, *English Hammered Coinage*, I, 3rd edn (London 1994) and II, 3rd edn (London, 1991).
PRO	Public Record Office (now The National Archives, Kew)
PSIA	*Proceedings of the Suffolk Institute of Archaeology*
Regesta	*Regesta Regum Anglo-Normannorum* I. *1066–1100*, ed. H. W. C. Davis (Oxford, 1913). II. *1100–1135*, ed. C. Johnson and H. A. Cronne (Oxford, 1956). III. *1135–1154*, ed. H. A. Cronne and R. H. C. Davis Oxford, 1968).
RLC	*Rotuli Litterarum Clausarum in Turri Londinensi Asservati, 1204–1227*, ed. T. D. Hardy, 2 vols (London, 1833–4).
RLP	*Rotuli Litterarum Patentum in Turri Londinensi Asservati, 1201–1216*, ed. T. D. Hardy (London, 1835).
RS	Rolls Series
SCBI	*Sylloge of Coins of the British Isles*
SCMB	*Seaby's Coin and Medal Bulletin*
TRHS	*Transactions of the Royal Historical Society*

PREFACE

This book is based upon a doctoral thesis written between 1986 and 1989, using material collected from 1976 onwards, when the writer first became interested in the mint at Bury. In its present form it takes account of the healthy stream of more recently published work and the emergence of many new coins up to the end of 2004. It also incorporates the (hopefully) more mature reflection of the author on a number of topics.

The book's content is concerned as much with the history of Bury and its abbey as with the abbot's mint and its output. Too often historical and numismatic writers underestimate or even largely ignore the synergy to be derived from combining both disciplines. Bury St Edmunds was one of the greatest Benedictine houses in England. It owed its importance and wealth to St Edmund himself, whose shrine was an object of deep veneration. Its abbot, besides his spiritual leadership, had feudal jurisdiction over West Suffolk and the right to strike coins of the realm, both privileges originating with grants by Edward the Confessor. The history of the abbey and its mint is traced from its beginnings to 1279. It is planned that a second volume will deal with the period from 1279 to closure of the mint in the early years of Edward III's reign.

Although the output from the mint at Bury was modest it is of the highest numismatic significance. From late Anglo-Saxon times many urban centres, including a few under ecclesiastical authority, had issued coins. In the twelfth and thirteenth centuries, however, most of these centres, with the exception of major cities such as London and Canterbury, had their minting rights progressively withdrawn, even though a number of mints were temporarily reinstated to meet the demands of a recoinage, as in 1205 and 1248. The abbot of Bury was immune from this trend because he could demonstrate to the exchequer that successive kings had confirmed his right to receive dies for striking currency, and was doubtless also able to draw continuing benefit from the repute of St Edmund. Thus between 1042 and 1279 coins bearing a Bury mint-inscription are known for all reigns except those of Harold II, William II and Richard I. The modest output at the Bury mint over its periods of operation makes it feasible to carry out a detailed analysis of the surviving coins, a monumental task for major mints in more or less continuous operation, such as London and Canterbury. The Catalogue to this study nevertheless records well over 3,000 Bury coins, which have been identified to the individual dies from which they were struck.

Wokingham
2005

ACKNOWLEDGEMENTS

The first debt is owed to my tutor at Birkbeck, Dr Emma Mason, for flattering me into the belief that completion of my thesis, as a respite from the rigours of life in industry, was a worthwhile objective, and to my examiners, Professors David Carpenter and Michael Metcalf and Dr Antonia Gransden, for encouraging me to revise and update it for publication.

My second, but no less important debt is owed to those who kindly agreed to read and comment on each draft chapter, namely Dr Stewart Lyon (Chapters 1 and 2), Hugh Pagan (Chapter 3), Marion Archibald (Chapters 4 and 5), Dr Mark Blackburn (Chapter 6), Tim Crafter (Chapter 7), Glen Gittoes (Chapter 8), and Ron Churchill and Bob Thomas (Chapter 9). Dr Martin Allen has also shown an unswerving interest in the work, and provided much food for thought from his prolific writings. In these pages a light sprinkling of contentious views may be encountered. I have decided to include them to stimulate the unending quest for deeper knowledge, even though I have not, in all cases, been able to persuade the chapter readers to my way of thinking. It is thus more than mere convention to state that any errors and follies to be found are of my own making.

Many persons have contributed to the corpus of coins which form the bedrock of this work. In particular, David Palmer has provided a steady flow of information and images from his outstanding (and still burgeoning) collection of Bury coins. The late Christopher Blunt also made his coins (now in the Fitzwilliam Museum) available for study, honed my self-critical faculties and entertained me memorably at his wonderful Wiltshire home. Debts of gratitude are also owed to the late Roy Osborne, who selflessly offered me his entire collection of Bury coins, to Peter Woodhead and Glen Gittoes, who allowed me to acquire choice pieces from their collections, and to Lord Stewartby, who lent me his Bury coins for study.

Amongst the dealers, Peter Mitchell and Michael Sharp were assiduous in supporting my project and, with Edward Baldwin, kindly allowed me to have my pick of Bury coins from the great Brussels hoard. Other dealers who also helped greatly were the late Patrick Finn, May Sinclair, Chris Martin, Michael Trenerry and Robert Sharman. The late Kenneth Jacob made my life easier, especially when I was based in Brussels, by lending me catalogues from his fine numismatic library.

Invaluable help has also come from professional numismatists and curators, including (again) Mark Blackburn and Martin Allen at the Fitzwilliam Museum,

Marion Archibald and Dr Barrie Cook at the British Museum, Graham Dyer and Dr Kevin Clancy at the Royal Mint Museum, Professor Nick Mayhew at the Ashmolean, Nick Holmes at Edinburgh, Dr Donal Bateson at Glasgow, Dr David Symons at Birmingham and Philip Wise at Colchester.

A special debt is owed to the museums and private collectors who have kindly permitted me to use their coins for illustration in the Plates. The Catalogue entries show the extent of this indebtedness.

My greatest thanks of all are saved for my former Secretary, Mandy Peel, who typed the original thesis and for my wife, Jenny, who has retyped parts of this work so many times that she could doubtless write her own version of it. Finally, I am grateful to the British Numismatic Society for agreeing to publish my work and to Mark Blackburn as President of the Society and Martin Allen as my editor for so expertly and energetically assuming the burden of bringing it into print.

CHAPTER 1

ORIGINS OF THE ABBEY

St Edmund

Documents referring to the Benedictine abbey at Bury St Edmunds survive in profusion. They include remarkable details of the life, death and resting-place of the abbey's patron saint, Edmund, king of East Anglia. Unfortunately, even after discounting such clearly conventional stories as the severed head of the king attracting his followers by calling out 'here, here, here',[1] much of what remains invites caution because the details appear to have been first recorded long after Edmund's death. Caution deepens into suspicion when contradictions are found between the various accounts.

The scholar is then left with a daunting task. It obviously may not be assumed that everything written down long after the period to which it relates can be safely discarded as fanciful. Certain facts could be handed down to the writer's time by oral tradition or copied from earlier lost writings. By the same token, a contradictory later report of events could nevertheless be correct through being derived from an antecedent but lost record of greater reliability than the earliest surviving record. The challenge with the material at the scholar's disposal is thus to distinguish fact from fiction with any certainty.

The manuscript of the *Anglo-Saxon Chronicle* known as the Parker Chronicle records that Edmund died in the winter of 869, slain by the Danish army quartered at Thetford.[2] The account of this event occurs in the first section of the *Chronicle*, written in a hand of about the year 900,[3] taking the text up to the end of 891. It is thus nearly contemporaneous with the events it describes. The *Chronicle* is ambiguous, however, as to which army launched the attack and whether the king died in or after the battle. Abbo of Fleury, writing in about 985,[4] first records the date of death as 20 November.[5] No other date has at any time been suggested and it has been generally accepted as accurate by modern authorities.[6] The preservation of the date by oral tradition in the years immediately following must, moreover, have been helped by the cult of the saint. This

1 *Memorials*, I, p. 18. See Gransden 1985, p. 6 and n. 6 on legends concerning severed heads.

2 *AS Chronicle*, p. 70; see also *The Anglo-Saxon Chronicle. A Collaborative Edition*. III, *MS A*, p. 47.

3 Gransden 1974, p. 39.

4 Ridyard 1988, p. 63, n. 221, dates Abbo's work to 985–7.

5 *Memorials*, I, p. 16.

6 E.g. Stenton 1971, p. 248, n. 3, and Whitelock 1967–9, p. 220, n. 13.

had developed sufficiently for the earliest coins of a large issue to be struck in his memory within a generation of his death,[7] and thus comfortably within the lifespan of his contemporaries.

Abbo of Fleury was also the first to relate that Edmund had died as a martyr after the battle, tied to a tree by his captors and pierced with arrows. His severed head was purportedly cast into a bramble thicket in Hæglisdun wood.[8] This has been identified with Hellesdon, on the outskirts of Norwich.[9] After recovery, according to Abbo, the rejoined head and torso were placed in a tomb, implicitly near the site of his martyrdom, over which a crude wooden chapel was constructed. At a later, unspecified date the remains were moved to Beadericesworth, by which name Bury was then known, and a more elaborate wooden church constructed. Hermann, a monk of Bury, however, writing about a century later than Abbo,[10] recorded the first resting-place of Edmund as Suthune (Sutton), close to where he was killed.[11] Today no place in the vicinity of Hellesdon can be identified with Sutton. This has led to speculation that the place referred to may have been Sutton Hoo, two miles north east of Ipswich.[12] Shortly after Hermann wrote, Bishop Herbert Losinga of Norwich, in the foundation charter of Norwich Priory of 1101, refers to yet another site, Hoxne in Suffolk, as the place where Edmund died and was first buried.[13] It has been shown, however, that this tradition was almost certainly cultivated to support an unsuccessful claim by Bishop Herbert to exercise episcopal control over the abbey at Bury.[14] The reference to Hoxne was intended to demonstrate that the saint's remains had once lain in a church serving as one of the seats of the bishops of East Anglia.

In the 1980s, in the *Proceedings of the Suffolk Institute of Archaeology*, an ingenious hypothesis was advanced, reconciling the references to Hellesdon and Sutton.[15] In the parish of Bradfield St Clare, about five miles from Bury, a field was marked as Hellesdon in the 1840 Tithe Map. This field lay one mile north of Sutton Hall,

7 See Chapter 2 pp. 13–16.

8 *Memorials* I, p. 16. Similarities with the death of St Sebastian will immediately strike the modern reader, and were noted by Abbo himself (I, p. 15) who also compared him with St Lawrence (I, p. 23) and St Cuthbert (I, p. 4). Modern scholars have also found parallels with St Olaf of Norway, St Ælfheah and St Mary of Egypt (Gransden 1985). However, conventional hagiographical details would not only serve the writer to make up for his want of hard facts but also, by implicit or stated analogy, tend to enhance the standing of the saint being celebrated. Gransden has also drawn attention to the close parallel between the incorrupt state claimed for the body of St Edmund and that of St Cuthbert late in the eleventh century (Gransden 1981, pp. 73–4).

9 Whitelock 1967–9, p. 220.

10 Gransden 1974, p. 125, dates his work as 'some time after 1095' and Ridyard 1988, p. 70, to 'within a few years of . . . 1097'.

11 *Memorials*, I, p. 27.

12 *The History of King Eadmund the Martyr*, p. 14 ; Clarke 1960, p. 156. But cf. Galbraith 1925, p. 223, n. 3, where there is reference to a 'Sutton in Wymondham'.

13 Whitelock 1967–9, p. 223; *Monasticon*, IV, pp. 15–17.

14 Galbraith 1925, p. 222–3.

15 West 1981–4, pp. 223–5. This hypothesis is given further circumstantial support in Ridyard 1988, pp. 218–19 and n. 34.

on the boundary between the parishes of Bradfield Combust and Cockfield. It is plausible that this was indeed the site of Hæglisdun wood and that the king was buried at Sutton (Hall), only to be moved to the more populous settlement at nearby Beadericesworth once his cult had begun to flourish.

Translation to Beadericesworth

As already mentioned, Abbo gave no date for the translation of Edmund's body from its earlier, uncertain resting-place to Beadericesworth, and his contemporary, Ealderman Æthelweard, simply observes that Edmund was buried there.[16] About a century later Hermann relates that in the reign of Æthelstan, Edmund, who then reposed at Beadericesworth, was already revered as a saint. His remarks have been taken to imply that the body was moved there in the reign of Æthelstan, but the text as such does not warrant this construction. Hermann's dating of events possibly occurring at least a hundred and seventy years before must be treated with caution. Moreover, his statement that Edmund was already known as a saint by the time of Æthelstan, although literally true, refers to a dignity to which Edmund had aspired more than thirty years earlier, as is borne out by the St Edmund Memorial coinage discussed in Chapter 2.

Roger of Wendover, writing in the early part of the thirteenth century,[17] states vaguely that the body was moved to Beadericesworth after the lapse of many years.[18] For more definite dating, we must turn to regrettably late sources. Bodley MS 240 compiled towards the end of the fourteenth century[19] gives a date around 900 in the reign of Alfred or, 'according to others' 906 in the reign of Edward the Elder, as the year in which the saint was moved to Beadericesworth, to repose in a great wooden church.[20] The even later Register of Abbot Curteys, completed just before the abbot's death in 1446,[21] categorically places the translation in the year 903. Except for the vital addition of the dates, however, the text of Bodley MS 240 is virtually identical with the words used by Abbo about four hundred years earlier. Apart from this implicit debt, no authority is given in either Bodley MS 240 or Curteys' Register for the dates cited.

Importance of Beadericesworth in the ninth and tenth centuries

It is difficult to capture an impression of Beadericesworth either at the time of Edmund's death or even in the succeeding century. A tradition of uncertain origin,

16 *The Chronicle of Æthelweard*, p. 36.

17 Gransden 1974, p. 359.

18 Roger of Wendover, I, p. 314.

19 The document cites, for example, miracles occurring in the year 1375 (see *Memorials*, III, p. 337).

20 *Corolla Sancti Eadmundi*, p. 407.

21 BL Add. MS 14848, fol. 211; *Archives*, p. 35.

recorded in abbey registers from the thirteenth century onwards,[22] claimed that King Sigebert of East Anglia built a monastery there, to which he retired in 633. No less authority than Bede (672/3–735) had indeed related Sigebert's withdrawal from the world to a monastery of his founding, but without identifying its whereabouts.[23] Bede's account is repeated in the *Liber Eliensis*, compiled after 1131,[24] with the words 'in Betrichesworde' significantly added in a later hand.[25] The abbey registers, moreover, may naturally be expected to emphasise the long-standing importance, not to say royal associations, of the place where the monastery was sited. Excavations in 1972 at Bury St Edmunds of sixty-seven 'Pagan-Saxon' graves ranging from the early fifth to mid/late seventh century bear witness to settlement at that period, but do not confirm this earlier Christian tradition.[26]

In his account of about 985 Abbo says that the wooden church to house St Edmund's remains was constructed in the royal vill (*villa regia*) of Beadericesworth, a phrase repeated in Bodley MS 240. Gransden has pointed out that the surviving copies of Abbo's work (two from Bury and one from St Denis, Paris) date from the late eleventh century and that the passage referring to Edmund's translation to the royal vill of Beadericesworth may well have been interpolated at the time the abbey was resisting the attempt by Bishop Herbert Losinga to assert control over it. A reference to royal origins would under such circumstances be a useful argument against later episcopal subordination.[27]

There is, however, circumstantial evidence that Beadericesworth was not an important settlement in the ninth or tenth centuries. Two lists of saints' resting-places compiled in the early and the mid eleventh century show how unusual it was for the name of a saint to have influenced the name of the place where his or her remains were laid at rest.[28] Of forty-seven named places only two bore place names originally derived from that of the saint, Congresbury and Malmesbury. More significantly, in only four or possibly five further locations did the saint's name exert sufficient influence to cause a subsequent change in the name of a settlement. These were Waeclingcestre (St Albans), Cicc (St Osyth), Eanulfesbirig (St Neots), Cecesege (Hibaldstow?) and Beadericesworth (Bury St Edmunds). The implication is that only in relatively unimportant settlements was the presence of an illustrious saint's remains likely to bring about a change of name.

As shown later in this Chapter, the change of name from Beadericesworth to Bury St Edmunds occurred in the first half of the eleventh century,[29] rather than in the

22 See Yates 1805, p. 18.

23 Bede, Book III, Chapter 18, p. 269.

24 *Liber Eliensis*, p. xlviii.

25 *Liber Eliensis*, p. 11.

26 Owles 1970–2, p. 283.

27 Gransden 1985, p. 4, n. 4; p. 13, n. 2; Gransden 1981, p. 72. Cf. Ridyard 1988, p. 220, arguing for the traditional belief in Bury as a *villa regia*.

28 Rollason 1978, pp. 87, 89–93.

29 Accordingly, the name had already become anachronistic by the time of the second of the two lists of saints' resting places.

period of fervent adulation for St Edmund reflected in coinage struck in his memory by the turn of the tenth century. It could be argued that the stability of the name Beadericesworth during the earlier period hints at a reputation enjoyed by the settlement not susceptible to be submerged by that of the saint. I believe it more significant, however, that the saint's prestige, in hand with monastic development, was able to bring about a change of name more than a century later.

The conclusions thus far to be gleaned are that Edmund died, during or after a battle against the Danes on 20 November 869, and that he was not buried to begin with at Beadericesworth but moved there at a later date from an uncertain resting place. It is logical to associate his translation with the growth of his cult and the extensive coinage struck in his memory, from the early to late 890s. These events are most unlikely to have been widely separated in time. Since it appears that Beadericesworth was not a place of great importance before St Edmund was moved there, it is also most unlikely that his remains would have been conveyed a large distance to be enshrined there. This adds weight to the suggestion of Bradfield St Clare as the first resting place rather than Hellesdon (Norwich), or Hoxne or Sutton Hoo. If Hellesdon had been the first resting-place translation to nearby Needham or Northwic (Norwich)[30] would be far more probable than to Beadericesworth. It has already been shown that Hoxne can be dismissed on other grounds and removal of the body to Beadericesworth from distant Sutton Hoo appears doubly questionable if, as it appears, Sutton Hoo was itself a significant Anglo-Saxon location.[31]

The religious community at Beadericesworth in the tenth century

The development of a religious community associated with St Edmund remains obscure, even in outline, until after the accession of Edward the Confessor in 1042. Documents mainly of a later date or in late copies afford evidence of earlier religious organisation but must be treated with customary caution.

The supposed founding of a monastery at Beadericesworth by King Sigebert in the seventh century has already been mentioned. Whether he did so or not, organised monastic life, at least outside the heartland of Wessex, is not thought to have survived intact the incursions of the Danish invaders in the decade which witnessed the death of Edmund himself.[32]

Formal monasticism only reappears from about 940, gathering momentum in the period immediately following the accession of Eadgar in 959.[33] It is,

30 Carter 1978, p. 201.

31 Clarke 1960, p. 156.

32 Stenton 1971, p. 445; Knowles 1966, p. 24.

33 Knowles 1966, pp. 31, 40–52. Recent research has shown that secular communities existed after the Viking invasions with many attributes of monasticism. See Blair 1985, p. 117.

therefore, not to be expected that St Edmund would be consigned to the care of an organised monastic community upon his translation to Beadericesworth. Hermann in fact tells us that his remains were at first attended by four priests and two deacons and, as if to enhance the credibility of his account, he even gives their names.[34] Battely, the eighteenth-century antiquarian, conjectured the founding of a college of secular priests by Æthelstan in about 925 to care for the saint's shrine,[35] whereas others[36] have associated the existence – but not necessarily the establishment – of a clerical household or college with the reign of his half-brother Edmund. This association has been prompted by a charter in the name of King Edmund, dated 945, giving possession of a defined area around the shrine 'to the monastery situated in the place called Beadericesworth' to be held free from burdens, dues and interference. Although it has been argued that the charter is genuine, it must be viewed with the gravest suspicion.[37] The coincidence, offered in support, that the boundary marks described correspond, after allowing for directional errors, with those of the medieval *banleuca* or urban boundaries of the abbey possessions manifestly does not qualify as evidence of authenticity.[38] Moreover, the isolated reference to a monastery as such in existence at that early date is at variance with abbey records discussed below giving a later date for the foundation. It is hard to imagine the monks would readily have abandoned earlier, authentic proof of their monastic origins and royal patronage to rely upon claims to a later foundation in the reign of Cnut or Edward the Confessor. Although the charter of Edmund does not refer to freedom from episcopal control as such, which became such a consuming concern to the monks after the Norman Conquest, it is difficult not to dismiss the charter as an illegitimate child of this later concern.

Whereas the supposed charter of Edmund refers to a 'monastery', the earliest extant will to mention St Edmund's, that of Bishop Theodred in 942 x *c*. 951 as recorded in the later Sacrist's Register, refers simply to 'Sce Eadmundes Kirke'.[39] To the extent that this document can be relied upon it shows no more than that by the mid-tenth century those who cared for St Edmund were a sufficiently well-defined body to become a beneficiary under Theodred's will.

The next period to attract the attention of scholars considering the religious and urban community at Beadericesworth is the reign of Edward the Martyr (975–8). This is not because the period yields any reliable facts, but because of the wide-

34 *Memorials*, I, p. 30.

35 Battely 1745, p. 28.

36 E.g. Page 1907, pp. 57–8. Ridyard 1988, p. 223, considered that a religious community of sorts very probably existed at Bury as early as the mid 890s. The evidence so far available, however, does not justify this conclusion.

37 See, for example, *AS Charters*, p. 192, no. 507; Lobel 1935, p. 2, n. 7. The charter is not listed by Thompson (*Archives*) but C. R. Hart considered it substantially genuine (*The Early Charters of Eastern England*, no. 74, pp. 54–8).

38 *The Early Charters of Eastern England*, pp. 54–8.

39 *AS Wills*, no. 1, p. 4.

spread belief among historians that coins were minted there in Edward's name. The fallacy of this belief is explained in Chapter 2, but it has been misleadingly quoted as proof that Beadericesworth was already an important centre at that date.

Role of Cnut

Although important details remain obscure, the reign of Cnut (1016–35) undoubtedly saw a marked development in the religious community at Beadericesworth, if not in its urban settlement. Three important circumstances have been recorded as occurring in his reign. Firstly, the foundation of the monastery in 1020; secondly, the granting of a charter of privileges to the monastery in 1021 x 1023 and, thirdly, the consecration of a new monastic church in 1031/2.

The earliest authority for Cnut's foundation is to be found in a marginal note to the Easter Tables in the Bury Psalter.[40] Although it appears against the years 1020–4, the Tables in this version at least were not executed before 1044.[41] Opinion is also divided on whether the marginal note was contemporaneous with the main text.[42] Nevertheless, it appears to offer mid-eleventh century testimony of Cnut's foundation. Later in the century Hermann relates that with the support of Ælfwine, bishop of East Anglia, and Earl Thurkil, the king replaced the secular priests at the shrine by monks in 1020, with Ufi becoming the first abbot.[43] This account is repeated in the interpolated version of Florence of Worcester's Chronicle written at Bury towards the mid-twelfth century, adding that the move had the support of Queen Emma and that some of the priests took the habit and stayed on.[44] A number of writers have expressed scepticism that a bishop of East Anglia should have encouraged the setting up of an independent monastery within his diocese.[45] Gransden has suggested, however, that, whether true or not, Hermann may have gathered the story when in service with Bishop Arfast of Elmham and incorporated it into his account, apparently oblivious of its being potentially damaging in the abbey's struggles with the bishops of East Anglia.[46] The fact that the story was potentially damaging appears to lend support to its veracity because it would have been a foolish fabrication. Most writers have in fact tended to accept that Cnut founded the monastery. Certainly the marginal note in the Easter Tables cannot have been spawned during the episcopal disputes of the Norman period when it suited the abbot to claim royal patronage extending further back than the reign of Edward the Confessor.

40 Vatican MS Reg. Lat. 12, fol. 16v. See Temple 1976, no. 84, p. 101.
41 Gransden 1995, p. 38.
42 Gransden 1994, pp. 159–60.
43 *Memorials*, I, pp. 47–8; Gransden 1974, p. 125.
44 *Liber Eliensis*, p. 155.
45 See Galbraith 1925, p. 226 (referring to Ælfric in mistake for Ælfwine); *AS Writs*, pp. 140–1.
46 Gransden 1985, p. 14.

The late fourteenth-century Bodley MS 240 elaborates further that the secular priests were replaced by monks from Ely and St Benet's Holme, and that Abbot Ufi had formerly been the prior at Holme.[47] This account also states that Bishop Ælfwine had abrogated all episcopal power over the monastery. The tradition of monks being transferred from Ely and Holme appears to have first arisen elsewhere than at Bury itself. The tract written in 1103 x 1119 in support of Bishop Herbert Losinga's jurisdictional struggle against St Edmund's[48] states that a monk of Holme was the first prior (*sic*), and the second book of the *Liber Eliensis*, not completed before 1154, in a copy from the early thirteenth century,[49] mentions the transfer of monks from both Holme and Ely at the instigation of Bishop Ælfwine. Once again, therefore, it is disquieting to find new details emerging from these later accounts.

A mid-twelfth century manuscript, Bodley MS 297, provides the earliest record that Æthelnoth, Archbishop of Canterbury, consecrated a new monastic church at Beadericesworth on 18 October 1032.[50] The later Bodley MS 240 gives the date as 1031 in one place and 1031/2 in another.[51] Bodley MS 297 also mentions that some years before, in 1028, a charter of privileges was granted to St Edmund's by Cnut. The authenticity of this charter has divided historians, but with a preponderance in favour of its being spurious or at least questionable in its surviving versions.[52] The charter states that the monastery at Beadericesworth shall always be inhabited by monks, free from jurisdiction by the bishops of the shire, and gives to the monks the benefit of taxes otherwise payable to maintain the army or warships. However, the parts of the charter assigning to the abbey an annual grant of fish due to Cnut, rights in a fishery, benefit of the pleas in vills owned by St Edmund's and confirming the gift of 4,000 eels a year from Queen Emma have been considered as possibly copied from a genuine charter.[53] It would be natural for Cnut and his queen to be seen to venerate St Edmund and atone for his reputed death at the hands of Danish forces and the harm inflicted by Cnut's father, Sweyn, on religious communities during his campaigns in England between 994 and 1013.[54]

Further evidence of a monastic community having come into being in Cnut's reign is found in the wills of Thurketel Heyng, dated possibly after 1020, referring to the 'abbot on Byri',[55] and of Bishop Ælfric, dated 1035–7, referring to the

47 *Memorials*, I, p. 359.

48 Galbraith 1925, pp. 222–8; recorded in BL Harl. MS 1005, fol. 197 (*c.* 1275).

49 *Liber Eliensis*, pp. xlviii, 155.

50 *Memorials*, I, p. 342. See also BL Harl. MS 447 (*Memorials*, II, p. 3).

51 *Memorials*, I, pp. 360, 362. Hermann (*Memorials*, I, pp. 84–5) records that the church (presumably the new one) was clad in stone during the reign of Cnut.

52 *AS Writs*, pp. 141, 433–4; *AS Charters*, no. 980, p. 294; *Archives*, p. 45; *contra* Hart, *The Early Charters of Eastern England*, no. 86, pp. 63–4.

53 Gransden 1985, p. 11.

54 Hermann (*Memorials*, I, pp. 32–8) even attributes the sudden death of Sweyn to his attempted imposition of tribute upon St Edmunds.

55 *AS Wills*, no. XXV, p. 70.

'munecas on Byrig'.[56] These documents, it will be noticed, refer to Bury rather than Beadericesworth, and this change is traced in the next section.

From Beadericesworth to Bury

As we have seen, Abbo and Ealderman Æthelweard mention Beadericesworth by name towards the end of the tenth century. Although an earlier reference in the charter of 945 in the name of Edmund[57] must be discounted because of its doubtful authenticity, it may nevertheless be assumed that the name Beadericesworth substantially pre-dates the time of Abbo and Æthelweard. The change of name from Beadericesworth to the equivalent of St Edmundsbury can be traced most clearly in the Anglo-Saxon wills and writs published respectively by Whitelock and Harmer. Our knowledge of many of these documents derives from later copies in the Sacrist's Register compiled at Bury late in the thirteenth century but, fortunately, not in every case.

Whitelock's collection of wills includes nineteen which contain gifts to St Edmund's.[58] The two earliest, of Bishop Theodred and of Ælfgar, datable to 941 x *c.* 951, both in fact derive from the Sacrist's Register, but the place name description used in the will of Ælfgar is similar to that in the will of Æthelflæd, from the late tenth century and written in an early eleventh century hand. This latter refers to 'Scae Eadmundes stowe [place or foundation] to [at] Bydericeswyrthe'. The will of Æthelric *c.* 995, in a contemporary version also refers to 'Sce Eadmunde on [at] Bedericeswyrthe'. These documents clearly show the name of the saint beginning to assert itself over the old name of the settlement. Harmer in turn reproduces eighteen Anglo-Saxon writs which in various forms and spellings refer to St Edmundsbury, the earliest of which is dated 1042–3.[59] Although Harmer considered one of these writs not to be genuine and most of the remainder again derive from late copies in the Sacrist's Register, two of the writs she judged to be entirely authentic and one possibly an original deed. The latter of these two, granting the privilege of sake and soke over his men to Abbot Leofstan and datable to the years of his abbacy (1044–65), refers to 'Eadmundes byrig'[60]. The other, dated late in 1065 or the beginning of 1066, after the appointment of his successor, Abbot Baldwin, and granting him soke over the eight and a half hundreds constituting modern West Suffolk, refers to the 'Mynstre [monastery] innto [at] Sce Eadmundes byrig'.[61] There can be no serious doubt – quite apart from the evidence of the coins to be considered later – that by the reign of Edward the Confessor (1042–66) the name of St Edmundsbury had become firmly established.

56 *AS Wills*, no. XXVI, p. 72.

57 *Corolla Sancti Eadmundi*, p. 588 (see n. 37 above).

58 *AS Wills*, nos I, II, XIV–XVI, XXIV–XXIX, XXXI–XXXVIII.

59 *AS Writs*, nos 8–25.

60 *AS Writs*, no. 11, p. 156.

61 *AS Writs*, no. 24, p. 164.

Closer precision is difficult but the will of Bishop Ælfric, dated to 1035–7 but in a copy made possibly up to twenty or thirty years later, refers several times simply to 'Sce Eadmunde' and once – strikingly – to the 'munecas [monks] on [at] Byrig'[62] . Two further wills, one in the name of Thurketel of Palgrave,[63] dated before 1038, and the other of Thurketel Heyng,[64] possibly after 1020, also use the forms 'Seynt Eadmund, Seynt Eadmundesbiri, Byri' and 'Biry', without reference to Beadericesworth. Copies of these wills again derive from the Sacrist's Register but in cases where earlier versions exist to be compared with those contained in the Register the spelling of the place names is consistent. There is, moreover, no reason why the transcribers should have actively set out to modernise place names which were variable in spelling but not otherwise confusingly obscure. If the evidence of the Sacrist's Register is accepted as valid both in terms of the writs cited by Harmer and the wills cited by Whitelock, the picture emerges of the name (Seynt) (Sce) Eadmundes (Byrig) being adopted after the start of the eleventh century but before the death of Cnut, and probably in the course of his reign. The two lists of saints' resting places which Rollason attributes to the first half and middle of the eleventh century respectively both refer to Beadericesworth rather than St Edmundsbury, [65] but at least one of these could have been reproducing outdated usage from earlier listings. It is inconceivable that testators were less aware of the proper name of the foundation remembered in their wills than the compilers of general lists of saints' resting places.

In studying the coinage emanating from Bury it is important to define as closely as possible when the change in name occurred. The placing of mint names on Anglo-Saxon coinage did not enter into general, if sporadic use until the reign of Æthelstan (925–39), and it was not until the reign of Eadgar (959–75) that it became established practice.[66] The search for a 'Bury' mint signature thus depends, in the early period up to Cnut, upon identifying an abbreviation of the name 'Beadericesworth', and in the reign of Edward the Confessor of the name 'St Edmundsbury.' During the period from about 1016 to, say, 1045 abbreviations of both names would be theoretically feasible.

Conclusion

From the foregoing it will be clear that important details of the early development of the abbey depend upon later and possibly suspect accounts. Despite this, there seems little doubt that a Benedictine house was founded in Bury in about 1020. In consequence, it would be natural for the monastery to be granted privileges to ensure its viability, even if the precise nature of the benefits is

62 *AS Wills*, no. XXVI, pp. 71–2.
63 *AS Wills*, no. XXIV, p. 68.
64 *AS Wills*, no. XXV, p. 70.
65 Rollason 1978, p. 61.
66 See North 1994, *passim*.

debatable. It is also very plausible that a new monastic church was consecrated during this period, even if contemporary evidence is lacking. There are, moreover, other circumstances to show that the religious community was growing in importance in Cnut's reign, thereby qualifying itself to receive the honours accorded some years later by Edward the Confessor.

Firstly, Whitelock shows that, after a lapse of at least twenty years at the beginning of the eleventh century, St Edmund's became once more the beneficiary of a number of gifts in the period 1020–42.[67] These continue unabated in the immediately following decades. Secondly, apart from Cnut's apparent role as founder of the monastery, both he and his queen appear for reasons suggested above to have been keen to endow St Edmund's. Thirdly, there is evidence of a general revival in the cult of St Edmund in the 1020s.[68] These influences undoubtedly played upon each other and increased the renown of St Edmund to the extent that at this time his name ousted that of Beadericesworth. Obviously, this remarkable development is more readily explicable if the royal couple's patronage towards the religious community is believed to extend well beyond the gift of eels and the like, however welcome to the monks. Unless further records for this period come to light, a deeper knowledge of the early history of St Edmundsbury may depend upon the archaeologists. It is only to be hoped that whenever the possibility of a promising excavation arises they will be given scope for their work.

With the reign of Edward the Confessor we reach landfall and coins from St Edmundsbury first appear. Before disembarking, however, it is necessary to deal with the claims deriving from erring numismatists and embraced by unsuspecting historians that earlier coins emanated from what is now known as Bury.

67 *AS Wills*, nos XXIV–XXIX.

68 Gransden 1985, p. 11.

CHAPTER 2

PUTATIVE BURY COINAGE

Introduction

This chapter deals with coins from earlier periods attributed by numismatic writers over the years incorrectly to Bury.[1] Unfortunately, the reasons for such attributions have not always been explained and, equally regrettably, later writers have not always troubled to give their reasons for rejecting them. Most seriously of all, past attributions have depended upon identifying mint names which could be interpreted to signify St Edmundsbury, whereas at least until the early years of Cnut's reign, as shown in Chapter 1, they should have denoted Beadericesworth. In part, therefore, this chapter entails rousing and exorcising spectres. Thankfully, at least no one has suggested that coins of Edmund as king of East Anglia were minted at Bury.

St Edmund Memorial coinage

The earliest coins suggested to emanate at least partly from Bury are those known collectively as the St Edmund Memorial coinage. The issue, already referred to in Chapter 1, has been dated between 895 and 915, with a few years latitude either side, and consists mainly of silver pennies struck in the weight range of 1.10 to 1.50 g.[2] They are mostly similar in style, bearing variants – often blundered – of the inscription SCE EADMVND REX within two circles around a central letter A on the obverse and, on the reverse, a cross surrounded by a legend within two circles giving the moneyer's name and status. Figure 1 shows an example, with the reverse reading +VVIDBVLD MOIIE for Widbald Mone(ta).

Ruding in his *Annals* conjectured that these coins were minted by the abbot at Bury some time after Edward the Confessor's reign.[3] He was writing, however, before his contemporary, Hawkins, had published an account of the large Viking hoard deposited *c.* 905 and found at Cuerdale in Lancashire in 1840 containing over 1,800 examples, which constitute the bulk of the coinage known today.[4]

---

1 The term 'Bury' is applied for convenience to St Edmundsbury, even for the period when the settlement was still known as Beadericesworth.

2 Blunt 1967–9, pp. 250, 253; Grierson and Blackburn 1986, pp. 319–20; Blackburn 1989, p. 25.

3 Ruding 1840, II, p. 218. The coinage is also briefly discussed by Blunt, Stewart and Lyon 1989, pp. 100–2.

4 Hawkins 1842–3, pp. 23–38; also *Inventory*, no.112, pp. 39–42.

Figure 1

Penny of St Edmund Memorial coinage (enlarged x1.5)

Although most of the surviving coins are in the form described above and thus coy about their date and place of issue, possible exceptions have been noted. In particular, three coins from Cuerdale combine an obverse die of St Edmund with a reverse of Alfred the Great (871–99) reading AELFRED REX DO. This legend has been construed as referring to Dorovernia, or Canterbury, and the coins as providing a clue to the origins of the coinage both in date and place.[5] More recent work, however, suggests that these three coins are Viking imitations.[6] Amongst other exceptional coins two from Cuerdale reading ERIAICEVIV have been attributed to York and another found at Northampton with an obverse legend containing the letters NORDVICO, dubiously to Norwich.[7]

Based on Hawkins' work, Golding in his slender volume on the *Coinage of Suffolk* realised that the forty-eight moneyers he recorded without any ostensible mint provenance were far too many to be attributed to Bury alone, but he did not question Bury's involvement.[8] More guardedly, Keary in the introduction to his *Catalogue of English Coins in the British Museum* considered that the coinage was issued 'chiefly in East Anglia' as the fame of St Edmund could hardly, within thirty-five years of his death, have become more widespread.[9] Although the reason given for Keary's conclusion is not convincing, and the coins themselves appear to have been minted at least in small numbers as far afield as York, Blunt in the only serious modern study of the coinage concludes that the bulk were indeed issued from one or more mints in East Anglia and circulated primarily

5 Blunt 1967–9, p. 242.

6 Grierson and Blackburn 1986, pp. 319–20.

7 *SCBI* Midlands Museums, 100. This coin is illustrated by Blunt 1967–9, Pl. XXXI, 8, where it is mistakenly said to have come from excavations at Thetford. Blunt, whilst unable to link the word NORDVICO with the name of any known moneyer, was nevertheless troubled that apparently only one coin had come to light with the Norwich signature, if, as he surmised, it was a centre of output for the coinage. Although the inscription is on the obverse rather than the reverse, it begins +NORDVICO and is followed by space for two or three further letters. These letters, for example, could be MON or CIV or DE but the fragment for the missing section of the coin is more easily reconcilable with the first of these readings. Peculiarities in the inscriptions encountered in this coinage are sufficiently widespread for this interpretation not to be dismissed simply because the moneyer's name would thereby be construed as appearing on the obverse. See also Smart 1985, p. 86. Blackburn and Pagan 2003, p. 5, dismiss an obverse inscription reading +NVRITCVI as probably 'a meaningless collection of letters'.

8 Golding 1868, p. 3.

9 Keary 1887–93, I, p. xxx.

in the Danelaw.[10] However, apart from the possible contribution from mints located in the Mercian Danelaw, which by 883 had accepted Alfred the Great as its overlord,[11] and proceeded to mint coins in imitation of Alfred's own from a number of centres including Lincoln,[12] actual identification of minting places in East Anglia responsible for the coinage has so far eluded numismatists. Blunt, in addition to Norwich, suggested Thetford as a possible location. Interestingly, the earliest mint names from eastern England presently known to appear on regal coinage are Maldon and Norwich under Æthelstan (924–39),[13] followed by Cambridge, Ipswich and Thetford under Eadgar (959–75).[14] Any of these places could be candidates, with Norwich taking pride of place owing to the number of its moneyers recorded on known coins, as Table 1 illustrates.

Table 1. Moneyers at eastern mints, 925–975

Mint	*No. of known moneyers*	
	Æthelstan[13]	*Eadgar*[14]
Cambridge	–	2
Ipswich	–	2
Maldon[15]	1	1
Norwich	7 or 8	4
Thetford	–	1

The claims of Bury to be included in the list of possible minting places must, however, be rejected. As shown in the previous chapter, it was not a settlement of importance in the period of the Memorial coinage, or for some long time after, and was possibly not even the resting-place of St Edmund for much of the period of the coinage. Moreover, as this chapter will show, there is no evidence of mint activity at Bury in the next century or more, unlike the other East Anglian locations named above. Nevertheless, regardless of the uncertainties

10 Blunt 1967–9, pp. 252–3. See Brooke 1950, p. 30; Oman 1931, pp. 40, 46. Blunt, Stewart and Lyon 1989, p. 102, considered that the coinage was also likely to have been struck in the southern and central Danelaw.

11 Stenton 1971, pp. 259–60.

12 North 1994, p. 107.

13 Blunt 1974, pp. 78, 80.

14 North 1994, pp. 149–50. Andrew 1901, pp. 229–30, stated (without supporting reasons) that a mint was established at Bury by Eadgar.

15 The name Abonel appears on the coinage of Guthrum/Æthelstan II of East Anglia who died in 890 (see *BMC* 90, in the form Abenel), the St Edmund Memorial coinage (*BMC* 110–28), and at the mints of Hertford and Maldon in the reign of Ælthelstan (Blunt 1972, pp. 25–6). This would support the hypothesis of Maldon as a mint for the Memorial coinage. However, the time span of these issues suggests more than one generation bearing the name Abonel must have been involved and this is borne out by the recurrence of the name at Hertford through to the reign of Eadgar (Chester (1950) Hoard, 483 – see Blunt and Dolley 1952–4, p. 159 and Pl. V). Unlike Maldon, the mint of Hertford is nevertheless an improbable contributor to the Memorial coinage since the Parker version of the *Anglo-Saxon Chronicle* records that only in 912 did Edmund the Elder order a fortress to be built there (*AS Chronicle*, p. 96).

surrounding it, the Memorial coinage represents a remarkable expiation by Danish settlers in East Anglia for the conduct of their pagan fellow countrymen. It also appears to have formed the model for coins issued in commemoration of St Martin at Lincoln and St Peter at York.[16]

Æthelstan to Eadgar

The attribution to Bury of coins from the reign of Æthelstan of the moneyer Eadbald at a place designated as SMRIE or S.MRIE[17] was suggested in an unpublished paper read by Dolley to the Royal Numismatic Society in 1960.[18] He ventured that the inscription was a contraction of SANCTI MARTYRIS EADMVNDI. Dolley repeated the suggestion with some misgivings in a little booklet published in 1964.[19] Quite apart from the incredibility of a loosely organised ecclesiastical community at Beadericesworth enjoying rights from Æthelstan to mint coins bearing the name of the saint or the community rather than the place name, an example with the extended reading SMRIERL[20] (the L being inverted) effectively destroys Dolley's epigraphic interpretation. Blunt in a detailed study of the coinage of Æthelstan conceded the mint as quite uncertain,[21] but Dolley's suggestion has continued to exert an unjustified influence on numismatic publications.[22]

In the Crowned Bust type (*BMC* vi) of Edmund (939–46) rare coins are to be found incorporating mint names into the reverse legend, including the East Anglian mint of Norwich.[23] In this series, reverse inscriptions on coins of the moneyers Nother and Boe include the letters BA and BI respectively which, if intended as mint references, could theoretically allude to Beadericesworth. However, Brooke gave the former, reading +NOÐER IIOHEBA,[24] to Bath.[25] This was logical given the existence of coins of the moneyer Biorhtulf in the reign of Eadwig (955–9) reading BA[26] and in the reign of Eadgar reading

16 North 1994, pp. 109, 116. Ridyard 1988, pp. 214, 217, 226, suggests that the cult of St Edmund may have arisen as a symbol of opposition to the Danes. However, if this had continued to signify in the eyes of the indigenous population it would have been a foolish gamble by the Danish rulers to encourage the cult through the St Edmund Memorial coinage. Given that Guthrum only gained control of East Anglia in 878 and the Memorial coinage was only issued some twenty-five years after St Edmund's death, it is likely that the Danes were associating themselves with a tradition that – if born of protest – had by then lost its original significance. It is even conceivable that the Danes revived a flagging interest in St Edmund for their own purposes.

17 BM (1950); *SCBI* Copenhagen I, 703; Rome, Forum hoard 2, 93. See Blunt 1974, p. 78.

18 Blunt 1961, p. xiv.

19 Dolley 1964, p. 22.

20 National Museum of Wales, ex Lockett 565.

21 Blunt 1974, pp. 78–9.

22 See *Standard Catalogue of British Coins* 2000, p. 127.

23 E.g. *BMC* 3, 4.

24 Blunt 1971, Pl. IV, 9.

25 Brooke 1950, p. 61.

26 Chester (1950) hoard, 262 (Blunt and Dolley 1952–4, p. 150 and Pl. III).

BAĐV,[27] an unambiguous rendering. Blunt subsequently suggested a north-easterly provenance for Nother's coin: firstly, because the Crowned Bust type is otherwise unknown from the west country and, secondly, because this unusual moneyer's name occurs on coins in a style identified with the north-east under Æthelstan and, as Nothe, on a coin struck on behalf of the Viking King Anlaf.[28] This also makes an East Anglian provenance very improbable and Blunt's alternative tentative suggestion of Bedford equally so.[29] It is likely that IIOHEBA in the reverse inscription is simply a blundered rendering of IIOHETA (Moneta).

Blunt's analysis of Nother's coin as emanating from the north-east affords grounds for rejecting a Bury origin for Boe's coin of the same type reading BOEMONETABI.[30] Common sense also suggests that 'I' would not have been a preferred choice of letter to follow the initial 'B' in reference to Beadericesworth, regardless of the precise spelling of the place-name being abbreviated. Quite apart from stylistic arguments, the same reasoning could, incidentally, be applied to the dubious attribution of Nother's coin to Bedford, where the obvious combination of letters would be BE rather than BA.[31]

Under Eadred (946–55) the only mint-signed coins so far known originate from Norwich and Lincoln.[32] The number of mint signatures increase under his nephew, Eadwig (king of England, 955–7 and of Wessex, 957–9) but none could possibly allude to Beadericesworth.[33] Under Eadwig's brother, Eadgar, the coinage falls into two phases. In the first there is a further increase in mint-signed coins but many remain without any indication of mint origin.[34] From this period Hawkins attributed to 'St Edmundsbury' a coin from the Reverend Christmas collection purportedly reading, on the reverse, SIC (or ZIC) EADMONIT and thus omitting the moneyer's name.[35] When sold in 1864 the legend was construed as SIGEDMONET with no reference to Bury.[36] Such a reading clearly typifies a coin with a moneyer's name but no mint signature,[37] and the coin type (Circumscription Rosette, *BMC* iv) is otherwise unknown from East Anglia.[38] In the second phase dating from *c.* 973, represented by Eadgar's Reform Portrait issue, all the coins bear a mint signature. From this period the only

27 Chester (1950) hoard, 490 (Blunt and Dolley 1952–4, p. 158 and Pl. V).

28 Forum hoard 385; Blunt 1971, pp. 18–19. In Blunt, Stewart and Lyon 1989, p. 229, the latter coin is designated as 'Southumbrian'.

29 Blunt 1971, p. 20. See also Blunt, Stewart and Lyon 1989, p. 197.

30 Blunt, Stewart and Lyon 1989, Pl. IV, 10.

31 Seven moneyers are known to have been active at Bedford in the reign of Eadwig, with the mint name being rendered BEDA or BEĐA (Blunt and Dolley 1952–4, p. 150).

32 North 1994, p. 142; Blunt, Stewart and Lyon 1989, p. 198. See also *BNJ* 67 (1997), Coin Register 127.

33 North 1994, pp. 144–5; Blunt, Stewart and Lyon 1989, pp. 154–5, 181.

34 Dolley 1961, p. 142.

35 Hawkins 1887, p. 148.

36 Sotheby, 1 February 1864, 201.

37 Cf. *SCBI* Oxford 416 (ZIFERDMONET).

38 Dolley 1961, p. 142; Blunt, Stewart and Lyon 1989, pp. 186–90.

known coin having a possible link with Beadericesworth is a fragment reading +[ ]VLF M-O BEA. This coin has been attributed to Barnstaple,[39] and given that the mint reading BEARDA occurs under Eadwig[40] and, importantly, the moneyer Beorthulf is associated with the mint reading BEORHTVLF MO BARD in the First Hand type of Æthelred the Unready (978–1016),[41] there is no justification to proffer Bury in place of Barnstaple as the likely mint.

Edward the Martyr

The short rule of Edward the Martyr (975–8) is dignified by a separate section because the shrillest siren voices are heard in his reign for coinage at Bury in the period before Edward the Confessor. To choose but one example, Lobel in her study of urban Bury stated that:

> 'Another indication of the flourishing condition of the vill and that its character was not purely agricultural at this time is the presence of the mint which Edward the Martyr (975–9) [*sic*] is known to have set up.'[42]

Lobel cited in support of her statement a review by York Powell in 1896 of Keary's recently published catalogue of coins in the British Museum. The passage relied upon reads:

> 'Eadweard the Martyr seems only to have set up three new mints – Buckingham, Lydford and St Edmundsbury, the last a place which had at the end of the ninth century probably been the minting place for East England but for which we find no direct evidence since East England came into the hands of the West Saxons till Eadweard's days.'[43]

This curious and inaccurate statement – implying, for example, that Bury was the minting place for the Memorial coinage although Keary himself was careful to avoid making this claim – has misled subsequent historians and archaeologists alike.[44] The error made by York Powell, however, was not originated by him but has an earlier lineage in numismatic literature. Ruding gave in his list of mints for the Martyr's reign the reading SC.EDMD which he innocently ascribed to St Edmundsbury. He also included the name MEN in his separate list of moneyers for the reign.[45] Later, Hawkins in turn cites Ruding,[46] but Keary in the catalogue reviewed by York Powell makes mention of neither Bury nor the moneyer

39 Tingstäde hoard, Gotland, 1970–1. See Jonsson 1975–6, p. 76; illustrated on p. 70.
40 Chester (1950) hoard, 368 (Blunt and Dolley 1952–4, p. 153 and Pl. IV).
41 Brettell sale, Glendining, 18 June 1975, 409 (illustrated).
42 Lobel 1935, p. 3.
43 York Powell 1896, pp. 760–1.
44 Besides Lobel, other references include Andrew 1901, p. 386; Davis 1909, pp. 419, 420; Cam 1963, p. 100; Suffolk County Council Planning Department 1975, p. 48; Gottfried 1982, p. 82.
45 Ruding 1840, I, pp. 132–3.
46 Hawkins 1887, p. 148.

MEN. The coin referred to by Ruding in fact resided not in the British Museum but in the Hunterian Collection at the University of Glasgow. It reads:

O. +AИLRED RED REX A
R. +MEИ HO FCERИ·D·

and is now reassigned from the style of die-cutting to the First Small Cross issue of Æthelred the Unready and tentatively to the mint of York.[47] This mint attribution need not concern us here, but examination of the coin[48] shows that it could plausibly be read as FCEDMD, although the misreading of F as S at the beginning of the mint signature is difficult to excuse. Any lingering doubt in identifying the coin as that referred to by Ruding is dispelled, however, when the list of Hunter's coins prepared by Taylor Combe in 1807,[49] before the collection was moved to Scotland, is consulted. This list includes the coin under Edward the Martyr. Whatever the mint intended, it cannot possibly refer to Beadericesworth, which should be looked for at this period rather than St Edmundsbury. Nevertheless, the pretence of Bury to be the mint has again exercised a malign influence on numismatic as well as historical writings.[50]

Æthelred II and Harold I

Æthelred II and Harold Harefoot (1035/7–40) are the only other monarchs before Edward the Confessor to whom coins of Bury have been attributed. Hawkins,[51] following Lindsay,[52] cites the mint reading 'STED' under Æthelred II as referring possibly to St Edmundsbury. The present writer has been unable to trace this reading on any coins known today, but Hildebrand lists the following closely related readings:[53]

+ÆGENVLF MΩO STÆB (Hild. 3418)
+GODRIC M'O STÆD (Hild. 3426)

He gives these coins to Stafford and there is no reason to doubt this is correct on orthographic or stylistic grounds. Another coin of the moneyer Godric reads STÆÐ (Hild. 3425), whereas coins of Alfwold read STÆÐ and STÆF respectively (Hild. 3422, 3420). Besides, even at this late period the earlier objection to a St Edmundsbury mint signature still holds good, whereas coins of Æthelred II with

47 *SCBI* 1 Glasgow 780. See Jonsson 1987, pp. 176–7, where FCERND is listed as a York reading under the Reform issue and MEN is interpreted as signifying the moneyer Manna, known from other coins in the First Small Cross issue.

48 *SCBI* 1 Glasgow 780, Pl. XXV.

49 *SCBI* 1 Glasgow 780, p. xi.

50 See North 1980, pp.119, 189, 193, but corrected in North 1994.

51 Hawkins 1887, p. 153.

52 Lindsay 1842, pp. 89, 108.

53 Hildebrand 1881, pp. 137–8.

mint signatures beginning BA or BE may, on the basis of other coins with more extended mint signatures under the same moneyers' names, be confidently assigned to Barnstable, Bath or Bedford.

For Harold I, Brooke lists Leofwine as a Bury moneyer.[54] Once again the reason for the attribution is not obvious. He could have had in mind a coin of the Fleur-de-Lis type recorded by Hildebrand as reading +LEOFPINE ON BV (Hild. 38), but this is improbable, since the only two coins assigned by Hildebrand to Buckingham from the systematic collection at Stockholm were this coin and another, of the Jewel-Cross type, reading +BRIHTPINE ON BV (Hild. 37), both being moneyers shown by Brooke as active at Buckingham under Harold I. Also, if Brooke was being guided purely by the mint signature, Peterborough – known from late in the tenth century as Burh[55] – might have been a more obvious suggestion than Bury.[56] Leofwine was in fact one of the commonest moneyer's names in the reigns of Cnut, Harold I and his brother Harthacnut[57] but, apart from the Buckingham coins, it is difficult to see which other mint readings could have attracted Brooke's special notice. A coin reading +LEOFPINE ON E (Hild. 134) was placed by Hildebrand under Exeter, and this is supported by a moneyer of that name striking the posthumous Arm and Sceptre type of Cnut, reading +LEOFPINE ON ECXC (Hild. 401). Hildebrand also placed the coins of the Fleur-de-Lis type reading +LEOFPNE ON SEO (Hild. 831) and +LEOFSTAN ON SE (Hild. 830) to Shrewsbury. His judgment is again supported by a coin of the Jewel-Cross type reading +LEOFSTAN ON SCRO (Hild. 829) and a coin reading +LEOFPINE ONN SCRO (Hild. 3147) in the posthumous Arm and Sceptre issue. These apparent relationships must take precedence over a fanciful interpretation of the reading SE(O).

In the absence of being able to identify actual obverse die-links between clear and unambiguous reverse mint readings, however, or of pointers derived from different regional die-cutting styles discernible in certain Anglo-Saxon issues, it must be admitted that a number of mint attributions may depend upon a mixture of deductive logic and common sense. Cases may accordingly arise where the attribution is not correct, especially where a moneyer's name is common. Despite this caveat, however, the present writer is confident that none of the coins discussed in this chapter can have emanated from Bury.

54 Brooke 1950, p. 70.

55 Ekwall 1960, p. 364; Stewart 1955–7, p. 106.

56 As will be seen in Chapter 9, the mint signature Bury – in the form BERI – only occurs fleetingly in the reign of Henry III. Otherwise, abbreviated variants of SCI EADMVND prevail until the new coinage of Edward I.

57 Hildebrand 1881, pp. 327, 381, 413; North 1994, pp. 172–8.

CHAPTER 3

EDWARD THE CONFESSOR

The Liberty of St Edmund

The door to prosperity was thrust open for the abbey when Edward the Confessor granted to St Edmunds jurisdiction (sake and soke) over the eight and a half hundreds corresponding with the modern geographical area of West Suffolk. This grant, coupled with the fame of the saint, raised Bury to one of the foremost Benedictine houses in the country and so increased the standing of the abbot that he acquired the right to mint coins.

An amusing, if fanciful, account of the circumstances giving rise to the grant of the hundreds is to be found in the Red Vestry Register, compiled early in the fifteenth century.[1] It relates that in the first year of his reign, on the feast of St Edmund (20 November 1042), the Confessor came to Bury and seeing the monks eating barley bread for their midday meal asked why they were so poorly fed. The abbot explained that the resources of the monastery were insufficient for them to take wheat bread. The king is then supposed to have said to the abbot, 'Ask what you will and I will give it to you, so that they may be better nurtured and perform the service of God with the greater zeal and vigour'. Thereupon, the abbot after consulting the brethren asked from the king the Manor of Mildenhall and the eight and a half hundreds with all their liberties as held by him. Edward replied, 'Rashly you have demanded for yourself and your successors a great and unending travail. I would willingly have given you three or four manors. Nevertheless, I will freely grant your request out of the reverence I bear for my kinsman [*sic*] the saint'. The account in the Red Vestry Register, however, attributes this bold stroke of opportunism not to the abbot of the time, Ufi, but the more renowned Baldwin who became abbot in 1065.[2]

The eight and a half hundreds, which came to be known as the Liberty of St Edmund, consisted of the hundreds of Thingoe, Thedwastre, Blackbourn, Bradmore (later merged into Blackbourn), Lackford and Risbridge, together with the double hundred of Babergh and the half hundred of Cosford (see Figure 2). A writ notifying the grant is recorded in the fourteenth century Werketone Register (amongst others),[3] and is generally considered to be

1 Cambridge UL MS Ff.ii 29, fol. 65; *Archives*, no. 1284, p.130.

2 Ufi appears to have been succeeded in 1044 by Leofstan who died on 15 July 1065 (Knowles, Brooke and London 2001, p. 32).

3 BL Harl. MS 638, fol. 26. Other versions are listed by Sawyer (*AS Charters*, no. 1069, p. 319).

Figure 2

The Liberty of St Edmund

authentic, although the transcriber has modernised the language.[4] Harmer renders the writ as follows:

> 'King Edward sends friendly greetings to Bishop Grimketel and Ælfwine and Ælfric and all my thegns in Suffolk. And I inform you that the land at Mildenhall and the sokes of the eight and a half hundreds pertaining to Thingoe shall belong to St Edmund's with sake and with soke as fully and completely as my mother possessed it. And I will not permit anyone to take away from them any of the things that I have already granted to them.'[5]

Hermann gave 1043, rather than 1042, as the date of the grant[6] and among modern writers Davis[7] suggested that the Liberty was granted by the king after he had confiscated it from his mother, Queen Emma, following her disgrace on 16 November 1043.[8] If so, a further fact besides the mistaken identity of the

4 *AS Writs*, p. 117; *AS Charters*, p. 319.
5 *AS Writs*, no. 9, p. 155.
6 *Memorials*, I, p. 48.
7 Davis 1909, p. 418.
8 *AS Chronicle*, pp. 163.

abbot is discredited from the account given in the Red Vestry Register. A potentially important clue to the date of the writ is the reference to Bishop Grimketel. Harmer supported Davis' dating on the ground that Grimketel briefly held the bishopric of East Anglia (Elmham) when Bishop Stigand, the closest confidant of Queen Emma was deprived of his see when she fell from favour.[9] In the next year he was restored[10] and Harmer, following Florence of Worcester's assertion (*s.a.* 1038) that Grimketel held the see during this interval, dated the writ to 1043–4 and more probably 1044.[11] The *Handbook of British Chronology*, on the other hand, gives 1043 both as the year in which Grimketel acceded and that in which he was possibly ejected,[12] maybe because of plurality since he continued to hold the bishopric of Selsey throughout this time.[13] If the *Handbook* is correct, therefore, the Liberty would have been granted to St Edmunds in 1043 rather than 1044. If so, the abbot may have been encouraged to solicit the Liberty because he knew it had just come into the king's hands, upon Emma's disgrace. It is unfortunate that the wording of the grant does not refer to the abbot by name but merely to 'St Edmund's' since, if made in 1043, it could only have been to Abbot Ufi who is recorded as dying and being succeeded by Abbot Leofstan in the following year.[14]

Earlier history of the hundreds

Although the origins of the eight and a half hundreds as a unit of administration or jurisdiction are obscure, Davis surmised they were a morning-gift to Emma upon her marriage to Ælthelred the Unready in 1002 or to her second husband, Cnut, in 1017.[15] Confirmatory grants in favour of St Edmunds by the Confessor to Abbot Leofstan and by William the Conqueror to Abbot Baldwin add that Ælfric, Wihtgar's son, and Orthgar had administered the hundreds on behalf of Emma.[16]

Besides its greetings to Grimketel, the writ of King Edward quoted above is also interesting in that the hundreds are described as 'pertaining to Thingoe'. Apart from being a hundredal name, 'thingoe' was also the name given to an artificial mound lying north-west of Bury itself.[17] The word derived from the old Norse 'thing-haugr', or assembly hill with the word 'thing' suggesting judicial significance.[18] Whatever its original standing, therefore, it was clearly an assembly

9 *AS Chronicle*, p. 162.
10 *AS Chronicle*, p. 165.
11 *AS Writs*, p. 436.
12 Fryde, Greenaway, Porter and Roy 1986, p. 223, where the date on which Grimketel was deprived of his see is qualified by a question-mark.
13 Fryde, Greenaway, Porter and Roy 1986, p. 221.
14 See n. 2 above.
15 Davis 1909, p. 419.
16 *AS Writs*, no. 18, pp. 160–1; *AS Charters*, no. 1078, pp. 321–2 and *Feudal Documents*, no. 3, p. 48.
17 Gage 1838, p. xi, identified it with Shirehouse Heath.
18 *AS Writs*, p. 437; Skeat 1913, p. 69.

point of some antiquity. Hermann referred to it in his story, set in the time of King Ælthelstan, of a sheriff who was stricken with madness when he tried to remove a woman from sanctuary at St Edmund's shrine.[19] These references and the siting of the 'thingoe' have led to acceptance of Bury as the natural administrative centre of the eight and a half hundreds when in Emma's possession and even before.[20] The accident of proximity, however, is not sufficient to justify this conclusion, particularly when bolstered by a misconceived impression of Bury's importance at that time. As was often so,[21] the names of the eight and a half hundreds, other than Lackford,[22] do not refer to centres of population at all but, as their derivations show, to physical features presumably chosen as a distinctive rallying point at which to conduct the administrative or judicial business of a hundred or group of hundreds.[23] Thingoe is a perfect example. Against this background, the choice of the 'thingoe' as the hub of the eight and a half hundreds was almost certainly dictated originally by its location in the midst of the geographical area covered by the hundreds rather than its proximity to Bury. Moreover, although the name evidence, the writ quoted above and even the story told by the often fabulous Hermann point clearly to the special status of the 'thingoe', it is clear that Bury itself was treated as separate from the eight and a half hundreds.[24] To the extent that the distinct identity of Bury existed before the abbot received jurisdiction over the Liberty – and such a distinction could hardly have originated at the time the Liberty came into his hands – it is most improbable that a settlement not forming part of the eight and a half hundreds would have served as their administrative centre. The separation could in theory have occurred as late as the reign of Cnut, either when Emma was granted the eight and a half hundreds or, if they were indeed a morning-gift, when Cnut and Emma together became benefactors of the newly-founded Benedictine monastery.[25] However, had Bury been the centre of the hundredal organisation at that time it is incredible that it would have been separated at all. It is equally incredible that as late as the reign of the Confessor the administration of the hundreds should be attached simply to the 'thingoe'. This suggests that somewhere other than Bury may have been important in the hundredal structure.

Although the hundreds were in one of the more densely populated areas of the country,[26] they contained scarcely any substantial settlements, pointing to

19 *Memorials*, I, pp. 30–1.

20 Cam 1963, p. 100; Davis 1909, pp. 418–19; Hurnard 1949, pp. 319–20.

21 Loyn 1984, p. 144; Blair 1977, p. 238.

22 By Domesday (DB II, fol. 357a) Lackford was across the border in Thingoe hundred, but this must have arisen from some earlier redrawing of the boundary between the hundreds of Lackford and Thingoe.

23 See Blair 1977, p. 237.

24 *AS Writs*, p. 437. The grant of jurisdiction to Abbot Leofstan and the brethren over all their men within the borough (byrig) and without (*AS Writs*, no. 11, p. 156), was distinct from that over the eight and a half hundreds (*AS Writs*, no. 18, p. 160). See also DB II, fol. 372a.

25 *The Kalendar of Abbot Sampson*, p. xxv, and Finn 1967, p. 116, suggest 1021 or even earlier.

26 Hill 1981, p. 19, where Map 26 shows the population in 1066, based on the work of H. C. Darby.

agrarian-based prosperity. By far the most important centre of population in the Liberty was Sudbury, which Domesday Book records as having 138 burgesses, a market and 'moneyers.'[27] Clues also exist pointing to its importance within the hundreds. Pursuing an observation by Round,[28] R. H. C. Davis noted that Sudbury, lying on the boundary of Essex to the south and the double hundred of Babergh on its other three sides, was by the time of the Domesday survey recorded as forming part of Thingoe hundred, whose closest boundary lay seven miles further to the north. Davis concluded that since the geld assessment for taxation purposes of Sudbury at 60 pence corresponded with that of Bury, Sudbury had been transferred to Thingoe hundred to compensate for the loss of Bury's geld contribution when it was separated. This explained, after allowing for minor clerical errors, the 75 pence shortfall in the full geld assessment of 480 pence for the double hundred of Babergh. Davis also considered that the deficit against the 240 pence contribution of Thingoe as a single hundred had been made up in this way because the impact of such a deficit was less marked upon a double than upon a single hundred.[29] This explanation is neat but by no means convincing. Since hundred boundaries could be and were modified,[30] an adjustment of that kind would have been a more obvious and convenient expedient to mitigate the effect of the loss of contribution than a geographically remote substitute for Bury. It is thus far more probable that Sudbury had been chosen in preference (or substitution) for Bury simply because it was the most suitable choice of administrative centre for the group of hundreds under Emma, and had it not been for the grant of the hundreds to St Edmunds, Sudbury may well have emerged as the county town for West Suffolk. It certainly enjoyed minting rights for coinage some thirty years before Bury,[31] although a clear picture is bedevilled by uncertainties between the mint inscriptions for Sudbury and Southwark,[32] and by gaps in continuity possibly explicable by the scarcity of surviving coins.

Confirmatory grants under the Confessor and beyond

The original grant of the eight and a half hundreds to Abbot Ufi was confirmed to his successors, Leofstan and Baldwin. The writ surviving from the abbacy of Leofstan has been dated to 1052 or 1053–7,[33] which may appear strange since he had succeeded Ufi in 1044. One explanation offered[34] is that the hundreds had been returned to Emma after the grant of 1043 x 1044, her death on 14 March

27 DB II, fols 40a, 76b and 286b. Clare, although smaller, also had a market and was the only other place in West Suffolk for which burgesses as such are recorded in Domesday Book (DB II, fol. 389b).

28 Round 1895, p. 101, n. 187.

29 *The Kalendar of Abbot Samson*, pp. xxv–xxvi.

30 See n. 22 above.

31 North 1994, pp. 155, 166.

32 Dolley 1955–7a, pp. 264–9.

33 *AS Writs* no.18, p. 161.

34 Barlow 1997, p. 77.

1052[35] accounting for the timing of the writ. If this were correct the writ should sensibly be dated to 1053–7 since it states specifically that Edward himself held the hundreds after his mother had done so. However, it is unlikely that the abbey would have been able to recover the Liberty after a lapse of some years. The explanation may simply be that Edward held the hundreds briefly in 1043 or 1043–4 before granting them to St Edmunds. The wording of the writ is consistent with this interpretation in that it was not so much confirming the sokes of the Liberty to Leofstan as clarifying that the rights of 'hamsocn, grithbreach, foresteall, fihtwite and æbæretheof' had not been alienated from St Edmunds to anyone else.

The grant was confirmed to Baldwin[36] by a writ of Edward the Confessor between the date of Leofstan's death on 16 July 1065[37] and of the king himself on 5 January 1066. Copies of later confirmations resulting from the accession of a new king or the appointment of a new abbot have also survived. It is not always possible, however, to match the writs precisely with these events because the wording affords insufficient clues by which to date them accurately. In spite of this, the confirmations granted by William I and II – placed by Douglas between 1066 and 1070,[38] and 1087 and 1100,[39] respectively – may safely be attributed to the beginning of their reigns as it is inconceivable that, in the absence of an abbatial vacancy, the jurisdiction enjoyed by St Edmunds over the hundreds could have been held long in abeyance or doubt.[40] In practice, administrative chaos may have been avoided by allowing St Edmunds to exercise its rights on a provisional basis until confirmation was received. This consideration would not apply to a change of abbot because, at least after the Conquest, the revenues collected from his temporalities (including fines derived from the hundredal jurisdiction) were simply made over by the abbey's officials to the king until a successor was appointed.[41] Since until early in the reign of Henry I no distinction was drawn between the temporalities attaching to the monastery and to the abbot himself,[42] the king stood to gain handsomely from any vacancy. This probably explains why Baldwin, who died in 1097/8, was not replaced until 1100.

Grant of minting rights

During the reign of Edward the Confessor the first coins appear with an incontestable Bury mint signature. Those examples known to exist are noted and each die is illustrated in the Catalogue. These are from the fourth through to the

35 Fryde, Greenaway, Porter and Roy 1986, p. 28.

36 *AS Writs*, no. 25, pp. 165–6.

37 *Memorials*, I, p. 344. This citation is incorrectly used in Knowles, Brooke and London 2001, p. 32, to give 15 July 1065 as the date of Leofstan's death.

38 *Feudal Documents*, no. 3, p. 48.

39 *Feudal Documents*, no. 18, p. 60.

40 The eminence of Abbot Baldwin (see Chapter 4 below) must have contributed to a rapid confirmation of St Edmunds' privileges.

41 Howell 1962, pp. 10–11, concluded that the practice was imported from the Duchy of Normandy.

42 See Chapter 5 below.

ninth main issues of the reign, namely, the Small Flan, Expanding Cross, Helmet, Sovereign-Eagles, Hammer Cross and Facing Bust types.[43]

No copy has come to light of a charter or writ originating the abbot's privilege to strike coins, but copies have survived of Edward's grant of one moneyer to Baldwin, between the date of his becoming abbot upon the death of Leofstan on 16 July 1065 and the death of the king on 5 January 1066. Besides its cardinal importance for the history of the Bury mint, the writ is also the earliest extant record of a specific grant of coinage rights in England.[44] Harmer renders it as follows:

> 'King Edward sends greetings to Bishop Æthelmær and Earl Gyrth and Toli and all my thegns in East Anglia. And I inform you that I have granted to Abbot Baldwine a (or one) moneyer within St Edmund's Bury, to have with the same freedom from restriction as I have my own anywhere in any of my boroughs where I have them more freely than anywhere else. May God be the friend of you all.'[45]

Certain writers, construing the wording of the writ literally, have concluded that it originated rather than confirmed the minting rights of the abbot.[46] Since coins can be attributed to Bury from six of the ten main types issued by Edward, it would necessarily follow from such construction that a royal mint had operated at Bury until the abbacy of Baldwin at the end of the Confessor's reign. This view was indeed taken by Ruding,[47] who knew of only one Bury coin from the reign, a Hammer Cross penny then, as now, in the Ashmolean Museum at Oxford.[48] However, although the dating, as opposed to the sequence, of the types has not been satisfactorily determined, the earliest known coins from Bury, of the Small Flan type,[49] are generally agreed to have been in issue no earlier than about 1048.[50] By this time the king had already granted the eight and a half hundreds, confirmed the privileges of the monastery,[51] and possibly accorded sake and soke to Leofstan and the brethren over their men within Bury and without.[52] It is, therefore, most unlikely that the king would have set up his own mint in the vill. Moreover, during Edward's reign, the recurrence of individual moneyers' names at neighbouring mints suggests some interchange took place between mints under royal control.[53] At Bury, however, Morcere is

43 For the provisional dating of the types see Table 2 below.

44 Cribb 1986, p. 48.

45 *AS Writs*, no. 25, pp. 165–6, from Cartae Antiquae Roll P, no. 4. For a list of manuscripts containing versions of the writ, see *AS Charters*, no. 1078, pp. 323–4.

46 E.g. Davis 1909, p. 420; Lobel 1935, p.11 (who refers to Leofstan in mistake for Baldwin).

47 Ruding 1840, II, pp. 217–18.

48 Catalogue, 5 (1).

49 Catalogue, 1 (1)–(3).

50 See Table 2 below.

51 *AS Writs*, no. 8, pp. 153–4, and no. 13, pp. 157–8.

52 *AS Writs*, no. 11, p. 156, dated by Harmer to 1044–65. Although there is no direct evidence for a closer dating, it is likely to form one of a group of privileges granted or confirmed upon the appointment of Leofstan.

53 Freeman 1985, I, p. 264 and *passim*.

the only moneyer known to have been active and his name is not associated with any other mint.

Features of Edward's coinage

Although some features of late Anglo-Saxon coinage are now well understood, there remain important areas of debate and uncertainty. One eminent historian of the period has suggested that it is difficult to explain the monetary system satisfactorily without attributing to the government a grasp of economics which seems unlikely in the eleventh century and that, even ignoring foreign trade and exchange, there is so much we do not know that economic analysis is hardly worthwhile.[54] In avoiding the danger of importing modern ideas into Anglo-Saxon minds, however, there may be a corresponding risk of underestimating the ability of the king and his advisers to manage the economy or, at least, their belief in their ability to do so.

An outstanding feature of late Anglo-Saxon coinage was, as has been frequently pointed out, the level of central control asserted by the king.[55] His officials designed the coin type, laid down the weight and purity at which the coins were to be struck and issued the dies to the moneyers responsible locally for minting the actual coins. The link between the royal officials and the mint officials is less clear. The Domesday Book entry for Huntingdon implies that there were three moneyers TRE, accountable to the king, but that William I farmed the mint out to the burgesses. Under the earlier arrangement the king had shared the ancient payment of 40 shillings from the moneyers with the local earl, presumably in the proportion of 2:1, resulting in the so-called 'earl's third penny'.[56]

How far this cameo is representative of mint organisation under the Confessor and the Conqueror respectively is not known. Distinct from these 'royal' mints, from as early as the reign of Æthelstan, a very limited number of ecclesiastics were also granted the privilege to strike the official coinage. The rights of the abbot, described above, fall into this category and are considered in the next section. The minting process as such was thus devolved upon individuals and legislation introduced to control their activities and impose heavy penalties for dishonest or negligent conduct. The moneyers were made directly accountable for the coins struck under their authority by the system of inscribing their name and mint location on the reverse dies issued to them. The position of moneyer was sought after not only because of the profits to be earned, but also for the prestige attaching to the office and freedom from taxes.[57] Indeed, for the

54 Barlow 1997, pp. 182–3.

55 e.g. Craig 1953, p. 8; Oman 1931, p. 73; Loyn 1961, pp. 124–9; Barlow 1997, p. 181; Challis 1992, p. 49.

56 DB, fol. 203b; Eaglen 1999, pp. 84–5.

57 *Norman Kings*, I, pp. cxli–cxlii; Challis 1992, p. 69.

moneyers at minor mints or less active moneyers at major mints, the prospect of profits could well have been the least of the incentives to become a moneyer.

Control of the internal monetary system was further enhanced because circulation of foreign coin appears to have been forbidden.[58] A single currency was, of course, more easily maintained in an island kingdom than in Continental Europe. The system was further simplified by having one denomination, the penny, struck in silver at a high level of purity.[59] To meet the need for a smaller denomination pennies could legitimately be cut into halves or quarters. These features created confidence in the coinage both within the kingdom and abroad, and may have enabled the government to modify the weight from issue to issue without causing a general reluctance to accept the coins at their face value. Such weight variations nevertheless remain the most difficult feature of the monetary system to explain.

It is generally recognised which designs constituted the substantive coin types issued in the reign of the Confessor but, although the sequence is clear, the dating of each successive type is not. Pursuing the thesis of Dolley that from the Reform Coinage of Eadgar the coin type was changed at regular intervals, whereupon the old type ceased to be legal tender,[60] Seaby suggested that a biennial cycle applied in the early part of the reign, followed by triennial in the latter part.[61] Dolley further suggested that the change of type probably occurred at Michaelmas (29 September) rather than at the turn of the year.[62] This refinement is certainly plausible because from no later than the twelfth century it was one of the two dates in the year on which the sheriffs had to make their returns of revenues to the king, and therefore provided a suitable occasion on which details of the new type could be announced.[63] In spite of the criticism this scheme of dating has provoked,[64] it provides a useful framework until better knowledge enables us to confirm or modify the dates put forward. Table 2 shows the sequence of types and for each type the dates derived from Seaby with

58 Dolley 1966, p. 8. That indigenous regal coin alone should be allowed as currency was promulgated by Æthelstan in the decrees of Grately (see *EHD*, I, p. 420). The lack of foreign coins in tenth and eleventh century English hoards is testimony of how successfully this policy was pursued by succeeding kings (Dolley and Metcalf 1961, p. 149).

59 A surprising level of debasement has been found in the Last Small Cross issue of Æthelred II and Quatrefoil issue of Cnut (Eaglen and Grayburn 2000, pp. 22–6, confirmed by Metcalf and Northover 2002, pp. 217–36), using coins of the same types from the trays of the Ashmolean Museum and referring to analytical results from a sparse sample of coins from early issues of Edward the Confessor obtained by Harris 1962, pp. 5–7. See also Forbes and Dalladay 1960–1, pp. 82–7.

60 Summarised in Dolley and Metcalf 1961, pp. 156–7.

61 Seaby 1955–7, pp. 128–9.

62 Dolley 1955–7b, p. 284, resuscitating an hypothesis suggested by Carlyon-Britton 1905, pp. 203–4.

63 Barlow 1997, p. 186, who remarks pointedly (p. 181) on the absence of any surviving laws on legal tender.

64 Brand 1984 for an impassioned numismatist's view and Barlow 1997, p. xxviii, n. 1, and pp. 182–3, for an historian's.

Table 2. Provisional chronology and summary of mint activity under Edward the Confessor

Type	*Date*	*No. of Years*	*No. of coins*	*No. of mints*	*Standard weight* gr.	g
1 PACX	1042–4[a]	2	679	53	18	1.17
2 Radiate	1044–6	2	972	56	17	1.10
3 Trefoil	1046–8	2	784	56	18	1.17
4 Small Flan	1048–50	2	770	55[b]	18	1.17
5 Expanding Cross (light)	1050–1	1	996	53[b]	18	1.17
(heavy)	1051–3	2			27	1.75
6 Helmet	1053–6	3	979	59[b]	21.5	1.39
7 Sovereign	1056–9	3	744	53[b]	20.5	1.33
8 Hammer Cross	1059–62	3	1280	63[b]	21.5	1.39
9 Facing Bust	1062–5	3	895	53[b]	17	1.10
10 Pyramids	1065–6	–	606	50	21.5	1.39

Notes
(a) Harthacnut died on 8 June 1042, but Edward was not crowned until the following Easter.
(b) Including Bury.

Dolley's refinement, the number of surviving coins and mints represented, as identified by Freeman,[65] and the weight standard(s) in grains for each type as suggested by Grierson.[66]

Key to Seaby's dating scheme was the dramatic increase in weight from 18 to 27 gr. during the Expanding Cross issue.[67] He associated this with abolition of the unpopular heregeld,[68] a tax to pay foreign mercenaries, recorded in the *Anglo-Saxon Chronicle* in 1051.[69] Taking this year as the fulcrum, the remaining types were distributed mathematically on either side. This produced a neat two-year timespan for the first four types, a further two years for the heavy emission of Expanding Cross coins, on the heels of one year for the light, and three years for each of the next four types. This left just over three months for the Pyramids type at the end of the reign, on Dolley's reckoning. Although Dolley had over-estimated the rarity of the Pyramids type,[70] it would be natural to expect a considerable output of coin in the early months of the new type, especially if it were needed to meet tax commitments following the harvest of 1065.

65 Freeman 1985, II, Appendices II, p. 530, and IV, p. 538. Freeman is likely to have recorded the majority of coins currently known to exist, although his statistics may, in some cases, be distorted by separate references which allude to the same coin. For Bury he cited 20 coins, compared with 30 listed in Catalogue 1–7 below.

66 Grierson 1961, p. 275.

67 Seaby 1955–7, p. 128. Lyon 1976, p. 204, has accepted Seaby's thesis, but Brand 1984, pp. 6–7, treated it as questionable.

68 Dolley 1966, p. 10.

69 *AS Chronicle*, p. 173, where the passage is translated as if to refer to the danegeld. Barlow 1997, p. 106, n. 5 and p. 184, suggests the geld was suspended rather than 'abolished', as the *AS Chronicle* recorded.

70 Eaglen 2001a, pp. 309–10.

As will be seen from Table 2 and the Catalogue, no Bury coins of the Pyramids type are known to exist. This could be owing to the accidents of survival or discovery and, despite the small number of known coins from the mint in the Confessor's reign, the number of dies represented suggest that further dies remain to be discovered. These could indicate an increased output of known types or extend the activity of the mint back beyond the earliest type at present known or forwards to the Pyramids type. It is also possible that an interruption in the activity of the mint arose because of the death or resignation of the moneyer Morcere. All this, however, is speculative compared with the knowledge that Abbot Leofstan died in the summer of 1065, about the time that preparations for the new type would have been under way. A possible explanation, therefore, is that the four months of the reign remaining were insufficient for the installation of Abbot Baldwin, confirmation of his right to mint coins, (both of which occurred) and the engraving, issue and bringing into use of Bury dies for the Pyramids issue. On this hypothesis it would be purely a coincidence that the type is likewise at present unknown from the neighbouring mint of Sudbury. More remarkably , however, at both mints the first known type after the Facing Bust issue is the second, Bonnet type of William I.[71]

That in late Anglo-Saxon times coins of the old type ceased to be legal tender on or shortly after the introduction of a new type has become widely accepted amongst numismatists,[72] but has been treated more cautiously by some historians.[73] However, in the reign of Edward the Confessor a policy is evident of clearly distinguishing between the consecutive types, especially where a change of weight standard between types was also involved. Thus, the reduction of the standard on introduction of the Helmet type was marked by the king's bust facing right whereas hitherto it had pointed to the left, and the further reduction from 21.5 to 17 gr. later in the reign was marked by a hitherto unique facing bust and smaller diameter coin. There could be no doubt, even among the illiterate or unobservant, that the type had changed. The slightly lower weight of the Sovereign type, compared with the immediately preceding and succeeding issues, was also signified by a unique design. This contrasts strikingly with the close similarity between, for example, the Bonnet and Canopy types of William I, which will be considered later.

The contents of hoards including coins of the Confessor for which details of the types exist do not afford clear evidence on the circulation of a single design as legal tender at any one time. With the exception of Soberton,[74] and the tiny

71 North 1994, pp. 186, 196.

72 Lyon 1976, pp. 194–5, is more cautious in his views, intimating that new coin was possibly obligatory only for the payment of taxes, but that this would lead to the unacceptability of old coin for general use as well.

73 E.g. Barlow 1997, p. 181.

74 *Inventory*, no. 334, pp. 125–6. For convenience, J. D. A. Thompson's *Inventory* is generally used in this work for hoards published before 1956. For more detailed investigation of the statistics summarised by Thompson, reference should be made to the authorities cited in the *Inventory*, together with any published after 1956.

Stockbridge Down hoard,[75] the others contain a number of types. These hoards nevertheless probably represented savings systematically put aside in peaceful times, the saver treating his accumulation of coin as bullion until such time as he had need of current coin when it would be melted and re-struck, to incur only one set of minting charges. The remarkable absence of wear and of the later habit of clipping away the edges of the coins in circulation,[76] especially when a heavier issue was replaced by a lighter, are further pointers to a single type circulating at any one time, at least following such a weight change.

Against this background, however, the most dramatic weight difference in the Confessor's reign occured, as Table 2 shows, not between types but within the Expanding Cross issue, struck at two weight standards: 18 and 27 gr. Although the lighter coins have marginally smaller flans, the use of the same obverse and reverse designs proves conclusively that one weight was not intended to supersede the other in general use, but it was foreseen that both would circulate together.[77] There is no more elegant evidence that for the populace, as opposed to merchants or tax collectors dealing with large amounts of money, the face value and not its weight was the dominant feature of a coin. This may seem extraordinary, but in the recent past Æthelred II and Cnut in particular had systematically lowered the weight of coins struck during the life-span of a type.[78]

Bearing in mind the inevitable fluctuation of up to 5 per cent or even more in the weight of individual coins produced to a particular standard,[79] it is doubtful if the average person who had occasion to use money would have been concerned or even conscious other than at a change of type of official weight variations falling within the limits of 5–10 per cent. The inflexibility of the penny as a unit of relatively high value, being susceptible only to halving or quartering, would also have helped its use at face value for small transactions. For merchants, however, especially if involved in significant transactions or foreign trade where the bullion content of any payment would have been important, although the volume of money passing hands would tend to average out discrepancies in the weight of coins struck approximately to a particular standard, it seems very likely that the coin was weighed. This would have been done either to verify the accuracy of a payment by tale, as is current banking practice, thus ensuring that the payment was not constituted with coin light in bullion content, or even as a practical means to establish an amount due without resorting

75 Dolley 1955–7b, pp. 283–7.

76 Lyon 1976, p. 216.

77 Eaglen 1999, p. 77. The traditional assumption that the light Expanding Cross issue preceded the heavy has been questioned by Williams 1998, pp. 152–3, and defended by Lyon 1998, pp. 426–8.

78 See, for example, Eaglen 1999, pp. 54–5, 59, 61, 65, 72.

79 The vast majority of coins of one type from the Lincoln mint under the Confessor were within 5–10% of the median weight, although the number of coins in the 5–10% divergent bands were also more than double the number falling within the narrow weight range constituting the median weight (see Mossop 1970, Table 5). At Huntingdon, in the Long Cross type of Æthelred II, the outer limits of deviation from a standard of 1.63 g appear to have been +5% and −7% (see Eaglen 1999, p. 55).

to a laborious count by tale. In this case the coin could simply be spread on a flat surface after weighing to check that it was uniformly of correct currency.

A major role for coinage was still to facilitate the collection of taxes and other dues owing to the king.[80] When this liability was expressed in terms of weight, manipulations in the standard would be neutral in their effect, but not so when liability was expressed by tale. It is hard to see weight changes other than as a means whereby the king could increase his revenues, or reduce the tax burden on his subjects. This in turn suggests that at this period tax liabilities were customarily expressed by tale. If this picture is correct, Edward may have taken steps to channel the monies hitherto paid as heregeld into his own coffers, instead of leaving them as a windfall to his subjects, by requiring dues to be met in coins of the heavier standard. If so, the large weight increase in the Expanding Cross issue may have been both unpopular in itself and have artificially depressed the quantity of coin in circulation with a consequent effect on prices. The co-existence of widely disparate standards may also have caused problems. Against this background it is not surprising that the weight standard in the next, Helmet type was reduced to 21.5 gr. Only six Bury coins of the Expanding Cross type have so far come to light (see Table 3 below), and none is known to have been struck at the 18 gr. standard. On the above hypothesis, given that the abbey at this point was exempt from taxes and dues, it would appear that the coins were struck for mint clients who did not enjoy such immunity.

Apart from the payment of a fee by moneyers on the issue of new dies, which is clearly documented,[81] it is not known at this period what levy was imposed upon owners of coin or bullion to cover minting costs and profits at a recoinage or whenever unusable coin or silver was taken to a mint workshop for striking into current coin.[82] Logically, the moneyers' men would have deducted as coining fees either a proportion of the melted silver or of the coins produced or producible from the silver, or both, to be shared in the royal mints with the king, and, possibly, the local earl. To reduce delays, the mint may have maintained a stock of ready-coined pennies to issue against silver brought into the mint. The mint officials would still have had to satisfy themselves by assay or melting that an appropriate quantity of coin was being offered in exchange. Upon the approach of a recoinage at least, unless the king had specific need of coin, his share in the minting profits would probably have been retained as bullion, in order to prime the system when the new type was introduced. This may explain why at later recoinages the franchisal mint at Bury was not significantly involved at the outset. In any event, as already noted, initial demand for the new type must have been lively, followed by only fitful activity at the lesser mints thereafter until the next type change.

80 Dolley and Metcalf 1961, p. 154.

81 *Norman Kings*, I, p. cxxxv.

82 Petersson 1969, p. 101, following Bolin's theories, calculated a standard surcharge up to the Conquest of one third. This suggestion has been criticised by Lyon 1976, p. 206, and Lyon 1971, pp. 101–20, and appears exceedingly unlikely, especially as late as the reign of the Confessor.

It has been claimed that the currency in late Anglo-Saxon England was substantially overvalued,[83] but this is difficult to prove, particularly in periods of weight variation which have prompted this very theory. If, as already suggested, significant business transactions were conducted by weight rather than by tale, changes in the weight of a penny would be irrelevant to its value in such transactions.[84] Similarly, weight changes would have no direct effect on the face value of the penny when used to pay royal taxes and dues whether by weight or tale. On this analysis only coin used by tale by the populace for small transactions would be over (or under) valued at the time of the transaction. It is hard to imagine, however, that the populace in general would have perceived any difference between the actual purchasing power of English pence and their approximate bullion value. There is at least no evidence either in the make-up of coin hoards, or from clipping or the like, to suggest that such a situation was recognised as existing and being capable of exploitation.

Ecclesiastical mints

In late Anglo-Saxon England nearly all of the fifty to sixty or so mints known to have operated in each type appear to have been under the direct or indirect control of the king, who had at least a share in the profits derived from their activity.[85] Then as in other periods, however, a few select ecclesiastics were granted the privilege of having their own moneyers. The nature of their entitlement is not clear and may have varied from time to time and place to place. At Hereford, according to Domesday Book, the bishop received 20 shillings from his moneyer when new dies were issued at a recoinage.[86] How far, if at all, he otherwise shared in the profits is not mentioned. At a later date the archbishop of Canterbury is known to have shared in the expenses and profits of the mint at Canterbury in proportion to the number of moneyers he employed alongside those of the king.[87] At Bury, however, apart from having to obtain approval for the appointment of his moneyer and other mint officials, and to return old dies against the issue of new,[88] the abbot appears to have been free to organise the internal economics of the mint to his liking and to strike his own deal to cover the costs and profits of the moneyer and his workmen. It would be sensible to assume, however, that his mint applied financial terms to its customers corresponding with those offered by mints under royal control.

83 E.g. Dolley and Metcalf 1961, p. 158.

84 Such weight changes would also not affect the inflow or outflow of silver in foreign trade transactions.

85 According to DB (I, fol. 203), at Huntingdon in the time of the Confessor three moneyers paid 40 shillings for their rights, shared equally between the king and the earl.

86 DB, fol. 179.

87 See Chapter 8 below.

88 These limitations on his freedom of action are spelt out in the exchequer records relating to the Long Cross coinage of Henry III (see Chapter 9 below), but might well have originated considerably earlier. For example, the use of single sets of dies (one obverse with one or two reverses) is apparent during the Short Cross coinage at the beginning of Henry's reign (see Chapter 8 below).

Not only the scope of entitlement, but also the actual operation and mint output of a number of these ecclesiastical franchises, is difficult or impossible to gauge with any certainty. This arises because in the late Anglo-Saxon period coins issued under ecclesiastical authority had no special distinguishing marks: the right was to mint the king's coinage, not their own. At Bury, where only the abbot had a mint workshop, the name of the town of issue on the reverse was sufficient to identify the abbot's coinage. But in places where both royal and ecclesiastical moneyers were at work, in the absence of documentary evidence, no distinction can be drawn from the names of the moneyers active there. Canterbury is an example of this difficulty. By the decrees of Grately, Æthelstan had granted two moneyers to the archbishop and one to the abbot of St Augustine's to operate in the city in addition to four moneyers of the king.[89] No documentary evidence exists to show if this allotment applied in the Confessor's reign. Nevertheless, recent work suggests, on the basis of surviving coins, that for each type of the Confessor seven moneyers were plausibly active, except in the Sovereign and – not surprisingly – the Pyramids type.[90] The value of this evidence, however, must be treated cautiously because the 251 coins recorded by Freeman produce 75 different monetype combinations, including 18 combinations represented by a single coin,[91] so this may not be a comprehensive sample. Moreover, owing to the lack of distinctive marks or written records of his moneyers' names, even if one of the moneyers was, for example, in the employ of the abbot of St Augustine's, it is not possible to identify him.

Turning to Hereford, Domesday Book records that there were again seven moneyers of whom one was in this instance allotted to the bishop.[92] The picture emerging here from surviving coins is less clear than at Canterbury owing to the smallness of the sample, 67 coins producing 38 different monetype combinations; 15 of these coins, however, are of the Hammer Cross type and conveniently provide seven moneyers' names.[93] According to Domesday Book the bishop of Norwich could if he wished have one moneyer,[94] but again there is no means of knowing if the right was exercised. The archbishop of York was entitled to two moneyers from no later than the reign of William I, whose coins cannot usually be distinguished from those of the royal moneyers in York,[95] and the bishop of Durham first had the right to a moneyer in the 1080s.[96] The abbot of Peterborough appears to have been granted by Eadgar the right to employ one moneyer at the neighbouring mint of Stamford,[97] and a coin of Æthelred II

89 *EHD*, I, p. 420.

90 Freeman 1985, pp. 512–14 and Appendices, where somewhat different conclusions are drawn from the statistics.

91 Each monetype represents the distinct combination of a moneyer at a mint and the type in which he struck coins. Thus Morcere striking in six types at Bury represents six monetypes.

92 DB I, fols 179, 181b.

93 Freeman 1985, pp. 376–7.

94 DB II, fol. 117b.

95 Allen 2004a, pp. 25–9.

96 Allen 1994, pp. 384–6; Allen 2003, pp. 3, 14, 17, 165–6.

97 *AS Charters*, no. 787, p. 251, where its authenticity is questioned.

has been erroneously and another of Cnut very dubiously identified with Medeshamstede, the Anglo-Saxon name for Peterborough.[98] So far, moreover, no coins with readings capable of attribution to Peterborough have come to light for the Confessor's reign. This grant was analogous to that accorded to the abbot of Reading in the reign of Henry I to have a moneyer operating on his behalf at London.[99] In contrast, there is no evidence of the abbot of Bury having a moneyer at work away from his vill.

In this brief survey of ecclesiastical coinage it is also convenient to deal here with coins of the Conqueror reading SAGSTI STEFANII without a moneyer's name and GODRIC ON SINTSTFNI. Brooke accepted the attribution of these by Carlyon-Britton to the Canons of St Stephen at Launceston,[100] but Blunt, in his review of ecclesiastical mints, passed over them in dismissive silence.[101] If Carlyon-Britton were correct, these coins of the canons would constitute the only examples from this period of coins clearly identifiable as the output of an ecclesiastical authority apart from those of the abbot of Bury.[102]

Surviving coins of Bury

The Catalogue gives details of 30 coins of Edward the Confessor known to survive from the Bury mint. These are summarised in Table 3. As in other parts of the Catalogue the number of references to coins is greater but descriptions in auction catalogues and elsewhere which cannot be verified from actual coins, photographs or casts must be treated as suspect or at least uncertain. Without such physical evidence, even where a description tallies with a coin known to exist, it may still be impossible to say if the known coin is being referred to or another, otherwise unrecorded specimen.

According to Seaby's dating scheme, the first known coins of Bury in the Small Flan type were struck between about 1048 and 1050. This would have been from five to seven years after the grant of the eight and a half hundreds, suggesting that rapid enrichment of the abbey and increasing influence led to the grant of minting rights closely upon that of the Liberty. The dies throughout the reign appear to have been issued in sets of one obverse with one reverse. Only in the

98 Blunt 1960, p. xv. The coin of Cnut, however, is suspiciously late to bear the Medeshamstede signature since the name Burh had supplanted it by the eleventh century (see Ekwall 1960, p. 364). Moreover, a coin of Æthelred II, reading +HILDE M-O MEÐELTV (Dunger 1999) has been attributed by Mark Blackburn to Melton Mowbray (Blackburn 2000). This must increase doubts over later coins with MEÐ readings having emanated from Peterborough.

99 Blunt 1961, p. v; *Regesta* II, pp. 192–3. See *Reading Abbey Cartularies*, I, pp. 33, 35, for the view that the text, although spurious as it stood, possibly represented an 'improved' version of a genuine original.

100 *Norman Kings*, I, p. clxxiii.

101 See Blunt 1960 and Blunt 1961.

102 No coins can be attributed to the minting rights granted to the bishop of Bath by William II (see *Regesta* II, no. 362, p. 85, and Grinsell 1973, p. 33).

Table 3. Known Bury coins of Edward the Confessor by *BMC* type

Moneyer: Morcere

BMC type		*No. of coins*	*No. of dies*		*Mint reading*
			O.	*R.*	
ii	Small Flan	3	1	1	ED
v	Expanding Cross				
	(light)	–	–	–	–
	(heavy)	6	1	1	EDHVN
vii	Helmet	6	1	1	EDM
ix	Sovereign-Eagles	1	1	1	EADM
xi	Hammer Cross	10	2*	2*	EADMVN
xiii	Facing Bust	4	1	1	EAD
xv	Pyramids	–	–	–	–
Total		30	7	7	

Note
*Hammer Cross dies only found as unlinked pairs.

Hammer Cross issue is more than one set of dies known to have been used. This results in a tally of six monetypes, similar to the mints of Watchet and Buckingham, and ranking Bury as fifty-fourth of a total of seventy-six mints active in the reign.[103] Those below Bury tended to be single moneyer mints not active (from the evidence of survival) from type to type. Two of the Bury dies are worthy of particular notice, the Hammer Cross reverse with small crosses saltire in two of the quarters (Catalogue 6) and the reverse of the Facing Bust type which has been modified by the addition of two vertical lines connecting the central cross with the inner circle (Catalogue 7 and 8). The cross saltire is found on other coins of the Confessor, for example, a Facing Bust type from Dorchester[104] but the significance of these and other symbols such as pellets and crescents is not known.[105] The neat modification of a conventional die by the addition of two bars is equally curious but must have been carried out at the mint to indicate that some aspect of the coins struck from the dies had altered. This could only signal a change in weight from the standard, a change in purity of the silver or a change in responsibility for minting the coins. There is no suggestion of a different weight standard between the coins recorded in the Catalogue and, although it has not been possible to test the purity of coins struck from the conventional and modified die, the likelihood of such a change by the abbot's mint is remote. Thus, most probably the die was being used by someone other than Morcere, perhaps as a temporary expedient until dies in

103 For the basis of this calculation see Eaglen 2001b, pp. 361–2.

104 *BMC* 199, Pl. XXIV, 2.

105 For a discussion of the possible ecclesiastical significance of crosses on the reverse of Anglo-Saxon coins, see Eaglen and Grayburn 2000, p. 27.

Table 4. Weights of Bury coins compared with Lincoln and the standards under Edward the Confessor

	Lincoln No. of coins	*Median wt (g)*	*Postulated standard* (g)*	*Bury Mean wt (g)*	*No. of coins*
Small Flan	44	1.12	1.10	1.09	3
Expanding Cross (Light)	40	1.12	1.14	–	–
(Heavy)	86	1.67	1.72	1.61	4
Helmet	55	1.27	1.36	1.32	3
Sovereign-Eagles	29	1.27	1.30	1.29	1
Hammer Cross	58	1.32	1.36	1.25	4
Facing Bust	33	1.12	1.07	1.04	4

Note
*Standards reduced by 0.03 g (0.5 gr.) for wear.

the name of a newly appointed moneyer could be issued. All of the coins are in the name of the moneyer Morcere, spelt variously as MARCERE, MORCEP, MORCERE, MORCARE, MORCEREE or MORCRE. Marcer is known as a moneyer in the reign of Eadgar,[106] but otherwise there is no other closely resembling name on late Anglo-Saxon coinage. Nothing is known of Morcere's identity. A Morcar is recorded in Domesday Book as a freeman of Edric, holding 30 acres at Burston in the half-hundred of Diss,[107] and another is mentioned as a freeman of Roger Bigot under the entry for Burgate in East Suffolk.[108] A more renowned Morcar or Morkere, the younger son of Ælfgar of Mercia, was elected earl of Northumbria on 3 October 1065 following the deposition of Tostig.[109] His family links with Suffolk appear to have been close in that his mother held Sudbury before 1066 and manors in the double-hundred of Babergh.[110] That the future earl had held the position of abbot's moneyer, even if in some honorary capacity, must nevertheless be considered highly improbable at this late date.

As Table 3 shows, the mint signature appears as (or as contractions of) EADMVN, being most abbreviated in the Small Flan type as ED. The mean weight of the surviving Bury coins where known, but excluding corroded and damaged specimens, is compared in Table 4 with the median weight of coins from the Lincoln mint,[111] and with the standard postulated by Grierson.[112] These figures show a tendency for both mints and particularly Bury to be striking marginally below the standard, although the Bury sample is very small.

106 *BMC* 128.
107 DB II, fol. 154b.
108 DB II, fol. 339b.
109 Freeman 1870–6, II, p. 481.
110 DB II, fols 286b, 287a, 374a.
111 Mossop 1970, Table 5.
112 Grierson 1961, p. 275.

Conclusion

It is clear from the foregoing that the mint of the abbot at Bury was of minor significance and may well have been mainly employed for his own monetary needs at this period. Nevertheless, the growing importance of Bury during the Confessor's reign, clear from the Domesday Book entry to be considered in the next Chapter, may have been inadequately reflected by the surviving coins simply because St Edmunds inland had from about 1051 been exempted – amongst its other substantial privileges – from taxation.[113] Without such exemption the abbot's mint could well have been more active.

113 *AS Writs*, no. 15, p. 158; *AS Charters*, no. 1075, pp. 320–1.

CHAPTER 4

WILLIAM I AND II

Introduction

This chapter steps from the reign of the Confessor into those of William I and II. The brief rule of Harold II is passed over because none of his known coins is attributable to Bury.[1] It remains doubtful whether this is explained by the accidents of survival or the right of the abbot to mint coins not having been confirmed between the coronation of Harold and his downfall at Hastings. Admittedly, later confirmations of minting and other privileges enjoyed by the abbot refer specifically to earlier grants by Edward the Confessor but are silent about Harold. This may nevertheless simply reflect the fact that once William was secure upon the throne Harold was referred to as an earl and not acknowledged, as a usurper, to have ruled as king.[2] In Norman times, to cite any rights granted or confirmed by Harold would thus have been not merely irrelevant but even prejudicial. Barlow has suggested that Baldwin was at court in Christmas 1065, during Edward the Confessor's fatal illness.[3] If so, he would doubtless have stayed on to attend Harold II's coronation on 6 January 1066, the day after Edward died.[4] He would thereby have been well placed to obtain the earliest possible confirmation of Bury's privileges, including minting rights, from the new king. The manifestation of Bury coins from Harold's reign would give substance to this surmise.

Confirmation of privileges

Chance undoubtedly nurtured the growing fortunes of Bury after the Norman Conquest. William must have been acutely aware of the fragile substance of his conquest. Necessity even obliged him for a time to depend on the precarious allegiance of the defeated earls, Edwin and Morcar.[5] It must, therefore, have been some consolation to know that the abbey and Liberty of St Edmund were already in sympathetic hands.[6] Abbot Baldwin had been born in Chartres, became a

1 North 1994, pp. 182–6, records 48 mints as issuing coins of Harold II.

2 See Chibnall 1986, p. 21. Garnett 1986, pp. 91–116, draws attention to some early references to Harold as king. Examples of the later form occur in *Regesta* I, nos 162–4, pp. 44–5, dated by Davis as no earlier than 1070.

3 Barlow 1997, p. 245.

4 *AS Chronicle*, pp. 192–3, 197.

5 *AS Chronicle* (*s. a.* 1066), p. 200.

6 Douglas 1999, p. 215.

monk of St Denis, Paris, and subsequently prior of Leberaw in Alsace. Having acquired a reputation in medicine he came to England at an unknown date as physician to Edward the Confessor, who invested him with the church of Deerhurst in Gloucestershire and the manor of Taynton in Oxfordshire.[7] Fortunately both for William and for the abbey, shortly before his death Edward had appointed Baldwin as abbot at Bury. It is thus reasonable to assume that William confirmed the privileges of the abbey with minimal delay in order to secure support from the abbot in a part of the kingdom exposed to counter-invasion from Scandinavia besides the risk, existing everywhere, of insurgence among those he had just vanquished.[8] The nearby abbey at Ely became the focus for disaffected parties and, aided by the Danes, Earl Morcar and Hereward the Wake withstood William until 1071.[9] Confirmation of the eight and a half hundreds, freedom of the abbey demesne lands from gelds and other dues, jurisdiction of the abbot over St Edmund's men and lands within and without the confines of Bury, and the grant of a moneyer to Baldwin have all been dated to between the years 1066 and 1070.[10] It is likely, however, that these measures were taken between William's coronation on Christmas day 1066[11] and his departure to Normandy on about 21 February 1067, or upon his return to England the following December,[12] when the *Anglo-Saxon Chronicle* records him as having given away every man's land.[13]

From a later grant of Henry I it appears that Baldwin also had the right to hold a market at Bury and that he may not have been the first abbot to do so.[14] From Domesday Book it also appears that when a geld was collected the abbot was entitled to levy 60 pence in the pound from the vill for sustenance of the monks. Since in 1086 the town was valued at £20, this would have resulted in a periodic windfall of £5.[15]

7 Gransden 1981, p. 65; *Regesta* I, no. 26, p. 8.

8 Chibnall 1986, p. 30. The threat of Scandinavian attack materialised in 1069–70 (*AS Chronicle*, pp. 202–5). The statement in the Worcester Chronicle (*AS Chronicle*, p. 204, and repeated in *The Peterborough Chronicle*, p. 205) that the king plundered all of the monasteries in England at that time was undoubtedly an exaggeration (Knowles 1966, p. 117; *Feudal Documents*, p. lxiv).

9 *AS Chronicle*, pp. 207–8.

10 *Feudal Documents*, nos 3–6, pp. 48–50; *Regesta* I, no. 12, p. 4 (where the grant of jurisdiction is dated to *c.* 1067) and nos 41–3, p. 12; Davis 1909, pp. 423–4.

11 Fryde, Greenaway, Porter and Roy 1986, p. 34.

12 Fryde, Greenaway, Porter and Roy 1986, p. 34; *Regesta* I, p. xxi.

13 *AS Chronicle*, p. 200. Douglas also cites a writ of 1066–70 (*Feudal Documents*, no. 1, p. 47) in which the land of St Edmund's tenants who died fighting against William was declared confiscated. This writ must have been of very early date in the reign and, as with the confirmation of the Liberty of St Edmunds and a moneyer, was significantly in Anglo-Saxon rather than Latin, which quickly came into general use. The same writ is included in *Regesta* I, no. 40, p. 12, where the language is construed by Davis to mean that the confiscated lands were handed over to the abbot.

14 *Regesta* II, no. 1914, p. 292 (dated '1135?'); *Feudal Documents*, no. 42, p. 73 (dated 1123–9); Davis 1909, p. 428 (dated 1123–35). The grant confirmed the right as held by 'Abbot Baldwin or any predecessor of him'.

15 DB II, fol. 372a. See translation of entry in next section.

In contrast with such well-documented confirmations no written record survives on the creation of the *servitium debitum*, or knight service, owed by the abbot of Bury in common with other leading ecclesiastics. It has been suggested that such service evolved after 1070 from the actual military resources of each abbot,[16] or from the needs of defence occasioned by rebellions in the early years of the reign.[17] Either explanation could account for the 60 knights to be maintained by the abbots of Glastonbury and Peterborough and 40 by the abbots of Ely and Bury.[18] The latter explanation, however, would not account for the origin of the 40 knights at Ely until at least 1071. It is also plausible, however, particularly to the extent that such service was based on existing military resources, that the obligations were imposed on certain monasteries very early in the reign in return for confirmation of the valuable privileges they had hitherto enjoyed.[19] The imposition of knight service unconnected with an act of largess could otherwise have been regarded as an unjust burden upon the religious houses. At Bury itself, the obligation of knight service could also have been linked to monastic freedom from geld payments otherwise attaching to the demesne lands.

The good relationship existing between William and Baldwin resulted in his continuing to act as physician both to the Conqueror and to his son, Rufus.[20] The latter, who had a constructive policy towards the Benedictine monasteries for most of his reign,[21] had no hesitation in reaffirming the possessions and privileges of St Edmund's.[22] Intimacy with the monarch must also have helped Baldwin to thwart the attempt by Bishop Arfast to re-site his East Anglian see at Bury. The designs of Arfast were evidently supported by Archbishop Lanfranc,[23] and were eventually laid to rest only by the personal intervention of the king in 1081.[24] Nevertheless, confronted by such influential adversaries Baldwin left

16 Knowles 1966, pp. 610–11. Chew 1932, p. 3, suggested that knight service was extended to ecclesiastical tenants between 1070 and 1072.

17 Chibnall 1986, p. 30; Douglas 1999, p. 325.

18 The quotas of service due, compiled by Round 1895, pp. 249 and 251, and reproduced by Chew 1932, pp. 4–5, shows Ely as a bishopric because it was based on information derived from the reign of Henry II (see Chew, p. 4).

19 Chibnall 1986, p. 29, hints at this. See also *Feudal Documents*, p. lxxxvi.

20 See Gransden 1981, p. 66.

21 See Mason 1999, pp. 113–44.

22 E.g. *Feudal Documents*, no. 12, p. 57, and *Regesta* I, no. 291, p. 76 (referring to the abbot's possessions and men), dated by Davis to 1087 and Douglas as 'probably 1087'; *Feudal Documents*, no. 13, p. 58, and *Regesta* I, no. 293, p. 77 (sac and soc) dated by Douglas as '1087–1098; probably early during this period', and by Davis as '?1087'; *Feudal Documents*, no. 18, p. 60, and *Regesta* I, no. 292, p. 77 (eight and a half hundreds), which are dated by Douglas '1087–1100' and Davis '?1087'; and *Feudal Documents*, no. 14, p. 58, *Regesta* I, no. 392, p. 99 (grant of moneyer and exchange) dated by Douglas '1087–1098' and by Davis between 1087 and 1097, although the witness Hugh de Grantmesnil is recorded (Freeman 1882, I, p. 473) as having died in 1094. The suggestion that Hugh de Grantmesnil witnessed this last writ early in the reign receives added credibility if, as is likely, he fell out of favour temporarily after taking part in the revolts of 1088 (Poole 1955, pp. 100–1). For reasons given elsewhere, dates very soon after Rufus' accession must be assumed for all these confirmations.

23 Gransden 1981, p. 70, n. 66–9.

24 *Memorials*, I, pp. 65–7; *Regesta* I, nos. 138–9, pp. 36–7.

nothing to chance and his *scriptorium* appears to have fabricated a number of documents to prove the independence of the abbey from episcopal influence, derived from supposed long-standing royal sanction.[25] The victory over Arfast must also have made the renewed attack by Bishop Herbert Losinga at a later date that much easier to repel.

The favourable conditions created by the Confessor and thus sustained after 1065 were clearly conducive to the growing importance of Bury, both as a monastic establishment and a centre of population. This is reflected in the Domesday account to be considered below. An important remaining question is how far at this period such conditions had also encouraged the growth of Bury as a centre of trade. Its importance as a prestigious shrine, as a privileged and wealthy monastery, and as the judicial and administrative centre for an extensive geographical liberty, is beyond doubt. These advantages in themselves were already favourable to increasing secular economic activity.[26] Bury had its market and its mint, traditional yardsticks of urban development at this period. But significantly its fair came later and there is nothing to suggest its market served wider interests than the abbey, the town and the immediately surrounding countryside. This supposition is reinforced when the inactivity of the mint – to be considered below – is reconciled with the evidence to be winnowed from Domesday Book.

Domesday Book

The Domesday Book entry for Bury is so detailed and yet so cryptic that it merits quotation in full:[27]

> 'In the town (*villa*)[28] where the king and glorious martyr St Edmund lies buried Abb(ot) B(aldwin) held 118 men in the days of King Edward to provide for the needs of the monks. They were entitled to grant and sell their land and had under them 52 bordars from whom the abbot could command some service. There were also 54 somewhat impoverished freemen and 43 almsmen, each with 1 bordar. Now there are 2 mills and 2 stews or fish ponds. The town was then valued at £10 and is now valued at £20. It is 1½ leagues in length and likewise in breadth and when £1 of geld is levied on the hundred 60 pence is paid from the town to provide sustenance for the monks. This applied to the town as it was in the time of King Edward but still remains so now that it is within a larger boundary encompassing land formerly sown and ploughed. On this land are 30 priests, deacons and clerks, together with 28 nuns and paupers who

25 Gransden 1981, pp. 70–2. Forgery by monastic houses was not an uncommon occurrence (see, for example, *Reading Abbey Cartularies*, I, p. 19).

26 Maitland 1897, p.195; Tait 1936, pp. 64–5.

27 DB II, fol. 372a.

28 Although the modern word 'town' is here used instead of 'vill', it is clear that Bury, despite its mint, market and population, had a distinctive status from other towns of the period, derived from the control exercised by the abbot and obedientiaries over its affairs (see Lobel 1935, pp. 16–18). Once it ceased to be the custom to place the name of the moneyer on English coinage, during the reign of Edward I, the mint inscription of Bury became VILLA SCI EDMVNDI.

> daily pray for the king and all Christians. There are also 75 (literally 80 less 5) bakers, ale brewers, tailors, launderers, shoe makers, robe makers, cooks, porters and storemen, and all these are daily in attendance upon the Saint, the abbot and the brethren. Besides these, 13 rural reeves have their houses in the said town and under them are 5 bordars. Now there are 34 knights, both French and English, and under them 22 bordars. Likewise, in total there are 342 houses on demesne land of the Saint which was under the plough in the time of King Edward.'

Darby counted up 310 persons as recorded in the time of the Confessor and 207 occupying the new town, although he recognised that not all of these were likely to have been householders (or, he might have added, the head of family units).[29] However, since 342 houses were said to have been built since the Conquest, Darby concluded that the description of inhabitants in Domesday Book was incomplete and estimated, by adding 342 householders to the figure of 310 in Edward's day, a total population of over 3,000 at the end of the Conqueror's reign. This estimate he admitted was 'very conjectural'. The reliability of his calculation is suspect not only because a house count is an imprecise measure of urban population or importance, particularly in a religious centre, but also because Abbot Baldwin (1065–97/8)[30] embarked upon a radical redevelopment of the abbey and town.[31] Although it is likely that the layout owed something to the earlier Saxon vill,[32] the alignment of the abbey church with the grid pattern of streets supports the view that both were conceived before construction of the new church began in 1081.[33] However, the work on the main body of the church and on the monastic buildings extended between 1081 and 1142 and it is unknown how far the town developed in tandem.[34] An obvious impetus towards an increase in permanent residents would have been the translation of St Edmund's remains into the partly completed church in 1095. It is thus perhaps not surprising that the value of Bury had no more than doubled between 1066 and 1086. Against this background it is uncertain how many of the 342 new houses were built to cope with expansion or simply to replace those demolished in the redevelopment.[35] At Lincoln 160 houses were destroyed to make way for the Conqueror's new castle.[36] At Bury it has been suggested that the original settlement was formed as a narrow strip beside the Rivers Lark and Linnet.[37] If so, this area must have been requisitioned by Baldwin to form part of the monastic precincts, as it remained in later times, its inhabitants

29 Darby 1971, p. 198. In contrast with Darby's estimates, Gottfried 1982, pp. 28, 35, 37, calculated the tenement densities in the *banleuca* of Bury as follows: thirteenth century, 286; fourteenth century, 373; fifteenth century, 582.

30 Knowles, Brooke and London 2001, p. 32.

31 Lobel 1935, p. 8.

32 Gauthiez 1998, p. 93.

33 Fernie 1998, p. 12.

34 Statham 1998, pp. 99–101, has emphasised the importance of developments during Anselm's abbacy (1121–48) when, according to the *Gesta Sacristarum*, the walls round the abbey precincts and the town were built. See *Memorials* II, pp. 289–90.

35 Ellis 1833, p. 488, believed that 342 represented the total number of houses in Bury.

36 Douglas 1999, p. 313; Darby 1971, p. 78.

37 Lobel 1935, p. 8.

being resettled on higher ground to the west. Their numbers in the new town may also have been augmented by those engaged in constructing the new abbey buildings and other urban works not completed by the date of the Domesday survey. This area of the town to this day bears the mark of deliberate planning, with its regular pattern of roads. The Domesday account also states that there are 'now' two stews or fishponds and the map of Bury St Edmunds engraved by Thomas Warren in 1748, on which Figure 3 is based, shows the old monastic fishponds down by the River Lark in an area known as the Crankles, owing to their zig-zag layout.

Figure 3

The street layout of Bury

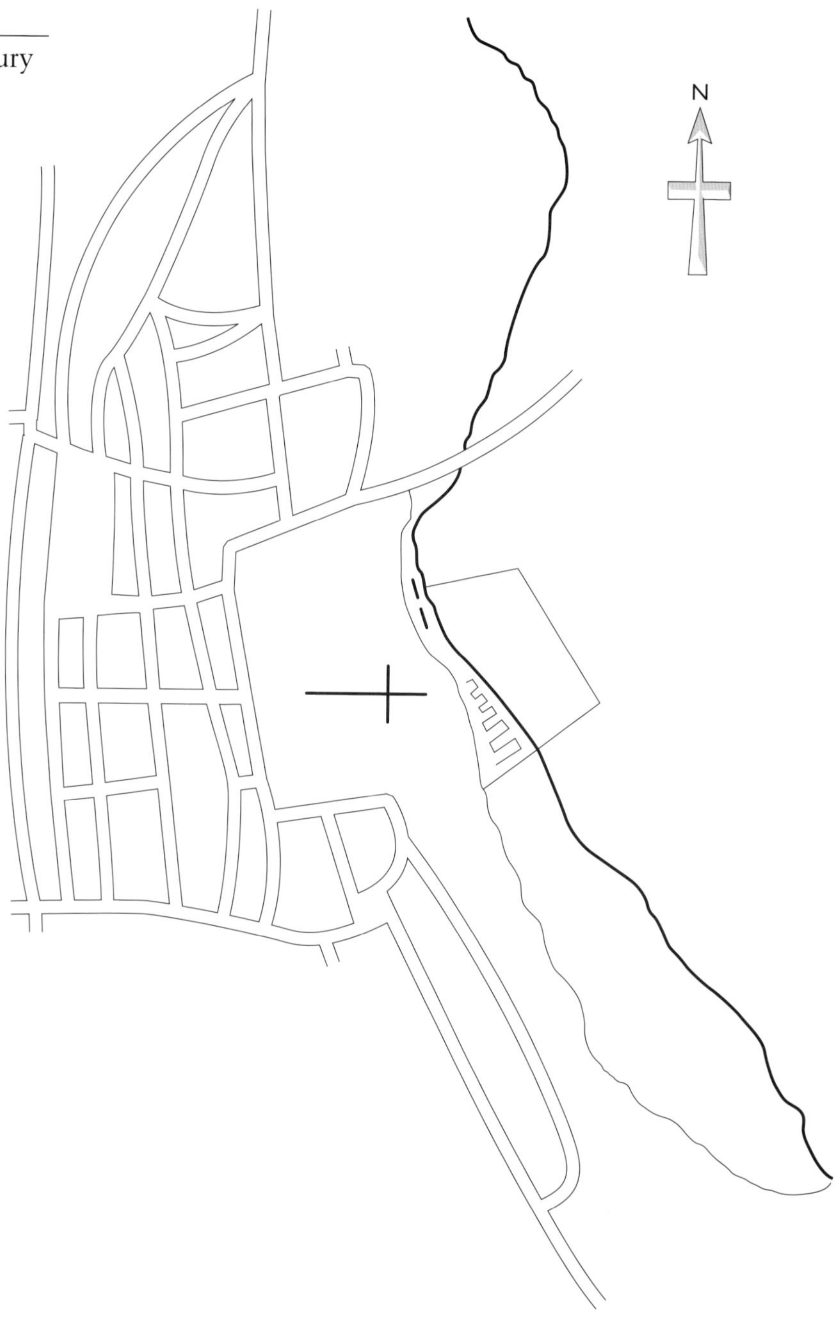

The clearest fact offered by Domesday Book is that the value of the town had doubled between the two reigns from £10 to £20.[38] Other background circumstances to be considered below also point to a steady rise in the importance of Bury in the closing decades of the eleventh century. Whether this indicated a vigorous commercial community is altogether another question. The Domesday account in fact fits very well the description of a settlement becoming more active under the influence of a phenomenally prosperous abbey. The persons whom Bury attracted in the Conqueror's reign were those whose livelihood could be made by serving the abbey and visitors to the shrine. This is a salient feature of Bury as described before 1066 and in 1086. There is also in Domesday Book no indication that economic activity dissociated from the abbey and its immediate needs had developed to any extent. The 54 freemen in the Confessor's reign are significantly described as 'somewhat impoverished'. The very presence of skilled trades would nonetheless have made Bury a congenial place in which to live and this doubtless accounts for the 13 rural reeves and 34 knights who had houses there. The latter may well have enjoyed special privileges as residents through belonging to the complement of 40 knights maintained by Baldwin as a feudal baron. If, as is suggested above, the *servitium debitum* arose at the beginning of the Conqueror's reign, the knights' dwellings may have followed shortly afterwards.[39]

Finally, Domesday Book points clearly to the wealth enjoyed by the abbot and brethren at Bury. An estimate was made by Corbett of the gross income receivable by the leading monasteries mentioned in Domesday Book,[40] and Knowles later made similar calculations for all the monasteries so mentioned.[41] A comparison of their figures is set out below.

Table 5. Income of leading monasteries in 1086 (£ p.a.)

Monastery	*Corbett*	*Knowles*[42]
Glastonbury	840	828
Ely	790	769
Christ Church, Canterbury	635	688
Bury	655	640
St Augustine's, Canterbury	635	635
Old Minster, Winchester	640	600
Westminster	600	584

38 Reynolds 1977, p. 43, has suggested that the higher values attributed by Domesday Book to cities such as Norwich and York are likely to have represented increased tax burdens rather than prosperity. This argument, if valid for the cities referred to, is not likely to have applied to Bury.

39 The text implies that the knights had separate establishments and were not housed in the abbey precincts.

40 Corbett 1926, p. 509.

41 Knowles 1966, p. 702.

42 The figures in this column are rounded to the nearest pound sterling.

On these figures Bury was in wealth the fourth or, according to Corbett, the third house in the country at the end of William I's reign. Obviously this league table bears no necessary correlation with the urban significance of the settlements surrounding these abbeys. For example, Darby in *The Domesday Geography of England: Eastern England* offered no estimate of the population of Ely, which did not even qualify by any recognised yardsticks as a borough at this period.[43]

Coinage from the Bury mint

Domesday Book contains no reference to a mint at Bury, either in the reign of Edward the Confessor or William I. Lobel noted this but suggested that 'the strangest part about the Domesday entry is not so much its omissions as the fact that it was made at all, for the demesne lands of St Edmund were exempt from geld payments'.[44] Fortunately, however, the texts of writs issued under William I and II granting a moneyer to Abbot Baldwin are preserved in the White Register[45] and the Sacrist's Register[46] of the abbey and have been published by Douglas and others. They are transcribed by Douglas, respectively, as follows:

> 'William kyng [William I] gret Aylmer bisscop and Rauf earl and alle mine theynes on Norf' and Suff' frendlike. And ic kithe ou that ic habbe unnen [I have granted] Baldwine abbot with innen seynt Eadmundesbiri to thene minsteres beofte one munetere also frelike on alle thing to habben also Eadward kyng mine mey him humeuthe alder frelikest. God be mid ihu.'[47]

> 'Willelmus rex Anglorum [William II] Henrico de Ferers et Godrico dapifero et Goscelino et ministris suis de Norf' et de Suff' salutem. Precipio vobis constater ut faciatis quod Baldwinus abbas de sancto Eadmundo terras suas omnes et omnes consuetudines suas infra burgum et extra et de monetario et de cambiatoribus habeat sicut ipse illos umquam melius habuit tempore regis Eadwardi et tempore patris mei . . . Teste Hugone de Grantemainilo.'[48]

The latter writ could be taken to refer to a moneyer or a mint (*monetario*), but since it also refers to exchangers (*cambiatoribus*) the translation 'moneyer' must be preferred, consistent with the single-moneyer status of the mint in other reigns except those of Henry I and Stephen.[49] This writ also contains the first known

43 Darby 1977, p. 364.

44 Lobel 1935, p. 13.

45 BL Add. MS 14847, fol. 38.

46 Cambridge UL MS Ff ii.33, fol. 28.

47 *Feudal Documents*, no. 5, p. 50. See also Davis 1909, p. 424; *Regesta* I, no. 42, p. 12 and no. V, p. 119.

48 *Feudal Documents*, no. 14, p. 58. See also Davis 1909, p. 424; *Regesta* I, no. 392, p. 99 and no. LXIII, p. 134.

49 See Chapters 5 and 6 below.

mention of the activity of exchange although it is expressed in confirmatory language.[50]

Given such evidence, it is extraordinary that only one coin positively attributable to Bury is known to exist from the reigns of William, father and son. This is of the third, or Canopy, type of William I, with a reverse reading + GODINC ON EIID-MII (see Catalogue, 8). The British Museum acquired this previously unrecorded piece of the moneyer Godinc from Spink and Son Ltd in 1960. Perhaps the most remarkable void is the lack of any coins of Bury in the extensive Beauworth hoard, which was predominantly of the PAXS type (*BMC* VIII). This strongly suggests that the Bury mint was inactive at that time because virtually every other mint known to have been engaged in the reigns of William I and II is represented.[51]

The Domesday entries for Suffolk contain no reference to Godinc (or plausibly relevant reference to Goding), but under Norfolk it is recorded that:

> 'Godinc, a freeman held Quidenham[52] of whom the abbot of St Edmund's had patronage only before 1066 . . . the same Godric [*sic*] held this land (for) three years from the abbot after King William came. Godwin, Earl Ralf's uncle, took this away from him unjustly . . . .'[53]

The Feudal Book of Abbot Baldwin, compiled between 1087 and 1098,[54] also contains two references to a Goding:

> 'Ad Bertune [Great Barton, three miles north east of Bury in Thedwastre Hundred] Goding Godwinii filius XII acras XI denarios et obulum.'[55]
> 'Ad Chethelburnestun [Kettlebaston, just over ten miles south east of Bury in Cosford Hundred] Godingus I carracutam et X solidus.'[56]

It is quite possible that the Godinc of Domesday Book was the self-same person as the abbot's moneyer. The name is also known on coins of London in the second (Bonnet)[57] and fourth (Two Sceptres)[58] types, and of the neighbouring

50 Ruding 1840, II, pp. 218–19, had only found one reference to an exchange at Bury, in the Kempe Register (BL Harl. MS 645) at the time of Henry III's great recoinage in 1247, although he noted (p. 220) that an exchanger (*cambiator*) was listed as one of the mint officials in the Sacrist's Register (Cambridge UL MS Ff ii.33).

51 *Inventory*, no. 37, pp. 11–13. Thompson lists 6,264 coins of the PAXS type.

52 Lying about ten miles east of Thetford, Quidenham is listed under the lands of the abbot of Bury in Norfolk (see DB II, fol. 209b).

53 DB II, fol. 127b.

54 *Feudal Documents*, p. lxxx. For the text of the Feudal Book, derived from Cambridge UL MS Mm iv.19, fol. 124, see *Feudal Documents*, pp. 3–44.

55 *Feudal Documents*, p. 25. 'Bertuna' was a manor of the abbey before 1066 (DB II, fol. 361b) and still shown as 'Berton' in the edition of Saxton/Kip's map of Suffolk published in 1610.

56 *Feudal Documents*, p. 44. 'Bitelbeomastuna' was also listed among the lands of the abbot before 1066 (DB II, fol. 369a).

57 *NCirc* May 1973, 3993.

58 *SCBI* Stockholm, 16 and, possibly, *BMC* 259 reading GODIC, which Brooke expanded to 'Godric?' (*Norman Kings*, II, p. 50), a moneyer in the preceding and subsequent type, (*Norman Kings*, I, p. ccxxii) rather than Godinc.

mint of Thetford in the PAXS type[59] and Cross in Quatrefoil type[60] of Rufus. It is also possible, but not demonstrable, that the coins refer to the same person, whose career took him briefly from London to Bury and later still from London to Thetford. It may seem improbable that Bury, as a franchisal mint, should engage royal moneyers but, particularly if the mint had been inoperative for several years, the abbot would undoubtedly prefer to enlist an experienced man.[61] There is documentary evidence from the reign of Henry III that new moneyers had to be vetted by the officials of the exchequer and this practice could well have originated well before his time.[62] Coincidences of names also arise at the end of Henry I's reign with the moneyer Oddo at Bury in types XIII and XIV and at Thetford in type XV and type I of Stephen, with the moneyer Gilebert at Bury and Sudbury during the reign of Stephen, and with the moneyer Fulke at Bury and London in the reign of John. These coincidences will be further discussed below.[63]

Besides the solitary coin of Godinc, various others have been suggested as emanating from Bury between 1066 and 1100, but rightly failed to gain numismatic respectability. Ruding observed, without adducing evidence, that coins of the royal (*sic*) mint of St Edmundsbury under William I were 'still extant'.[64] Hawkins simply followed Ruding in listing Bury as a mint under William I and II.[65] Golding, writing in 1868, thought that coins of the Conqueror bearing the inscription SCIE were minted at Bury, although he admitted the equal claims of Shaftesbury.[66] An obverse die link pointed out by Brooke between the coin reading +CINIHTPINE ON SCIE of the PAXS type and reverses of Ælnoth with mint readings SCIEF and SIECF and of Godesbrand reading SCI, SC and SCF places the Shaftesbury attribution of this group of coins beyond doubt.[67] Under Rufus, Golding attributed coins reading SC.EA unreservedly to Bury.[68] Brooke recorded no coins with this reading in his *Norman Kings* but placed an isolated coin of the Cross in Quatrefoil type with the reverse inscription +PIILFGIED ON SCE under Shaftesbury, presumably as a plausible contraction

59 *BMC* 1009, 1010.

60 *BMC* 156.

61 Where details are available about the appointment of mint officials at Bury in the reign of Edward II, the office of moneyer tended to be filled by an official working under the previous incumbent (see *The Pinchbeck Register*, II, pp. 16–17). This possibility would not arise, however, if – for some reason – the mint was inoperative for a number of years. Marion Archibald has raised the possibility that Godwine, the father of Goding (see text to which n. 55 refers), could have been the London moneyer of that name, whose coins are not known beyond the *Hammer Cross* issue (see Freeman 1985, I, p. 150).

62 See Chapter 9 below.

63 See Chapters 5, 6 and 8 below.

64 Ruding 1840, II, pp. 217–18.

65 Hawkins 1887, p. 172.

66 Golding 1868, p. 4.

67 *Norman Kings*, II, p. 172, where *BMC* 924 is linked with *BMC* 919–20 and *BMC* 927–29. Another coin of the moneyer Cnihtwine in the fifth (Two Stars) type of William I reads +CNIHTPINE ON SE (*Norman Kings*, II, p. 68, *BMC* 366).

68 Golding 1868, p. 4.

of SC(I)E(FT).[69] A more problematical candidature would arise from a PAXS penny reading +GODPINE ON SIIN,[70] were it not for the further reading of SIIND for the same moneyer,[71] supporting Brooke's attribution to Sandwich. These readings would also provide some justification for assigning coins of William II reading +PIILFPORD ON SN and +PIILFPOR ON SIIN to Sandwich.[72] Brooke, however, displayed uncertainty in admitting that he had assigned to Bury coins reading 'SA, SAN, etc', of moneyers who could be shown by other coin readings to have struck at the mint in the period up to the death of King Stephen and – whilst accepting this might not be correct in every case – the remainder to Sandwich.[73]

The most serious pretenders to attribution to the Bury mint undoubtedly are those coins of the Conqueror's second, or Bonnet type, reading LEOFPINE ON BVR(I),[74] a cause zealously espoused by Carlyon-Britton.[75] In *Norman Kings* (published in 1916) Brooke preferred to place the British Museum coin, reading BVR, under Barnstable,[76] although in his *English Coins* (last revised in 1950) he appears to have changed his mind since under William I and II he records: 'BURY ST EDMUNDS (Buri, Byri in A.S. documents; coins read Buri): Leofwine.'[77] This, however, is not convincing. The use of 'Buri' or 'Byri' appears to have enjoyed a brief currency at the time 'St Edmundsbury' was supplanting the place-name 'Beadericesworth' in the reign of Cnut.[78] It would thus have been bizarre for the die-cutter several decades after this change to have used the element in St Edmundsbury signifying simply the word 'town'. It would have been doubly inappropriate in that Bures St Mary, less than twenty miles south southeast of Bury, was itself then known as Buri.[79]

Wells formed the view that these coins were struck at Peterborough, or at Stamford on behalf of the Abbot of Peterborough,[80] and this is the most plausible attribution on straightforward orthographic grounds.[81] Wells' view gains further force from the fact that a moneyer with the name Leofwine was active at Stamford in the first six types of William I.[82] Despite these arguments conclusive

69 *Norman Kings*, II, p. 236, *BMC* 132.

70 *Norman Kings*, II, p. 170, *BMC* 915.

71 *BMC* 914.

72 *Norman Kings*, II, p. 258, *BMC* 249 and p. 264, *BMC* 272.

73 *Norman Kings*, I, p. clxiv.

74 *Norman Kings*, I, p. 15, *BMC* 74; Elmore Jones collection (now in the BM).

75 Carlyon-Britton 1912, p. 143.

76 *Norman Kings*, II, p. 15, *BMC* 74.

77 Brooke 1950, p. 83.

78 See Chapter 1 above. The maverick reading RAND ON BERI is, however, found on one reverse die from the extensive Long Cross coinage of Henry III, see Catalogue 322.

79 *Regesta* I, no. 116, p. 30.

80 Wells 1934–7b, pp. 69–70.

81 See *The Peterborough Chronicle, 1070–1154*, pp. 2–3, where the name 'Burh' is used three times (*s. a.* 1070).

82 *Norman Kings*, I, p. ccxxxviii.

proof that BVR(I) does not represent Bury must await the discovery of further coins, either of Godinc or Leofwine.[83] For example, if a coin of Leofwine at 'Bur(i)' came to light in the fourth type of William I, in addition to the second, it would be anathema to a Bury attribution owing to the single-moneyer status of the mint. Were it not for the existence of the coin of Godinc, unambiguously attributable to Bury, the authenticity of the writs of William I and II, confirming the grant of a moneyer and an exchange, would fall under suspicion.[84]

Features of early Norman coinage

Brooke as early as 1916 established the sequence of types between 1066 and 1100.[85] It has also been recognised that the weight of the penny was standardised, purportedly at 1.39 g (21.5 gr.) for the first five issues and at 1.46 g (22.5 gr.) thereafter.[86] Continuation from late Anglo-Saxon times of a regular, periodic change in the design of the coinage has likewise gained widespread if not universal acceptance.[87] On current knowledge, however, many questions remain unanswerable about mint activity and the charges and profits associated with coinage in the early Norman period. The scattered references in Domesday Book tend to obfuscate rather than clarify the problems.[88] Apart from textual ambiguities, it is not clear if the entries are an incomplete record of general practices or an attempt to highlight exceptional circumstances. As in the reign of the Confessor, the dating of each type again remains uncertain and, in consequence, the clear identity of the first type of William Rufus is also uncertain.

Numismatic writers have tended to stress the continuity in mint activity and policy between the closing years of Anglo-Saxon England and the early Norman period. This idea has taken root mainly because many moneyers remained in office after the Conquest, and their Anglo-Saxon names continued to predominate on the coinage.[89] This is not really surprising since the skills required and the social standing of the late Anglo-Saxon moneyer were not likely to make his office sought after by the elite among settling invaders who had richer pickings within their reach. Despite this, the changes to the coinage

83 A coin reading LIFPINE ON BIIIRD is discussed in Stewart 1986. Although the article evinces uncertainty, this coin must be attributed to Barnstable, despite removal of Brooke's attribution of *BMC* 74 from this mint and the moneyer Seword being known in types *BMC* VI (Sword) and VIII (PAXS).

84 The authenticity of these writs was not doubted by H. W. C. Davies or by D. C. Douglas.

85 *Norman Kings*, I, pp. lxvi-lxxi.

86 *Norman Kings*, I, p. cliii; Grierson 1961, pp. 274–5. Some doubt has, however, been expressed on the actual weight levels resulting from standardisation (see Metcalf 1987, p. 282, n. 12).

87 See for example North 1994, pp. 191–3, where the dates are properly suffixed by a question mark; but cf. Brand 1984, pp. 5–6.

88 The references to pre- and post-Conquest mints in Domesday Book are listed by Grierson 1987, p. 76.

89 Ruding 1840, I, pp. 146–7; Oman 1931, p. 80; Brooke 1950, p. 79; Craig 1953, p. 17.

wrought by William I were in fact more radical than at first might appear. He achieved what Edward the Confessor strove towards, particularly in the latter part of his reign, namely, a coinage of consistent weight. He also appears to have granted the design of coins and engraving of dies as an hereditary monopoly to Otto the Goldsmith and his family.[90] The date is not known when this sergeanty was set up. Douglas[91] traced its origins to two goldsmiths and tenants of the king by the name of Otto, father and son, the elder of whom married an English widow, Leofgifu, in the reign of Edward the Confessor.[92] If it is assumed that Otto the elder would himself have prepared the designs and cut or closely supervised the cutting of the dies, the origins of his activity may possibly be revealed if an exceptional change in design were identifiable after, say, 1042 and was then maintained. Applying this test, one such change occurred with the PAX issue of Harold II. In that type linear representation of the bust was superseded by an attempt to portray modelled features. This technique was used, although less skilfully, in the issues of William I that followed.[93] On this hypothesis it is conceivable that Otto was able to convert a role he had assumed before the Conquest into an hereditary right after the Conquest.

Another notable development was the greater similarity between the design of coins of consecutive issues under William I and II compared with the late Anglo-Saxon era. Most strikingly of all, the obverse design of the first (Profile Left) type of William I closely resembled that of Harold II, especially in the variety without a sceptre. The obverses of the second (Bonnet) and third (Canopy) types and the reverses of the fifth (Two Stars) and sixth (Sword) types are further examples of this phenomenon. Indeed, homogeneity of design is apparent also in the similarity between certain non-consecutive types, such as the reverses of the first (Profile Left) and third (Canopy) and the second (Bonnet) and fourth (Two Sceptres) types. Possibly these affinities were simply the by-products of unimaginative design. It is, nevertheless, strange that greater effort was not made to differentiate the consecutive types more clearly. This could be construed as meaning that differentiation had ceased to be important, possibly because a change in type was no longer tantamount to a recoinage disqualifying the previous type as legal tender. If this hypothesis were true its consequences would have been far-reaching. An important potential source of revenue to the crown by appropriating a proportion of the coins struck at a recoinage would have been extinguished. It could also have followed that the mysterious *monetagium* tax, discussed below, was introduced to mitigate this loss rather than, as suggested by Grierson, to compensate for

90 *Norman Kings*, I, pp. cxxxiii–cxxxiv.

91 *Feudal Documents*, pp. cxxxix–cxl.

92 *Feudal Documents*, no. 133, pp. 127–8 (for Otto the father) and no. 29, p. 66 (for the son).

93 See, for example, North 1994, Pl. 15. In contrast, the Pointed Helmet type of the Confessor, showing the king bearded, has been seen as a novel move towards greater realism, at a time when design was apparently being influenced by German models. See especially, Archibald 2004, pp. 131–50.

standardisation of the weight of the coinage.[94] Such standardisation itself would, of course, have reduced the need for recoinages, and could even be seen as integral to their abandonment.

Against the foregoing, the objection could be raised why, in the absence of a complete recoinage, periodic changes of type should have continued to occur. The revenues from wholesale issue of new dies to the mints could scarcely be a sufficient motive. The most obvious reason would have been the continued need to pay royal dues in the latest coin type.[95] But even this is not decisive, either in support or rejection of the hypothesis outlined above. If tax liabilities were met by weight rather than by tale, payment in the latest type would not appear to be necessary regardless of whether the new type constituted a recoinage or not. The coin user, however, would probably have been predisposed towards the latest type, and that, allied to payment of taxes in the latest type, could have contributed to keeping the currency in good shape by driving older worn coins out of circulation.

Frustratingly, there is scant direct evidence about the operation of the monetary system immediately after the Conquest and projection from earlier and extrapolation from later periods is hazardous.[96] Nevertheless, a new tax, variously described as *'de moneta'*, *'de monetariis'*, *'geldum moneta'* and *'geldum regis de monedagio'*, appears to have superseded the range of payments due from moneyers in the reign of the Confessor for annual minting rights, fees for enrolment and the issue of dies on a recoinage and the like.[97] The annual amounts involved in the new tax, however, were so substantial that they clearly also compensated for greater revenue losses, possibly resulting from standardising the weight of the coinage (as Grierson maintains) or from abandoning recoinages. The extra impost fell upon the moneyers or the burgesses of the centres at which the moneyers operated.[98] Regrettably, no information is available to show how these burdens were passed on to the population at large, or what element of profit was allowed and in practice accrued to the moneyers at this period. In the case of Bury, it may be assumed that the abbot enjoyed the profits of coinage and was free to make his own deal with his mint officials. At no stage in the history of the mint at Bury is there evidence of payment being made by, or requested from the abbot or his obedientiaries for the issue of dies or other minting privileges. There is likewise no evidence of the financial benefit derived by Otto and his

94 Grierson 1961, p. 275, more extensively developed in Grierson 1985, pp. 84–94, where it is suggested the tax was imposed after the revised standard weight of 22.5 gr was established in the sixth (Sword) type of William I.

95 A somewhat ambiguous passage in the *Dialogus de Scaccario*, pp. 9–10, appears to imply that in the reign of Henry I, apart from counties without their own moneyers, payments to the exchequer had to be in coin of the current type (*solos usuales et instantis monete legittimos denarios*).

96 For further discussion on the relationship between type changes, weight standards and taxation, see Eaglen 1999, p. 85.

97 Grierson 1987, p. 77; cf. Metcalf 1987, p. 290.

98 Grierson 1987, p. 77, considered that the burden was transferred to the burgesses, but Metcalf 1987, p. 292, suggested that it remained with the moneyers.

family from exercising their privileges.[99] It must be presumed, however, that some form of payment was normally due on the issue of dies, quite separately from the charges levied in the Confessor's reign on a recoinage.[100] At Bury this may have been an obligation placed on the moneyer. As prominent landowners and goldsmiths to the king, it may well be that the sergeanty was as important for the influence it conferred as for the profits of the office as such.

The measures associated with the *monetagium* tax show that the king and his advisers were aware that manipulation of the coinage as practised in the Anglo-Saxon period was both a clumsy route to taxation and brought with it other ills. The experience of raising gelds to buy freedom from Viking destruction and to maintain forces against the threat of invasion had not only demonstrated the efficiency of direct taxation but also accustomed eleventh-century England to gelds as a fiscal expedient. Like most forms of taxation it was naturally unpopular,[101] but the combined effect of not using recoinage as an excuse for taxation and standardising the weight of coins would have at least resulted in the coinage having the same value whether used for everyday transactions or the payment of dues. William may have felt comfortable to venture upon such experiments with taxation and the currency system because his wealth was derived overwhelmingly from the fruits of conquest. It is estimated that at the time of the Domesday survey William held twenty per cent of all land in England, compared with twenty-five per cent held by the church as a whole,[102] of which the monasteries' share was two thirds.[103] He thus had no pressing need to swell his coffers by the cumbersome currency manipulations of his predecessors. Nevertheless, the king and his advisers were shrewd enough to maintain and use the efficient administrative system developed during the Anglo-Saxon period as epitomised by the Domesday survey itself, in defining rights and liabilities and collecting taxes, fines and other dues.[104]

Against this background any attempt to determine the dates on which the coin design was changed and, thereby, those dates between which the coin of Godinc would have been struck are thwart with difficulty. The problem is easily demonstrated by simple arithmetic. Approximately thirty-four years elapsed between the coronation of William I on Christmas Day 1066 and the death of William II

99 Craig 1953, p. 18, quotes, without giving his source, a price of seven shillings per dozen dies in the thirteenth to fifteenth centuries, representing a profit of six shillings after paying one to the workmen.

100 Metcalf 1987, p. 290.

101 Four of these are recorded in the *Anglo-Saxon Chronicle*, under 1066, 1067 (*AS Chronicle*, p. 200), 1083 (p. 215) and 1085 (p. 217). These are described as '(very) heavy', and the geld in 1083 is specified to have been at six shillings per hide. The implication is that 'normal' gelds were levied at other times and various historians, including V.H. Galbraith (1961, pp. 97–8) and F. Barlow (2000, p. 240) believe that gelds of one or two shillings in the pound were levied annually.

102 Douglas 1999, p. 269.

103 Lawson 1982, pp. 226–7.

104 Campbell 1975, p. 49; Warren 1984, pp. 113–32.

on 2 August 1100, during which time thirteen substantive changes in design were made. These numbers cannot be fitted into any logical, periodic scheme. Amidst this uncertainty, most attention has been given to the dating of the eighth (PAXS) type which has been treated as the last in William I's reign on proportionate grounds in that each of the thirteen types averaged approximately two and a half years.[105] This calculation was compatible with the suggestion that the large Beauworth Hoard, containing well over six thousand PAXS pennies, represented one of the donations made by William Rufus to monastic houses for his father's soul.[106] Brooke, however, was sceptical of this explanation,[107] and Dolley preferred to date the type to 1083–6, thereby associating it with the six shilling geld levied after Christmas 1083, and the Beauworth Hoard with the emergency in 1085 when a Danish invasion was thought to be imminent.[108] In accommodating this dating, Dolley reduced the duration of the second, third and fourth types of William I from three to two years to produce the following tentative datings:[109]

Table 6. Tentative dating of coin types by Dolley, 1066–1100

King	*Type*	*Description*	*Dates*
William I	I	Profile Left	1066–8
	II	Bonnet	1068–70
	III	Canopy	1070–2
	IV	Two Sceptres	1072–4
	V	Two Stars	1074–7
	VI	Sword	1077–80
	VII	Profile Right	1080–3
	VIII	PAXS	1083–6
William I/II	I	Profile	1086–9
William II	II	Cross in Quatrefoil	1089–92
	III	Cross Voided	1092–5
	IV	Cross Pattée and Fleury	1095–8
	V	Cross Fleury and Piles	1098–1100

There must be serious reservations about Dolley's tentative dates, not least because of the arbitrary juggling with two and three year periods and the tenuous link of the PAXS type with the six shilling geld. Upon logical grounds alone it would, in fact, make more sense to place the PAXS issue at the beginning of Rufus' reign.[110] The symbolism of a *'pax'* coinage was far more appropriate to the beginning rather than the unforeseen end of a reign. It had

105 *Norman Kings*, I, pp. lxvii-lxix; Brooke 1950, p. 81.

106 Packe 1893, p. 135; Andrew 1903–4, p. 27.

107 *Norman Kings*, I, pp. xxi–xxii.

108 Dolley 1966, p. 17.

109 Dolley 1966, pp. 15–18, 20–1.

110 Keynes 1978, pp. 165–73, has suggested that the symbolism was two-fold, alluding to both Christ and peace by combining A (alpha) with a chrismon.

already been used for the first substantive issue of Edward the Confessor and – ironically in the event – for the first and only type of Harold II. It is even conceivable that the type was, besides being a prayer for the reign ahead, also – or even alternatively – a prayer for the peace of the Conqueror's soul, a *Pax Sempeterna*. Insofar as Dolley was correct in believing the PAXS issue was of extensive output, it is tempting to embrace the traditional view linking it to the distribution of wealth recorded in the *Anglo-Saxon Chronicle* in the following terms:

> '. . . the king went to Winchester and inspected the treasury and the riches which his father had accumulated: untold wealth was gathered together there in gold, in silver, in vessels, in costly robes and in jewels and in many other precious things which are difficult to enumerate. The King then did as his father had commanded him before he died: he distributed these treasures to each monastery in England for his father's soul; to one monastery ten marks of gold, to another six, and to each country church sixty pence; and into every shrine he sent a hundred pounds in money to be distributed to poor people for his soul.'[111]

However, although the PAXS type was very plausibly a commemorative issue, it is very unlikely that the Beauworth hoard was part of the distribution recorded by the *Anglo-Saxon Chronicle*. William I had died on 9 September 1087.[112] Rufus, the second of his three sons, was crowned in Westminster Abbey on 26 September and appears to have carried out his father's wishes for the distribution of arms before the end of that year.[113] Barlow has estimated that this amounted to £8,600, exclusive of church ornaments.[114] Even given the speed with which Harold II was able to introduce an extensive coinage in his own name, William would have been hard pressed to arrange for the PAXS issue to be minted widely throughout the country so soon after his father's death. Yet the Beauworth hoard contains coins from 59 mints.[115] On this evidence the date of the hoard should be no earlier than 1088.

Regardless of these considerations, in the absence of evidence to the contrary, there seems no reason to doubt a three-year periodicity in the reign of William I, which may possibly have been shortened from some point in the reign of William II. There is ample evidence (not least from the obverse inscriptions on the coinage) that Rufus intended at the outset of his reign to continue his father's policies and system of government in England, and change – in the form of harsher, extortionate conduct – crept in later.[116] Possibly a more frequent change to the design of the coinage was allowed to Otto's family at a price. Thus,

111 *AS Chronicle*, *s. a.* 1086 (= 1087), p. 222.

112 Fryde, Greenaway, Porter and Roy 1986, p. 34.

113 *AS Chronicle*, p. 222.

114 Barlow 2000, p. 64.

115 *Inventory*, no. 37, pp. 12–13. The implications of the representative nature of the hoard is also considered by Metcalf 1988, pp. 13–14, where it is argued that the PAXS issue was essentially complete at the time of William's death.

116 Barlow 2000, pp. 60, 66.

the following chronology may have applied, dating the coin of Godinc to 1072–5:

Table 7. Suggested tentative dating of coin types, 1066–1100

King	*Type*	*Dates*
William I	1	1066–9
	2	1069–72
	3	1072–5
	4	1075–8
	5	1078–81
	6	1081–4[117]
	7	1084–7
William II	8 (PAXS)	1087–90
	9	1090–3
	10	1093–5
	11	1095–7
	12	1097–9
	13	1099–1100

Dolley, in another of his writings,[118] suggested that the period of legal tender of an issue was unaffected by the accession of a new king. He thus treated the Pyramid issue of Edward the Confessor, the PAX type of Harold II and the first type of William I as one issue, ending at Michaelmas 1068. Although it may seem unlikely that Harold II would have taken the inconvenient and unpopular step of withdrawing his predecessor's Pyramid type when it had only been in issue for some three months, it seems even less likely that William would have recognised the reign and coinage of Harold II in calculating the period of an issue once Harold had been stigmatised as a usurper. For this reason termination of William I's first issue is placed in 1069 rather than 1068. The similarity of the obverse of Harold's penny and that of William I still demands some explanation. The resemblance in the royal bust, despite William being portrayed as clean-shaven, is hard to imagine as a deliberate act of policy to emphasise William as the legitimate successor to the throne. It is more probable that at the outset William may not have contemplated withdrawal of Harold's coins from circulation but could have done so later as a symbolic gesture because a distinctive reverse design had been used.

Ranking of Bury as an urban and minting centre

It remains to consider the importance of Bury as an urban and minting centre during this period, taking the end of William I's reign as a convenient point, and

117 Boon, 1988, pp. 13–14, argues that type VI was introduced as the first type to be struck at Cardiff in 1081.

118 Dolley 1955–7b, p. 284.

that at which the most information is available. Various attempts have been made to rank boroughs on the basis of Domesday Book. Stephenson made an assessment of forty-six urban centres from the estimated number of houses (*mansiones*),[119] excluding Bury which in common with other writers he treated as not having borough status.[120] Darby and his collaborators in the *Domesday Geography* series made broad estimates of population for the main urban centres.[121] The results were summarised in *Domesday England*, which listed 112 towns, including Bury.[122] For those at which coins were struck a further insight can be obtained from the level of mint activity. Unfortunately, the surviving coinage is scanty for the first seven types after the Conquest but a helpful résumé has been published by Harris of the known moneyers and the types in which they struck.[123] This enables the monetypes[124] to be calculated as a pointer to relative importance. The results based on the first seven types and the next, more plentiful PAXS issue are set out in Table 8. The rankings of the urban centres in the Table are primarily based on the population estimates contained in the *Domesday Geography* series and *Domesday England*. Towns for which no estimates could be hazarded have been inserted subjectively, according to the level of mint activity suggested by the monetypes. For comparison the Domesday Book rankings calculated by Stevenson for relevant centres in 1086, plus London and Winchester, are also included. As a check against possible distortion from including type VIII (with its bias towards southern mints derived from the Hampshire Beauworth hoard) the equivalent dies for the type, calculated by Metcalf, are also shown.[125] Finally, the monetypes for the five types usually attributed to William II are included, based on Harris' résumé, to help to assess if any apparent increase or diminution in mint activity in the PAXS issue appears to be reflected in later types.

Given the tentative nature of the statistics it would be foolish to interpret Table 8 too literally. It does show, however, that as in the Anglo-Saxon period, coins of Norwich are fewer than the importance of the city would lead one to expect.[126] It also illustrates the decline of York by the end of William I's reign, from the equivalent dies in type VIII; also the decline of Oxford and possibly Lincoln and

119 Stephenson 1933, Appendix III, p. 221, omitting London and Winchester, gave an estimate of '*mansiones*' in forty-two boroughs 'TRW'.

120 Stephenson 1933, p. 127. See also Ballard 1904, pp. 117–120, but cf. Lobel 1935, pp. 12, 15. An attempt to classify urban centres in this period according to yardsticks developed at a later period seems somewhat pointless, especially when dealing with a town like Bury which had distinctive characteristics derived from the power and privileged position of the abbot. For the purposes of this section Bury will be considered (as it was by Darby) alongside generally accepted boroughs.

121 Darby 1971; Darby and Terrett 1971; Darby and Maxwell 1962; Darby and Campbell 1962; Darby and Finn 1967.

122 Darby 1977, pp. 296–309, Fig. 102 and Key; Appendix 16, pp. 364–8.

123 Harris 1983–8. A revision and updating of these lists by T.G. Webb-Ware so far remains unpublished.

124 See Chapter 3, n. 91.

125 Metcalf 1981, pp. 79–85. Where Metcalf has given a range for estimated equivalent dies, the mid-point of the range has been used for creating the rankings shown in Table 8.

126 Loyn 1961, p. 127.

Table 8. Ranking of boroughs, *c.* 1086 x 1090

	Place name	*Population estimate ('000s)*	*Stephenson DB ranking*[a]	*Monetypes*		*Ranking by type VIII equivalent dies*	*Monetypes (William II) IX–XIII*
				I–VIII[b]	*Ranking*		
1	London (+ Southwark)	10.0+	1	74^{12}	1	1	65
2	Winchester	6.0–8.0	2	45^{8}	2	2	23
3	Norwich	4.0–5.0+	3	26^{7}	9	4	15
4	York	4.0–5.0	4	37^{5}	3 =	30 =	9
5	Lincoln	4.0–5.0	5	34^{2}	5	17	17
6	Thetford	<4.0 (+)	6	37^{6}	3 =	12	20
–	BURY	[3.0+]	–	1^{-}	62 =	–	–
7	Gloucester	2.5–3.0 (?)	7	14^{3}	19 =	9 =	6
8	Stamford	2.0–3.0+	12	17^{3}	15 =	33 =	6
9	Wallingford	2.0–3.0	8	19^{2}	11 =	16	5
10	Oxford	2.5++	11	32^{3}	6	13	12
11	Canterbury	2.5	18	28^{8}	8	3	27
12	Bristol	?	–	17^{5}	15 =	6 =	9
13	Exeter	2.0+	17	29^{3}	7	8	11
14	Colchester	2.0+	13	19^{4}	11 =	25 =	15
15	Wilton	?	–	19^{3}	11 =	27 =	6
16	Sandwich	2.0	14	13^{3}	21 =	33 =	10
17	Lewes	2.0	–	12^{3}	23 =	11	9
18	Worcester	?	–	24^{4}	10	22 =	10
19	Dover	(1.0–3.0)	–	14^{4}	19 =	5	9
20	Salisbury	?	–	7^{2}	36 =	6 =	9
21	Hastings	(1.0–3.0)	–	7^{2}	36 =	21	12
22	Hereford	?	–	15^{4}	17 =	22 =	10
23	Nottingham	1.0–2.0+	30	10^{2}	28 =	30 =	4
24	Leicester	1.5–<2.0	9 =	6^{1}	39 =	44 =	6
25	Huntingdon	<2.0+ (?)	–	10^{1}	28 =	53 =	4
26	Dunwich	2.0 (?)	9 =	$-^{-}$	–	59 =	–
27	Cambridge	1.6+	15	8^{2}	32 =	53 =	4
28	Ipswich	1.6+	22	19^{5}	11 =	14 =	7
29	Northampton	1.5+	16	6^{1}	39 =	59 =	3
30	Chester	1.5+	21	11^{3}	25 =	9 =	8
31	Warwick	<1.5	19	11^{3}	25 =	14 =	7
32	Chichester	1.2–1.5	26	10^{2}	28 =	19	11
33	Bedford	(1.5+)	–	8^{1}	32 =	39 =	6
34	Buckingham	(1.5+)	–	$-^{-}$	–	59 =	–
35	Southampton	1.2++	–	$-^{-}$	–	27 =	–
36	Maldon	1.1++	24	5^{3}	45 =	39 =	3
37	Shrewsbury	1.0++	27	13^{3}	21 =	24	10
38	Stafford	?	23	5^{2}	45 =	44 =	6
39	Hythe	1.0+	20	2^{1}	58 =	33 =	3
40	Shaftesbury	1.0+	25	12^{3}	23 =	18	6
41	Bath	1.0+	38	6^{3}	39 =	33 =	1

Table 8. Ranking of boroughs, *c.* 1086 x 1090 (continued)

Place name	*Population estimate ('000s)*	*Stephenson DB ranking*[a]	*Monetypes*		*Ranking by type VIII equivalent dies*	*Monetypes (William II) IX–XIII*
			I–VIII[b]	*Ranking*		
42 Hertford	1.0	–	4^{2}	49 =	44 =	6
43 Romney	0.8+	–	7^{2}	36 =	25 =	7
44 Derby	0.7+	28	10^{2}	28 =	39 =	5
45 Wareham	0.7+	29	15^{4}	17 =	20	2
46 Guildford	0.75	37	3^{1}	53 =	57 =	2
47 Sudbury	<0.7+	–	3^{1}	53 =	30 =	3
48 Steyning	0.6++	31	6^{2}	39 =	27 =	4
49 Dorchester	<0.7	35	8^{2}	32 =	33 =	5
50 Rochester	0.5++	–	5^{2}	45 =	39 =	7
51 Pevensey	0.5++	–	2^{1}	58 =	57 =	3
52 Bridport	0.5+	34	3^{2}	53 =	39 = (?)	–
53 Malmesbury	0.4–0.5+	36	6^{2}	39 =	33 =	2
54 Ilchester	0.5	–	11^{1}	25 =	44 =	4
55 Barnstable	0.35	43	4^{2}	49 =	44 =	–
56 Taunton	0.3	42	8^{1}	32 =	44 =	3
57 Marlborough	?	–	6^{1}	39 =	59 =	1
58 Cricklade	?	–	5^{1}	45 =	53 =	2
59 Launceston	?	–	4^{1}	49 =	59 =	2
60 Tamworth	?	–	4^{2}	49 =	44 =	4
61 Winchcombe	?	–	3^{1}	53 =	44 =	–
62 St Davids	?	–	3^{3}	53 =	59 =	–
63 Cardiff	?	–	2^{2}	58 =	59 =	–
64 Watchet	?	–	2^{1}	58 =	53 =	1
65 Bedwyn	?	–	1^{-}	62 =	59 =	–
66 Christchurch	?	–	1^{-}	62 =	59 =	–
67 Durham	?	–	1^{1}	62 =	59 =	2
68 'Maint'	?	–	1^{-}	62 =	59 =	–
69 Rhuddlan	?	–	1^{1}	62 =	59 =	–

Notes:
a. London and Winchester added as nos 1 and 2.
b. The smaller figures show the monetypes in the PAXS issue only.

Stamford. In contrast, towns such as Bristol, Dover, Chester, Gloucester and Lewes appear to have prospered. It is also noticeable that certain mints are more active than the population estimate would suggest: for example, Shrewsbury, Shaftesbury and Wareham. Although in theory this could be accountable to unrepresentative survival rates for their coins, abnormally active mints for the size of the place or understated population estimates, the last is the most likely explanation.

The most remarkable entry in Table 8 remains that of Bury. Darby estimated its population at over 3,000. At this level it would have arguably been the seventh largest urban settlement in the country. Its mint, however, represented by only one monetype – and indeed only one coin – places it amongst the least of minting centres such as Bedwyn and Christchurch, and far below Taunton with an estimated population of no more than 300. Set against the activity under Edward the Confessor and the confirmation of minting rights by William I and II, this apparent lack of coinage is an enigma. As intimated above, the population was possibly exaggerated at least two-fold by Darby, but centres with estimated populations of 1,500, such as Chester, Warwick and Northampton, still had fairly active mints. Even allowing for an unrepresentative survival rate, the discovery of sufficient coins to lift Bury substantially up the monetype rankings to the half-way point, say with 8–10 monetypes, seems only remotely likely. The conclusion must be that the mint was largely quiescent between the Conquest and 1087 and from then until the death of Rufus, for whose reign no coins of Bury are at present known. Preoccupation with the building programme, and the disruption entailed once the work started after 1081,[127] does not appear to be a very convincing explanation for the lengthy suspension of mint activity, yet it is hard to think of an alternative. It has to be borne in mind that the sacrist of the abbey was responsible for both activities and the building works and his other essential duties may have commanded all his attention.[128] As will be seen below, mint activity revived under Henry I but, on the evidence of known coins, did not become buoyant until the later part of the reign. By this time the building programme initiated by Abbot Baldwin was nearing completion and the town was able, at last, to prosper under settled conditions.

To end this section, Table 9 shows the monetypes for the reigns of Edward the Confessor (taken from Freeman)[129] and the first eight issues and final five issues between *c.* 1067 and 1100 (taken from Harris),[130] assuming that the ninth issue was introduced not in 1087 but in 1090, as suggested in Table 7. These figures illustrate how relatively less well represented the coinages of William I and William II are than that of Edward the Confessor. The higher figures for William II (types VIII–XIII) result partly from the inclusion of type VIII (PAXS) but more importantly from the greater frequency of type changes.

Conclusion

In 1094, towards the end of Baldwin's life, the rebuilding of the abbey church had reached the stage where the abbot could apply to the king for permission to return the body of St Edmund to his resting place and to dedicate the building.[131] According to Herman, the king at first agreed but later perversely withdrew his

127 Fernie 1998, p. 4.

128 *Memorials*, II, pp. 289–90. On duties of the sacrist, see Knowles 1966, pp. 429–30.

129 Freeman 1985, II, Appendix III.

130 See n. 123.

131 The stone for the church (the earlier church, according to Davis, having burnt down in 1078) was provided by the abbot of Peterborough (*Regesta* I, no. 369, p. 95).

Table 9. Comparison of monetypes between the reigns of Edward the Confessor and William I and II

	Edward the Confessor	*William I and II*		
		I–VII	*VIII–XIII*	*I–XIII*
Dates of coinage	1043(?)–65*	*c.* 1067–87	*c.* 1088–1100	*c.* 1067–1100
No. of years	23	21	13	34
No. of coin types	10	7	6	13
No. of monetypes	2,064	638	642	1,280
Average no. of monetypes (per type)	206	91	107	98
Average no. of monetypes (per year)	90	30	49	38

Note
* Although Harthacnut died on 8 June 1042, Edward was not crowned until the following Easter.

consent to the dedication and departed abroad. This resulted in a delay until the next year, by which time rumours were circulating at court that the incorrupt body of the saint was not at Bury and that the ornaments of the shrine should be stripped away to pay the soldiers. Relief came with the unexpected arrival of Bishop Wakelin and Ranulf Flambard on 25 April 1095 who, despite opposition from Bishop Herbert Losinga, performed the ceremony of translating the saint on Sunday, 29 April.[132] The conduct of the king was symptomatic of a less considerate attitude towards the monasteries as his reign progressed. This may have been partly prompted by his need of money for his continental projects.[133] The abbey was to suffer a heavier blow at his hands after Baldwin's death at the end of 1097,[134] when the king delayed appointing a successor and kept the abbatial revenues for his own benefit, leaving the community to fend for itself under the prior.[135] The vacancy continued until the death of William in 1100, when Bury numbered among eleven abbeys and three sees retained or farmed out by the king.[136]

132 *Memorials*, I, pp. 85–8.

133 Prestwich 1954, pp. 19–43.

134 Knowles, Brooke and London 2001, p. 32: Baldwin died between 28 December 1097 and 1 January 1098.

135 Barlow 2000, pp. 184–5, 234, assesses the effects of vacancies as less serious than suggested (for example) by Freeman 1882, I, p. 350 and II, Appendix W, pp. 564–7.

136 *AS Chronicle*, p. 235 ('from all of which he was drawing revenues'); cf. *EHD*, II, p. 184 ('all let out for rent'). See also n. 21 above.

CHAPTER 5
HENRY I

The abbots and their privileges

Within three days of Rufus' death on 2 August 1100 Henry had himself crowned as king.[1] Knowing very well the claims of his elder surviving brother, Robert Curthose, duke of Normandy, to the succession he immediately and systematically set out to show to his new-found subjects that he would be a just and worthy ruler. In an expedient Coronation Charter he condemned the exactions of his predecessor, restored the laws of Edward the Confessor, introduced a number of reforms and made certain commitments for the future. Besides abolishing the *monetagium* tax, he made free the Church in the opening clause of his charter in the following terms:

> ' . . . I will neither sell nor lease its property, nor on the death of an archbishop or a bishop or an abbot will I take anything from the demesne of the church or from its vassals during the period which elapses before a successor is installed.'[2]

This wording was far from clear in the letter, if not the spirit, and did not – for example – actually promise that an ecclesiastical vacancy would be speedily filled. Nevertheless, Henry gave a token of his good faith by immediately filling the sees and abbacies which Rufus had held in abeyance.[3] He recalled Archbishop Anselm of Canterbury from exile in Rome and on his coronation day appointed Richard, grandson of Count Gilbert of Brionne,[4] as abbot at Ely and Robert, illegitimate son of his cousin Hugh, earl of Chester,[5] as abbot at Bury.[6] Pragmatism was evident in these appointments since they would have helped to cement good relations with the baronial families from whom these appointees were drawn. They were not, however, to go unchallenged.

Unluckily for Henry, Anselm had returned from Rome imbued with the Church's views of the impropriety of lay investiture.[7] The lengthy ensuing dispute

1 *AS Chronicle*, pp. 235–6.
2 *EHD* II, p. 433.
3 The view of Green 1986, pp. 3, 7, that Henry's coronation promises to the Church were sincerely meant, must be questioned from his later conduct. At Bury there were two lengthy vacancies, in 1107–14 and 1119–21, only the latter of which could be excused by the king's absence in Normandy (*Regesta* II, pp. xxix–xxx).
4 Round 1895, p. 472 and chart facing p. 473.
5 *DNB*.
6 Bodley MS 297 (*Memorials*, I, p. 353); *Liber Eliensis*, p. 225.
7 Barlow 1979, pp. 297–342; Poole 1955, pp. 177–80.

widened to embrace whether the king should even have a voice in who was elected to ecclesiastical office. The settlement reached in August 1107 was nevertheless a satisfactory outcome for Henry.[8] Spiritual investiture was recognised as a prerogative of the Church but the king's right to invest a bishop or abbot with his temporalities, and to receive homage from him as a feudal baron, was reaffirmed. The more delicate issue of who selected the candidates for preferment was left unresolved, but does not appear to have been a further cause of friction in Henry's lifetime.[9]

Against this background of his dispute with the Church, although the king's appointment of Robert as abbot at Bury paid lip-service to his coronation promises, it was not to the liking of the monks.[10] The previous incumbent, Baldwin, had been influential through his knowledge of medicine and experienced in the exercise of monastic office. Robert, however, had merely served as a monk of St Evroult in Normandy[11] and was little more than a youth.[12] Consequently, it is not surprising to find him amongst those who were deposed from office at the Council of London, held by Anselm about 29 September 1102.[13] Any annoyance to the king arising from this move may have been somewhat mollified since Earl Hugh had died the previous year.[14] It was also during this period that Bishop Herbert Losinga made his final but unsuccessful bid to relocate his East Anglian see at Bury.[15]

After Robert's removal the abbey was administered at least until late September 1103 by Ralph the chaplain on behalf of the king, with Prior A(lfere) assuming responsibility for the brethren.[16] The writ yielding this information is also of numismatic interest since it confirms a gift to the abbey of land at Hawstead by Oddo and his wife. It has been suggested that because a later confirmation described Oddo as a goldsmith he may have been employed in the mint of the monastery.[17] Although Oddo appeared as the name of a moneyer at Bury late in the reign, Douglas has identified the reference with Otto the elder, the first hereditary die-sinker. As, however, he had probably died by 1098,[18] it could have referred to his son, also named Otto.

Either late in 1102 or in the following year,[19] Robert, prior of Westminster – generally known as Robert II – was appointed abbot, but because of the dispute

8 Barlow 1979, p. 301.

9 Chibnall 1986, p. 70.

10 BL Harl. MS 447 (*Memorials*, II, p. 4), *'renitentibus monarchis'*.

11 *Memorials*, II, p. 4.

12 *Memorials*, I, p. xxxvi, n. 1; Brett 1975, p. 78.

13 Knowles, Brooke and London 2001, p. 32; BL Harl. MS 447 (*Memorials*, II, p. 4).

14 Fryde, Greenaway, Porter and Roy 1986, p. 454; Brett 1975, p. 78, n. 2.

15 Bodley MS 297 (*Memorials*, I, pp. 353–4).

16 *Regesta* II, pp. x, 34 (no. 653); *Feudal Documents*, p. 61 (no. 20).

17 Gage 1838, p. 406.

18 *Regesta* II, p. xxv, following *Feudal Documents*, pp. cxxxix, 61 (no. 20).

19 *Memorials*, III, p. 5 (*'anno Domini M°CII°'*); cf. BL Harl. MS 447 (*Memorials*, II, p. 4 (*'annis iiii, tranactis obiit'*), indicating the following year. The temptation to place the appointment of Robert II

between Henry and the church he was not blessed by Anselm until 15 August 1107.[20] Very soon afterwards, on 16 September 1107, he died.[21] By this time Henry had become neglectful of the expectations raised by his Coronation Charter and kept the abbey vacant until 1114 when the *Anglo-Saxon Chronicle* records:

> '. . . he came to Winchester and while he was there he gave the archbishopric of York to Thurstan, his chaplain, and the abbey at Bury St Edmunds he gave to Al(e)bold who had been a monk of Bec, on 16 August.'[22]

The *Chronicle* omits to mention that at the time of his appointment Alebold was prior of St Nicaise at Meulan in the Vexin.[23] After election by the monks he was blessed by the recently appointed archbishop of Canterbury on 1 November 1114.[24] He is said to have died on 1 March 1119,[25] following which another vacancy occurred of two years.[26] It appears that on this occasion Maurice, the king's steward, had custody of the temporalities and the community was in the hands of a monk named Ednod.[27] The next abbot was Anselm, nephew of the late Archbishop Anselm, who had been a monk of Chiusa and abbot of S. Saba, Rome.[28] His tenure, although interrupted in 1138 when he served for a time as bishop of London, continued well into the reign of Stephen.[29]

A strangely worded writ, datable between 1100 and 1107 owing to its being witnessed by Roger Bigod,[30] is addressed to the abbot of St Edmunds and the lords (*dominis*) of the monastery. This raises the question whether, during the early years of the reign, the temporalities were in fact enjoyed by the abbot. Despite

after the date of the writ addressed to Ralph the Chaplain in late September 1103 should be resisted. For the reasons given later in this section (concerning the writ addressed to the 'Lords' of the monastery), until the separation of the abbot's and convent's property, in the time of Robert II, Ralph would have administered the convent on the king's behalf simply because the abbot could not be invested during the king's dispute with Anselm and the church. The writ does, however, indicate that this separation had not taken place by September 1103. The writ dated by Douglas as between 'September 1102 and Easter 1103' (*Feudal Documents*, p. 62, no. 21) and by Johnson and Cronne to '1102–3, 3 Apr.' (*Regesta* II, p. 31, no. 644), referring both to the abbot and the convent, may have been an expedient to ensure that the rights of the convent were confirmed in the hands of the king's officials.

20 Bodley MS 297 (*Memorials*, I, p. 355).

21 *Memorials*, I, p. 356.

22 *AS Chronicle*, p. 245.

23 Bodley MS 297 (*Memorials*, I, p. 356) and BL Harl. MS 447 (*Memorials*, II, p. 5), giving the year incorrectly as 1115. The latter source nevertheless stated that Alebold held office for five years, dying in 1119. See also Knowles, Brooke and London 2001, p. 32.

24 Bodley MS 297 (*Memorials*, I, p. 356); *Memorials*, III, p. 5.

25 *Memorials*, III, p. 5.

26 *Memorials*, III, p. 5.

27 *Regesta* II, p. 150 (no. 1226).

28 *Memorials*, III, p. 5; Knowles, Brooke and London 2001, pp. 32, 242.

29 See Chapter 6 below.

30 *Regesta* II, p. 6 (no. 511) where it is assigned to '*c.* 1100' on the untenable grounds that the abbey was vacant, even though the writ is addressed to the abbot(!); *Feudal Documents*, p. 65 (no. 26).

the reference to '*Dñis*' (which both Gage and Douglas appear to have suspected to be a scribal error),[31] it is not credible that the king would have appointed a new (albeit inappropriate) abbot in the immediate pursuit of his election promises only to retain the temporalities in his own hands. That Henry had, as Arnold believed,[32] withheld recognition and thus also the temporalities from his successor, Robert II, is equally implausible. The dispute between Henry and Anselm was conducted without vindictiveness and, as the eventual outcome showed, admitted the possibility of distinguishing between ecclesiastical and temporal investiture.[33] The explanation for the reference both to the abbot[34] and the lords of St Edmund must lie in the abnormal conditions created by the dispute between Henry and the Church. The king was able to confer their temporalities on both Robert I and II but not, without precipitating a dangerous confrontation with Rome, to install them as head of the monastic community. This led to the affairs of the convent being administered by the king's officials, whether an individual, such as Ralph the Chaplain, or several persons, as with the lords referred to in the writ. This situation, if allowed to persist, would have prejudiced the convent's interests as greatly as the hated vacancies of William Rufus. Undoubtedly Henry was sufficiently embarrassed by these circumstances to allow the property and revenues of the abbot to be separated from that of the convent. The effect of this change, however, extended far beyond its original cause in enabling the convent's portion also to remain under its control when the abbacy fell vacant. That this separation of the abbot's and convent's property and revenues occurred at Bury in the days of Robert II is clearly attested by Jocelin of Brakelond.[35] He describes how at the end of the twelfth century the anniversary of Robert II was solemnly observed in recognition of this 'great deed'.[36]

It should not be assumed that before its separation the convent had no recognisable possessions or revenues distinct from those enjoyed *ex officio* by the abbot, but these were limited in extent. A charter in Baldwin's time distinguishes between the abbot's personal books and those of the monastery, and Baldwin himself, for example, made charitable gifts out of his revenues for the sustenance of the monks which were intended to be in perpetuity.[37] It is questionable, however, how far the king's officials would have felt bound to honour the terms of such gifts during a vacancy. It also appears that Bury may have been unusual in the extent of protection secured for the convent's property and

31 *Feudal Documents*, p. 65; Gage 1838, p. 275, n. 1.

32 *Memorials*, I, p. xxxvi.

33 Barlow 1979, pp. 298–9.

34 Apart from the writ addressed to Roger Bigod (see n. 30 above) the king addressed Robert as abbot in writs dated 25 December 1103(?) (*Regesta* II, p. 34, no. 655) and 10 February 1106 (*Regesta* II, p. 51, no.739).

35 *Jocelin*, pp. 81, 90.

36 The separation appears to have been made prior to 31 July 1106, the latest date for the writ referring to 'St Edmund and Abbot Robert' (*Regesta* II, p. 58, no. 777); see also *Feudal Documents* p. 67, no. 32, dating the writ to 1104–6.

37 Robertson 1939, no. CIV, pp. 196–9.

revenues during a vacancy,[38] which doubtless explains why the monks' veneration of Robert II was so fervent. At about this time, the abbots were also beginning to live in separate quarters apart from their community. It was again Robert II who initiated this practice at Bury.[39] The natural result of these developments was to increase the power of the obedientiaries, such as the sacrist and the cellarer, within the community.[40] There is no doubt, however, that the right to mint coins continued to attach to the person of the abbot. An extraordinary view has nevertheless been propounded that not only were such rights personal and therefore lapsed with the death either of the king as grantor or of the grantee but that they were even in suspense when, for example, the grantee was out of the country.[41] This view does not bear examination. Mints were needed for practical reasons as well as being a convenient source of profit or privilege to the individual.

From the foregoing it will be apparent that between 1100 and 1107 a number of events occurred upon which a confirmation of rights could have been expected by the abbot. These were the appointments of Robert I and II, the separation of the abbot's and conventual property and revenues and, less probably, the investiture of Robert II. In fact, during the years spanned by Robert I and II three writs survive referring to the eight and a half hundreds and the same number to freedom of the abbey demesne lands from gelds. One of each of these can definitely be associated with Robert II and probably to the moment of separation, since both St Edmund and the abbot are specifically mentioned.[42] Of the remainder one grant of the eight and a half hundreds, which refers to the abbot (but not by name), the monastery (which is described as enjoying soc within the hundreds) and for the first time the burgesses (*burgeses*), appears to have been associated with the time of Robert II before the property separation.[43] By a process of elimination, the confirmation of eight and a half hundreds to 'St Edmund' dated by Douglas as 1100–7 but probably 1103 and in *Regesta* as 25 December 1103(?), but witnessed by Robert Malet who could have done so in 1100, 1102, 1103 or 1005, may well be assignable to the abbacy of Robert I at Christmas 1100.[44] It cannot at least have related to the investiture of Robert II. It is impossible to date precisely the two remaining writs on freedom from gelds but one of them, witnessed 'after Christmas' by Robert Malet,

38 Howell 1982, pp. 173–92.

39 *Memorials*, I, p. 356 (Bodley MS 297).

40 Barlow 1979, p. 193.

41 Andrew 1901, pp. 2–3.

42 *Feudal Documents* p. 67 (no. 32), dated by Douglas to '1104–1106' and *Regesta* II, p. 58 (no. 777), dated by Johnson and Cronne to '1103–1106, 31 July' on the eight and a half hundreds, and for the gelds *Feudal Documents* p. 68 (no. 33), dated to '1104–1107' and *Regesta* II, p. 76 (no. 861), dated likewise to '1104–1107' but where the reference to Abbot Robert (II) is unjustifiably used to argue for 1107, ignoring – for example – the evidence of writ no. 739 (*Regesta* II, p. 51).

43 *Feudal Documents*, p. 62 (no. 21), dated to 'Sept.1102 – Easter 1103', and *Regesta* II, p. 31 (no. 644), dated to '1102–3, 3 April'. See also n. 19 above.

44 *Feudal Documents*, p. 63 (no. 22) and *Regesta* II, p. 34 (no. 656).

was probably associated with the other writ already tentatively given to the year 1100.[45]

Most importantly for the present study a further writ dated by Douglas between 1104 and 1107 and similarly in *Regesta* but with an unexplained predisposition for 1106,[46] grants 'St Edmund' the right to a mint. Douglas cites it as follows:

> 'Henricus rex Anglie [*sic*] Herberto episcopo et Rogero Bigot et Radulfo Passelewa et omnibus fidelibus suis de Norfolc et Sudfolc et Othoni aurifabro de Lund salutem. Sciatis quod volo et concedo ut sanctus Ædmundus habeat monetarium suum in villa sua cum omnibus consuetudinibus monete sicut habuit tempore patris mei et sicut frater meus per breve suum sibi concesserat. Teste Rogero de Curcella [*sic*]. Apud Sanctum Ædmundum.'

The interest of this writ is heightened because it was promulgated at Bury and directed to Otto (presumably Fitz Otto, son of Otto the elder), undoubtedly to notify him that the abbot would be legitimately applying to him for dies. No Bury coins from this part of the reign have so far come to light to show if Otto was in fact called upon to prepare dies for the abbot. The terms of the grant to 'St Edmund' suggests that it was made very early in the reign during the confused period before the separation of the abbot's property from that of the community.

With the abbacy of Alebold no writs can be positively identified, but the confirmation of the eight and a half hundreds given at Woodstock to 'the abbot of St Edmund' and dated (somewhat unhelpfully) by Douglas between 1100 and 1133 may have been in his favour.[47] Anselm, however, is mentioned by name in a similar confirmation given at Rouen between 1121 and 1129, but almost certainly datable to 1121/2, soon after his election as abbot.[48] Confirmations of the eight and a half hundreds also survive in other forms from the rest of the reign but the reasons for such repetition are not apparent.[49] From Anselm's abbacy writs of Henry I also survive confirming the right to a market,[50] and granting an

45 *Feudal Documents*, p. 64 (no. 24), dated to '1100–1107; probably 1103', and *Regesta* II, p. 34 (no. 657), dated '1103?'. The remaining writ is cited in *Feudal Documents* p. 65 (no. 27) and *Regesta* II, p. 35 (no. 658), dated similarly to the preceding pair of writs.

46 *Feudal Documents*, p. 66 (no. 29), *Regesta* II, p. 55 (no. 760).

47 *Feudal Documents*, p. 70 (no. 37). Andrew 1901, p. 389, speculated that Henry did not confirm the temporalities on Alebold, but there is no reason for suggesting this, apart from the lack of identifiable references to him in writs of the period. The discovery of a Bury coin of type *BMC* VII (according to Brooke's classification in *Norman Kings*) unknown to Andrew also points to mint activity at this period; see Catalogue 9.

48 *Feudal Documents*, p. 71 (no. 40).

49 *Feudal Documents*, p. 72 (no. 41), dated to '1121–1129'; p. 73 (no. 42), dated to '1123–1129'; p. 74 (no. 45), dated to '1121–1133'; p. 75 (no. 48), also dated to '1121 to 1133', and pp. 76–7 (no. 50), dated to '1129–1133'.

50 *Feudal Documents*, p. 73 (no. 42), dated to '1123–1129', and *Regesta* II, p. 292 (no. 1914), improbably dated to '1135?'

annual fair.[51] Also from this period survives the only other writ of Henry I referring to the coinage at Bury.[52] Douglas again renders it thus:

> 'Henricus rex Anglorum Evrando, episcopo de Norwic et Roberto filio Walferi et omnibus baronibus et fidelibus suis francis et anglis de Sudfolc salutem. Concedo quod abbas de Sancto Ædmundo habeat in villa de Sancto Ædmundo monetam et monetarium et cambium suum sicut hucusque habuit peracta iusticia de monetario suo sicut facta est de aliis monetariis Anglie. Teste episcopo Lexoniensi et episcopo de Sancto David et Roberto de Sigillo. Apud Rothomag.'

This writ was attributed by Douglas to Abbot Anselm without closer precision. In *Regesta* a date of October 1125 was proposed, the words *'peracta iusticia de monetario suo sicut facto est de aliis monetariis de Anglie'* being identified with the purge of moneyers between Christmas 1124 and Epiphany (6 January) 1125 described in the *Anglo-Saxon Chronicle*.[53] The significance of the purge and its implications on the dating of the coin types of Henry I will be considered in the next section. The writ, it will be observed, grants the mint to the abbot as such, compared with the writ in Robert II's day addressed simply to St Edmunds. This greater precision was clearly felt necessary because of the separation of the abbot's temporalities, with which the minting rights were associated and shows that after 'the great deed' the right to coinage continued to attach to the abbot and was not passed over to the convent. As under William II the writ also spelt out that the abbot enjoyed the right to operate an exchange for coin or bullion brought to the mint, in addition to coining for his own purposes.[54]

The coinage of Henry I

Our state of numismatic knowledge takes a backward step in the reign of Henry I. The only comprehensive study so far undertaken, published as a volume of the *Numismatic Chronicle* in 1901,[55] is badly flawed, apart from obviously taking no account of coins coming to light in the course of the twentieth century. Amongst these the important Lincoln hoard found in December 1971 and January 1972 and containing at least 744 coins of Henry I, still awaits full publication.[56] Modern numismatists may have been discouraged from detailed work

51 *Feudal Documents*, pp. 73–4 (no. 43), dated to '1124–1129', and *Regesta* II, pp. 229–30 (no. 1599), similarly dated. The fair lasted six days beginning on 22 July.

52 *Feudal Documents*, p. 77 (no. 51), *Regesta* II, p. 194 (no. 1430).

53 *AS Chronicle*, p. 255, *s. a.* 1125, the date also given by *The Peterborough Chronicle*, p. 46.

54 See *Regesta* I, p. 99 (no. 392).

55 Andrew 1901. Brooke's *Norman Kings*, covering the period 1066–1158, based on the British Museum collection as it stood in 1916, is the work of a distinguished numismatist but is now in need of revision and updating. The lists of moneyers by type and mint published by E. J. Harris in *Seaby's Coin and Medal Bulletin* between January 1983 and March 1988 (Harris 1983–8) represents the only attempt to bring together the material recorded since Andrew and Brooke wrote.

56 A summary is set out in *Coin Hoards* 1 (1975), p. 90 (no. 359) and Fig. 20, p. 91. The more recent so-called 'Beauvais' hoard, containing 119 pennies of Henry I, received partial publication when 100 of these coins were auctioned by Glendining on 4 November 1987.

owing to the considerable rarity of surviving coins except from the latter years of the reign.[57] It is from these years that all but one of the small number of coins known from Bury occur.

A die study conducted into the Lincoln mint shows a remarkable decline in known examples of the coinage between the accession of Edward the Confessor and that of King Stephen:[58]

Table 10. Known dies from the Lincoln Mint

Period	*Known reverse dies*	*Average no. of dies per annum*
Edward the Confessor	384	16.7
Harold II	14	14.0 (9 months)
William I, types I–VII	78	3.7
William I/II, types VIII*, I–V	47	3.6
Henry I	26	0.7

Note
* 17 reverse dies are known of type VIII.

This decline in available material from Lincoln cannot be explained simply by reduced activity at the mint. The decline occurs also at other mints, and the remarkable figures for Henry I must in part reflect the incompleteness of survivors as a representation of coinage in his reign.[59] Nor is there evidence at this period of a material reduction in the number of mints operating. When Dolley wrote his brief survey of the Norman Coinage in 1966 he counted 51 known mints, 8 fewer than under William II, listed 10 he believed had closed for good and 3 more he surmised were active since coins were known from such locations in the reign of Stephen.[60] One mint (Cambridge) has since come to light in the former category,[61] and two (Stafford and Watchet) in the latter.[62] It nevertheless remains unclear whether the resources of silver in England shrank in the early decades of the twelfth century.[63] Sufficient wealth existed to support the king's policy in Normandy,[64] and this in itself may have caused a nett outflow of coin.

57 Apart from short papers, referred to elsewhere in the footnotes, the most detailed study is that of Blackburn 1990, pp. 49–81.

58 Mossop 1970, Table 4.

59 Brooke listed 1,437 coins from the reigns of William I and II in *Norman Kings*, but only 307 from the reign of Henry I. Stewart Lyon has calculated that the surviving reverse dies at Lincoln under Henry I represent approximately twenty-six percent of the total employed (Mossop 1970, Table 4).

60 Dolley 1966, pp. 28–9.

61 *SCMB* 716 (April 1978), p. 104 (type *BMC* V).

62 Both coins were in the Lincoln Hoard; see *Coin Hoards* 1 (1975), p. 90 and Fig. 19.9 (for a Stafford coin of type *BMC* X), and Fig. 19.19 (for a Watchet coin of type *BMC* XIV).

63 Spufford 1988, p. 97, infers that the currency in England at the beginning of the eleventh century amounted to twenty million pennies and was rising, but that by 1158, when Henry II introduced his 'Tealby' coinage, it had shrunk to half that volume.

64 Green 1986, p. 18.

Objection to the quality of pence used to pay his mercenaries is even suggested[65] as the reason why Henry angrily instructed Roger, bishop of Salisbury, before Christmas 1124 to punish all the moneyers in England by mutilation.[66]

It is also unclear how far the actual number of moneyers employed at each mint town may have altered independently of the level of mint activity. For London Brooke records between 5 and 13 moneyers at work for each type he ascribed to William II, compared with 7, 11 and 17 respectively for the last three, least scarce types of Henry I.[67] Taking Brooke's listing of moneyers for the last two types at London, however, there is only one, Ordgar, common to both types. This species of evidence, based on all the moneyers by type and mint known to Brooke, has been used to argue that a wholesale replacement of moneyers took place between the last two types of Henry's reign.[68] Walker, who produced this evidence, suggested that an unrecorded purge of moneyers had taken place in the early 1130s.[69] Subsequently, it was suggested that the 'crisis' identified was none other than the purge of Christmas 1124.[70] The listings produced by Harris usefully provide a more up-to-date picture of the known moneyers by mint and type than Brooke recorded.[71] Selecting the ten mints recorded by Harris as having seven or more different moneyers in types XIII to XV – on the grounds that the sample is likely to be more complete – the results are shown in Table 11.

The relationship between the total number of moneyers (122) and the aggregate of those known for types XIII–XV (173) suggests that a relatively broad sample has been obtained. More remarkably, the continuance into type XV of 25 (38%) of the 66 moneyers known for types XIII and/or XIV demonstrates a significant degree of continuity.[72] Although amongst the 40 further mints with fewer than seven known moneyers, only five have the same moneyer striking in type XV as well as in XIII or XIV, in 16 of those mints no coins are at present known of type XIV and in 29 of them no coins of type XV. Blackburn treats the mints not represented in type XV as having closed, but a number of the gaps could equally reflect the accidents of survival. It may be pertinent that, as Blackburn himself notes, most of the missing mints emerge again under Stephen.[73]

65 William of Jumièges, p. 297.

66 *AS Chronicle*, p. 255, *s. a.* 1125.

67 *Norman Kings* I, pp. ccxx–ccxxv.

68 See Walker 1984. It should be noted that London is omitted in error from Table 1, the figures for which should read from left to right as 10–15–1. Table 2, derived from Brooke, showed at those mints where types XIV and XV were both known, 62 monetypes in type XIV, 72 in type XV and only 11 common to both.

69 Walker 1984, p. 284.

70 See Gomm 1985a. This evoked a response from Walker (1985), expressing reservations about Gomm's arguments, and a rejoinder from Gomm (1985b). Seaby 1988, pp. 34–6, accepted the thesis of Walker as modified by Gomm.

71 See n. 55 above.

72 Blackburn 1990, pp. 66–9, reaches broadly similar conclusions.

73 Blackburn 1990, pp. 68, 70, Table 6. Brown 1997 also emphasises the decline in mints operating.

Table 11. Mints with seven or more moneyers in types XIII–XV of Henry I

Mint	*Total moneyers*	*XIII*	*XIV*	*XV*	*Monetype total*	*XIII and/or XIV*	*XIII and/or XIV + XV*
Canterbury	10	3	7	5	15	8	3
Chester	9	–	5	5	10	5	1
Gloucester	9	–	4	5	9	4	1
Lincoln	12	3	5	8	16	5	3
London	29	8	13	20	41	13	5
Northampton	7	4	3	6	13	3	3
Norwich	15	2	5	11	18	3	0
Thetford	11	5	10	4	19	11	3
Winchester	12	5	7	8	20	8	4
York	8	2	5	5	12	6	2
Total	122	32	64	77	173	66	25

These figures are at variance with the *Anglo-Saxon Chronicle*, which categorically states that the moneyers 'were . . . taken one by one, and each deprived of the right hand and the testicles below'.[74] Other writers have suggested that the moneyers' purge occurred between types XI and X (reversing the order proposed by Brooke),[75] XI and XII,[76] and XII and XIII,[77] but the even lower survival rate for these types precludes putting these hypotheses to the test. However, it would be unwise to take the entry in the *Anglo-Saxon Chronicle* too literally. It is not credible that such a punishment should have been visited indiscriminately upon the innocent and guilty. A number may have exonerated themselves, some may have fled to escape punishment and some may have been able to obtain a pardon, with or without a fine,[78] and, as Stewart has shown,[79] a number of moneyers may have moved to other mints. Chronicles frequently appear to make unreliable or inaccurate references to the subject of coinage.

On our current state of knowledge, the argument for linking the large influx of new moneyers in type XV with the purge of 1124–5 must be plausible. Nevertheless, niggling doubts remain. First, it means attributing fourteen types to the first twenty years of Henry's reign. If this is accepted, the average life of a type under Henry is considerably shorter than otherwise encountered since the accession of Edward the Confessor, as Table 12 illustrates:

74 *AS Chronicle*, p. 255.

75 Dolley 1966, pp. 26–7.

76 Brooke 1950, p. 87.

77 Oman 1931, p. 101; Archibald 1984, pp. 332–3, in which the widespread replacement of moneyers between types XIV and XV was noted, but not linked to the purge of 1124.

78 See *Norman Kings*, I, pp. cxliv-xclvi.

79 Stewart 1991 p. 6.

Table 12. Average duration of coin types

Reign	*Length in Years*	*No. of types*	*Average duration (years)*
Edward the Confessor	23	10	2.3
Harold II	–	1	–
William I	20	7[a] or 8	2.5 or 2.9
William II	13	5 or 6[a]	2.2 or 2.6
Henry I (types I–XIV)	24[b]	14	1.7

Notes
(a) Assuming type VIII to have been an emission of William II.
(b) On the hypothesis that type XV was introduced, as the first of the so-called immobilised types, in 1125.

Secondly, there are so many obvious gaps in the patterns of survival before types XIV and XV that one or two major hoards of earlier coins could have a revelationary – not to say revolutionary – effect. Thirdly, if type XV was indeed in issue from 1125 to 1135, it would be expected to cause not only a substantial number of new moneyers' names to crop up but also surviving coins of type XV to far outstrip those of the other types. Fourthly, in the period between 1128 and 1130 the local government machinery was audited and overhauled, resulting in many sheriffs losing their positions.[80] It could even be that this was the unrecorded event which Walker believed occurred in the early 1130s and led to the removal of a number of moneyers. If so, a number of years may have separated the moneyers' purge and introduction of type XV. In so far as an influx of moneyers may have been associated with a reduction in the number of mints operating, it would be as tenable to connect these moves with carefully thought out administrative reforms as to an earlier sudden move against dishonest moneyers. Stewart has offered a somewhat different hypothesis, namely that even if the purge of 1124–5 is associated with the removal of a large number of moneyers, further upheavals in the mint personnel could have occured in the course of type XV, as a consequence of the later administrative reforms.[81]

The writ attributed in *Regesta* to the time of the moneyers' purge, since it grants to the abbot at Bury his mint, moneyer and exchange 'after justice has been done (*peracta iusticia*) upon his moneyer',[82] could equally imply a form of screening rather than enforcement of a punishment. It would be strange for the threat of mutilation to have been triggered by the abbot's desire to reopen the mint, especially if, according to *Regesta*, the writ was issued in late October 1125, many months after the purge. The writ may be requiring the abbot to satisfy himself of the suitability of his previous moneyer to remain in office.

80 Green 1986, pp. 47, 64, 216.
81 Stewart 1991, p. 6.
82 See n. 52.

The regrettable paucity of material from Henry's reign may partly be explained by the peace which prevailed, and was so much envied in the following reign, once Henry had taken possession of Normandy after the Battle of Tinchebrai on 28 September 1106.[83] In such times there was less need to hide an accumulation of wealth and less likelihood that the owner would fail to retrieve it owing to a violent end. The lamentable state of the coinage referred to by chroniclers in 1108,[84]and a failure to cure the root causes implicit in the purge of moneyers at Christmas 1124, may also have rendered coinage up to that date less acceptable as a medium for long-term savings, particularly where the defects lay in debasement rather than poor workmanship or even short weight. The extent of this problem may also be cloaked by the hoard material since, insofar as coins from this period were deposited, they may well represent a careful selection of the less obviously defective. Stray coins may, from this point of view, eventually provide a more balanced picture of the state of the coinage in general use.

The dearth of coins and dateable historical events against which the coin types can be confidently placed has led to debate on both the sequence and dating of the fifteen types. The most noteworthy essays have been made by Brooke,[85] Dolley,[86] Archibald[87] and Seaby,[88] and most recently by Conte and Archibald,[89] and Blackburn.[90] Although Brooke did not attempt to place dates of issue against every type, their conclusions – excluding the earlier chronology suggested by Archibald – are summarised in Table 13.

From this table it will be apparent that unanimity exists upon the identification of the first, fourth to sixth, and twelfth to fifteenth types of the reign, and near unanimity on the seventh, tenth and eleventh types. This leaves in doubt the order of the second and third types (*BMC* II and III) and the eighth and ninth types (with *BMC* VII to XI all in contention). A detailed discussion of the sequence and dating is not appropriate here,[91] but the positioning of the PAX type (*BMC* III) as the second or third of the reign is at odds with the practice in earlier reigns.[92] Modern numismatists have, however, identified the so-called Annulets type, owing to its affinities in style and workmanship with the last type of William II, as the first of the reign. Nevertheless, association of the PAX

83 *AS Chronicle*, p. 241.

84 See *Norman Kings*, I, pp. cxliii–cxliv. Seaby 1988, pp. 37–9, voices caution about attributing, on current evidence, a reform of the coinage to 1108.

85 *Norman Kings*, I, pp. liii, lxvi–lxvii, lxix, cliv–clv.

86 Dolley 1966, pp. 22–8.

87 Archibald 1984, pp. 329–33.

88 Seaby 1988, pp. 27–43.

89 Conte and Archibald 1990, p. 236.

90 Blackburn 1990, p. 72.

91 Unfortunately Dolley does not set out detailed arguments in support of his dating schemes. Seaby relies for his sequence and dating heavily upon an analysis of the design of the coins. It is a considerable assumption, however, that similar design features in different types should be grouped together.

92 See Chapters 3 and 4 above.

Table 13. Henry I: sequence and dating of types

Brooke		*Dolley*		*Seaby*		*Conte/Archibald*		*Blackburn**	
BMC	*Dates*	*BMC*	*Dates*	*BMC*	*Dates*	*BMC*	*Dates*	*BMC*	*Dates*
I	1100–1	I	1100–1?	I	1100–1?	I	1100–1	I	1100
II		II	1101–4?	III	1101?-1103?	III	1101–3	II?	*c*. 1102
III		III	1104–7?	II	1103?-1105?	II	1103–5	III?	*c*. 1103
IV	-1108	IV	1107–8?	IV	1105–7	IV	1105–7	IV	*c*. 1105
V		V	1108–10?	V	1107–9	V	1107–8	V	*c*. 1106
VI		VI	1110–13?	VI	1109–11	VI	1108–9	VI	*c*. 1107
VII		VII	1113–16?	IX	1111–13	IX	1109–10	IX	*c*. 1109
VIII	1108–25	VIII	1116–19?	XI	1113–15	VIII	1110–11	VII?	*c*. 1111
IX		IX	1119–22?	X	1115–17	VII	1111–13	VIII?	*c*. 1113
X		XI	1122–4?	VII	1117–19	XI	1113–15	XI	*c*. 1115
XI		X	1124–5?	VIII	1119–20	X	1115–18	X	*c*. 1117
XII	1125–35	XII	1125–8?	XII	1120–1	XII	1118–20	XII	*c*. 1119
XIII		XIII	1128–31?	XIII	1121–3	XIII	1120–2	XIII	*c*. 1121
XIV		XIV	1131–4?	XIV	1123–5	XIV	1122–5	XIV	*c*. 1123
XV		XV	1134–5?	XV	1125–35	XV	1125–35	XV	1125–35

Note
*Blackburn gives a margin of error of +/− 3 years.

type with known events early in Henry's reign have so far failed to provide a satisfactory explanation of its significance. Oman attributed it to the period following the Treaty of Alton in 1101, which secured Henry against the claims of his brother, Robert, to the English throne and deprived the restive amongst the nobility of a rallying cause.[93] A PAX issue in such circumstances would appear highly improbable, amounting to an implicit admission that the crown had not hitherto sat securely on Henry's head. In her earlier article Archibald mentioned but, on the grounds of her dating scheme, dismissed as unlikely its celebrating the Treaty of Tinchebrai.[94] The Treaty would in any case have affected conditions in Normandy rather than in England. Another possibility (if all claim to its being the first type of the reign is rejected) is commemoration of the settlement in 1107 of the differences between the king and the Church discussed in the previous section. But such an explanation would not fit any dating scheme other than the skeletal one of Brooke. Yet another possibility is that Henry used the PAX type as an overt form of propaganda during his dispute with the Church. Such an explanation would be compatible with the dating schemes set out in Table 13.

93 Oman 1931, p. 95. Oman also considered the type to be stylistically similar to the coins of William Rufus and distinct from the following types of Henry I, associating this with the death of Otto, the hereditary die-sinker whom he stated to have been succeeded by his son, Otto Fitz-Otto in 1101 (cf. *Regesta* II, p. xxv, 'probably dead in 1098').

94 Archibald 1984, p. 329.

Interestingly, if the Annulets type is the first of the reign, its superficial resemblance to the last type of William Rufus is further evidence that each type was not, at this period, replaced as legal tender by the next issue.[95] Apart from considerations of design there are two more pointers to the same conclusion. Firstly, poor workmanship in striking which is very evident from surviving coins would have further complicated the task of differentiating readily between the types. Indeed the fact that in everyday transactions it was no longer necessary to do so could have helped create a slack attitude towards the quality of workmanship. Secondly, not only have numismatists sought to date at least two of the types by reference to the events of 1108 and 1124–5 through identifying a marked improvement in style and execution amongst the likely candidate issues,[96] but they have also accepted, not unreasonably, that a withdrawal of the unsatisfactory coinage in circulation also ensued.[97] If this view is accepted it is axiomatic that demonetisation was not normal.

The ordering of *BMC* VII and VIII as the eighth and ninth issues of the reign, or vice-versa, remains undetermined. Blackburn leaves Brooke's order unchanged.[98] The key argument adduced by Conte and Archibald for reversing this order appears to be based on an unproven date (1110) by which the Winchester moneyer Wimund was already dead, and the assumption that 'his last known coins are of *BMC* type VIII', thus discounting the likelihood of other types, such as *BMC* VII coming to light in his name, and accepting the speculative dating of *BMC* IX to 1109–10. A secondary argument by Conte and Archibald was that reversing Brooke's order would result in facing and profile busts alternating, thereby facilitating recognition on change of type.[99] In retrospect this looks to be the stronger argument of the two. The order suggested by Seaby, to place types VII and VIII after X has been demonstrated by Blackburn as untenable, from an analysis of inscriptions on coins from the mints of Lincoln and York.[100]

In the previous Chapter it was suggested that towards the end of Rufus' reign the type may have changed at two-yearly intervals. The abandonment of demonetisation may also have resulted, at some stage, in the type being changed at Christmas, rather than the fiscally important date of Michaelmas (29 September). It was at Christmas in 1100 when an ordinance was promulgated against false money and other abuses,[101] and again at Christmas in 1124 when

95 From his dating scheme Dolley clearly took type I of Henry I as completing the third of the three year cycle begun by the last type of William II (Dolley 1966, p. 22). Seaby 1988, p. 28, also held the same view. On this argument no type differentiation would be needed, but it would be expected that the resemblance would have been made as close as possible between the two related types.

96 On this basis the Voided Cross and Fleurs type (*BMC* V) is generally dated from 1108 (see Table 13), but see n. 84 above.

97 Craig 1953, p. 27.

98 Blackburn 1990, p. 60.

99 Conte and Archibald 1990, p. 234.

100 Blackburn 1990, p. 59, Table 2.

101 *Regesta* II, p. 4 (no. 501).

the moneyers were summoned to Winchester. Whether the average life of a type continued into the reign of Henry I at two years depends on whether type XV was introduced in 1125 or during a reorganisation of local government, *c.* 1129. Whatever the answer, it seems clear that the last issue of Henry I remained in use for a number of years, forming a model for the so-called immobilised types that became a feature of subsequent reigns, evident from the very first issue of Stephen.

Mint activity at Bury

Given that at this period the right to mint coins was enjoyed by the abbot personally rather than by the convent of Bury, it would be natural to expect the mint to cease operating on the death or removal of the abbot. If so, no coins should have been minted at Bury, possibly from 29 September 1102 to late September 1103 and, more certainly, during the vacancies between 16 September 1107 and 1 November 1114, and again between 1 March 1119 and Anselm's appointment in '1121'. Thus, coins of Bury from the reign could potentially help clarify the dating of the types. It has to be conceded, however, that the king, having control of the abbot's temporalities, could doubtless have arranged for the mint to continue operating during a vacancy through his appointed custodians if he considered it sufficiently worthwhile to do so. At present, however, the earliest known coin from Bury in the reign of Henry I is a cut farthing of type *BMC* VII (Quatrefoil and Stars), reading] :ED[and therefore giving no clue to the moneyer's name.[102] Ironically, the preferred dates given for this type by Conte and Archibald are 1111–13 and by Blackburn *c.* 1113, and thus within the long vacancy from 1107 to 1114. This illustrates (if proof is needed) the difficulty in making something of the slender evidence so commonly at the numismatist's disposal. The conclusion has to be either that the dates suggested for type VII are too early (thereby vindicating Dolley), or that Henry did indeed on this occasion keep the mint in operation.

The next coin arguably attributable to Bury is in type *BMC* X (Full Face/Cross Fleury). It reads +GODRIC: OH:SAH and is placed in the British Museum trays under Sandwich.[103] Confusion between this mint and Bury is a problem in the latter part of Henry's reign because some coins in the name of Godric definitely originate from Bury, such as those reading ON:S:EDM (type XIII)[104] and ON:SA'E (XIV),[105] but equally a coin reading SAHD has reasonably been assigned to Sandwich.[106] In the absence of obverse die links,[107] this leaves homeless those

102 Catalogue, 9.

103 See Catalogue, under Henry I, *BMC* X.

104 Catalogue, 10.

105 Catalogue, 13.

106 See Catalogue, under Henry I, *BMC* XIV.

107 Catalogue, 10, 11.

coins reading SAN (or SAH) or SAN[[108] with any subsequent letters illegible. The problem is not made easier by the use of SA(N) under type XV at Bury,[109] where the moneyer, Gilebert, is not otherwise known as a Sandwich moneyer. The rendering of St Edmunds as SA(N)(T), as an alternative to (S)EDM(VND), is also found under Stephen (in the name of Gilebert),[110] and in the later Short Cross coinage.[111] None of the dating schemes set out in Table 13 helps in identifying the mint source of the coin reading GODRIC:OH:SAH because each could accommodate type X outside the periods when the abbacy was vacant.

The coins of Godric at Bury, in type XIII (Star in Lozenge Fleury) reading ON:S:EDM,[112] and type XIV (Pellets in Quatrefoil) reading ON SA'E,[113] have already been mentioned. The obverse of the first of these types is die linked to a reverse reading GODRIC. ON. SAN[.[114] This shows clearly that coins of Henry I with such readings should not be lightly dismissed as emissions from Bury. Another coin of Godric in type XIV has the reading ON:SAN[ ] but shares an obverse with another coin reading, on the reverse, GODRIC:ON:SAHD.[115] Although the next letter of its legend is not legible, the former coin has been logically placed in the British Museum trays under Sandwich. At 1.41 g it is, perhaps coincidentally, heavier than other coins of type XIV from Bury.

Also in types XIII and XIV, the moneyer Oddo makes his appearance at Bury, seemingly to operate alongside Godric.[116] Apart from the reign of Stephen[117] this is the only occasion in the mint's history when more than one moneyer was conceivably at work, but this circumstance in Henry's reign is not alluded to in any surviving records. It may nevertheless be that Stephen, in granting a second and third 'die' to the abbot at Bury, was merely continuing a practice begun by his uncle. The name Od(d)e also appears on coins of nearby Thetford in the last type of Henry I and the first of Stephen.[118] If, as is likely, we are looking at the same man, it is an unexpected instance of a Bury moneyer operating at another mint. The association of his name with the family of hereditary die-sinkers should not be ignored and may account for his unusual career. If indeed his activity extended into the reign of Stephen, he cannot have been Otto the younger who had died by 1128, to be succeeded by his son William.[119] But he must surely have been another member of the family. Possibly because his

108 See Catalogue, under Henry I, *BMC* XIV.

109 Catalogue, 18, 19.

110 See Catalogue to Chapter 6 below.

111 See Catalogue to Chapter 8 below.

112 Catalogue, 10.

113 Catalogue, 13.

114 Catalogue, 11.

115 See Catalogue under Godric (*BMC* XIV), Other references.

116 Catalogue, 12, and 14–17. Archibald 1984, p. 333, suggests, improbably, that the two moneyers were working 'consecutively'.

117 See Chapter 6 below.

118 *BMC* 289 (Henry I, type XV); *BMC* 108, 109 (Stephen, type I).

119 *Feudal Documents*, pp. cxxxix–cxli. On the Otto family (or families) see Biddle 1976, Addenda, pp. 551–2.

name was so short, Oddo's coins result in some interesting representations of the Bury mint signature, as may be seen from Table 16 below.

All the dating schemes would accommodate type XIII at Bury without having to argue that the king was operating the mint during a vacancy. It has the semblance of the first type introduced after Anselm became abbot in '1121'.

In the last type (*BMC* XV, Quadrilateral in Cross Fleury) only one moneyer, Gilebert, is known at Bury. It is tempting to look upon him as the moneyer installed after the purge of 1124–5. In Gilebert's name are found coins reading SA[N],[120] EDM[ ]N,[121] EDMV.,[122] and EDM[:],[123] a further salutary warning when construing the reverses of Godric. Gilebert remained in office as a moneyer of the abbot into the reign of Stephen. There is also one coin recorded by Andrew of type X, from the Lawrence collection, purportedly reading '+GILEBERT:ON..N',[124] but its whereabouts is not known. If substantiated as emanating from Bury, it would begin to appear that it became a three-moneyer mint under Henry I as well as under Stephen.

The surviving coins of Bury from the reign, although few in number, suggest that the mint may have been fairly active, as Table 14 shows:

Table 14. Moneyers active at Bury under Henry I

	No. of known coins (and no. of reverse dies)			
BMC type	*Unknown moneyer*	*Godric*	*Oddo*	*Gilebert*
VII	1(1)	–	–	–
X	–	1(1)?	–	1(1)?
XII	–	1(1)?	–	–
XIII	–	4(2)	1(1)	–
XIV	–	5(1)	7(4)	–
XV	–	–	–	19(6)

Other types and moneyers given incorrectly or dubiously to Bury by Andrew include an unspecified moneyer in type *BMC* I (Annulets), Adalbot in VII (Quatrefoil and Piles), Wulfwart in IX (Cross in Quatrefoil) and, by the cataloguers of the Murdoch sale in 1903, Aldred in type XIV. The coin of Adalbot in type VII, reading +ADALBOT :ON: SAN[125] from the Smith, Reynolds and Lockett collections, and its die duplicate at Stockholm,[126] have been generally accepted as emanating from Sandwich, on the straightforward, if insecure ground that a

120 Catalogue, 18, 19.
121 Catalogue, 20.
122 Catalogue, 21.
123 Catalogue, 22 and 23.
124 See Catalogue, under Henry I, *BMC* X.
125 Andrew 1901, p. 390 and Plate VIII, 3. Andrew also mentioned (p. 390) another coin with the same reading but no punctuation from the Murrell Sale, 1886. See Catalogue, under Henry I, type VII.
126 *SCBI* Stockholm 275.

'SAN' reading alone should be allotted there rather than to Bury. The moneyer is also known in the last type of the reign with the reading SANDP.[127]

A coin of Wulfwart in type IX, reading +PVLFPART :ON: SAN,[128] was described by Andrew as in the Bury St Edmund's Museum and as having been found less than five miles away at Whepstead. Further details of this coin are unknown since the undocumented collection was stolen in 1965 and not recovered.[129] Brooke, however, recorded under Sandwich another coin of the same type in the Wells collection, and this coin reading +PVLFPART :ON:SAN[130] subsequently passed into the hands of Mack.[131] The assignment of this moneyer to Sandwich must be based on similar reasoning to that applied to Adalbot. Wulfwart (or Wulfword) appears to have been an active moneyer in the last two types of William Rufus with mint readings of SN (type IV)[132] and SIIN (type V),[133] and in the following reign (type VII) with the reading SA.[134] If these coins were incorrectly placed under Sandwich the picture of Norman coinage at Bury would be dramatically transformed. Given the variety of these readings and that none specifically points to a Bury provenance, however, Sandwich must remain as the probable mint.

A coin of type XIV was included in the Murdoch sale in 1903, where the reverse reading is transcribed by the cataloguer as +ALDRED ON SANTIE.[135] Brooke, however, considered the coin was probably from Shaftesbury,[136] doubtless owing to other coins of the same moneyer and type with an unambiguous Shaftesbury reading.[137]

To conclude this review of incorrect or debatable attributions to Bury mention should be made of the coins of Godhese in type XIV. A coin read as +GO[—]SE :ON: SA[-]D was placed hesitantly by Andrew under Sandwich,[138] with which Brooke sensibly concurred, whilst noting a further coin in the Carlyon-Britton collection reading +GODhESE:OH:SAH.[139]

In summary, Tables 15 and 16 show the possible moneyers active at Bury under Henry I and the mint readings for those coins allotted to the mint in this study. Both Tables may expect to undergo some change as more coins from the reign come to light:

127 *SCBI* Mack 1576. The moneyer Adalbot is also recorded under William II in type *BMC* IV and V (see Harris 1983–8, December 1986, p. 374).
128 Andrew 1901, p. 392. See Catalogue, under Henry I, type IX.
129 *SCBI* Museums in East Anglia, p. 103.
130 *Norman Kings*, I, p. ccxxxv.
131 *SCBI* Mack 1529, and Mack (1977) 253.
132 *BMC* 249, Pl. XXXVI, 9.
133 *BMC* 272, Pl. XXXVII, 12.
134 *SCBI* Mack 1524; Mack (1975) 269.
135 Murdoch (1903) 226. See Catalogue, under Henry I, *BMC* XIV.
136 *Norman Kings*, I, p. cci.
137 E.g. *BMC* 165, *BMC* 166.
138 Andrew 1901, p. 405.
139 *BMC* 163 and *Norman Kings*, II, p. 311.

Table 15. Possible moneyers active at Bury under Henry I

Moneyer	*Type*						
	VII	*IX*	*X*	*XII*	*XIII*	*XIV*	*XV*
Unknown	+	–	–	–	–	–	–
Adalbot(?)	(+)	–	–	–	–	–	–
Wulfwart(?)	–	(+)	–	–	–	–	–
Gilebert	–	–	(+)	?	?	?	+
Godric	–	–	(+)	(+)	+	+	–
Oddo	–	–	–	–	+	+	–
Aldred(??)	–	–	–	–	–	(+)	–

Notes
+ clearly
(+) conceivably
? improbably

As Table 15 implies, if coins of Gilebert were attributable to Bury in type X, the likelihood of his having operated in types XII to XIV would be much increased. As intimated above, the effect of this would be to raise the complement of moneyers operating in types XIII to XIV to three, as under Stephen.

From the Catalogue it will be seen that, so far, only one die link is known (Godric, type XIII, Aab), the remaining coins all being struck from free-standing pairs of dies. In type XIV Oddo (known from four sets of dies) may have been more important than Godric (with one set). The nineteen coins of Gilebert in type XV, struck from six pairs of dies, are regrettably too few in number to justify more extensive statistical analysis.

Table 16. Bury mint readings under Henry I

Type	*Moneyer*			
	Unknown	*Godric*	*Oddo*	*Gilebert*
VII	S*:ED[			
X		SAH(?)		
XIII		SAN[	SANTEEDMV	
		S:EDM		
XIV		SA'E	SANCADM	
		SAN[ ] (?)	SANCEDMVN	
			SANTIED[	
			]ANE[	
XV				EDM
				EDMV
				EDM[ ]N
				S*A
				SAN

Note
* S reclines?

The importance of Bury under Henry I

What coin evidence there is, compared with the surviving coins of Edward the Confessor, points to increasing mint activity at Bury at least in the latter years of Henry I, particularly in the employment of more than one moneyer at a time. This, in turn, suggests economic growth stimulated by the revenues derived from the privileges of St Edmunds. The abbots were thereby enabled to embark upon an ambitious building programme, itself a stimulus to urban development but more importantly underlining the eminence of Bury as a religious centre, attracting the devout and ordinary traveller, and tradesmen to supply their wants. The continuing religious allure of St Edmund for the monarchy is illustrated by Henry's vow in 1131 to make a pilgrimage to Bury if he realised a safe sea crossing to England.[140] The loss of his son with the White Ship in 1120 had clearly implanted an abiding fear in the king's mind.[141] The growing temporal importance of the town was already evident from the Domesday entry, and is reflected by the existence of a regular market in the town.[142] The grant, under Henry I, of an annual fair,[143] moreover, is clear proof that the economic importance of St Edmunds was no longer purely local. These influences would have had their effect on the activity of the mint and dissemination of its output to other parts of the kingdom.

At this period, the inhabitants of Bury were well placed to take advantage of the favourable environment in which they found themselves. Although largely holding their urban properties from the abbey, or more accurately from certain obedientiaries of the abbey, in particular the cellarer and the sacrist,[144] their very subservience as the abbot's men meant they enjoyed his protection and obtained vicarious or even direct benefit from the privileges heaped upon him and his house. This is demonstrated by certain of the writs granted by Henry I,[145] and by Stephen,[146] confirming release from tolls and other burdens as enjoyed under Henry. In the second half of the century, however, as other urban communities without religious institutional ties began to acquire both privileges of their own and the independence to regulate their affairs, the protection afforded by St Edmunds and other religious communities came to be viewed as too high a price to pay for their lack of freedom.[147]

Apart from continued construction of the abbey church, which was incomplete apart from the presbytery upon the translation of St Edmund in 1095,[148] the

140 *Anecdota Oxoniensa*, pp. 33–4; Hollister 2001, p. 462.

141 Poole 1955, pp. 125–6.

142 See Chapter 4 above.

143 See n. 51 above.

144 Lobel 1935, pp. 16–59.

145 E.g. *Feudal Documents*, pp. 62–3 (no. 21) and pp. 65–6 (no. 28).

146 *Feudal Documents*, pp. 80–1 (no. 58).

147 Lobel 1935, p. 16, who nevertheless believed that the town's greatest period of freedom was in the twelfth and early thirteenth centuries. The pressures were already well in evidence by the abbacy of Samson (1182–1211), as shown by *The Chronicle of Jocelin of Brakelond* (see Chapter 7 below).

148 BL Harl. MS 1005, fol. 120; *Memorials*, II, p. 289. See Gransden 1991b, pp. 59–86.

next important phase of building activity occurred during the abbacy of Robert II when the cloister (*claustrum*), chapter house (*capitulum*), refectory, dormitory and abbot's quarters (*cameram suam*) were commissioned to be constructed[149] under the supervision of Godfrey, the sacrist.[150] The need to ensure adequate uninterrupted revenues to finance these projects would have been an important reason for Robert II to safeguard St Edmunds' resources from depredations during any vacancy between abbots. Thus, despite the vacancy from 1107, the new crypt was finished and dedicated in 1114.[151] Anselm continued the building activity with the able support of two sacrists, Ralph and Henry. Their works included walling around the precincts, the church of St Mary with its tower, and the tower of St James' church, now known as the Norman Tower, both of which churches were within the abbey boundaries, and an unidentified bell tower (*clocarium*).[152] St James' church itself was apparently also begun by Anselm at the behest of the monks instead of his making a pilgrimage to Santiago de Compostela in Spain.[153]

With the exception of Robert I, the abbots of this period appear, at a parochial level, to have been worthy successors of Baldwin, although little is known, favourably or otherwise, of Alebold. Certainly, Robert II was revered by later generations of monks at Bury. It is more difficult to judge how influential these abbots were in the wider world compared with, say, Baldwin. At this period, the richest abbeys could naturally expect to attract noteworthy heads,[154] particularly as long as the king exercised a major influence on the choice of abbot and abbacies remained a recognised route to bishoprics. This is illustrated by the appointment at Bury of Anselm, who as nephew of Archbishop Anselm must have been well-connected at Court and, with the abbot of Glastonbury, accompanied William of Corbeil, archbishop elect of Canterbury, to Rome to receive the *pallium*.[155] Nevertheless, it may be significant that the number of writs and charters witnessed by the abbot of Bury and printed in the first two volumes of *Regesta* declines from ten in the reigns of William I and II to two under Henry I.[156] On the other hand, although there is no evidence of either the Conqueror or Rufus visiting the abbey, a number of writs of Henry I were apparently issued there.[157] Any apparent falling away may well reflect the incomplete state of the monastic buildings rather than a difference of attitude towards St Edmunds by those monarchs, whose writs show unswerving respect for its privileges.

149 *Memorials*, I, p. 356 (Bodley MS 297).

150 BL Harl. MS 1005, fol. 120; *Memorials*, II, p. 289, referring also to the construction of the *aulam* of the abbot.

151 Whittingham 1971, p. 5.

152 BL Harl. MS 1005, fol. 120; *Memorials*, II, p. 289.

153 *Memorials*, I, p. xxxvii.

154 Knowles 1966, p. 175; Barlow 1979, pp. 177–8.

155 *AS Chronicle*, p. 252, *s. a.* 1123.

156 *Regesta* I (excluding those described as spurious or inflated): p. 6 (no. 22), p. 8 (no. 28), p. 17 (no. 64), p. 32 (no. 122), p. 34 (no. 129), p. 50 (no. 182), p. 78 (no. 301), p. 81 (no. 315), p. 83 (no. 319), p. 86 (no. 328); *Regesta* II, pp. 192–3 (nos 1426–7).

157 *Regesta* II, pp. 54–5 (nos 759–62), dated '1106?', p. 135 (nos 1144–5), dated '1106–1116', and p. 256 (no. 1733), dated '1132?'.

CHAPTER 6

STEPHEN

Bury during the Anarchy

Apart from one episode in 1153,[1] St Edmunds appears to have escaped the ravages of Stephen's reign and even prospered despite the unsettled times.

Writs from the reign afford an incomplete picture of the privileges enjoyed by the abbey and no actual confirmation of the eight and a half hundreds is known to exist. Nevertheless, writs do survive addressed to the barons of the hundreds (*omnibus baronibus de viii hundredis et dimidio Sancti Ædmundi*),[2] and to the men of the honour of St Edmund (*omnibus hominibus de honore Sancti Ædmundi*).[3] It is also clear that during the reign Stephen gave to the convent (*ecclesie Sancti Ædmundi et monachis*) the hundred of Stow in Suffolk. The grant survives in two forms, addressed to distinct audiences.[4] Stephen also gave the half hundred of Harlow expressly to Abbot Ording and his successors.[5] These territorial accessions, however, were not reaffirmed when Henry II came to the throne.[6]

Apart from a general confirmation to Ording, who succeeded Anselm in 1148,[7] of the possessions and immunities of the abbey,[8] other writs show the continuing advantage derived by the townsfolk at this period from attachment to Bury and the abbey in that the men of St Edmund were not to be impleaded outside his court,[9] and the burgesses were to be free from all levies other than those due to the abbot.[10]

Arnold offered a plausible explanation for the favour with which Bury was considered by the king in suggesting that Ording had had charge of Stephen's

1 See last paragraph of this section, p. 92.

2 *Feudal Documents*, p. 86 (no. 68); *Regesta* III, p. 278 (no. 753).

3 *Feudal Documents*, p. 90 (no. 75); *Regesta* III, p. 284 (no. 771).

4 *Feudal Documents*, p. 85 (no. 66); *Regesta* III, p. 280 (no. 758), addressed to notable subjects at large, and *Feudal Documents*, p. 88 (no. 71); *Regesta* III, p. 280 (no. 759), addressed to the hundred.

5 *Feudal Documents*, p. 90 (no. 76); *Regesta* III, p. 281 (no. 761).

6 See Chapter 7 below.

7 *Memorials* III, p. 6, giving simply the year. The granting of the abbey to Ording, however, must be dated before 16 April 1148, when Robert, bishop of Hereford, one of the witnesses to the grant, died at Rheims (*Regesta* III, pp. 280–1, no. 760).

8 *Feudal Documents*, p. 87 (no. 70); *Regesta* III, pp. 280–1, (no. 760).

9 *Feudal Documents*, p. 82 (no. 61); *Regesta* III, p. 278 (no. 752).

10 *Feudal Documents*, p. 89 (no. 74); *Regesta* III, p. 279 (no. 756).

upbringing. This was construed from the opening words of the prologue to a tract on the Infancy of St Edmund by Galfridus de Fontibus: *'regiis excubiis a puero insistenti domino Ordingo, abbatis praerogativa praecellenti. . .'*.[11] Besides the ambiguity of the language, Jocelin of Brakelond, although writing some decades later, described Ording as unlearned (*homo illiteratus*), whilst at the same time disarming any suspicion of prejudice by adding that he was nevertheless a good abbot who ruled his house wisely.[12] When to this evidence is added the fact that Ording had only attained the abbacy relatively late in the reign,[13] and had been a monk and then cellarer at Bury from as early as 1100–7,[14] the likelihood of his having supervised in any sense the upbringing of Stephen can be safely discounted. It is also probable that Stephen did not come to England until about 1113, when he was around seventeen years old.[15] The significance of Ording's appointment is as the first abbot at Bury whose career had been made within the community of St Edmund. As such it illustrates two related trends: firstly, the greater voice monasteries were acquiring in the choice of abbot and, secondly, that with bishops being increasingly appointed from among lay clerks rather than from within the monastic community,[16] abbacies – even important abbacies – were less attractive to the ambitious as a path to preferment. The role of the Benedictine order as a force in national affairs was in decline, although later abbots, such as Samson at Bury, could still attain eminence beyond the scope of their calling.

Stephen may have had a perfectly natural inclination to show favour to Bury as one of the greatest Benedictine houses in the kingdom. His magnanimity is well documented.[17] He would also have been conscious of following an honourable tradition set by Edward the Confessor and the Norman kings. Beyond inclination and emulation of his predecessors, however, very practical considerations gave the king good reason to secure and nurture loyal support from St Edmunds, as a bastion against his declared or prospective opponents in East Anglia.

Troubles for Stephen started shortly after his accession, and although the main support for Henry I's daughter, the Empress Matilda, as rival claimant to the throne became centred upon the West Country from 1141, parts of East Anglia were either actively or passively sympathetic to her cause until her final departure from England early in 1148.[18] The threat posed in East Anglia arose from two

11 *Memorials*, I, pp. xxxv, 93.

12 *Jocelin*, p. 11; *Memorials*, I, pp. xxxvii, 219.

13 Ording had been appointed as abbot briefly in 1138, when Anselm was named but not subsequently confirmed as bishop of London (*Memorials*, III, pp. 5–6).

14 See *Feudal Documents* p. 106 (no. 109). Douglas dates this writ witnessed by Ording as 'monk and cellerar' to 1098–1102 or 1107–14 but since it was issued by 'Abbot Robert' it must have been between 1100 and 1107.

15 Davis 1967, pp. l, 7.

16 See *AS Chronicle*, pp. 251–2.

17 E.g. *Gesta Stephani*, pp. 206–7, relating how Stephen gave money for young Henry of Anjou to pay off the army he had brought to England for his abortive attempt to unseat Stephen in 1147.

18 Davis 1967, p. 96; Cronne 1970, p. 58.

quarters. One of these was Hugh Bigod, an unprincipled and self-seeking nobleman with extensive lands in Norfolk and Suffolk and castles at Framlingham, Bungay, Walton[19] and Ipswich.[20] Ironically, he had played a key role in Stephen's accession. The leaders of the church and lay nobility had at the behest of Henry I shown allegiance to Matilda as his heir in 1126, after the death of Henry's only legitimate son, William, in the White Ship.[21] However, Hugh Bigod and two knights from Lyons la Forêt, where they had been in attendance on the king, testified publicly before the archbishop of Canterbury that on his deathbed Henry had disinherited Matilda and named his nephew Stephen as his successor. This removed a critical obstacle to Stephen, who was crowned on 22 December 1135.[22] Hugh Bigod's opposition to Stephen may well have arisen in part from disappointment at the recognition he received from the king after his accession. In any event, he gave early notice of his subsequent conduct when in the following year, upon a rumour of Stephen having died, he seized Norwich castle and only handed it back after the arrival of the king in person.[23]

In 1139 Stephen created further difficulties for himself in East Anglia by also alienating Nigel, bishop of Ely. Nigel's uncle Roger, bishop of Salisbury, had become in effect justiciar or chief minister of Henry I, a position he continued to hold on the accession of Stephen.[24] His 'nephew' Roger was appointed chancellor,[25] and another relative, Athelhelm, acted as treasurer,[26] as Nigel himself had done from 1127 to 1133.[27] Yet another nephew, Alexander, was bishop of Lincoln.[28] This enormously influential family was toppled from power under the pretext of a brawl implicating Bishop Roger's knights at Oxford in June 1139.[29] Nigel thereupon fled to his uncle's castle at Devizes and prepared to defend himself against the king.[30] The Church was incensed by the events and Stephen's brother Henry, bishop of Winchester and papal legate, temporarily alienated.[31] In the midst of the confusion and with consummate timing Matilda landed at Arundel on 30 September 1139 to claim the throne.[32] This heralded the period of greatest insecurity for Stephen, leading to his capture at Lincoln in 1141,[33] and imprisonment at Bristol.[34] Nigel himself, after capitulating at Devizes, was

19 Davis 1967, p. 80
20 Cronne 1970, p. 65.
21 Cronne 1970, p. 28; Davis 1967, p. 18.
22 Fryde, Greenaway, Porter and Roy 1986, p. 35.
23 Roger of Wendover, II, p. 219; Cronne 1970, p. 33.
24 *Regesta* II, p. xvii; III, p. ix.
25 William of Malmesbury described him as '*nepos . . vel plusquam nepos*' of Roger (*Historia Novella*, p. 27).
26 *Regesta* III, p. xix.
27 *Regesta* III, p. ix.
28 Davis 1967, p. 31.
29 *Gesta Stephani*, pp. 76–7.
30 *Gesta Stephani*, pp. 78–9.
31 Cronne 1970, p. 38.
32 Cronne 1970, p. 39.
33 *Gesta Stephani*, pp. 112–13.
34 *Gesta Stephani*, pp. 114–15.

stripped of his castles[35] but allowed to return to Ely, which he set about fortifying after the death of his uncle on 11 December 1139.[36] Stephen besieged him there and caused him to flee to the Empress' party at Gloucester.[37] Less than two years later, the king had to oust the bishop's knights who had once more established themselves at Ely.[38]

The problems created by Bishop Nigel early in 1140 were followed in June of that year by a new insurrection in East Anglia, led by Hugh Bigod. Stephen captured his castle at Bungay but had to return again in August to assert his authority.[39]

These events illustrate vividly the instability of East Anglia within Stephen's sphere of influence early in the reign. They also point to the importance of the abbot at Bury with his *servitium debitum* of 40 knights, equal to that of the bishop of Ely, as an ally and supporter of Stephen's cause. The ability of the abbot both to defend himself and act as a check upon Bishop Nigel and Hugh Bigod was increased early in the reign when he was released from the obligation to provide groups of knights for guard duties at Norwich castle, to enable such duties to be performed at Bury.[40] Figure 4 shows the castles held by Hugh Bigod and his adherents, and their relationship to the Liberty of St Edmund, and the abbot's tenant, Adam of Cockfield, whose castle was located at Lindsey.[41] It also suggests that Stow hundred may have been added to the abbey's possessions as a further buttress against Hugh's territorial interests in East Anglia.

That important monasteries were not immune from the effects of the conflict between Stephen and his adversaries, or those taking advantage of the disturbed times to further their own ends, is shown by the example of Ramsey, in the east Midlands. Its abbot, Walter, had been forced as a sympathiser of the Empress to resign late in 1143 in favour of a monk called Daniel, who had guided the royal army across the fens to confront Bishop Nigel at Ely in 1140. This served as an excuse for Geoffrey de Mandeville to take over the abbey by force, but instead of reinstating Walter he dismissed the monks, appropriated the treasures of the monastery and used the buildings as a base from which to devastate the surrounding countryside.[42] It appears that at this time he was in close touch with Hugh Bigod,[43] and these events have been associated with the reference in *Jocelin* to the defence of the abbot's interests in Groton and Semer

35 *Gesta Stephani*, pp. 78–9.
36 *Gesta Stephani*, pp. 98–9.
37 *Liber Eliensis*, pp. 314–15, 433.
38 *Liber Eliensis*, p. 319. *Liber Eliensis* records that at this time irregular coins (*drachmam*) were struck at Ely (p. 322).
39 Davis 1967, p. 45.
40 *Feudal Documents*, pp. lxxxvii-lxxxviii (especially n. 1) and pp. 83–4 (no. 64).
41 Davis 1967, p. 84, misconstrues the reference to Lindsey Castle in *Jocelin* (p. 138) and represents it as hostile to the king.
42 Davis 1967, pp. 82–3.
43 Davis 1967, p. 84; Cronne 1970, p. 54.

Figure 4

Castles in East Anglia *c.* 1140

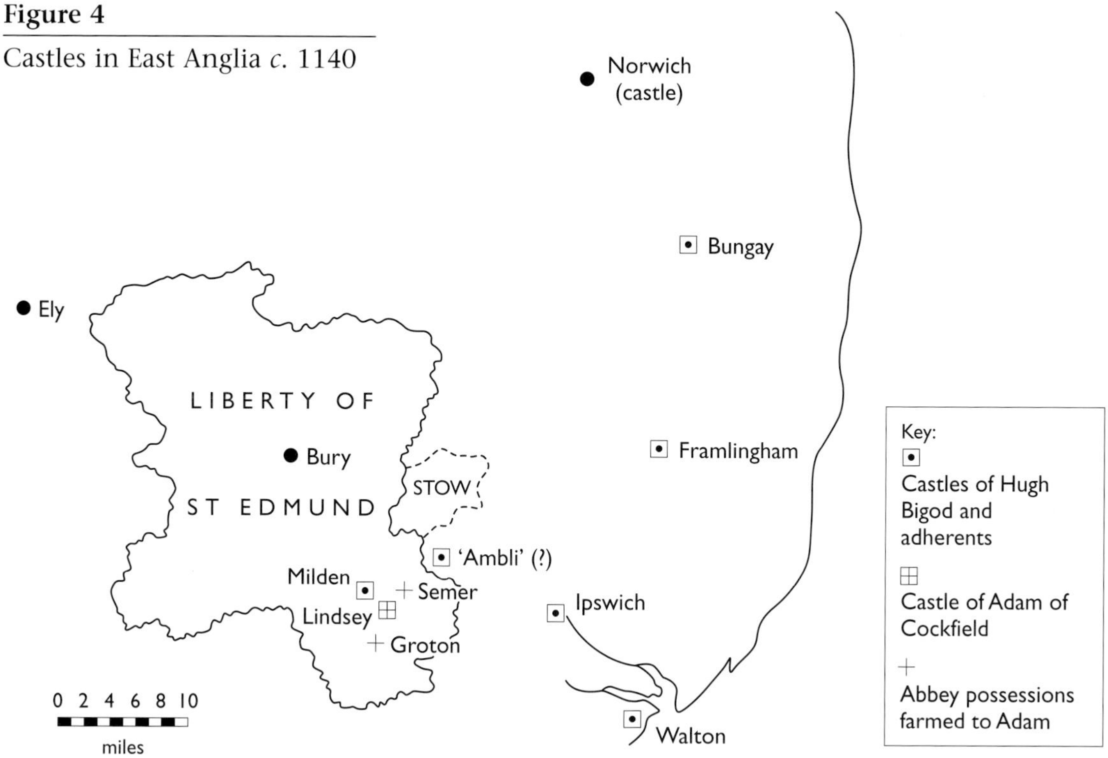

against the hostile castles held by William of Milden and William of Ambli from the fortification at Lindsey.[44]

Such happenings formed the backcloth to the well-known description of the Anarchy under Stephen given in the *Peterborough Chronicle*.[45] Nevertheless, as has been pointed out,[46] the passage is immediately followed by a description of how the abbey of Peterborough itself had prospered 'during all these evil days' under the energetic leadership of Abbot Martin:

> 'He provided everything necessary for the monks and the visitors . . . he extended the church and set apart the income from various estates and also other moneys for the building costs, and greatly adorned it and had it roofed . . . He recovered monastery property in the shape of lands which great men held by force.'[47]

44 *Jocelin*, p. 138. 'The Castle of William of Ambli' has been identified with an 'entrenched mount, covered with wild shrubs' at Offton, about seven miles north-west of Ipswich (Redstone 1908, p. 33.); see Fig. 4.

45 *Peterborough Chronicle*, p. 56; *AS Chronicle*, pp. 264–5.

46 Cronne 1970, p. 14.

47 Peterborough had a *servitium debitum* of sixty knights, compared with four at luckless Ramsey (Round 1895, p. 251).

The building activity at Peterborough was probably paralleled at Bury where the works started by Anselm presumably continued into the reign of Stephen. However, a major effort of reconstruction was required following a fire in about 1150 damaging the abbot's hall, refectory, dormitory, chapter house and old infirmary. The programme was put in hand by Ording's nephew, Helyas, as sacrist of the abbey.[48]

As the reign advanced Hugh Bigod was still capable of making a nuisance of himself but never enough to cause Stephen to move decisively against him. Hugh, on the other hand, did not attempt to cross the abbot at Bury, possibly recognising it as likely to rouse the king. In 1148, however, he entertained Archbishop Theobald in defiance of Stephen on his return to England and allowed him to set up his headquarters at Framlingham.[49] He also recovered Ipswich castle but was unable to hold it.[50] In spite of this, and although his status as earl of Norfolk appears equivocal,[51] he apparently enjoyed the earl's 'third penny'[52] and was, for example, a witness to the settlement reached between Stephen and Henry, for the latter's succession to the throne.[53]

Apart from thus living in the shadow of a hostile and unpredictable neighbour, the only documented harm inflicted on St Edmunds directly as a result of the disturbed times occurred as late as 1153 when Eustace, the disappointed and embittered son of Stephen, ravaged the lands of the abbey. Echoing the traditional fate of Sweyn, some said that the sudden death of Eustace on 17 August 1153 was brought about by the vengeance of St Edmund.[54] It may reasonably be assumed that if an abbey as celebrated as Bury had suffered depredations at other times these would have found their way into the chronicles of the period. The absence of any such evidence will be important in the next section when considering the coinage at Bury during the reign. Moreover, if Ording had not, like Abbot Martin of Peterborough, steered his monastery skilfully through the troubled reign of Stephen, it is highly improbable he would have won the approbation of Jocelin of Brakelond.

The coinage under Stephen

As would be expected, the coinage of Stephen reflects the divided and unstable state of the country. The chroniclers recorded that the weight and purity of the currency was so impaired by forgery and a lowering of official standards that

48 *Memorials*, II, p. 290.

49 Gervase of Canterbury, I, pp. 135–6; Davis 1967, p. 105.

50 Cronne 1970, p. 89.

51 In 1148/9 Stephen appears to have appointed his illegitimate son, William, as earl of Norfolk (*Regesta* III, p. 98, no. 272).

52 Cronne 1970, p. 147.

53 *Regesta* III, p. 98 (no. 272).

54 Cronne 1970, p. 65; Gervase of Canterbury, I, p. 155.

in ten shillings a silver value of twelve pence could scarce be found,[55] and that with the breakdown of central authority the barons issued their own money.[56] Although, as mentioned elsewhere, hoard material may represent a flattering selection from the coin actually in circulation, both statements of the chroniclers appear from surviving coins to be exaggerated, if not devoid of truth.[57]

Before judging the extent to which royal control of the coinage had broken down it is important to establish what the official weight of the coinage was intended to be. Grierson's assertion that 22.5 gr. (1.46 g) was the standard from type VI of William I through to the recoinage of 1279, and that light coins in the reigns of both Henry I and Stephen were the result of misconduct by moneyers and not of changes in the standard, has to be qualified in the light of more recent research.[58] Of the coins recorded by Brooke in the British Museum the preponderance from the PAXS issue through to the end of Stephen's reign weighed between 21.0–21.9 gr. (1.36–1.42 g),[59] and there is no reason to suppose that they represented a below average sample. The difference cannot be explained by margins of error in production (since they should have averaged out), or by weight loss during circulation. It may also be doubted if, for example, William of Malmesbury in his *Historia Novella* would have characterised as an act of policy weight reductions arising purely from Stephen's failure to regulate the moneyers. In particular, it may be doubted if the abbot of St Edmunds would have risked the loss of his franchise by authorising or condoning his moneyers to ignore the official weight standard. Yet at Bury, as the Catalogue (24–49) shows, there were marked differences in weight throughout the reign, the highest so far recorded being 1.44 g (22.2 gr.) and the lowest for intact coins 1.03 g (15.9 gr.).[60] Weight differences at Bury in the first type of the reign are discussed in the next section.

Thus the reason offered by William of Malmesbury that weight reductions resulted from a shortage of silver, as Stephen's maintenance of a mercenary army emptied the royal coffers of the large fortune amassed by Henry I, must at least afford a partial explanation. This does not mean that some moneyers may not have risked striking coin at even lower weight than the reduced standard in the expectation that they would not be brought to account. These explanations are certainly preferable to the suggestion that such coins were issued by the barons,

55 William of Malmesbury gives forgery as the reason for the lamentable purchasing power of the coinage in his *De Gestis Regum* (p. 562), *s. a.* 1140, but in his *Historia Novella* (p. 42) he places at least part of the responsibility upon a weight reduction ordered by the king as his treasury became depleted.

56 William of Newburgh, I, p. 69, *s. a.* 1149.

57 Cronne 1970, pp. 236–7, has pointed out that the language used by William of Malmesbury was very similar to that of the *Anglo-Saxon Chronicle* in 1124 and may therefore represent a conventional rather than precise description of the unsatisfactory state of the coinage.

58 Grierson 1961, pp. 274 and 282, n. 57 and 58. See especially Blackburn 1990, p. 52, referring to Seaby 1988, pp. 39–41, and Blackburn 1994, pp. 169–73.

59 *Norman Kings*, I, p. cliii. On the weights of the PAXS type, see Metcalf 1988, pp. 24–6.

60 One coin, with an erased obverse die (see Catalogue, p. 233) weighs only 0.76 g, but is chipped and is unlikely to have been an issue of Bury.

at least from minting centres held on behalf of the king.[61] At other centres, more immediately obvious than variations in weight (or purity) is that a proportion of coins reflect abnormalities in the dies employed. The most striking example, understandably absent from the Bury mint, is a series of coins bearing the obverse inscription 'PERERIC' in place of the king's designation, which has teased numismatists for generations. Other examples include the use of reverse dies incorporating roundels (or large pellets) into the design and of so-called erased obverse dies, where the design has been 'cancelled' by a cross or other means of obliteration.[62] These latter abnormalities will be further considered below in reviewing the output of the Bury mint. Apart from such deviant issues of the first type, coins were struck in the West Country in imitation of the first type but bearing the name of Matilda and possibly Duke Henry of Anjou.[63] A number of overtly baronial issues also appeared, and not merely in those parts of the kingdom over which Stephen was unable to exercise effective control.[64] These interesting coins, however, fall outside the scope of this study.

Brooke in 1916 identified seven types (*BMC* I to VII) for the nineteen years of Stephen's reign, but owing to the great rarity of *BMC* III, IV and V he was undecided if they should be classified as regular issues or not.[65] Subsequently doubt was expressed whether *BMC* VI qualified as a regular issue, and if so, whether it was struck concurrently alongside *BMC* II.[66] The majority of numismatic students of the reign now appear to accept that there was a sequence of four official types, namely *BMC* I, II, VI and VII.[67] Consensus has not yet been reached, however, on the dating of these types.

The main debate centres upon the duration of the first issue, *BMC* I, generally known as the Watford type from a hoard found there in 1818 containing well over 600 specimens of *BMC* I.[68] Mack, following Brooke,[69] considered that it continued to be struck until 1141, attributing the irregular coins (such as those with erased obverse dies) to the period when Stephen was captive to the Empress. He was not, however, sufficiently confident of its termination date to suggest a firm chronology for *BMC* II.[70] Writing a couple of years later, Dolley

61 Seaman 1978, pp. 62–3. A proportion of underweight coins is also to be found in earlier reigns (see table in *Norman Kings*, I, p. cliii).

62 *Norman Kings*, I, pp. lxxi-lxxxviii.

63 North 1994, pp. 213–14. The attribution of 'Henry' coins to Duke Henry of Anjou has come under increasing doubt: see Blackburn 1994, pp. 188–90.

64 North 1994, pp. 212–15.

65 *Norman Kings*, I, p. lxxiv. Brooke catalogued only four coins in total for the three types (*BMC* 176–9).

66 Mack 1966, p. 56. Mack believed the issues could have been concurrent because of two coins he and Elmore Jones construed as having *BMC* VII reverses with a *BMC* II obverse to which the beard, indicative of *BMC* VII, had been added (Mack 1966, p. 49 and Pl. II, T 1–2). This obverse, however, should be looked upon as of type *BMC* VII.

67 E.g. Elmore Jones 1955–7, pp. 542–3; Seaman 1978, p. 66; Seaby 1980, p. 50; Archibald 1984, pp. 333–4 and Blackburn 1994, p. 152; cf. Cronne 1970, pp. 243–4, and Warren 1987, p. 97, both of whom rely on Brooke's original classification of seven substantive types.

68 *Inventory*, pp. 143–5 (no. 372).

69 *Norman Kings*, I, p. lxix.

70 Mack 1966, pp. 40–1, 48.

suggested the first issue may have continued beyond the mid 1140s.[71] More recently, in a detailed analysis of hoards containing coins of Stephen, Seaman advanced arguments that *BMC* I lasted in eastern England until about 1150 and in the west (where no evidence of *BMC* II or VI was to be found) until 1152.[72] This thesis subsequently received support from Seaby, who controversially identified the coins with erased dies with the interdict towards the end of 1148, and gave the end of 1149 or early 1150 as the latest closing date for the issue.[73] Proponents of the 1141 (or 1142) termination nevertheless remain.[74]

The difficulties of dating were compounded because it was not possible to fit four issues over a nineteen year period into any systematic and frequent change of types as identified in preceding reigns. Regular changes of type were, however, already beginning to break down in Henry I's reign,[75] and it would have been surprising if, amidst his many other distractions, Stephen had reversed this new trend. So far, despite the talent and ingenuity devoted to the problem of dating, the arguments are founded on hypotheses without support from clear bench-marks in the coinage linked unequivocally to datable events in the reign. In this situation common sense dictates that given the predominance of *BMC* I amongst surviving coins, its weight variants and the deviant and imitative issues it spawned, the type must be assumed to have been struck for a substantial part of the reign.[76] It is indeed quite likely that Stephen only decided to change what had become an immobilised coin type once he saw his position more secure after the departure of Empress Matilda.

In addition to suggesting the span of the first type in the east as 1135–50, Seaman also espoused a theory first expounded by Andrew,[77] that the king's designation within that type was abbreviated step by step from STI(E)FNE REX to plain STIEFNE as the reign advanced:

Table 17. Abbreviation of Stephen's title in *BMC* type I

Title sequence	*Dates of issue suggested by Seaman*[78]
STI(E)FNE REX	1135–41
STIEFNE RE	1141–5
STIEFNE R	1145–7
STIEFNE	1147–49/50

71 Dolley 1968, p. 34.

72 Seaman 1978, p. 66.

73 Seaby 1980, p. 60.

74 Archibald 1984, p. 333. Her views were elaborated and suggested chronology slightly altered in Archibald 1991, p. 21.

75 See Chapter 5, above.

76 Blackburn 1994, p. 149, has shown that *BMC* I makes up 78% of known coins from hoards, but only 56% of the single finds.

77 Andrew 1913, pp. 57, 63–4.

78 Seaman 1978, p. 67. Blackburn 1994, p. 194, Table 5.5, prefers a closing date for *BMC* I of 1145, as Table 18 shows.

The neat execution of the 'REX' coins, allied to the desire of Stephen to stress his legitimate kingship, support their being placed as the earliest emission. The date and manner in which the king's title became abbreviated must be more speculative and may not have followed a strictly logical progression.[79] In particular instances, the appearance of RE(:) and R(:) at the end of obverse inscriptions could have been influenced as much by the space left to the die-sinker as adherence to a strict format. The abbreviations appearing on Bury coins, discussed below, are relevant to this question.

To conclude this section the main alternative dating systems for the reign are set out below, from which it will be seen that no serious difference exists over the dating of *BMC* VI or VII.

Table 18. Dating of coin types under Stephen

BMC type	*Brooke*[80]	*Mack*[81]	*Archibald*[82]	*Seaman*[83]	*Blackburn*[84]
I	1135–41	*c.* 1135–41	1135/6–42	1135–*c.* 1150	*c.* 1136–45
II	ND	?	1142–*c.* 1148	*c.* 1150–2	*c.* 1145–50
(III)	ND	1143–52	–	–	–
(IV)	ND	1143–52	–	–	–
(V)	ND	1143–52	–	–	–
VI	ND	*c.* 1153	*c.* 1148–53	*c.* 1153	*c.* 1150–4
VII	–1154+	*c.* 1153–8	1153–8	*c.* 1153–8	*c.* 1154–8

Notes
(a) 1136 seems sensible as the starting date of *BMC* I, as Stephen was not crowned until 22 December 1135.
(b) ND = no date(s) suggested.
(c) *BMC* VII continued until 1158, see Chapter 7 below.

Bury mint activity

The Catalogue lists 76 coins firmly attributable to Bury in the name of Stephen compared with 37 for Henry I. Of these a majority belongs to the first type, *BMC* I, bearing witness to its predominance amongst surviving coins from the reign as Table 19 shows. Bury coins from the reign are known to have occurred in ten hoards. Owing to inadequate recording of the earlier finds and of the provenances of a number of coins both in public and private collections only a proportion can be definitely identified with such hoards, as set out in Table 20.[85]

79 The last type of Henry I (*BMC* XV) had described the king simply as 'hENRICVS' (North 1994, p. 198).
80 *Norman Kings*, I, p. lxxv.
81 Mack 1966, pp. 40, 50, 52, 55.
82 Archibald 1984, pp. 333–4; Archibald 1991, p. 21.
83 Seaman 1978, p. 66, for eastern England.
84 Blackburn 1994, p. 194, Table 5.5.
85 See Catalogue 24–49.

Table 19. Surviving Bury coins of Stephen by type

Type	*No. of coins*	*No. of known moneyers*
BMC I	55+	4+
BMC II	6	2+
BMC VI	7	3
BMC VII	8	3
Total	76+	7+

Table 20. Hoards containing Bury coins of Stephen

Hoard	*No. of Bury coins identified*	*No. of Bury coins traced*
Watford (1818)[86]	13	5
Sheldon (1867)[87]	1	0
Nottingham (1880)[88]	2	2
Linton (1883)[89]	1	1
South Kyme (pre-1922)[90]	4	2
Prestwich (1972)[91]	12*	11
Paris Region ('Beauvais') (*c.* 1987)[92]	2	2
Wicklewood (1989)[93]	7	7
Portsdown Hill (1995)[94]	1	1
Pimprez (France) (2002)[95]	3	3
Total	46	34

Note
* Excluding erased die.

86 *Inventory*, p. 144 (no. 372): Gilebert 9; Abelin ('Canterbury') 2; 2 ex 'Sandwich'. See Catalogue 24 (3), (5), 27 (4), (5)?, 35 (1).

87 *Inventory*, p. 123 (no. 329).

88 Danson 1968, pp. 49, 60; *Inventory*, p. 111 (no. 295). See Catalogue 30(1), 32(1).

89 *Inventory*, p. 84 (no. 235). See Catalogue 40(1).

90 *Inventory*, p. 126 (no. 337). See Catalogue 24(4), 27(9).

91 *Coin Hoards* 1 (1975), p. 92 (no. 360), where 12 Bury coins of type I are recorded besides one with erased dies. See Catalogue 24(7), 25(1), (2), (13), (15), 27(1), (8), 29(3), after [33] (1), 35(2), (4).

92 Glendining, 4 November 1987, 101. See Catalogue 25(6), [34] (1).

93 Not published. Details kindly provided by BM. See Catalogue 40(4), 42(1), 43(1), (2), 44(1), 49(1), (2).

94 Buckland Dix and Wood, 28 June 1995, 171–91.

95 The hoard was acquired by Spink and a number of coins were released by auction and private treaty in 2004 (see Catalogue 18, 19, 21, 23, 24, 25).

The Bury content represents less than 1.5 per cent of all the coins of Stephen in these hoards. In addition, Bury coins of Stephen found abroad are in collections in Dresden[96] and Moscow,[97] whereas stray finds in England have been made at, or in the vicinity of, Bognor Regis,[98] Cranwich (Norfolk),[99] Newmarket,[100] Saffron Walden[101] and Thetford,[102] and at other less clearly identified sites.[103] Blackburn calculated in 1994 that whereas only 17 per cent of hoard coins had been found in East Anglia compared with other areas of the country, 67 per cent of single finds came from there.[104] This points to a greater concentration of currency in East Anglia and more hoarding of wealth prompted by greater political and social uncertainty in areas outside Stephen's control. It could also mean that East Anglian mints are under-represented amongst surviving coins. Taking the first type at Bury, the only one for which meaningful analysis can be applied, Figure 5 shows the location of hoards containing Bury coins as well as stray finds. The only other substantial hoards without any Bury coins, found at Dartford in 1825[105] and at Coed-y-Wenallt in 1980,[106] are also shown. This Figure suggests that Bury coins of the first type circulated mainly in the areas of Stephen's influence.

No writ is known to survive confirming the grant of a moneyer to Anselm following the accession of Stephen but, uniquely for the mint, writs do exist granting a second die (*unum secondum cuneum cum illo cuneo antiquitus ibidem fuit*),[107] and a third die (*quendam tertium cuneum ad monetam faciendum in villa sancti Ædmundi*).[108] The former of these confers the second die ambiguously upon the church of St Edmund and its abbot, in addition to the die traditionally held, but the latter states that the abbot as such is to enjoy the third die in perpetuity, as with the other two dies (*qua habit alios duos cuneos suos*). The intention must thus have been for the dies to form part of the abbot's rather than the convent's portion. These grants, it will be noticed, refer to dies rather than moneyers, but the surviving coins show that the grant was intended to be equally applicable to moneyers, since at least Gilebert and Acelin, and Acelin and Hunfrei, were clearly in office at the same time, as Table 21 on page 100 shows.

If Gilebert is confirmed to have continued into the later types, a complement of three moneyers is achieved, at least in *BMC* I, II, and VI. Indeed, under that

96 Catalogue 48(1).
97 Catalogue 25(5), 29(1), [39] (1).
98 Catalogue 42(2).
99 Catalogue 25(8).
100 Catalogue 43(3).
101 Catalogue 38(l).
102 Catalogue 49(3).
103 Catalogue 25(9), 28(1), 29(2).
104 Blackburn 1994, p. 149.
105 *Inventory*, no. 176, pp. 64–5.
106 Boon 1986, pp. 37–82.
107 *Feudal Documents*, pp. 88–9 (no. 72); *Regesta* III, p. 281 (no. 762).
108 *Feudal Documents*, p. 89 (no. 73); *Regesta* III, p. 281 (no. 763).

Figure 5

BMC I: British finds of Bury coins

scenario, if the contraction of the king's name and title was chronological, as suggested by Seaman, there could briefly have been four moneyers incumbent at Bury towards the close of type *BMC* I. This anomaly suggests that either the tentative inclusion of Gilebert in type *BMC* II is misplaced or that the contractions were not strictly chronological, with Henri (O.]EFNE:) being succeeded by Hunfrei (O. -----NE R[ ). The moneyer Iun was also catalogued with an apparent Bury mint reading (-MV) in the Taffs Sale,[109] and was included by Mack in his important article on the coinage of Stephen,[110] but its present whereabouts is a mystery. Since the coins in the Taffs lot were described as mostly fair, the reverse

109 Taffs (1956) 137.
110 Mack 1966, p. 41.

Table 21. Moneyers active at Bury in each type of Stephen[a]

Moneyer	*Henry I XV*	*Stephen*						
		I				*II*	*VI*	*VII*
		REX	*RE*	*R*	–			
Gilebert	6	1	2		6	1?		1?
Acelin		1	1			1	1	1/2
Hunfrei				1[b]		1	1	
Henri					1			
Iun (?)			?					
Oddo (?)					1			
[ ]ric							1	
Willem								2

Notes
(a) Numbers indicate the number of obverse dies known.
(b) Obverse reading possibly incomplete.

may simply have been misconstrued. The attribution to Oddo at Bury of a coin in the Palmer collection, possibly reading]O (or D) []ON S:[, also is insecure, but there was a such a moneyer of the abbot in the penultimate issue of Henry I.

From the die links found in *BMC* I of Gilebert (Bb, Cb, Cc), it would appear that, unusually for the Bury mint, he had access to several pairs of dies at one point in his tenure. It is possible that he enjoyed these as a consequence of the grant from Stephen, which referred literally to an entitlement to three dies, rather than three moneyers. In fact, the known coins of Gilebert raise further doubts on the sequence of abbreviations to the obverse legends and questions about the weight standards employed at Bury in *BMC* I. So far, no indisputable contraction of the regal title to R(:) has been encountered on coins struck in the name of Gilebert, or any other moneyer at Bury, in the type. It is, however, exceedingly unlikely that no moneyer operated at the mint between 1145 and 1147, when Seaman conjectured this variant was in issue. More tellingly, Gilebert's obverse die B, reading RE:, is linked through reverse b to obverse die C, which is devoid of any regal reference.

Interestingly, if obverse dies A (REX:), B (RE:) and C (–), owing to its reverse link to B, are the earliest issues of Gilebert in *BMC* I at Bury, the twenty-seven known coins show a fairly consistent pattern, struck between 1.42 and 1.18 g, producing an average (mean) of 1.36 g, and a median of 1.39 g. This calculation excludes the only known specimen struck from obverse D (RE), weighing 1.15 g, the typicality of which is impossible to judge. However, the seven remaining coins of Gilebert in *BMC* I for which weights are known are all without suffix and range between 1.28 and 1.03 g, giving an average of 1.15 g. Notwithstanding the small sample, this hints at a lowering in the weight standard during the currency of *BMC* I, possibly necessitated by the shortage of silver alluded to above as civil war depleted Stephen's treasury.[111] The weight range of coins struck from obverse dies A, B, and C is nevertheless rather wide. It has been shown that in Anglo-Saxon England marked weight differences generally resulted from a gradual lowering of the standard in the course of an issue. The reductions could be closely controlled, as the moneyers were capable of striking to within weight tolerances of plus or minus 6 per cent. Usually, however, the coins from individual dies were clearly struck to one standard.[112] The variances applicable to dies A, C and D range between 7 to 13 per cent, if the standard aimed at was 1.36 g. This can only mean that less skill was exercised, or greater laxity condoned, in striking coins from a set of dies in the early years of Stephen's reign than had obtained in the late Anglo-Saxon period. Although the small number of known coins from types *BMC* II, VI and VII precludes robust analysis, the known coins suggest a return at Bury to the initial standard, the intact coins yielding an average weight of 1.39 g.

If the date or dates on which the second and third dies were granted could be pinpointed, considerable light might be thrown on the argument whether the first type (*BMC* I) ended in 1141 or later, since Acelin, Henri and Hunfrei were all active in the first type, either alongside or following Gilebert. In the body of *Regesta* the relevant writs were simply dated to the reign (1135–54),[113] but in the introduction the dating was admitted to be uncertain but conjectured to have been after 1141.[114] This suggestion was repeated by one of the two editors of *Regesta* elsewhere[115] but, equally in that instance, no supporting reasons were proffered. The coins of Acelin bearing the REX: suffix would appear to contradict this date, unless the writs could be construed as merely confirmatory. Douglas, on the other hand, dated the writs to 1148–54, believing that both were issued at the same time as a third which freed the burgesses from all levies other than those due to the abbot and a fourth addressed specifically to Abbot Ording concerning land at Hardwick.[116] Regrettably, apart from all four writs having been issued at Bury, there are no other compelling reasons to group them together. The identity of the witnesses does not support such grouping. The writs for the second die and in favour of the burgesses were attested by Adam de Beaunay, that for the third die by Adam with Henry of Essex and that on the land at Hardwick by Robert de Vere. The careers of Adam and Henry of Essex are equally unhelpful since both are found as addressees or witnesses of documents both early and late in the reign.[117] More importantly, if these writs were issued together an explanation is required as to why the second and third dies should have been granted separately, using distinctive wording and attestation rather

111 See n. 55 above.
112 Eaglen 1999, p. 56.
113 *Regesta* III, p. 281 (nos 762–3).
114 *Regesta* III, p. xxix.
115 Cronne 1970, p. 241.
116 *Feudal Documents*, p. 88, n. 10.
117 E.g. *Regesta* II, p. 120 (no. 318), dated 1135–41, and p. 154 (no. 402), dated 1147–9.

than in one document. The numismatic evidence scarcely admits that Acelin only joined Gilebert as a moneyer at or after 1148. Circumstantial evidence thus suggests that the second die was granted early in Stephen's reign (*cum illo cuneo antiquitus. . .*), and the third at a somewhat later date. Surviving coins of Bury also support the suggestion that the first type may have lasted some years after 1141.

Given the unswerving allegiance of the abbey to Stephen's cause and apparent freedom from hostile interference, it would be surprising if irregular, as opposed to lightweight, coins were found from its mint. This could only be expected to arise from remotely likely circumstances, such as die-cutting activity falling into the hands of Stephen's adversaries. As a corollary, any abnormal coins doubtfully attributed to Bury should be regarded with heightened suspicion. The only moneyer with whom such coins have so far been linked at Bury is Gilebert.[118] Three sets of dies are involved. Firstly, the obverse of dies Hh has a large roundel in the centre of the reverse.[119] This feature has been associated with Stephen's queen, Matilda, since three bezants were the badge of the house of Boulogne of which she was sole heiress.[120] However, if Matilda had wished to place her imprint on the coinage it seems highly improbable she would have chosen so discreet – even ambiguous – a means to do so. More importantly, the mark of her distinct authority would hardly be appropriate when the king was merely captive and had not been removed from the throne. As at earlier periods, added roundels, annulets or pellets are far more likely to have minting rather than political or other significance. The two coins struck from dies Hh each weigh 1.03 g, the lightest so far known at Bury. Secondly, a coin struck from dies Ii includes roundels in the centre of the reverse and on the four limbs of the cross amongst other unusual features. However, the attribution of these dies to Gilebert and to Bury are highly speculative, as will be obvious from the relevant Catalogue entry.

The third coin of Gilebert has the obverse die 'erased' by a bold cross extending to the flan's circumference, and a reverse reading +GILE[]ERT:ON[]EI. Besides being associated with the interdict of 1148,[121] the dies for these coins have normally been explained as having been mutilated before use by the supporters of Matilda, or by the supporters of the king upon fear of their falling into the hands of his enemies.[122] On the latter explanation, they would either have been

118 The moneyer Gilebert is found at Ipswich in type II: see *BMC* 151, a coin Brooke suspected of being struck from base metal (*Norman Kings*, II, p. 359). The name also occurs on the erased die coin reading ON[ ]EI, discussed in this section, and in type VII: see *BMC* 183, Pl. LV, 7, possibly reading [ ]I,EBE[ ]:ON:S [ ], now attributed to Sudbury (see Elmore Jones 1955–7, pp. 546, 550); *BMC* 211, Pl. LVI, 8, reading [ ]EBERT:ON:SVB[ ]; and Elmore Jones and Blunt 1967, p. 91, for a coin reading +GILE [ ]VD.

119 Catalogue 32.

120 Mack 1966, p. 66.

121 Seaby 1980, p. 60.

122 *Norman Kings*, I, pp. lxxviii-lxxx; Oman 1931, pp. 125–6; Brooke 1950, p. 95.

brought into use after capture, regardless, or by the king's supporters from necessity once the danger had passed. A further possibility is that the dies were mutilated in anticipation of their replacement by a new design of coin but for some reason, whether an upheaval or otherwise, introduction of the new design was at least temporarily deferred.[123] The reverse of this coin has been attributed to Eye in Suffolk rather than Bury, supported by a cut halfpenny of *BMC* VI which has now come to light with a reading +DV(N)(:) EIE, and two further coins, one of the moneyer Willelm, with a left-facing bust (reading EI[ ), and another of Gilebert (reading :EI), both acquired in 2002 by the Fitzwilliam Museum.[124] Eye is only twenty miles, as the crow flies, from Bury and Stephen's son-in-law, Hervey Brito, was lord of its honour.[125] It is, therefore, quite conceivable that Gilebert could have been engaged to strike coins there, or at Bury itself, on behalf of the honour. In any event, the moneyer's name without other corroboration is hardly grounds for attributing this coin to Bury, and no amount of ingenuity could persuade that EI(E) stands for Bury St Edmunds. If, however, this coin were in any way connected with Bury it would cast serious doubt on association with the interdict. There are other grounds for rejecting such association. Quite apart from the abbot's loyalty to Stephen, there is no evidence that the interdict was put into practical effect.[126] There is also no evidence at other times that the coinage was tampered with in the implementation of an interdict. Finally, the suggestion that the defacement was carried out by William, bishop of Norwich and Hugh Bigod, in support of archbishop Theobald in his dispute with Stephen, is hardly credible.[127]

Beyond their scarcity, the Bury coins of *BMC* II, VI and VII require little comment. *BMC* VI, represented by two moneyers, establishes beyond any lingering doubt that the type was a substantive issue of Stephen. In *BMC* VII unease once existed about the authenticity of a coin of Acelin, with a pedigree stretching back to Ruding's *Annals*,[128] owing to its having been heavily retooled. Reverse die links, however, now show that its origins were genuine.[129] Also in *BMC* VII, a coin of the moneyer Gilebert, reading]LLEBE[RT]: ON : S[, was placed by Brooke under Bury,[130] but has since been assigned to Sudbury on the basis of a die duplicate with a clear mint reading SV.[131] More recently a coin reading +[ ]RT:ON:S:E[may have revived Gilebert's credentials as a moneyer in the type at Bury.[132]

123 Archibald 1991, p. 21, has contended that the erased dies were brought into use during the king's illness in May and June 1142, which delayed introduction of his second type.

124 See coins described between Catalogue entries [33] and [34].

125 Cronne 1970, p. 145.

126 Cronne 1970, p. 61, describes the interdict as 'singularly ineffective'. See also Seaby 1980, p. 60, n. 20.

127 Seaby 1980, p. 59.

128 Catalogue 46A(1); Ruding 1840, III, Suppl. pt. II, Pl. II, 18.

129 Catalogue 46B, 46C.

130 *BMC* 183, Pl. LV, 7. See also n. 118 above.

131 Elmore Jones 1955–7, p. 546. The die duplicate referred to has not been seen by the author.

132 Catalogue 47.

CHAPTER 7

TEALBY COINAGE OF HENRY II

Introduction

From the accession of Henry II to the closure of Bury mint in the second quarter of the fourteenth century it no longer makes sense to treat English coinage by reign. On his accession Henry II did not immediately set about replacing the coinage of Stephen as, for example, Harold II had after the death of the Confessor, but deferred introducing a new coin type in his own name for four years.[1] This, the so-called 'Tealby' or 'Cross-and-Crosslets' coinage,[2] remained unchanged in design until eventually withdrawn from circulation in 1180. The 'Short Cross' coinage then introduced remained current a further sixty-eight years only to be withdrawn by his grandson in 1247. Apart from its unwonted longevity, the Short Cross issue maintained the obverse inscription HENRICVS REX throughout the reigns of Richard I and John until it became once more apt under Henry III. The issue thus approximated to an immobilised coin design, which had already become a feature of continental coinage. The next, 'Long Cross' coinage of Henry III was not superseded by Edward I's new or 'Edwardian' coinage until 1279, in the seventh year of his reign. The basic design of penny then introduced continued to be employed under Edward II and III, and thus beyond the demise of coining at Bury.

In this Chapter, therefore, it is convenient to look at Bury and its mint over the period of the Tealby coinage, and in the following two Chapters the period spanned respectively by the Short Cross and Long Cross coinages. The Edwardian coinage at Bury will form the subject of a separate monograph.

Bury and its privileges to 1180

Already under the settlement reached between Henry and Stephen at Winchester in November 1153, it was recognised that 'property which had been appropriated by trespassers should be restored to the legitimate possessors thereof in the time of King Henry [I]'.[3] However, these and other measures

1 See p. 112 below.

2 The name derives from a hoard of about 6,000 coins of the type found at Tealby, Lincolnshire, in 1807 (see Allen 1951, pp. xlviii–ix; Sturman 1989). Allen proposed the alternative name Cross-and-Crosslets, but the simple, earlier designation seems happily destined to persist.

3 Roger of Wendover, II, p. 256. See also Robert of Torigny, p. 177, cited by Warren 1973, p. 52.

such as reform of the coinage, referred to by the chroniclers,[4] were undoubtedly professions of good intent by Henry as the king designate rather than steps likely to be taken as long as Stephen remained alive. Certainly the Charter issued by Stephen after the settlement dealt only with the succession of Henry and its immediate effects.[5] Nevertheless, when Stephen suddenly died the following year, Henry confirmed in his Coronation Charter on 19 December 1154 that:

> '. . . for the common restoration of my whole realm I have granted and restored and by this present Charter confirmed, to God and the Holy Church, and to all my earls, barons and vassals all concessions, gifts, liberties and free customs, which King Henry, my grandfather, granted and conceded to them.'[6]

This promise was clearly more than a conventional declaration at the start of the new reign. Henry must have been well aware that he would be pressed with numerous suits arising from both the concession and the alienation of rights and privileges in the previous reign. Thus, to reinstate the grants made by his grandfather was clearly the most practical way out of the tangle he had inherited, and the least contentious. In the case of Bury the promises of the Coronation Charter were meticulously fulfilled, resulting in gains and losses for the abbey.

The privileges of the church of St Edmund, its abbot and monks, were generally confirmed by two writs issued early in the reign.[7] Although Douglas dates both to 1155–8, it is logical to suppose that one of these was issued before the king's first absence abroad, from 10 January 1156 to about 8 April 1157.[8] Shortly after his departure, on 4 February 1156, Abbot Ording died.[9] The election of his successor, Hugh, was not confirmed until the next year,[10] presumably following the king's return. With his appointment must be associated the other of the two writs quoted by Douglas. Both writs confirm the eight and a half hundreds, but not the one and a half hundreds of Stow and Harlow granted by Stephen. Against this loss, the abbey recovered possession of Coney Weston, Chepenhall and all other demesne lands taken from the abbey since the death of Henry I.[11] One of the two writs also confirms the right to a moneyer (*unum monetarium*), thereby implicitly eliminating the two additional moneyers permitted in the previous reign.[12] As a general confirmation the writ refers broadly to the church

4 See n. 54 below.

5 *EHD* II, pp. 436–9 (no. 22).

6 *EHD* II, pp. 439–40 (no. 23).

7 *Feudal Documents*, pp. 92–3 (no. 79) and pp. 93–4 (no. 80).

8 Fryde, Greenaway, Porter and Roy 1986, p. 36.

9 *Memorials*, III, p. 6; Knowles, Brooke and London 2001, p. 32.

10 *Memorials*, III, p. 6; Knowles, Brooke and London 2001, p. 32.

11 *Feudal Documents*, pp. 94–5 (no. 81).

12 *Feudal Documents*, p. 92 (no. 79). Of the two writs (nos 79 and 80) this is the most likely to have followed the appointment of Abbot Hugh.

of St Edmund and its abbot and monks, but the moneyer is bestowed remarkably vaguely upon the said church (*prefata ecclesia.*) Despite the closure of many mints in Henry II's reign,[13] it is not surprising that minting rights endured at Bury, reflecting both the terms of the Coronation Charter and the prestige of St Edmund in the eyes of the monarchy.

Other indications that both rights and obligations existing under Henry I were reinstated are revealed in the treatment of knight service. An assessment of 1166 showed that Bury held fifty-two and three-quarters knights' fees but, together with other feudal lords, the abbot was able to show that a *servitium debitum* of forty knights was due, as under Henry I.[14] There is also evidence that the obligation of St Edmunds' knights to perform guard duties at Norwich castle was revived.[15]

The reputation of Hugh, the new abbot at Bury, has suffered at the hands of Jocelin of Brakelond, the biographer of his successor, Abbot Samson. Hugh was characterised as a good and pious man, but a weak and gullible administrator who allowed the abbey, including its obedientiaries, to fall heavily into debt. The sums involved, if Jocelin's account is to be taken at face value, were enormous for the time. A bond for £1,040 was given to William FitzIsabel and another for £400 to Isaac, the son of Rabbi Joce. Borrowings by William Wardell, the sacrist, resulted in a bond for £880 being given to Benedict the Jew of Norwich, who was also a creditor for further debts to the value of £320, excluding interest.[16] Although the abbey's cellarer was dismissed from office for secretly borrowing £60,[17] the financial irregularities were generally condoned and hidden from official scrutiny by dissembling[18] and purchasing papal dispensation from ecclesiastical visitations.[19] There is little doubt that the weak leadership of the abbot during this period lessened the dependence of the obedientiaries and convent upon the abbot which not even the resourceful Samson was fully able to retrieve.

Notwithstanding all of the defects of administration, on the evidence of surviving coins, the mint became more active during Hugh's abbacy than at any time hitherto. This was doubtless kindled by the increased volume of coinage in circulation,[20] at a time when the number of mints was being drastically reduced. To the extent that output at the mint depended upon the needs of the abbey for

13 For the effect of the Coronation Charter on mint closures, see Eaglen 2003, pp. 5–6.

14 *Red Book of the Exchequer*, I, p. 394; Warren 1973, p. 277.

15 A writ of Henry II was addressed to Hugh Bigod, bidding him perform service at the castle of Norwich for the fee held from St Edmunds (*Feudal Documents*, p. 99 (no. 90) and p. lxxxviii, n. 1).

16 *Jocelin*, pp. l-3.

17 *Jocelin*, pp. 5–6.

18 *Jocelin*, pp. 3–4.

19 *Jocelin*, p. 5.

20 Allen 2001d, p. 606 and Table 2, p. 607.

coin, it may also have resulted from the melting down of monastic plate to relieve pressing debts.[21]

The financial difficulties of the abbey were at least partly brought about by the expense of remedial and new building works. The debt run up by William, the sacrist, with Benedict the Jew had originated as a loan to restore the monks' chamber (*camera*) which had fallen into disrepair.[22] At the beginning of the period the work undertaken by Helyas to repair the ravages of the fire in about 1150[23] was completed by his successor Frodo and possibly also William Wardell.[24] During the latter's term of office, the choir was virtually finished and one storey built of the great tower at the west end of the abbey church.[25] The Gesta Sacristarum, the source of this information, implies, however, that recognition for these works should be given to Samson, who became sub-sacrist under William. Samson is certainly credited by Jocelin with striving to keep the buildings in repair, erecting the choir screen and providing stone and sand for the great tower.[26] Animosity clearly developed between the two men and, after the death of Hugh, William apparently prevailed upon the custodians appointed by the king, Robert of Cockfield and Robert de Flamville,[27] to forbid any further building work during the vacancy.[28] Not surprisingly, William was removed from office when Samson became abbot in 1182.[29]

Bury as a military base

The importance of Bury in the reign of Stephen as a focus of royal support against Nigel, bishop of Ely, and more particularly Hugh Bigod has been described in the

21 There is some evidence in *Jocelin* (pp. 2, 5) that ornaments were not only pawned but also used to meet financial commitments. Allen 1951, p. xiii, observed that the coins of the latest types were 'particularly common' from East Anglian mints, which he tentatively connected with penalties imposed after the uprising of 1173–4 (see below). According to Allen's chronology, however, only the last of the six varieties he identified was struck at that time, between 1170 and 1180, and is found in some numbers from Ipswich mint but scarcely from Thetford and not at all from Colchester or Norwich (Allen 1951, pp. clxxix-clxxii). An alternative explanation that the last variety (F) was struck at Bury in numbers to pay the royal army is also not convincing since the evidence of die linking (see Table 28) suggests that mostly only one obverse die was in use at a time. It nevertheless appears from the number of single surviving specimens of variety F dies that mint activity at Bury between 1170 and 1180 was at higher level than earlier in the reign. This is more plausibly explicable as a consequence of the closure of neighbouring mints in eastern England.

22 *Jocelin*, p. 2.

23 See p. 92 above.

24 *Memorials*, II, p. 290.

25 *Memorials*, II, p .291.

26 *Jocelin*, p. 9.

27 Robert de Flamville witnessed a writ of Abbot Hugh as steward (*dapifer*) (*Feudal Documents*, p. 141, no. 153).

28 *Jocelin*, p. 10.

29 *Memorials*, II, p. 291; *Jocelin*, pp. 30–1.

previous chapter. Whereas Nigel proved an asset to Henry II in putting order back into the machinery of government,[30] Hugh Bigod nursed his discontent and awaited further opportunities to advance his territorial ambitions. Bury played no small part in frustrating him.

Earl Hugh can hardly have been reconciled by the settlement in 1153 under which Stephen granted to his son, William, the castle and town of Norwich in the County of Norfolk, 'except what pertains to churches and prelates and abbots and earls and excluding particularly the third penny which pertains to Hugh Bigod as earl . . . .'[31] Possibly conscious that this was less than just to Hugh, but also determined that limits should be placed on his powers in Norfolk, shortly after his coronation Henry confirmed Hugh as earl of Norfolk but left William in possession of Norwich and its castle.[32] This reservation, exceptionally confirming a grant by Stephen, rankled with Earl Hugh whose desire to possess Norwich became obsessive. Only two years later, at the Great Council held at Bury on 19 May 1157,[33] Henry required both Hugh Bigod and William of Blois to surrender their castles.[34] It has been suggested, although contemporary sources are silent, that this step may have been taken by Henry in the wake of unrest in East Anglia during his first period of absence abroad ending in April 1157. It was in any event some years before Hugh regained his castles.[35]

Hugh Bigod's main opportunity to advance his ambitions arose when Henry's eldest son and namesake rebelled against his father in 1173.[36] Spurred by a promise of the hereditary constableship of Norwich Castle,[37] Hugh joined forces with the earls of Chester, Derby and Leicester against the king. The earl of Leicester, with a force of Flemings, landed at Walton, rallied to Hugh at Framlingham at the end of September 1173, and helped him capture Haughley castle, held for the king by Ralf de Broc.[38] In response, a royal army under the justiciar, Richard de Lucy, was positioned at Bury, and when the earl moved north to relieve his own supporters at Leicester he was intercepted at Fornham on the outskirts of Bury on 27 October 1173 and his forces routed.[39] Afterwards the bodies of defeated rebels were displayed at Bury, Colchester and Ipswich.[40] This reverse was not sufficient to extinguish Hugh Bigod's hopes, and on 15 May

30 *Dialogus de Scaccario*, p. xiv; Warren 1973, p. 266.
31 *Regesta* III, pp. 97–8 (no. 272); *EHD* II, pp. 437–8.
32 Thomas Rymer, I, pt. 1, p. 42, cited by Warren 1973, p. 67, dating the charter to 1155.
33 When possibly the king was at Bury for the confirmation and installation of Hugh as abbot.
34 Robert of Torigny, pp. 192–3.
35 Warren 1973, pp. 67–8, n. 5.
36 Yates 1805, p. 142, states that the revolt was led by Henry's sons Richard (aged 16) and John (aged 5!).
37 *Gesta Regis Henrici Secundi*, I, p. 45.
38 *Gesta Regis Henrici Secundi*, I, pp. 60–1.
39 *Gesta Regis Henrici Secundi*, I, pp. 60–1. This battle is alluded to in the opening words of *Jocelin*. Hugh's son, Roger, is said to have carried the abbot's standard at the battle. Assuming this is correct, he must presumably have been ranged against his father (*Jocelin*, p. 57).
40 Norgate 1887, II, p. 150.

in the following year another contingent of Flemings landed at Whitsand and helped him to capture and sack Norwich on 18 June 1174.[41] By this time, however, the rebellion was all but over. On 7 July the king landed at Southampton from Barfleur and some days later was himself at Bury, where he divided his forces to attack simultaneously Hugh Bigod's castles at Bungay and Framlingham. In the peace made at the end of July, Hugh was fined 1,000 marks, but had his revenues restored, including his third penny.[42] He was nevertheless obliged once more to yield up his castles and Framlingham, the centre of his military power, was apparently razed to the ground.[43]

In dealing with struggles in East Anglia in the reigns of both Stephen and Henry II reference is made by historians to the castle,[44] or even the king's castle[45] at Bury. In fact, although the documentary and archaeological evidence is less clear than could be wished, it is sufficient to prove beyond reasonable doubt that Bury was a fortified town, but evidence for a castle within its defences is entirely lacking. Physically, as will be seen from Figure 6, the River Lark provided a defensive perimeter running north-south, extended by the River Linnet along the southern boundary of the town in a westerly direction. To the north-east the marshy district of Tayfen also constituted a natural barrier. This left the five access roads and exposed western side of the town to be protected. The former were doubtless policed by the inhabitants at North, East, South, West and Risby gates.[46] According to a tradition quoted by William of Malmesbury,[47] the town boundaries were marked and protected early in the town's history by a ditch excavated by the order of Cnut. The Gesta Sacristarum further relates that Henry the Sacrist had strengthened the fortifications by constructing a wall around the town in the time of Abbot Anselm (1121–48).[48] This may well have been in response to the disturbed conditions in Stephen's reign. In 1968, when an earthen rampart was excavated at Tayfen road, no evidence was found at that point of a wall, but during further excavations, in 1997, traces were found in the vicinity of walling datable to the twelfth century.[49] A speculative map of the town as it was in the fifteenth century shows the line of a ditch supplementing the natural defences provided by the river frontage between Eastgate and Southgate, and a wall protecting the exposed boundary between Westgate, Risbygate and Northgate.[50]

It would have been inappropriate for Bury, as the centre of a feudal liberty, to have hosted a royal castle, and incongruous with its status as a centre for

41 *Gesta Regis Henrici Secundi*, I, p. 68; Ralph of Diceto, I, p. 381.
42 See Norgate 1887, I, pp. 158–67, for details of the campaign and settlement, and references cited.
43 Warren 1973, p. 235.
44 E.g. Davis 1967, p. 74 (map).
45 E.g. Warren 1973, p. 66.
46 On the townsmen as gatekeepers, see Lobel 1935, pp. 89–90.
47 William of Malmesbury, *De Gestis Pontificum Anglorum*, p. 155.
48 *Memorials*, II, p. 290.
49 West 1970–2, pp. 17–24; Martin, Pendleton and Plouviez 1997–9, pp. 221–2.
50 Lobel 1935 (map).

Figure 6

Defensive perimeter of Bury

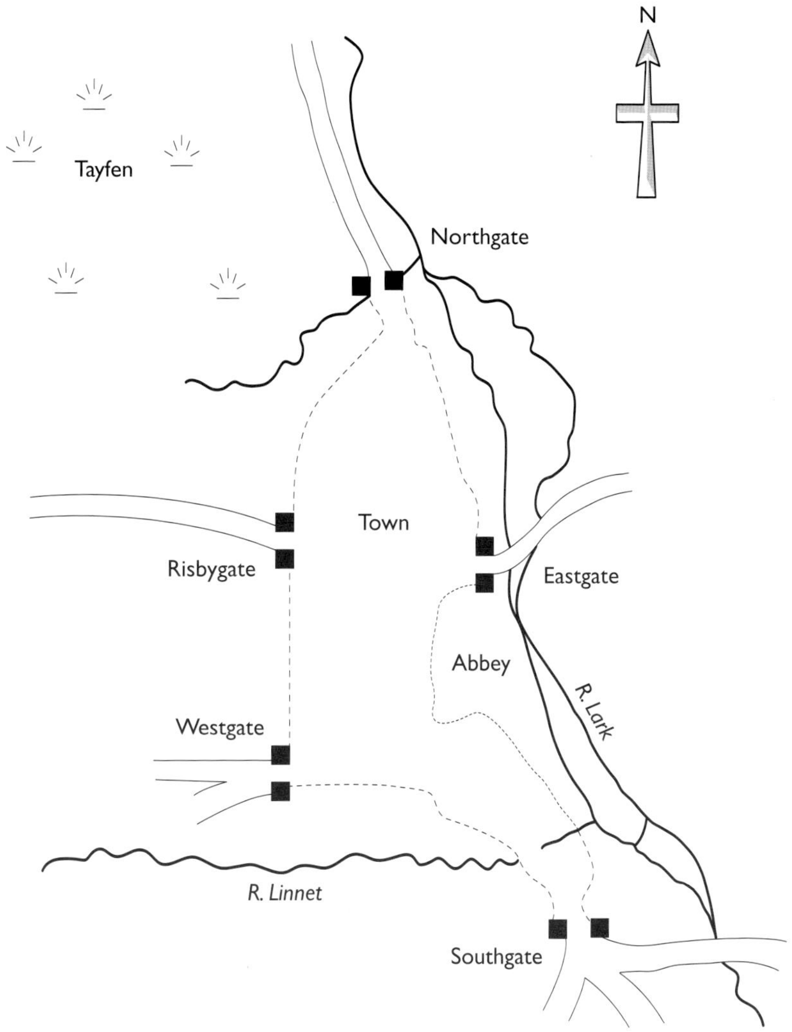

religious worship and pilgrimage for the abbot (even in his role as a feudal baron) to have set up his own castle alongside the abbey. The fundamentally religious standing of the town is shown during the rebellion of 1173–4 when, briefly, certain of the earl of Leicester's supporters took refuge there, although they must have been embarrassing visitors.[51] It was not, on the other hand, inappropriate for the boundaries of such a town to be defended. Strategically, St Edmunds was an obvious rallying point from which the king's forces could be deployed against his enemies in East Anglia.

51 Matthew Paris, *Chronica Majora*, II, p. 289, also recording that others took refuge at St Albans. Jocelin relates (p. 10) that 'in the days of the war' the children and wives of Jews also took refuge in the pittancery. In 1190, however, a year notorious for the massacre of Jews, Abbot Samson successfully petitioned the king to expel them from Bury since otherwise he would have had to accept them into the abbey for their safety (*Jocelin*, pp. 45–6 and p. 45, n. 5).

The Tealby coinage

The effects of administrative and legal reforms carried out under Henry II were far reaching, but the results were achieved by the cumulative effect of adaptive measures rather than implementing radical ideas.[52] This is illustrated by his treatment of the coinage. Two dates are of cardinal importance: 1158, when the Tealby issue was introduced and 1180,[53] when it was replaced by the Short Cross issue dealt with in the next Chapter. On his accession, Henry took no immediate steps to reform the coinage despite the chroniclers' recording that in the settlement of 1153 the objective was recognised of having only one type current in the kingdom.[54] This objective is in itself revealing, suggesting that the physical replacement of one issue by the succeeding had been abandoned long enough for it not to be seen as a normal arrangement.

Henry's delay in replacing the coinage of Stephen is unlikely to be explicable simply by the king's absence abroad between January 1156 and April 1157. Harold II, it will be recalled, was able to introduce a new coinage superseding that of Edward the Confessor in less than one year.[55] The further suggestion of one writer that the geld levied in 1156 drew the lamentable state of the coinage to the attention of the king and his advisers[56] is simply not convincing. There is, in any case, no evidence to show that the coinage at this time was in an abnormally poor state, whether through the continued circulation of baronial issues or otherwise. That Henry was in no haste to replace the currency even suggests the contrary.

Surviving coins, and this applies to the Tealby issue as much as to earlier emissions in the twelfth century, are nevertheless condemned in general for unimaginative design compared with, for example, the robustness of the Anglo-Saxon series, and the Tealby issue in particular for the inferior quality of the actual striking. The shapes of the silver blanks are often irregular and the obverse and reverse impressions unevenly struck up and frequently off-centre. The very fact that it was no longer necessary under Stephen, or relevant under Henry II, to distinguish between successive issues may have insidiously led to lackadaisical mint practices, and engendered an attitude of mind that as long as the impression on the coin was clear enough to indicate an official issue – as a stamp of approval for a piece of silver of given weight and purity – it was not necessary to strive towards exemplary workmanship. An obvious effect of the decline in standards was to invite tampering with the coinage by clipping parings of silver

52 Warren 1973, pp. 317, 360; Pollock and Maitland 1895, II, p. 673.

53 Roger of Howden, I, p. 215: *'novam fecit monetam quae sola recepta est et accepta in regno'*.

54 E.g. Roger of Wendover, II, p. 256: *'celebrus et publica moneta una et eadem erit in regno percussa'*; Allen 1951, p. xi.

55 See North 1994, pp. 182–6 and Chapter 3 above. As, however, Warren 1973, p. 54, points out, Henry came to the throne as undisputed king. He presumably therefore felt no pressure to introduce his name on to the coinage as a symbol of legitimacy.

56 Warren 1973, p. 264.

from the flans, a fraudulent practice that became a problem from this period onwards.

Although the actual weight standard (or standards) for the Tealby coinage is not known,[57] the surviving coins are predominantly of good weight. Allen found that, after discarding clipped, forged, fragmentary, pierced and tooled coins in the British Museum collection, of the 793 remaining, 523 (or two thirds) came within the weight range 21.6–23.0 gr. (1.40–1.49 g), and 245 (nearly one third) in the range 22.1–22.5 gr. (1.43–1.46 g).[58] As will be seen from Table 22, taking the 152 Bury coins in the Catalogue for which weights are known (excluding corroded and fragmentary coins), 96 are regular in appearance and of these 58 (at least 60 per cent) weigh at least 1.39 g. Interestingly, of the remaining 56 coins, having irregularly shaped flans, 30 (over half) also meet the same weight standard. This shows beyond reasonable doubt that many misshapen coins were issued in that state by the mint and not tampered with after issue. The blanks for a number of these appear to have been prepared with curved shears, resulting in a concave irregularity in the flan edge. It may be that it was easier to adjust the flan weight with such blades than straight edged shears. The weight of Bury coins is analysed further in the next section.

It is not clear at what date control of mint activity shifted from tracing coin actually in circulation back to an offending moneyer to inspecting and analysing samples of output retained by the mint, akin to the later Trial of the Pyx.[59] Certainly the assays described in the *Dialogus de Scaccario*[60] were designed to ensure that the exchequer was not cheated by payments in lightweight or debased coin, and not to monitor the operation of the mints as such. Significantly, the obviously better and inferior coins were not separated but were mixed together for the purposes of assay. Unless the coins had first been sorted into separate moneyers by mint before counting and weighing, or a sizeable batch of recently struck coin made under the authority of one moneyer had been paid into the exchequer before becoming mixed with other money, the culprit responsible for calculated irregularities would have been difficult to identify. Clipping and wear and tear once the coin had left the moneyer's nominal control would have been a further complication, whereas the final act of blanching, or melting twenty-shilling batches of coin to assay the purity of silver would, of course, have destroyed the very identity of the moneyers in the furnace. It may be that at this period regulation of mint activity was achieved indirectly. The sheriff was personally accountable for any shortcomings in the money he tendered to the exchequer.[61] This would make him vigilant when accepting coin to settle such dues. It is reasonable to suppose that equal caution

57 Allen 1951, p. xli.

58 Allen 1951, p. xliii, Table of Weights.

59 For the first recorded instance of such a Trial in 1248 see Chapter 9 below. See also *The De Moneta of Nicholas Oresme*, p. xix and references there cited.

60 *Dialogus de Scaccario*, pp. 36–8.

61 *Dialogus de Scaccario*, pp. 36–8.

Table 22. Weights of regular (R) and irregular (I) shaped Tealby coins of Bury

		Allen classification						
Weight (g)	*Shape*	*A*	*C*	*B*	*D*	*E*	*F*	*Total*
Over 1.45								
	R	–	1	1	–	–	3	5
	I	–	2	–	–	2	6	10
1.39–1.45								
	R	16	12	8	5	2	10	53
	I	1	5	2	3	2	7	20
1.35–1.39								
	R	2	1	1	2	–	4	10
	I	1	1	1	5	1	3	12
1.25–1.35								
	R	1	7	–	2	1	5	16
	I	1	–	1	1	–	3	6
1.16–1.25								
	R	2	3	1	–	–	3	9
	I	–	1	2	–	–	2	5
Under 1.16								
	R	1[a]	1[b]	–	1[e]	–	–	3
	I	–	1[c]	1[d]	–	–	1[f]	3
Total								
	R	22	25	11	10	3	25	96
	I	3	10	7	9	5	22	56
	R + I	25	35	18	19	8	47	152

Notes
(a) 1.14 g; (b) 1.00 g; (c) 1.08 g; (d) 1.14 g; (e) 1.11 g; (f) 1.08 g.

would be exercised by those paying him and, indeed, by anyone proffered other than trifling amounts of money. By this means a chain of vigilence would stretch back to the exchange originally issuing the coin.

The Tealby coinage has been characterised as a 'major' reform,[62] but its novel features were only two-fold, and they represented a change of degree rather than substance. Firstly, the number of mints was reduced from more than forty towards the end of Stephen's reign to only twenty-nine at the outset of the new coinage. As the issue progressed, however, the number was progressively reduced to fourteen at the end of the series,[63] never thereafter to increase to former proportions. This decline may have partly resulted from the second change, namely, the maintenance of a single basic design[64] throughout the twenty-two

62 Warren 1973, p. 264.

63 Allen 1951, p. clxxxiii.

64 Relatively minor design and inscription changes were made over the period of the issue which are valuable to the numismatist in putting such variants into sequence, but would have been unobserved and irrelevant to the contemporary user of the coins.

years of the issue. With a discontinuance of relatively frequent changes in the design of the coin there was less need to employ a battery of mints across the country, other than to carry out a total recoinage. Increased use of money by the population in general may also have reduced the need for widespread mint coverage because coin was circulating more readily in those areas where no mint was nearby. The maintenance of a single design, which had its precedents from the immobilised types circulating on the Continent,[65] was again not a sudden break with tradition in England because, as described above, there was already evidence of this happening at the end of Henry I's reign and in that of Stephen. It would also appear that the obvious consequence of these changes may not have been thoroughly thought out by Henry or his advisers: to the extent that a change in coinage was deferred, any revenues to the crown flowing from such changes would proportionately decline. A neat and simple measure to compensate for this loss of income was, however, introduced in 1180, as will be seen below.[66]

One advantage of an immobilised type, provided it gained and kept a reputation for good weight and purity, was its ready acceptance as a unit of currency or exchange in transactions outside its country of origin. This phenomenon was of no relevance in England where foreign coin was not permitted to circulate, but it did result in English coin becoming accepted on the Continent, although its full effect only began to be apparent during the Short Cross coinage.[67] On the other hand, for coin intended to circulate for many years without withdrawal, adequate standards of appearance and legibility would nevertheless make good sense. It is therefore strange that the Tealby coinage was generally allowed to be of such inferior workmanship, and this may have inhibited its use as an international currency, compared with succeeding coinages. The explanation may be that when the type was first introduced the king and his advisers did not in fact plan that it would remain current for such a long period. Despite the workmanship and condition of surviving coins, they are not difficult to die-study because the strictures of design were not so precise as to drive out the idiosyncracies of engraving, using a limited range of punches.[68] It is said that the late Elmore Jones was frequently able from examination of an obverse, to identify the moneyer and mint appearing on the reverse of a coin.

The Tealby coinage at Bury

Allen divided the Tealby coinage into six main varieties or classes,[69] all of which are represented from Bury. He also defined seventeen regular sub-varieties

65 Allen 1951, p. xi.

66 See Chapter 8 below.

67 See Chapter 8 and Chapter 10, Fig. 15 (map).

68 Allen 1951, p. xxxvi.

69 Allen 1951, pp. xxi–xxxii.

Table 23. Tealby sub-varieties at Bury

Class/sub-variety		*No. of obverse dies known*
A	1	2
	2	2
B	1	1
	2	0
	3	0
	4	0
C	1	2
	2	1
	3*	1
D	1	1 (+1?)
	2	0
	3	1 (+1?)
E	1	0
	2	0
	2/3*	1
F	1	6 } +4
	2	1 }
	3	0 }
		19 +6
		<25

Note
* See n. 70.

of obverse, of which at least nine have been identified from Bury.[70] Table 23 summarises their occurrence.

As will be seen from the Catalogue, the number of surviving coins increases markedly from 76 in the name of Stephen to 187 for the Tealby issue. From this point onwards the problems of presenting a corpus of coins from the mint changes completely. Until the reign of Henry II the rarity of surviving coins at least means that there is a good chance of their being recorded (although not always as accurately as might be wished) and even illustrated in auction catalogues and numismatic literature. But as the amount of surviving material progressively increases in Henry's reign and thereafter, only cursory details are noted and the coins themselves are not likely to be illustrated unless representing an atypically rare type. Thus the fears from the earlier period of not having traced all of the small number of surviving coins changes into certainty that an

70 See Catalogue. Crafter 1998, p. 45, has identified another sub-variety, designated as class C3. A further sub-variety, with two pellets in the left shoulder fold (see Catalogue 65, reverse die p) is intermediate between sub-variety E2, with three pellets and E3 with one. It must be doubted whether the number (or absence, as in E1) of pellets in this position has an intentional significance.

increasing quantity of relevant material has not been covered. This is illustrated from Table 24, which summarises the total number of Tealby coins known from the main and the most recent hoards containing examples of the coinage, the number identified with named mints (including Bury), and the number identified from the Bury mint itself. The quantity of material nevertheless means that, from Henry II onwards, a fair picture of coinage at Bury can usually be captured without taking the quest for surviving coins to absurd lengths.

Table 24. Tealby coins from hoards[71]

Hoard	*Total Tealby coins*	*Total with mint identification*	*Total Bury coins*
Bramham Moor (1753)	245?	12	1 (or 2)
Ellesborough (1777)	≥12	12	1?
Tealby (1807)	*c.* 6,000[72]	185	9 (or 10)
Outchester (1817)	<1,000[73]	20	–
Ampthill (1836)	146	85	7[74]
Daeli (Norway) (1840)	5	4	–
London Bridge (1850)	100s	29	≥4
Lark Hill (*c.* 1853)	217	167	7[75]
Awbridge (*c.* 1902)	104	65	6
Rome (pre-1917)[76]	11	?	?
Leicester (1927)	238	141	9[77]
Corné, Loire (*c.* 1930)[78]	>16	16	1
Thorpe Thewles, near Middlesborough (pre-1932)[79]	>12	12	–
Mile Ditches (1978)[80]	8	8	2
Brackley (1986)[81]	13	11	–
Near Brussels (1987)[82]	16	13	1
Norton Subcourse (1987–90)[83]	41	32	–

71 Unless otherwise stated, the details are taken from Allen 1951, pp. xlv-lx, supplemented by Thompson's *Inventory* and Allen 2002, pp. 46–8. The figures given by Thompson do not always correspond with those of Allen 1951.

72 5,127 coins from the hoard of approximately 6,000 were sadly melted down. A parcel of 59 coins from the hoard is described by Dolley and Elmore Jones 1958–9, p. 83. Sturman 1989 corrects the total for this hoard given by previous authors (5,700).

73 This hoard is reported to have consisted of 'nearly 1,000 silver coins which appeared to be pennies of Stephen and Henry II' (Allen 1951, p. xlix).

74 *Inventory*, pp. 2–3 (no. 7), lists only four Bury coins.

75 *Inventory*, p. 148 (no. 381), lists nine Bury coins, but only seven are identified in the Catalogue.

76 Lawrence 1918, p. 20; Brooke 1927, p. 320.

77 *Inventory*, p. 83 (no. 231), lists eight Bury coins, but nine are identified in the Catalogue.

78 Elmore Jones 1966a.

79 Information from W. Lean and T. C. R. Crafter.

80 Archibald and Cook 2001, pp. 10–11.

81 Archibald and Cook 2001, pp. 7–9.

82 Dawson and Mayhew 1987.

83 Archibald and Cook 2001, pp. 12–15.

Table 24. Tealby coins from hoards (continued)

Hoard	*Total Tealby coins*	*Total with mint identification*	*Total Bury coins*
Wicklewood (1989)[84]	141	88	4
West Meon (1992)[85]	34	27	3
Gayton (1998)[86]	315*	201	12
Total	±8,674	1,128	67–69

Note
* Includes fragments.

Apart from the huge difference between the first and second columns of Table 24, the number of Bury coins identified within the hoards (67–69) accounts for little more than one third of the 186 coins in the Catalogue. In spite of this incomplete picture the amount of recorded material from Bury still results in a fuller representation of the mint output than in earlier reigns. Moreover, the pattern of known surviving coins from individual dies, as set out in Table 28 below, suggests that nearly all the dies used at Bury during the Tealby coinage have already come to light. Metcalf has estimated the total obverse dies in use at Bury during the Tealby issue at 30, with the caveat that this may be an over-estimate.[87] In comparison, the Catalogue records 25 different obverses. Table 25 shows the respective breakdowns by class, compared with Metcalf's figures:

Table 25. Obverse dies at Bury compared with Metcalf's estimates

Classes	*A*	*B*	*C*	*D*	*E*	*F*	*All*
Metcalf	5	1	2	3	3	16	30
Catalogue of known dies	4	1	4	4	1	11	25

Applying Metcalf's formula to the larger number of coins in the Catalogue, an estimate of 26 obverses is reached. Both sets of figures highlight the predominance of Class F dies. This is particularly remarkable because, as the last class, it is the one most likely not to have survived the introduction of the Short Cross recoinage, in the form of hoarded savings. This reservation is supported by the number of singletons occurring, and hints at the class from which new dies may yet appear.

As already mentioned, one of the two writs confirming the privileges of St Edmunds, datable to 1155 or 1157, refers to minting rights, and provides:

84 Information from M. M. Archibald.

85 Archibald and Cook 2001, pp. 3–6.

86 Provisional statistics from T. C. R. Crafter.

87 Metcalf 1977, p. 31.

> '. . . that the aforesaid church (St Edmund's) shall have a (one) moneyer in the town of St Edmund as freely as it had enjoyed in the past . . .'.[88]

If minting of Stephen's coinage had ceased at Bury on Henry's accession then a date of 1157 would be appropriate for this confirmation, in time for the projected recoinage. Although it is impossible to say if this hypothesis is correct, the occurrence of Willem as moneyer for the last type under Stephen's name and the earliest Tealby coins from Bury suggests continuity of office. This, in itself, is noteworthy. From surviving coins it appears that at most mints there was a complete replacement of moneyers, if not of the personnel used to produce the coins. Even at London only three moneyers' names from Stephen's last type recur on Tealby pence. Elsewhere two moneyers' names recur at Canterbury, and single names at Hereford, Ipswich and Wilton, in addition to Bury.[89] Doubtless, at Bury, the king's officials would have been in the position to endorse or raise objections to the abbot's choice of moneyer under his franchise, but not to impose their own choice as if the mint were under royal control.

As the reign progressed Bury remained operative in shrinking but distinguished company,[90] a trend to be continued whenever the mint was active at later dates. Over the period of the Tealby coinage it was one of only five mints known to have struck all six varieties.[91] Its resilience is the more remarkable since other ecclesiastical minting rights, especially where not an adjunct of an otherwise busy royal mint, were being progressively eliminated. There is no evidence that the bishop of Lincoln at Newark,[92] the bishops of Hereford,[93] London[94] and Winchester[95] at their sees, or the abbot of Reading at London[96] exercised the right of coinage under Henry II. The mint of the bishop of Durham, however, was active in the first three classes of the Tealby coinage and then fell into abeyance until 1195.[97] Ecclesiastical moneyers also formed part of the total

88 *Feudal Documents* pp. 92–3 (no. 79). The order of the two writs varies in manuscripts from Bury, with Cambridge MS Ff ii, 33 and BL Harl. MS 743 placing no. 79 first and BL Add. MS 14847 placing it after no. 80.

89 See Allen 1951, pp. clxxix-clxxxiii.

90 Allen 1951, p. clxxxiii, summarises the number of mints active in the six main classes as follows: A (30), B (10), C (20), D (17), E (12) and F (11). The following new mint classes have come to light since 1951: B (Thetford); D (Colchester); E (Norwich, Thetford); F (Chester, Exeter, Norwich) (Dr Martin Allen, personal communication). The low figure for variety B supports Allen's belief (pp. lxii, lxxiv) that B and C were concurrent issues. By the latter part of the reign the centre of the country was completely denuded of mints, with the closure of Bedford, Gloucester, Hereford, Leicester, Northampton, Oxford and Shrewsbury. The eastern mints, particularly Ipswich, appear to have been relatively more active (see n. 21 above).

91 North 1994, p. 218.

92 Allen 1951, p. cxlviii.

93 Allen 1951, p. cxxxv.

94 Allen 1951, p. cxlvi.

95 Allen 1951, p. clxvii.

96 Allen 1951, p. cxlvii.

97 Allen 1951, p. cxxxii, suggests that the right to mint coins may have been lost when the bishop supported the uprising of 1173–4, but dated Classes B and C to 1161–5.

complement of moneyers at Canterbury and York. At Canterbury three of the eight moneyers appear to have belonged to the archbishop,[98] and one to the abbot of St Augustine's, but the latter's rights lapsed when the abbey was taken into the king's hands on the death of Abbot Sylvester in 1161.[99] At Bury, Abbot Ording had died in 1156, before the Tealby coinage was introduced, and his successor, Hugh, died in 1182, after it had been supplanted. Hugh may have avoided the fate that befell the abbot's minting rights at Canterbury by living this long. At York only two of the moneyers in the city belonged to the archbishop.[100] Since these moneyers did not place distinguishing marks on the coinage, however, it is generally not possible to distinguish them by name from the royal moneyers. Although the *British Museum Catalogue* lists the names of ten moneyers at York in class A, no more than three are known in subsequent classes. This could again mean that the ecclesiastical moneyers had disappeared. The archbishop's minting rights at Canterbury do not appear to have suffered in this way, although the revenues of the archiepiscopal dies were in the king's hands from Becket's flight to the Continent in 1164 until his successor was appointed in 1173.[101]

The *Dialogus de Scaccario* is tantalisingly silent on the organisation and control of the mints under Henry II, but the Pipe Rolls are a source of information hitherto lacking on the royal mints and their officials. Unfortunately they reveal nothing of Bury as a franchisal mint during the Tealby period.[102] Two charters of Abbot Samson, however, throw some light on the social standing of Henri the moneyer who struck in classes B to E at Bury. One concerns a shop (*sopa*) formerly belonging to him in the market (*foro*),[103] and the other two mills at Stow granted to his son Gervase for 60 shillings a year.[104] The names of two of the moneyers, Willem and Raul, also correspond with the names of two of the stewards of the honour of St Edmund, equivalent in the eight and a half hundreds to the sheriff of a county. However, their probable dates of office preclude the likelihood that the role of steward and moneyer were being combined in the same person.[105]

Allen considered that the Bury moneyers struck in the sequence shown in Table 26.[106] The peculiarity that class C appeared to precede B presented him with no difficulties because, on other evidence, he considered that they were concurrent issues.[107] Crafter has argued that class B was of short duration, more akin to A

98 Allen 1951, p. cxix.
99 Allen 1951, p. cxx, citing William Thorne, p. 94.
100 Allen 2004a, pp. 26–9.
101 Allen 1951, p.cxix.
102 Allen 1951, p. xcix, cxvii.
103 *The Kalendar of Abbot Samson*, pp. 77–8.
104 *The Kalendar of Abbot Samson*, p. 117.
105 See Ralph of Hastings (1155) (*Feudal Documents*, pp. 97–8, no. 87); William of Hastings (1164–6) (*Feudal Documents*, pp. 98–9, no. 89).
106 Allen 1951, p. cxvii.
107 Allen 1951, p. lxxiv.

Table 26. Sequence of moneyers at Bury in the Tealby coinage

	Stephen	*Tealby*					
Moneyer	*VII*	*A*	*C*	*B*	*D*	*E*	*F*
Willem	+	+	+				
Henri			+	+	+	+	
Raul							+

Table 27. Chronology of the Tealby coinage

Class	*D. F. Allen (1951)*	*M. Allen (1994)*	*Crafter (1998)*
A	1158–61	1158–*c.* 1161?	1158–*c.* 1163
B	1161–5	*c.* 1161–1165x9?	*c.* 1162–3
C	1161–5	*c.* 1161–1165x9?	*c.* 1163–7
D	1165–8	*c.* 1165x9–*c.* 1172	*c.* 1167–70
E	1168–70	–1172– ?	*c.* 1170–4
F	1170–80	?–1180	*c.* 1174–80

than C, and used in parallel with the later dies of class A until both were superseded by class C.[108] This is one example of the briar thicket presented by the Tealby coinage. Frustratingly, the increase in written evidence, in the form of Pipe Rolls and other records, is less easily reconciled with the evidence of the coins themselves than might have been expected and attempts to associate the hoards with datable historical events more equivocal than might have been hoped. As a result, uncertainties over chronology carry forward into Henry's reign. Table 27 shows the latest essay by Crafter,[109] compared with the dates suggested by Derek Allen in 1951[110] and Martin Allen in 1994.[111]

Applying Crafter's scenario for classes A to C to Bury as a single moneyer mint, various possibilities emerge. Most obviously, Willem could have ceased operating during class A, being succeeded by Henri with class B, returned to office, supplanting Henri at the outset of class C, only to be succeeded by him yet again later in class C. Although this is possible, it does seem to be highly improbable. Another possibility is that Henri received his class B dies from stock and thus out of chronological sequence. Since the Bury moneyer would have only rarely required new dies it is inconceivable that they would have been cut and stored against future demand. Because of this, if Henri received his class B obverse in the currency of class C, his reverse should be of a newly cut class C die. It is, however, clearly of the design associated with class B (see dies Kk). A further possibility is that class B is evidence of the activity of a distinctive die cutter who

108 Crafter 1998, p. 44.
109 Crafter 1998, p. 51.
110 Allen 1951, p. lxxiv.
111 Allen 1994, pp. 392–5.

was at work in a minor way at the time when class A was being superseded (in the hands of the main die cutter) by class C. This would accommodate Derek Allen's supposition that B and C overlapped, and be compatible with the dating scheme preferred by Crafter, if class B could be admitted to have overlapped class C, '*c.* 1163'.

The surviving coins of Bury (Table 28) show from the amount of die linking that the normal arrangement under Stephen of providing only one set of dies,

Table 28. Reconciliation of Tealby coins and dies in *BMC* and the Catalogue

Type	*Moneyer*	*BMC*			*Catalogue*		
A1	Willem	42	1	42	A	7	a
		43	2	43	B	10	b
				44		5	
			3				
A2	Willem	44			C		
		45		45			
		46	9	46	D	15	d
		47		47			
		48		48			
C1	Willem	49		49			
		50	7	50	E	13	e
		51		51			
		52	6	52	F	9	f
		53		53			
						4	
C1	Henri	16					
		17	2			10	
		18					
			3				
				16			g
				17			
				18			h
					I	4	i
C2	Henri				J	2	j
B1	Henri	19		19			
		20		20			
		21	13	21	K	26	k
		22		22			
		23		23			

Type	*Moneyer*	*BMC*			*Catalogue*		
D1	Henri				L	8	l
D?	Henri	27			M		
			1			3	
		24		24			
D3	Henri	25	3	25	N	11	m
		26		26			
D?	Henri				O	1	o
		28		28			
E2/3	Henri	29	4	29	P	11	p
		30		30			
F1	Raul	31	2	31	Q	3	q
		32					
			1			4	
				32			
F2?	Raul	33	3	33	R	7	r
F1	Raul	33A	1	33A	S	6	s
		34	2	34	T	5	t
		35		35			
		36	1			4	
				36			u
					V	2	v
					W	1	w
		36A	1	36	X	1	x
F2	Raul	37	1	37	Y	1	y
		38					
		39	3			10	
				38			
				39			z
F?		40	1	40	AA	2	aa
		41	1	41	BB	1	bb
					CC	1	cc
Total coins			71			187	

comprising one obverse and one or two reverses, for use at one time was by no means scrupulously observed. On at least three occasions two obverse dies were available for use with one reverse die (BCb, MNm, QRr), and on one occasion an obverse die was used by one moneyer (Willem) with a single reverse die, and afterwards by another (Henri) with his own pair of reverse dies (Ff, Fgh).[112] This clearly marks the moment when Henri finally took over from Willem as the moneyer at Bury. A number of dies appear to have been issued in sets of one obverse with two reverses, particularly late in the issue (Ttu, Yyz).

The relative importance of Bury as a mint location at this period is not easy to assess. Of 918 catalogue entries by Allen in his *British Museum Catalogue*, 40 relate to Bury. Although the collection was obviously not put together to reflect mint output, the entries result in the following table:

Table 29. *BMC* Tealby entries by mint

Rank	*Mint*	*No. of entries*
1	Canterbury	199
2	London	171
3	Ipswich	67
4	Lincoln	64
5	Norwich	49
6	Thetford	45
7	*Bury*	40 (4.3%)
8	Newcastle	37
9	York	36
10	Northampton	27
11	Winchester	26
12	Ilchester	14
13–32	Others	143
		—
Total		918

Thanks to Mossop, closer comparison is possible with the Lincoln mint:[113]

Table 30. Tealby coins known from the Bury and Lincoln mints

	Bury	*Lincoln*
No. of coins recorded	186	168
No. of moneyers	3	7[114]
No. of reverse dies	27	55

112 Allen 1951, p. cix, cites Henry passing an obverse die to Raul. This is, however, clearly a confusion.

113 Mossop 1970, *passim*.

114 Allen 1951, p. clxxx, knew of six moneyers.

Table 30 shows that Bury output is more fully represented in the British Museum cabinets than Lincoln. Table 29 may thus exaggerate the contribution of Bury to the coinage. Table 23 in turn also suggests that for most of the period an obverse die had an average life of about one year, indicative of very modest activity at the mint.

If Allen is correct in placing the weight standard for the Tealby issue at 22.5 gr. (1.46 g),[115] Bury is seriously anomalous. The average (mean) weight of 152 not obviously damaged or worn coins listed in Table 31 is only 1.37 g. This figure is strongly influenced by 33 coins recorded between 1.31 and 1.05 g. It is even possible that such bantams are under-represented in the hoards through being less welcome as savings. Theoretically, a number of reasons could lie behind the apparent discrepancy at Bury. It seems most unlikely that the mint was authorised to strike coins below the official weight standard, even if only for the abbey's own purposes. The wide spread of weights could conceivably result from the standard being infringed, either wilfully or – more plausibly – through carelessness. A further possibility, however, should not be rejected without examination.

Table 31. Weight distribution of Tealby pence of Bury

Wt (g.)	*No. of Coins*	*Wt (g.)*	*No. of Coins*	*Wt (g.)*	*No. of Coins*
1.48	3 ▲	1.33	6	1.18	1
1.47	5	1.32	2	1.17	3
1.46	7	1.31	6	1.16	1
1.45	5	1.30	2	1.15	–
1.44	11	1.29	–	1.14	1
1.43	11	1.28	1	1.13	–
1.42	10	1.27	2	1.12	–
1.41	14	1.26	2	1.11	1
1.40	11	1.25	1	1.10	–
1.39	9	1.24	1	1.09	–
1.38	10	1.23	–	1.08	2
1.37	4	1.22	1	1.07	1
1.36	3	1.21	3	1.06	–
1.35	7	1.20	3	1.05	1
1.34	2 ▼	1.19	–		

Table 22 shows that 56 (37%) of the 152 coins listed, well-distributed through the weight range, are struck on irregular flans. As already pointed out above, many of the latter must have been issued by the mint in that state. Table 31 shows that half of the 152 coins were struck in the range of 1.38 to 1.44 g, suggesting that a weight standard for the mint may have fallen within those limits.

115 Allen 1951, p. xli.

Table 32. Tealby: obverse readings on Bury coins

Class	*Reading*	*No. of dies*
A1,2	+hENRI REX ANGL	4
C1	+hENRI:R:AN	1
	+hENRI:R:AG	1
	+hENR[]R[	1
C2	+hENRI:RE	1
B1	+hENRI REX AN	1
D1	+hENRI:REX	1
	hENRI[	1
D3	+hEN REX AN	1
	+hENRIR[	1
E2/3	+hENRI REX	1
F1	+hEN REX AN	1
F1?	+hENRI REX	1
F1	+hENRI REX:	1
	]ENRI:REX	1
	]RI REX A	1
	+h[ ]REX	1
	]EX ANG	1
F2	+hENRI:REX	1
F?	]hENRI REX	1
	+hENRI[	1
	+hE[	1
		—
		25

The highest number of coins is found at 1.41 g. The highest recorded weight is 1.48 g which, upon a standard of 1.41 g, would produce a margin of error of 5%. This is not unreasonable.[116] On such an hypothesis, coins struck down to 1.33 g could also be considered within specification. Below this, 33 coins (22%) are encountered down to 1.05 g. It is extraordinary that those at the lower end of this range are struck on small, rounded flans, without any obvious signs of having been tampered with. Such coins are also struck from the same dies as used for coins struck to the putative 1.41 g standard.[117] This may reflect very lax workmanship – if so, erring unfailingly in favour of the mint – or, conceivably that more than one standard was in use at the same time, for reasons that defy explanation. The median weight of the thirty-three bantams is 1.21 g, the heaviest coin being 8% above that weight and the lightest 9% below.

116 The author has calculated a deviation of + or – 6% from standard in the Long Cross issue of Æthelred II at Huntingdon: see Eaglen 2000, p. 56.

117 Examples of such coins are Aa (1),(6), Cb(3), Ee(13), Ff(3), Fh(7), Ll(8), Qq(3), Ss(3) and Yz(8), thus occurring throughout the series.

Table 33. Tealby: reverse readings on Bury coins

Reading	*Class (and no. of dies)*					
	A	*C*	*B*	*D*	*E*	*F*
SC:EDM	1					
SC:ED[a]	2					
S:EDM[b]		1				
S:EDMVH		1				
S:ED'		1				
S:EDMV:		1				
S.ED		1				
S·E[		1				
S:EDM:			1			
S:EDMV[cd]				2		
S:ED.				1		
S:EDMV				1		1
]:ED[]V						1
S:EDM:[c] }					1	3 }
S[:]EDM:[c] }						
S:EDMV:[c]						1
S:EDM[c]						1
S:EDM'[c]						1
S:EDMV[c]						3
S[]ED:[c]						1
S:EDM[b]						1
S[]:[c]						1

Notes
(a) One die reading SC:ON:ED:, the other ON:SC:ED:
(b) S retrograde.
(c) S reclining.
(d) S tilted.

In conclusion, Tables 32 and 33 summarise the obverse and reverse readings of the Bury coins recorded in the Catalogue. The Tealby issue displays a diversity of obverse readings, even within the individual classes identified by Allen.[118]

The reverse readings on the Bury coins are all variants of S(C)ED(MVN), with or without abbreviation marks.

118 Allen 1951, pp. xxii–xxxiii.

CHAPTER 8

SHORT CROSS COINAGE

Bury under Abbot Samson

Abbot Hugh's unfortunate abbacy came to an end on 14 or 15 November 1180,[1] shortly after the introduction of the Short Cross coinage.[2] Samson was eventually elected as his successor on 28 February 1182 and installed at Bury on 21 March,[3] to preside over the resurgence of the abbey's fortunes until the end of 1211 and remain vividly alive to future generations through the pages of Jocelin's *Chronicle*.[4]

In order to bring the finances of the house under control he had an inventory prepared of all its customs, revenues and expenses,[5] surviving today as Samson's *Kalendar*.[6] Having established that the abbey had debts amounting to £3,052 13*s*. 4*d*., before interest, he came quickly to terms with its creditors and by skilful management liquidated the entire deficit within twelve years.[7] He also increased his resources sufficiently to repurchase the Manor of Mildenhall from King Richard for 1,000 marks (£666 13*s*. 4*d*.),[8] to fulfill his ambition to complete the abbey church,[9] and to adorn its interior and feretory.[10]

Before the turn of the century his sacrist, Hugh, finished building the great tower over the west end of the church and leaded the roof. He also carried out the stone work for one of the two lesser towers on either side of the great tower and for one storey of the other. Hugh's successor, Walter of Barnham, renewed the fabric of the church and finished one of the towers, but no record survives of when the second was completed.[11] The dimensions of the church were given in paces by the fifteenth-century antiquary, William of

1 Knowles, Brooke and London 2001, p. 32.

2 Allen 1951, pp. lxxii–lxxiii, accepted 11 November 1180 as the date on which the Short Cross coinage was introduced. Evidence has, however, been adduced by Brand and Elmore Jones 1966, p. 117, to show that the new coinage had begun in Winchester by the beginning of July 1180.

3 *Memorials*, III, p. 7; Knowles, Brooke and London 2001, p. 32.

4 Diana Greenway and Jane Sayers have made a more recent translation of *Jocelin of Brakelond* (Oxford, 1989), based on the Latin text edited by H. E. Butler (London, 1949).

5 *Jocelin*, p. 29.

6 *The Kalendar of Abbot Samson*.

7 *Jocelin*, p. 30.

8 *Jocelin*, pp. 45–7, 144.

9 *Jocelin*, p. 47; James 1895, p. 120.

10 *Jocelin*, pp. 87, 96–7.

11 *Memorials*, II, pp. 291–2.

Worcester.[12] From his description and physical evidence it is generally accepted to have been either 472 or 505 feet in length, and approaching 250 feet in width, and thus marginally greater by both measurements than Norwich cathedral.[13]

Although Jocelin wrote that Samson would have been happy to expend two thousand marks of silver to have the king present at the dedication of the building, no reference to the event survives, apart from the leave granted on 1 December 1198 by Pope Innocent III for the ceremony to take place.[14] Towards the end of Samson's abbacy part of his life's ambition was undone when, on 23 September 1210, the main tower collapsed, accounts of the disaster being at variance whether on a still day or during a storm.[15]

In addition to work upon the fabric and interior of the church, the abbey was also able to finance building activity elsewhere in the abbey precincts. After removing William Wardell from the office of sacrist, Samson had his houses in the cemetery razed to the ground because of their being used for 'frequent wine-bibbing and other things of which it is best to say nothing'.[16] This was followed by the erection of a new infirmary, guest hall and bath house and lodgings for the abbot and his own guests.[17] This marks one of the steps by which at Bury, as at other houses, the abbot set himself apart from the community. Extensive building also appears to have been carried out in the townships (*villis*) of the abbot's domain,[18] besides restoration work upon the halls and ruinous houses of his manors.[19]

Apparently, not all the abbot's outlay was productive since Jocelin records that Richard died before Samson had received the 'favour and grace' he had purchased from the king.[20] Despite this miscalculation, Samson's relationship with Henry II, Richard I and John was undoubtedly close, and beneficial to St Edmunds. When in 1188 Henry had engaged himself to embark on a crusade he came to Bury and during the visit Samson pleaded, unsuccessfully, to accompany him. The king's refusal was said to have been prompted by the bishop of Norwich, who considered that the security of Suffolk and Norfolk could have been at risk if both he and Samson were absent together.[21] Richard in turn also made a pilgrimage to St Edmund's shrine during both his short spells in

12 James 1895, pp. 163–5.

13 James 1895, pp. 120–1; Yates 1805, p. 13.

14 *Jocelin*, pp. 47 (n. 2), 48. Dedication and consecration may be taken as synonymous: see Gransden 1991b; at p. 59 Gransden concludes that, partly because of continuous civil works, the post-conquest church never was consecrated.

15 James 1895, pp. 159, 203.

16 *Jocelin*, p. 31.

17 *Memorials*, II, pp. 291–2; Whittingham 1971, pp. 6–7.

18 *Jocelin*, p. 95.

19 *Jocelin*, p.28.

20 *Jocelin*, p.116.

21 *Jocelin*, pp. 53–4, n. 4.

England,[22] and Samson visited him with gifts when he was captive in Germany in 1193.[23] Upon his accession, John set aside other calls on his time and came straightaway to Bury. He upset the monks, however, by limiting his largess to a silken cloth borrowed from the sacrist and thirteen pence donated at mass before his departure.[24] Samson showed greater magnanimity (or possibly gratitude) towards the king by leaving him his palfreys and personal jewels in his will.[25]

The importance of Samson to the abbey cannot be overestimated, and if the pages of Jocelin betray a gradual cooling in the writer's admiration, it must have been easy for the monks to forget his contribution once the abbey had been restored to affluence. But even Samson's shrewdness was not able to stem the growing influence of the convent and its obedientiaries, such as the sacrist and cellarer,[26] or to allay the burgeoning restlessness of the townsmen who were increasingly looking upon the abbey as oppressor rather than protector.[27]

The Short Cross coinage (1180–1205)

Some chroniclers recorded the introduction of the Short Cross coinage as occurring in 1181, but the evidence of the Pipe Rolls shows that the correct date was 1180.[28] The type then introduced and continuing in production until 1247 has been divided by numismatists into eight classes with a number of sub-divisions.[29] As these become increasingly refined they help clarify how the design evolved during the issue and ease the task of die-study.[30] They may also offer the prospect of dating the classes and sub-classes more precisely where the moneyers recorded on the coins are also mentioned in datable surviving records. However, many of the subtleties would have had no significance for contemporary officials or coin users and may thus appear to the layman to be over elaborate and even artificial. Although all the coins bear the royal title *Henricus Rex*, much to the confusion of early numismatists, class I is now generally attributed to Henry II, classes II and III to Richard I, class IV to Richard and John, class V to John, class VI to John and Henry III, and the remainder to Henry III.[31] The change in monarch was thus not decisive in the evolution of the classes, but 1205 was important as the year in which John reformed the currency, implementing measures to eliminate clipped coins and improve the workmanship of

22 Appleby 1965, maps on pp. 14 and 125.
23 *Jocelin*, p. 55.
24 *Jocelin*, pp. 116–17.
25 *Curia Regis Rolls*, VI, p. 189.
26 On the struggle of the convent to limit the abbot's power from Samson's time, see Gransden 1975, pp. 25–39.
27 For example, *Jocelin*, pp. 77–9.
28 Allen 1951, pp. lxxxix-xc.
29 Lawrence 1915b, especially pp. 62–6.
30 The classification systems are compared by Mass 2001, pp. 95–8.
31 North 1994, pp. 220–3; Brand 1964, pp. 68–9.

those newly minted.[32] This reform is clearly associated with the neat coins of class Va.[33]

During the first phase of the coinage, from 1180 to 1205, the number of mints in operation fluctuated between ten at the beginning of the period and seven in class III.[34] All the mints in class I had also been active in the Tealby issue with the exception of Worcester. A number of prominent Tealby mints, however, did not join in the recoinage, including Bristol, Canterbury, Durham, Ipswich, Newcastle, Norwich, Thetford and Bury.[35] Of the mints with earlier ecclesiastical links Canterbury was reopened in class II,[36] and Durham in class IV,[37] but Bury only once the reforms of 1205 were under way.

In contrast with the absence of Bury coins, the texts of writs from Richard I and John survive, confirming the abbot's minting rights.[38] Moreover, Jocelin relates that at the investiture of Samson 'the charters of the king concerning the donation of the abbacy were produced and read for all to hear'.[39] This implies that the customary privileges enjoyed by the abbot and convent had already been confirmed during the three weeks that had elapsed between Samson's election and his installation, otherwise the reading would have been pointless. The failure of St Edmunds to exercise its minting rights before class Vb has been attributed to Samson's preoccupation in the early years of his tenure with placing the abbey's finances on a sound footing.[40] This is, however, scarcely plausible. The mint was active in Hugh's abbacy and it is hard to imagine that it operated at a loss. Moreover, minting was such a familiar activity at the monastery, particularly to Samson as former sub-sacrist, that it could not have been perceived as other than a help in reviving the abbey's fortunes. He must also have been aware of the risk that if the customary right, so meticulously recorded in the abbey cartularies, was not exercised, it could be adjudged to have lapsed through desuetude.

The correct explanation clearly lies in a radical change introduced in 1180, whereby the operation of exchanging old coin for new was removed from the moneyers and placed under the direct control of royal officials (*cambiatores*).[41]

32 *The Great Roll of the Pipe for the Seventh Year of King John*, pp. xxvii–xxviii. The reform was initiated at Guildford on 9 November 1204 (*RLP*, pp. 47b-48).

33 Brooke 1950, pp. 104–5; Oman 1931, pp. 137–8.

34 North 1994, pp. 224–5.

35 Allen 1951, pp. clxxix-clxxxiii.

36 Archbishop Baldwin was granted three dies and moneyers on 1 December 1189 (Lawrence 1915b, p. 69). The evidence suggests that at this period, at least, exercise of the archbishop's privilege was subordinated to operation of the royal mint in the city.

37 Allen 1979, p. 46, concluded that the Durham mint was probably reopened during the vacancy in the bishopric for nine months from 2 April 1195.

38 BL Harl. MS 743, fol.11, 11b; see also BL Harl. MS 645, fo1.133b and Ruding 1840, II, p. 218.

39 *Jocelin*, p. 25.

40 Lawrence 1915b, p. 84.

41 Allen 1951, pp. lxxxvii–xciv.

This was, of course, at variance with the privilege to mint and exchange bullion hitherto enjoyed by the abbot at Bury, but the death of Hugh and ensuing vacancy possibly prevented St Edmunds from promptly asserting its claims based on precedent. Without the grant of an exchange the confirmation eventually obtained by Sampson may have entitled him to operate the mint to coin his own silver but not that of others. Because of this, he and the sacrist may well have decided it was not worthwhile to maintain a mint for such a limited purpose.[42]

A further administrative change appears to have occurred in 1191–2 with the creation of the *Cambium Totius Anglie*,[43] possibly as a step to reinforce central control. This development was based on the mints of London and Canterbury,[44] and may account for the latter's return to minting activity in class II in which the archbishop, with his three moneyers and three-eighths share in the costs and profits of coinage, was a coincidental beneficiary.[45]

Short Cross coinage at Bury (1205–1217)

The reform of John, besides bringing about an improvement in the appearance of the currency, was mainly designed to remove clipped and otherwise underweight coins from circulation. Penalties were proclaimed against those possessing clipped coin after 13 January 1205,[46] and on 26 January steps were taken to eliminate any pence not weighing more than seven-eighths of the standard. Weights were issued to any who wished to check their coins.[47] A Bury chronicler also recorded that the currency introduced in 1158 (i.e. the ' Tealby' issue) was in that year withdrawn from circulation (*renovata fuit moneta, anno Domini MCLVIII olim facta*).[48] Although the same statement occurs in the continuator of Florence of Worcester,[49] other chronicles date the withdrawal to St Martin's Day (11 November) 1180, an altogether more credible chronology.[50]

It was also provided that money could only be changed at the exchange of the king or archbishop of Canterbury, and that the profit on exchange should be no more nor less than six pence in the pound of fine and pure silver.[51] It is not precisely clear when the first coins of the new issue (known as class Va) were

42 When, however, the mint was farmed back to the king in the early years of Henry III it made sense for the abbot to obtain the right to use the dies to strike coins for his own use (see p. 147 below).

43 *The Great Roll of the Pipe for the Third and Fourth Years of the Reign of King Richard the First*, p. 148.

44 Tibbo 1954, p. 41.

45 Tibbo 1954, p. 72.

46 *RLP*, p. 47b.

47 *RLP*, p. 54b; Ruding 1840, I, pp. 178–9.

48 *Memorials*, II, p. 13.

49 Cited by Oman 1931, p. 137.

50 See 'Benedict of Peterborough' and Ralf of Diceto, quoted by Allen 1951, p. lxxiii.

51 See n. 45 above.

struck.[52] Abbot Samson was granted his dies on 12 June 1205,[53] together with all customary rights (thus presumably including that of exchange), paying 500 marks (£333 6*s*. 8*d*.) for this and other privileges, including entitlement to hold an eight-day fair at Beccles.[54] The wording of the writ expressly confirms the grant to the abbot and convent. The absence of known coins before class Vb1 reflects the fact that the abbey mint was not active from the outset of the recoinage.

The Bury coins of class Vb1, Vb2 and Vc, all bearing the name of the moneyer Fulke,[55] were studied in detail by Brand in the 1960s and the links between the dies in the British Museum and additional dies found elsewhere described.[56] Since then further die links have come to light but no additional dies. The updated earlier die study is set out at Figure 7.[57] The significant die combinations discovered are Xi and Ef, which link the break in the series, as recorded by Brand, occurring between class Vb2 and Vc. These links suggest that no Vb3 dies were issued at Bury, and that Brand's die sequence should be amended to place obverse X after and not before obverse D.

The way the dies were deployed shows clearly that the normal arrangement at Bury of one obverse with one or two reverse dies being issued against surrender of the old dies did not apply at this time. It is tempting to suppose that this arose because the king's officials wished to facilitate the operation of the mint during the recoinage without the inconvenience of regular journeys to London to collect replacement sets of dies. Although the pattern of die linking is not easy to interpret, and the dies were clearly not issued all together or according to any consistent grouping, the level of activity was clearly greater than normal. The first obverse die (A) appears to have been issued with three or four reverses (x, a, b and possibly c). The next four obverse dies (B, C, D, X) were issued with one or maybe two associated reverses (Bcd or Bd; Ce or Cef; Dh or Dgh; and Xg or Xfg). Most significant, however, is the extent to which reverses issued with an obverse were retained and used with later obverses. In contrast, the absence of class Vb3 dies, with so-called 'broken eyes,' and the issue of one class Vc obverse with possibly only one reverse (i) hints at a marked decline in mint activity by 1207, or even by 1206.[58] From the pattern of survival it is probable that all of the dies, and possibly all of the die combinations used in class V at Bury, have now come to light.[59]

52 See Allen 2001a, p. 6.

53 *ChR*, p. 156b.

54 *The Great Roll of the Pipe for the Seventh Year of King John*, p. 236.

55 A moneyer named Fulke operated at London in class V, but since he remained active there until class Vb2 he did not apparently move to Bury to reopen the mint.

56 Brand 1964, pp. 61–2.

57 His analysis was summarized in Brand 1994, p. 78.

58 Allen 2001a, p. 12, dates class Vb3 to *c*. 1206.

59 Allen 1989, Appendix 4, p. 65, shows the high frequency of obverse die survival at Bury compared with other mints, based on 71 coins (there are 107 in the Catalogue below).

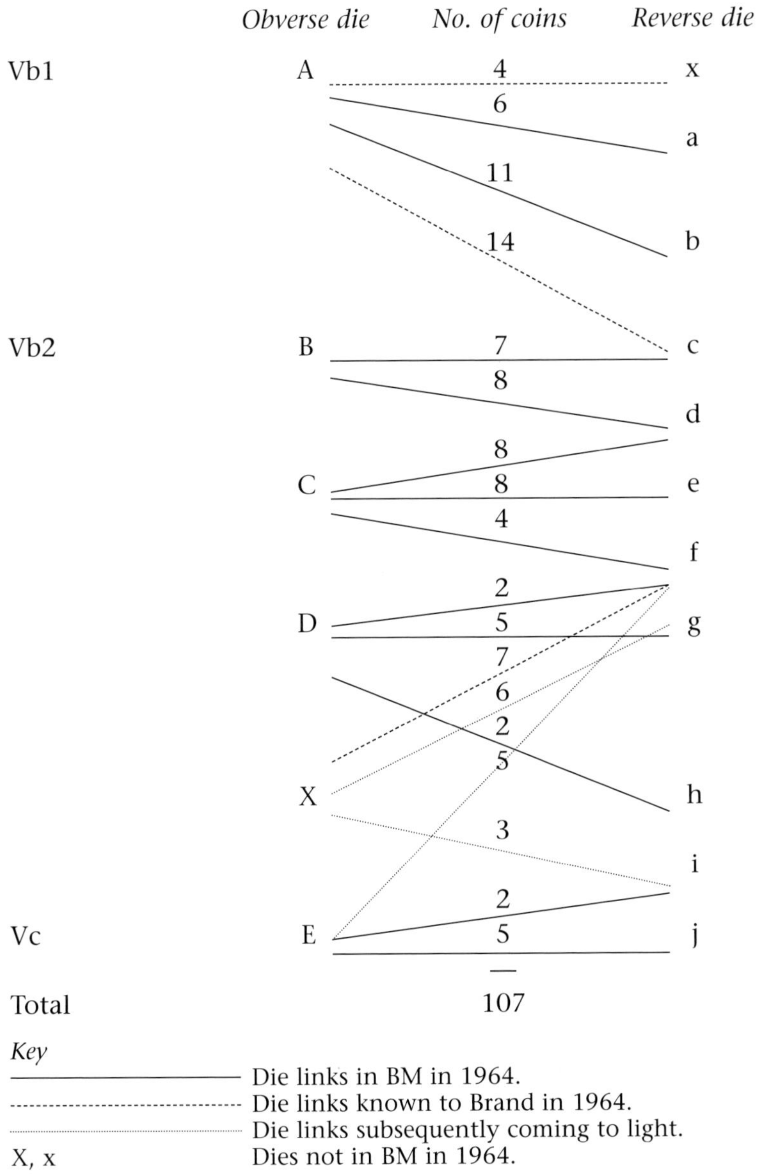

Figure 7

Bury dies in John's reign (class V)

On 7 October 1207 the well-known writ was issued summoning all mint personnel with their dies to a conference at Westminster.[60] Brooke gave the date of the meeting as 10 January 1208, but Martin Allen has shown that it was in fact scheduled to be held on 24 October 1207.[61] The summons must have marked the completion of the recoinage. Of the sixteen mints involved all struck coins in class Vb2/3 whereas only eleven are known in class Vc, and at the outset of class VI only two mints, London and Durham were operating.[62] It is thus likely

60 *RLP*, p. 76; Ruding 1840, I, p. 179.

61 Allen 1995, pp. 223–4.

62 Allen 2001a, pp. 8, 10.

that Carlisle, Exeter, Kings Lynn, Oxford and Rochester had already effectively completed their task of recoinage before the conference took place.[63] It is also safe to conclude that the majority of the remainder surrendered their dies at the conference. London and Durham were two clear exceptions. At the former, three of four moneyers active at the beginning of class VI are unrecorded before class Vc and seven moneyers disappear in that class. This suggests that these seven lost their positions at the conference, to be replaced by three others. If so, this is clear evidence that class Vc dies were issued and used both before and after the conference. At Durham, the bishopric became vacant on 22 April 1208, but the mint continued to operate, doubtless for purely practical reasons, under the royal custodians of the bishopric.[64]

At Canterbury, closure of the mint is in all likelihood linked to the interdict imposed on 23 March 1208,[65] arising from John's quarrel with the Pope over the election of Stephen Langton as archbishop of Canterbury.[66] A similar fate may have befallen the mint at Bury from whence, after class Vc, no coins are known until late in class VI. Certainly a vacancy in the abbacy cannot explain this gap, because Samson lived until 30 December 1211.[67] It would also be surprising, given the earlier and subsequent history of the mint, if the abbot had lost his mint franchise simply because the recoinage had been completed.

Although the king had immediately responded to the interdict by seizing the Church's property he appears to have rapidly come to an accommodation with the most important monasteries, including Bury, whereby they were farmed for the profit of the king after deducting the sums needed to maintain their establishments.[68] A Bury chronicle relates, perhaps with exaggeration born of hope, that out of reverence for St Edmund John confirmed the abbey in its entire liberties (*in omnibus libertate pristina*) when he was at Guildford for Easter in early April 1208.[69] It is unclear how the abbot's rights were affected by these writs, but hard to imagine that privileges deriving from his office, including that of coinage, were not placed in abeyance.[70]

Before the interdict was lifted in 1214[71] Samson had died, followed by a vacancy of over three years until the election of his successor, Hugh of Northwold, was

63 The mints striking in class Vc were Bury, Canterbury, Chichester, Durham, Ipswich, Lincoln, London, Northampton, Norwich, Winchester and York. Chichester is a recent addition to this list (*BNJ* Coin Register 2005, no. 255).

64 Allen 1979, p. 51.

65 Roger of Wendover, III, p. 222; *Memorials*, II, p.16. See also Norgate 1902, p. 127, n. 9 and pp. 127–8.

66 Stewart 1989, pp. 44–5.

67 *Memorials*, II, p. 19.

68 Norgate 1902, pp. 128 (n. 1), 129; Warren 1978, p. 167.

69 *Memorials*, II, p.16.

70 Brand 1964, p. 68, makes the same connection but unjustifiably extends the influence of the interdict to the closure of provincial mints generally.

71 Norgate 1902, p. 207 and n. 2.

confirmed followed by his blessing on 11 March 1215. The chronicle recording the events leading up to Hugh's investiture, besides describing how his candidature was eventually accepted by the king at Runnymede,[72] contains several oblique references to coinage. On 18 January 1214 the sacrist, Robert of Graveley, who with Richard the precentor led the opponents to Hugh's election,[73] told the chapter that he was going to the papal legate on convent business *'et maxime pro coyn et pro moneta adquirenda'*. This phrase, which Thompson translates as 'particularly to acquire equipment for the mint' is superficially puzzling.[74] So also are two later references in the chronicle, where the sacrist is described as offering to the bishop of Winchester, if expedient, to come to an accommodation with the king about the business of the house and the die for the mint (*eundemque regem super coyn . . . conveniret*), on which the bishop duly spoke to the king (*. . . et maxime pro coyn impetrando*).[75]

At first glance the reason given by the sacrist for his journey may seem to imply that the mint was already operational, but this is certainly not correct. The words *'pro coyn et pro moneta adquirenda'* refer to obtaining both the dies (*coyn*) and details of the standard (*moneta*) for the coinage. If the mint had been operating the standard would already have been known. Bearing in mind that Hugh's disputed election had taken place at Bury on 7 August 1213,[76] the partisan chronicler is possibly insinuating that Robert of Graveley was showing extreme duplicity by pretending to make an approach for dies for the new abbot, whose investiture in reality he opposed. Most interesting for the numismatist, however, is that Robert should have plausibly proposed to raise the question of coinage with the papal legate at all. The latter would normally not be expected to have any involvement in such matters. The obvious conclusion is that the lack of wherewithal for minting was still bound up with the interdict. Robert was therefore, for whatever motives, trying to lobby support from any quarters he could, including the legate and the bishop of Winchester.

The arrangement Robert was prepared to come to with the king about the 'dies for the mint' is impossible to know. He may have been prepared to trade the privilege of coinage against fulfilment of his personal ambition to become abbot at Bury, or to farm the privilege back to the king as in fact happened in the early years of the following reign. Another plausible, and more honourable, motive could have been to ask for the right of coinage to attach to the convent in place of the abbot, as a means to retain the right when the abbacy was vacant. Such an arrangement would, however, have been incompatible with the fact that the right clearly attached to, and derived from, the abbot's feudal barony. It would nevertheless not necessarily have followed that the abbot rather than the convent would inevitably have enjoyed the profits arising from exercise of the right,

72 *The Chronicle of the Election of Hugh*, pp. 170–1.
73 *The Chronicle of the Election of Hugh*, p. xvi.
74 *The Chronicle of the Election of Hugh*, pp. 36–7.
75 *The Chronicle of the Election of Hugh*, pp. 38–9.
76 *The Chronicle of the Election of Hugh*, pp. 10–11.

and by an uncertain date in the thirteenth century such profits were clearly attributed to the sacrist.[77] This could have been what Robert was seeking to accomplish, although he would have recognized that this source of revenue would not thereby be protected during a vacancy.

One further episode from this period should be briefly mentioned before turning to the revival of coinage at Bury. Roger of Wendover, after recording the return of John to England on 19 October 1214, related that at the same period (*sub eadem tempestate*) the barons met at Bury under the guise of worship, and swore to hold the king to the charter of Henry I which Stephen Langton, archbishop of Canterbury, had unearthed.[78] This episode has been popularly accepted as true (and is commemorated by a tablet in the abbey precincts),[79] but since the abbey was in the hands of the king's nominated custodians during the vacancy[80] it would have been a very risky place at which to assemble and plot against John. Gransden takes a different view, accepting the authenticity of Roger of Wendover's account and detecting that at least Hugh and his adherents were 'in some degree implicated with the barons' rebellion'.[81] Besides the presence of the king's custodians, this is not easy to reconcile with the fact that Robert of Graveley, who remained in office as sacrist, also led a strong faction in the abbey,[82] and was clearly for the king.[83]

The first type to be recorded at Bury after class Vc is that known as VIc1,[84] of which two obverse dies are known, used with reverses of the moneyer Rauf. The date of these coins must be after the confirmation of Hugh as abbot on 11 March 1215, and for reasons explained below is more likely to have been near to that date rather than '*c.* 1217' as suggested by Brand,[85] especially since confirmation of the right to a die was granted to Hugh on 19 July 1215.[86]

From this time onwards Bury is active in all of the main classes and varieties issued until the end of the Short Cross coinage.[87] The dating of these classes and

77 The sacrist's entitlement to minting profits (*una cum cuneo et eius profectu*) is confirmed in a charter of Edward I dealing with the division of the abbot's and convent's property (*Monasticon*, III, p. 157), and is implied in a Bury manuscript from early in the fourteenth century (*cuneus maneat in manu conventus, donec aliter ordinetur*) (Harl. MS 3977, fol. 52).

78 Roger of Wendover, III, pp. 293–4.

79 Warren 1978, pp. 227–8, appears to be sceptical of the story, in contrast with Painter 1949, p. 286. Norgate 1902, p. 221, states that John was at Bury on 4 November and the barons probably arrived after his departure. Whittingham 1971, p. 7, adhered to the popular view that the barons were there ostensibly to celebrate the martyrdom of St Edmund, on 20 November.

80 *RLC*, I, p. 212.

81 Gransden 1975, p. 38.

82 *The Chronicle of the Election of Hugh*, pp. 84–7; at pp. xxxiv-vi the editor construed 'opposition' to the sacrist's party amongst the more literate in the convent.

83 See for example, *The Chronicle of the Election of Hugh*, pp. 58–9.

84 The classification used for class VI is that of Stewart 1979a, pp. 29–35.

85 Brand 1964, p. 69.

86 *RLC*, I, p. 221, referring to a die (*cuneum suum*) but not specifically to an exchange.

87 Excepting class VIx, known only at Canterbury: Mass 2001 pp. 48–9.

varieties is not settled, but documentary or circumstantial evidence from Bury and other mints nevertheless provide some clear pointers. Brand first drew attention to the entry in the Lord Treasurer's Remembrancer's Memoranda Roll for 20 January 1218,[88] recording that the moneyer Willelm at Bury received one die on 7 December 1217, but with the name Willelm struck out and that of Norman inserted above. To date, coins of Willelm are known in class VIIa2 and VIIa3, and of Norman from VIIa3. Although it is possible that the correction to the Roll was made some time after 20 January 1218, it is not probable. Brand also adduced other evidence to demonstrate that dies of class VIIa were likely to have been in use by that date, mention in the same Roll of the Canterbury moneyer Roger of Rochester being particularly persuasive, because his earliest known coins were struck in Class VIIa.[89] Thus, unless he was in office but inoperative, class VIIa would certainly appear to have been in issue before the date of the Roll.

Willelm de Monasterio (*sic*) is also recorded as a moneyer at Bury in the King's Remembrancer's Memoranda Rolls for 1217–18.[90] This entry has further interest because Simon of Catteshale and Derman de Mercato are mentioned as keepers of the dies. It would thus appear that when not in actual use the obverse die was held by one person and the reverse(s) by another.

The activity of Rauf, Willelm and Norman at Bury is represented by surviving coins as follows:[91]

Table 34. Obverse dies used by Rauf, Willelm and Norman at Bury

Class	*Moneyer*	*No. of known obverse dies*
VIc1	Rauf	2
VIc2	Rauf	5
VIc3	Rauf	3
VId	Rauf	1
VIIaA	Rauf	1
VIIaB	Rauf	1
VIIaB–C	Willelm	6
		—
VIc1–VIIaC total		19
VIIaC and VIIbA–B	Norman	19

Thus, if indeed Willelm vacated his office at the end of 1217, Rauf and he would have used at least nineteen obverse dies in the intervening period from the reopening of the mint after 11 March 1215. Such a level of activity is surprising,

88 PRO, E368/1 [LTR 2 Henry III], m. 5; Brand 1964, p. 66.
89 Mass 2001, p. 93.
90 PRO, E159/1 [2 Henry III], m. 3.
91 See Catalogue for details.

bearing in mind that the country was disrupted during the greater part of this period by civil war. Although the hostilities were by no means unremitting,[92] London, as the normal source of dies, appears to have been occupied by the rebel barons from 17 May 1215[93] through to the Treaty of Kingston on 12 September 1217.[94] By mid-June 1216, after the arrival of Louis of France as claimant to the throne, John also lost control of Canterbury and Winchester.[95] It follows that even allowing for Bury being secured for the king's cause when rebel refugees were driven out of the town by mid-January 1216,[96] it is remarkable that the abbot's moneyer would have received an uninterrupted flow of dies at the rate of one set every five weeks or so. Further still, if, as suggested by Brand, class VIc were introduced in '*c.* 1217,' nineteen obverse dies would have been used at Bury in the space of twelve months. This level of activity, although not inconceivable, is far greater than anything previously or subsequently encountered, and was not even associated with a recoinage. Moreover, the sets of dies show scant evidence of inter-linking, indicating that they were generally issued sequentially against surrender of the previous set. Under Brand's scenario, assuming the return journey from Bury to London took at least four days, someone would have been sent there for new dies on average about every two and a half weeks, and during the envoy's absence the mint would have been unable to operate.

As Bury itself illustrates, Oman's view that coinage ceased at London, Canterbury and counties in the eastern shires during the conflict[97] is not borne out by the numismatic evidence.[98] There are also no obvious signs of disruption or abnormalities in the coinage, apart from the use of ornamental forms of lettering. Thus the outward semblance is that its administration was maintained in spite of the civil war.

As will be seen from Figure 8 and the Catalogue there was considerable variation in the number of reverse dies issued to Bury with each obverse in class VI, ranging from one to four. From class VId or shortly before, however, normally only one reverse was issued with each obverse and this remained the practice until the close of the Long Cross coinage at Bury under Edward I.[99] The dies of VId and early VIIa dies are also markedly superior in execution to those of VIc3. It is tempting to associate these changes with the accession of Henry III, but there is

92 Powicke 1962, p. 8.

93 Roger of Wendover, III, pp. 299–300; Norgate 1902, p. 229.

94 Roger of Wendover, IV, p. 31; Norgate 1912, p. 59.

95 Norgate 1902, p. 270 and n. 1, p. 271 and n. 7.

96 Norgate 1902, pp. 257–8.The abbey was, however, despoiled during a raid on East Anglia in the middle of 1217 by the Viscount of Melun and Eustace de Neville (Norgate 1912, p. 48). This episode has been associated with the supposed removal of St Edmund's remains from Bury to St Sernin, Toulouse (see, for example, Houghton 1970, p. 54 and *passim*).

97 Oman 1931, p. 139.

98 Apart from Bury, London with four moneyers and Canterbury with eight were both active in classes VIc to VIIa (Stewart 1979a, p. 38).

99 See this and the following chapter.

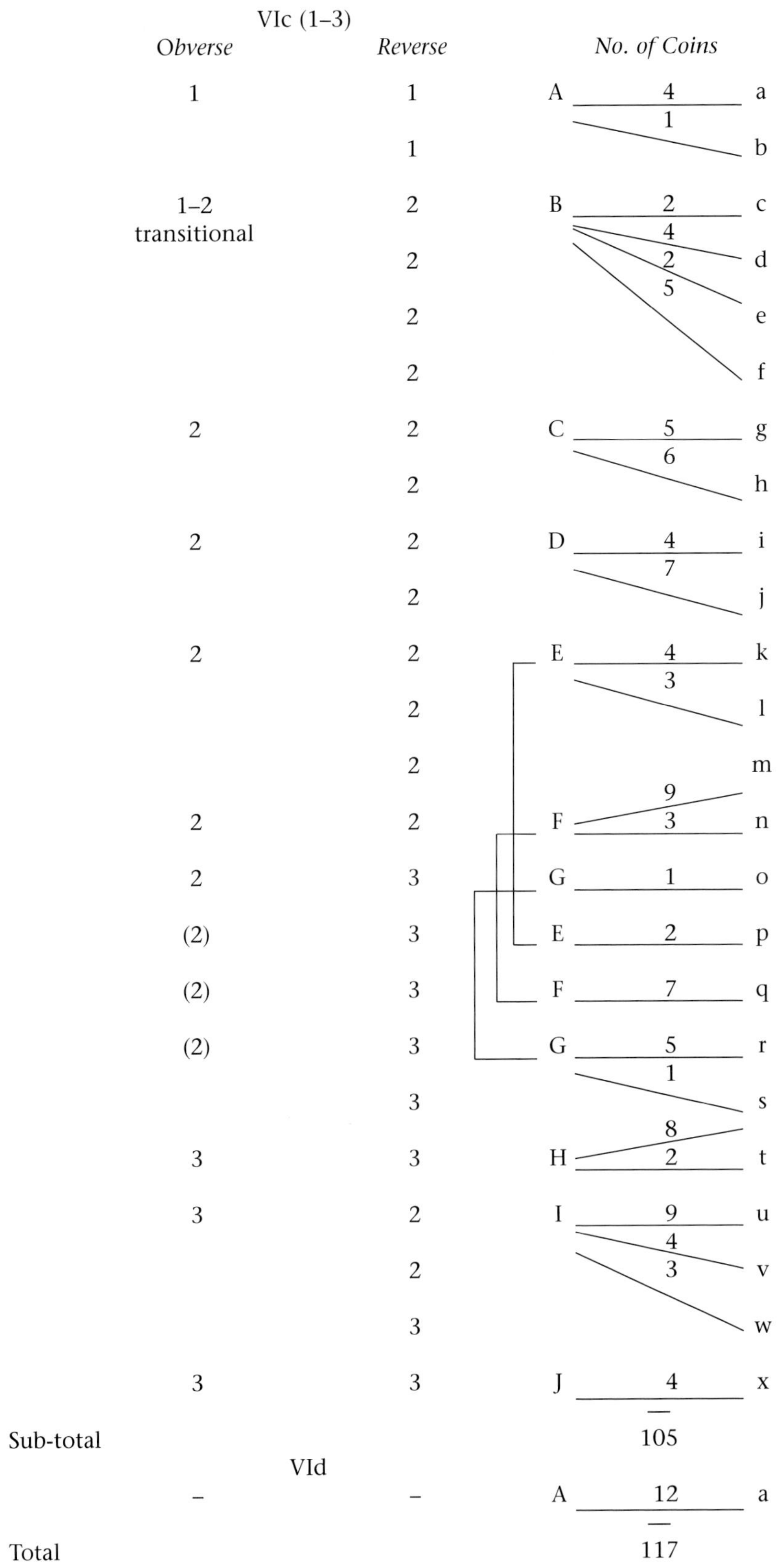

Figure 8

Short Cross class VI coins of Rauf

Table 35. Ornamental letters on class VIc2 reverses used with obverse B

Bc	+	R	A	V	F	·	O	N	·	S	A	N	T	A	D
Bd	+	R	A	V	F	·	O	N	·	S	A	N	T	A	D
Be	+	R	A	V	F	·	O	N	·	S	A	N	T	A	D
Bf	+	R	A	V	F	·	O	N	·	S	A	N	T	A	D

Note
As noted above, obverse B itself has an ornamental 'S', similar to that of reverse f, and so could be classified as VIc2, instead of VIc1.

no concrete support for such an hypothesis. Equally logically, renewed attention to the coinage could be expected once the supporters of the infant Henry III had recovered full administrative control after the Treaty of Kingston. This, however, would mean that at least nine sets of unlinked dies would have been in use between, say, October 1217 and January 1218 at Bury, an unbelievable number even if coining activity intensified in the more settled times after the Treaty. On balance it appears that VIc3 dies were introduced soon after Henry III came to the throne on 28 October 1216.

Although at this period there is only one link of different obverses with a common reverse at Bury (Gs, Hs) the pattern provided by the sets of one obverse with between one to four reverses demonstrates that the sequence of varieties VIc1 , VIc2, and VIc3, is correctly stated. A VIc1/VIc2 mule represented by dies Bf was noted by Stewartby in 1981,[100] but although this obverse has the double side curls typical of VIc1 it also has an ornamental R and S, the latter with a central pellet and conspicuous serifs. As such it is clearly transitional and was used with four VIc2 reverse dies (cdef). Reverse d is also the most ornamental of those from Bury, supporting the hypothesis that ornamentation was at its height at the outset of VIc2.[101] Table 35 illustrates the great variety in treatment of the reverse reading +RAVF·ON·SANTAD, which is extraordinary if all four reverses were supplied with obverse B. Figure 8 also shows that when VIc3 was introduced it was issued concurrently with VIc2 dies, mules being found both in VIc2/VIc3[102] and VIc3/VIc2 combinations.[103] So far only one set of VIc3 dies (Jy) has come to light of which neither the obverse nor the reverse is found linked with a VIc2 die. The ultimate variety of class VI, first identified by Brand and now classified as VId,[104] is known only from one obverse die at Bury. The other recently identified variety, VIx,[105] has so far only been found at Canterbury. It is attributed to the period of the baron's war (1215–17), and *inter alia* displays pellets on either side of the king's nose. This unusual feature is also found on VIc1, obverse A from Bury, datable to the same period.

100 Stewart 1981, p. 105, Addenda 2.

101 Stewart 1979a, pp. 32–3. See Catalogue for these coins.

102 See Catalogue 113–116.

103 Catalogue, 119–120. The same proposition is demonstrated by mules of VIc2 and VIc3 obverses and reverses with class VId (see Stewart 1981, pp. 101–3).

104 See *SCBI* 12, p. xiv, where the variety is designated 'VIc*'; Dumas and Brand 1971, pp. 32, 36–8.

105 Stewart 1979a, p. 30; Stewart 1981, pp. 91–4.

The mint signature for each reverse die is recorded in the Catalogue, but Table 36 summarises how Bury is denoted in classes V and VI:

Table 36. Bury mint readings in Short Cross classes V and VI

		Class (and no. of dies represented)						
Moneyer	*Mint reading*	*Vb1*	*Vb2*	*Vc*	*VIc1*	*VIc2*	*VIc3*	*VId*
Fulke	S·ADMV	1	1					
	S·ADMV	1						
	S·EDM	2						
	S·AD		1	1				
	S·ADM		3					
	S·AND		1					
Rauf	SANTAD				2	10	2	
	SANTEA					3	1	
	SANTE					1	1	1
	SANTA						3	

The last two sets of dies known for Rauf are of class VIIa, as are all of the coins known of Willelm and all but two sets of dies of his successor, Norman. The class VII coins of Norman will be dealt with in the next section, but the dies identified of Rauf and Willelm in class VIIa are summarised in Table 37 below. The bust of one of the two VIIa obverse dies of Rauf has close affinities with the VId obverse, but has no pellet on the chin. Some attempt has been made to place the dies of Willelm in sequence of issue, but because die links are absent the order cannot be certain. Mass,[106] following earlier work by Stewartby[107] and North,[108] has attempted to define sub-classes VIIaA-C more precisely, but the results for VIIaB and C do not fit comfortably with the known dies of Willelm at Bury. Willelm's obverses fall into two groups. The first somewhat resemble die B of Rauf but are usually (B, C) if not always (A) of coarser execution. The second has an exaggerated 'Hapsburg' chin with a copious beard (D, E, F). These are placed second because a similar style is found among the obverse dies of Norman. It is possible that the 'Hapsburg' chinned coins were the work of a particular die sinker, but they are here treated as having a sequential significance, since they are associated with other early features of class VIIa, such as a straight sided instead of a waisted letter 'I'. An inner circle on the reverse made up of fine rather than coarse pellets is also an early feature.[109] A number of dies use an S with curved serifs (B, Ee), and two reverses (b and d) bear pellets in the legend.

106 Mass 2001, pp. 50–4.
107 Stewart 1979a, pp. 35–6.
108 North 1988.
109 Stewart 1979a, p. 35, confirmed by unpublished die studies of the Canterbury and London mints by G. P. Gittoes.

Table 37. Short Cross class VIIa coins of Rauf and Willelm

Moneyer	*Class*	*Dies*	*No. of coins*
Rauf	VIIaA	Aa	2
	VIIaB	Aa	3
			—
			5
Willelm	VIIaB-C	Aa	4
		Bb[110]	22
		Cc	19
		Dd	5
		Ee	6
		Ff	14
			—
			70

To conclude this section, the following dates may tentatively be suggested for the inception at Bury of Short Cross issues between Vb and VIIa:

Vbl	after 12 June 1205
Vc	before the end of March 1208
VIcl	after 11 March 1215
VIc3	after 28 October 1216 (?)
VId	after 12 September 1217 (?)
VIIa	before 7 December 1217.

Short Cross coinage at Bury (1217–1242)

Since the known die sets of Willelm's successor, Norman, are all, except for the last two, of Class VIIa it is convenient to begin this section by considering his dies and attempting to trace their evolution from those used by Willelm. The 19 obverses and 20 reverses are summarised in Figure 9 and described in full in the Catalogue. Statistically, Figure 9 is likely to represent all or almost all the obverse dies used by Norman.[111] Apart from the initial cluster of linked obverses and reverses, the pattern under both Norman and his successor, Simund, was of one obverse die issued with one reverse.

Class VIIa presents challenges in classification that have not yet been convincingly met. Prospective diagnostic features, such as the presence or absence of pellets in the curls (either free standing and/or in the shape of commas) and on

110 Gittoes and Mayhew 1983, p. 25, suggest that Rauf's obverse A (Catalogue 125) is from the same die as an obverse of Willelm (B, Catalogue 127) but this does not appear to be correct.

111 All known obverse and reverse dies are represented by at least two examples.

Figure 9

Short Cross class VIIaC and VIIb coins of Norman.

Class	Obverse	Coins	Reverse
VIIaC	A	5	a
	A	12	b
	B	2	b
	B	1	c
	B	7	d
	B	1	e
	C	11	c
	E	12	e
	F	2	f
	G	5	g
	H	11	h
	I	8	i
	J	25	j
	K	9	k (CAN)
	L	3	l
	M	12	m
	N	4	n
	O	10	o
	P	19	p
Crude bust (VIIaD)	Q	5	q
	R	5	r
Total		169	
VIIbA	A	2	a
VIIbB	A	4	a

the chin, variations in the form of lettering, and bust design are not readily amenable to chronological ordering. It is difficult to avoid suspecting that some of the apparent inconsistencies arise from relaxed supervision over different die cutting hands. At Bury, Norman used a cluster of linked dies unique in extent for the mint, involving four obverses (A–C, E) and five reverses (a–e). These combine obverses both with and without pellets in the curls (A and B, C, E respectively) and on the chin (B and A, C, E), and three of the reverses read SANT (a, b, d) and two SAN (c, e). Nevertheless, taken as a whole, pellets on the chin of Norman's dies appear to be an earlier rather than later feature. Of the busts, A is akin to the 'Hapsburg' chin group used by Willelm. It also uses similar lettering, notably the thick, straight sided 'I' found on dies of Willelm, rather than the waisted 'I' of the remaining dies of Norman. These attributes prompt the placing of the cluster of dies at the outset of Norman's output. The size and shape of busts B, C and E are similar and resemble those found on obverses F to K. In contrast, obverses L and M, N, O are distinctive, and P heralds the crude bust, cut off at the chin (Q, R), which Mass does not differentiate but North designates as Class 7aD. The reverses from j onwards use the form SAN rather than SANT for the mint name, and may thus be a consistent late feature of Norman's dies. One reverse (k) mistakenly uses the form CAN. Three reverses have pellets in the legend (l, n, p). Amongst the lettering, A and S are particularly susceptible to variation. With the former it may be the result of casual die-cutting, but the usual, small-serifed S is occasionally replaced by one with wedge ends (I, d, n, p) or ornamented with a central pellet (Pp).

During the period from 1218 to 1247 there was no vacancy in the abbacy of sufficient duration to cause a recognisable hiatus in the coinage at Bury. Hugh of Northwold remained abbot until appointed bishop of Ely in 1229. His seal as bishop bore the effigies of St Edmund and St Ethelreda. Richard de Insula who had been prior at Bury before becoming abbot at Burton in 1222, was elected in his place on 5 June 1229.[112] The grant to the abbot and convent of a die (meaning one obverse die with accompanying reverse(s)) and of an exchange is recorded in the Close Rolls for 1230, and Richard Renger, then in charge of the exchanges at London and Canterbury,[113] was ordered not to annoy or interfere with the abbey in the exercise of its rights.[114] When Abbot Richard died on 29 August 1233 he was succeeded by Henry of Rushbrook, the prior, on 2 February of the following year.[115] He in turn outlived the end of the Short Cross coinage, dying on 19 June 1248.[116] Although the abbot's seat was thus almost continuously occupied, abnormal circumstances nevertheless affected the operation of the mint between 1218 and 1229.

On 21 February 1218 instructions were given to the mint officials at Winchester, London, Durham, York and Bury confirming them in office but requiring their exchanges to be yielded up to William Marshall junior.[117] Since, however, coins of class VIIa are only known from London, Canterbury, Durham and Bury, it would appear that the mints at Winchester and York were already inoperative when Marshall acquired control over their exchanges.[118] Durham may also have lapsed from activity by that time since the surviving coins are of the earliest variety,[119] and not the 'Hapsburg' chinned type associated with the latter part of Willelm's output at Bury, datable to 1217.

112 *Memorials*, III, p. 26.

113 Appointed as keeper of the king's dies in July 1227 (*RLC*, II, p. 194) and replaced by William Hardel in June 1233 (*CR 1231–1234*, p. 230).

114 *CR 1227–1231*, p. 299.

115 *Memorials*, III, p. 27. Battely 1745, p. 91, mistakenly gives the date of Richard's death as 27 August 1234. Abbot Henry may have been locally born since there is a village of Rushbrooke only a few miles outside Bury.

116 *Memorials*, III, p. 29.

117 *CPR 1216–1225*, p. 138 (cited by Lawrence 1915b, pp. 72–3).

118 Brand 1964, p. 67, noted that both Winchester and York were recorded as receiving dies on 1 and 3 December 1217 respectively (PRO, E 159/1 [KR 2 Henry III], m. 3; PRO, E 368/1 [LTR 2 Henry III], m. 5), which he related to known coins of class VIc3 (see Stewart 1979a, p. 40). Since class VIIa was already in use Stewart (p. 33) attributed this apparent anomaly to the dies being cut some time before being brought into use. It is equally possible that the class VIc3 dies had nothing to do with those issued in December 1217, which could have been class VIIa dies which were not brought into use. As Brand remarked (p. 67) the VIc3 moneyers were recorded as still in office in 1222 but, as the lack of coins avers, the holding of office is no proof of its exercise. Similarly, the issue of dies is no proof of their use.

119 Allen 1979, p. 41 and Pl. V, 100–4, but compare his comments on p. 52.

A further writ from 1218 survives, instructing William Marshall to allow the abbot at Bury to enjoy his die and exchange in peace.[120] From this it may be inferred that, encouraged by the terms of his grant, Marshall had attempted to take over the exchange at Bury or possibly close the mint but the abbot had successfully asserted his ancient privileges. In 1221, however, the rights of the abbot were reviewed,[121] and a writ subsequently issued forbidding him from admitting merchants at his exchange to the detriment of the king's exchange at London.[122] The writ instructed the abbot to operate within his authority (*auctoritate regia*) without defining what that authority was. Presumably the embargo would not have applied to merchants resident in Bury or to the abbot's tenants wherever they resided. With a semblance of normality, the Lord Treasurer's Remembrancer's Memoranda Roll for 1221/2 records Norman Rufus as moneyer, and once again two persons – Simon of Catteshale and Geoffrey son of Richard – as keepers of the dies.[123] Difficulties for the mint, however, may have increased rather than have been resolved during this period since a writ addressed on 13 February 1223 to certain continental cities informed them that exchange had been limited to the mints of Canterbury and London.[124] It is not clear if this in fact reflected a further restriction imposed on the franchisal mint at Bury, but a curious agreement reached at that time between the young king and the abbot and convent may have been a compromise reached by the abbot to avoid further erosion or total loss of his rights to a mint and exchange.

The agreement provided that the die and exchange should be farmed back to the king until his coming of full age.[125] Meanwhile the abbot and convent would receive a payment of £20 per annum, in two instalments at Easter and Michaelmas, and would be entitled to have use of the die for their own purposes (*fretinum suum*). If retained over night the die had to be placed in the abbey church under the custody of the sacrist. References occur to the half-yearly payments, from which it appears that although the king declared himself of age in January 1227,[126] the arrangement lasted until late in 1229,[127] but was not renewed after Richard de Insula became abbot.[128] This is the only period in the history of the mint when coinage can be shown to have been permitted other than under the aegis of the abbot. St Edmunds may have been happy to allow

120 *RLC*, I, p. 354b.

121 *RLC*, I, p. 456.

122 *RLC*, I, p. 476.

123 PRO, E 368/4 [LTR 6 Henry III], m. 4d. At the end of the Short Cross period, in the spring of 1246, the abbot chose personally to present Adam Absolon and William the Cleric (*sic*), son of William, as keepers of the dies (PRO, E 368/17 [LTR 30 Henry III], m. 6).

124 *CPR 1216–1225*, p. 366 (cited by Lawrence 1915b, p. 74).

125 *CPR 1216–1225*, pp. 405–6.

126 Fryde, Greenaway, Porter and Roy 1986, p. 38.

127 Payments are mentioned as follows: *RLC*, I, p. 554 (Easter 1223); *RLC*, II, p. 5b (Easter and Michaelmas 1224), p. 42 (Easter 1225), p. 68 (Michaelmas 1225) and p. 109 (Easter 1226); *CLR 1226–1240*, p. 4 (Michaelmas 1226), p. 29 (Easter 1227), p. 77 (Easter 1228), p. 113 (Michaelmas 1228), p. 126 (Easter 1229) and p. 148 (Michaelmas 1229).

128 *CR 1227–1231*, p. 299.

the arrangement to run on because even if a pair of dies, with careful use, was capable of producing 48,000 pence,[129] £20 per annum would have represented the profit from four dies calculated at 6*d*. in every £1 minted.[130] This estimate also ignores any advantage from the abbey's access to the dies for its own purposes. An enquiry, recorded in the Liber Albus at Bury,[131] probably dates from the period of the agreement, because otherwise the answers to a number of queries raised make no sense for a franchisal mint.

Although the replacement of Willelm by Norman at the end of 1217 is implied by the amendment of the Lord Treasurer's Remembrancer's Memoranda Roll, there is no clear evidence of when Norman was replaced as moneyer at Bury by Simund. This is particularly unfortunate because, as has been seen, of the 19 obverse dies known to be associated with reverses of Norman only two are of class VIIb. The date on which he vacated office could accordingly have been very helpful in fixing the introduction of class VIIb.

It has been seen that in classes VI and VIIa, up to the replacement of Willelm by Norman, the mint was particularly active, with 19 obverse dies in use over a period of about 33 months from April 1215 to December 1217, giving an average usage of about one die every 7 or 8 weeks, or approaching 7 dies a year. If the mint had maintained this level of activity under Norman his term would have lasted for a similar period, since he is also known to have used 19 obverse dies. This would have resulted in his leaving office in the autumn of 1220. The Rolls, however, record him as still in office at the end of September 1221.[132] There are also other pointers now to be considered, suggesting he may well have continued as moneyer for some time thereafter.

If class VII ended as is generally thought in 1242, its life span from the appointment of Norman was about twenty-five years. During this period it is estimated that about 100 obverse dies were used (19 by Norman, at least 60 by Simund and 20 by Ioan, respectively). Table 38 summarises this data and shows the number of dies of class VII and a calculation of equivalent dies for the three moneyers, with classes VIIb and c subdivided according to North's classification.[133]

129 Allen 2004b, superseding earlier work by Stewart 1964 and Mate 1969, calculates an average of 33,383 coins to have been to have struck from each obverse die at the London and Canterbury mints in the reign of Edward I, and 22,030–35,040 coins from each obverse die at six other mints in 1300. Tatler 1998, p. 73, in contrast, estimated that de Hadeleie may have struck an average of 64,000 coins per set of one obverse and two reverse dies at Bury early in the new coinage of Edward I. Reverse dies generally had a shorter life span than obverses, owing to being struck directly by the hammer. Accordingly, the useful life of an obverse die at Bury would have been limited by being issued with a single reverse in the Short and Long Cross periods.

130 *The De Moneta of Nicholas Oresme*, p. 51, from the *Red Book of the Exchequer*, fol. 246.

131 BL Harl. MS 1005, fol. 215. For text see *Monasticon*, III, p. 164. Allen 2001b, p. 115, associates the enquiry with the revival of the mint in 1215.

132 PRO, E 368/4 [LTR 6 Henry III], m. 4d.

133 North 1988, pp. 29–32.

Table 38. Obverse and equivalent dies in Short Cross class VII

Class	*Moneyer*	*No. of obverse dies*		*No. of equivalent dies*
VIIa	Norman	17		17
VIIbA		1		1
B		1		1
VIIbB	Simund	23		
C		12	47	52
D		12		
VIIcA		3	8	8
B		5		
VIIcB	Ioan	13	16	20
C		3		

The obverse die estimates in Table 38 would produce an average level of activity of one die within every quarter over the twenty-five year period. Such activity is markedly less than that of Rauf and Willelm, but the average could cloak interspersed periods of activity and inactivity. A fall or cessation in output at Bury might be expected at two periods after the appointment of Norman: during the moves towards central control between 1218 and 1223 and/or immediately thereafter, and during the term of the agreement with the king from 1223 to late 1229. Understanding the level of output at Bury between those years would be greatly helped if dates could be confidently given for the replacement of class VIIa by VIIbA and VIIbA by VIIbB. For the latter, the career of the moneyer William the Tailor at Canterbury is helpful because he succeeded the deceased Simon Chiche in April 1230,[134] and his first known coins are of class VIIbB.[135] So VIIbB would appear to have superceded VIIbA no later than that date. The replacement of VIIa by VIIbA is more problematical, and the circumstantial evidence provided by Bury itself is ambiguous.

The most widely held view is that VIIbA was introduced in *c.* 1222.[136] This is founded on the replacement of the moneyer Eudo Chic at Canterbury by Ioan Chic in 1221/2. Protagonists for this date equate the name Eudo with that of (H)iun on the coins, and point to both (H)iun and Ioan as having struck in class VIIb1.[137] The identification is, however, insecure and it is not certain that Ioan Chic began minting straight away. Turning to Bury, if class VIIbA originated in 1222, possibly all except Norman's last die (VIIbB) would have been used by 1223 when the agreement with the king came into force. This gives rise to two concerns: is it likely that he would have been so active, including having access to the cluster of VIIa dies at a time when St Edmunds was clearly having great difficulty in defending its very rights to coinage before the king's centralizing

134 PRO, E 368/11 [LTR 14 Henry III], m. 5, 6, 9d; *CR 1227–1231*, p. 350.

135 North 1988, p. 34.

136 North 1988, p. 33 (*c.* 1222–8) and Allen 2001a, p. 12 (1222–*c.* 1229).

137 Allen 2001a, pp. 9–10 and n. 54.

officials? And is it likely that only one (or possibly two) dies were used during the six year span of the agreement with the king?

It is clear from the terms of the agreement itself that St Edmunds had exacted a concession from the king that the abbey should have use of the dies for its own purposes. It would be surprising if they had not availed themselves of it. It does not follow, of course, that the royal officials themselves had any intention to exercise both minting and exchanging activities at Bury. Or possibly they may have originally had the intention to do so, but quickly realized that it would be more convenient and cost-effective to have any local needs for coin supplied from London for issue through the exchange at Bury. The Pipe Roll for 1227/8 records that between 25 March and 7 July 1226 a royal profit of £9 8*s.* 0*d.* arose from the Bury exchange,[138] under the joint keepership of Alexander of Dorset and Henry of St Albans.[139] It is perhaps more likely that Norman's cluster of dies represent a batch issued to Bury after the agreement had come into force. The subsequent return to supplying dies in single pairs would then have been to satisfy St Edmunds entitlement once minting at Bury under royal control had been abandoned. Under this hypothesis, class VIIa would have continued well beyond 1223. Indeed, Glen Gittoes, from unpublished die usage figures at Canterbury, has estimated that VIIa dies could have been employed there until at least 1226.[140]

The foregoing provides a logical argument for Norman having been relatively active at Bury during the term of the agreement with the king. But it also gives rise to a disturbing consequence. The cluster of dies includes one obverse (A) of the 'Hapsburg' chin type, associated with Willelm's coins. It must, therefore, have been engraved and issued shortly after Norman came into office at the end of 1217. This circumstance can only be reconciled to the cluster post-dating the agreement if Norman had retained dies Aa(b) during the wrangles between 1218 and 1222, and combined them with the remaining dies in the cluster (BCE, (b)cde) when they were issued to him in 1223.

A further theoretical possibility is that any dies used at Bury between 1223 and 1229 were inscribed with the London (or Canterbury) mint signature with any resulting coins not being identifiable. Such an arrangement, however, is scarcely credible, not least because it would have struck at the root of the abbot's customary claim to strike his own coinage at Bury.

In conclusion, although it cannot be claimed that the case for class VIIa having ended in 1221/2 has been refuted, considerable evidence can be adduced to support its continuation beyond the early 1220s. Further die studies by Gittoes reveal a ratio of Bury to London and Canterbury obverse dies in class VIIbA of 1:250 +, compared with 1:8 + in class VIIbB. Although the latter ratio implies a

138 PRO, E 372/72 [Pipe Roll 12 Henry III], m. 10.

139 *RLC*, II, p. 128.

140 Personal communication.

far higher contribution to the coinage than might be expected from Bury at any period, the former ratio clearly reflects low levels of activity at Bury during the period of the agreement with the king.

Returning to the design features of class VII, North first identified coins with realistic but 'broken' eyes[141] as preceding those with annulet eyes.[142] He also noted that the earliest of such coins (class VIIbB) bore a pellet on the chin – a feature confirmed by the second set of class VIIb dies of Norman – sometimes associated with pellets in the curls.[143] Since the coin of Norman referred to does not contain pellets in the curls, and dies also survive from Bury with pellets in the curls but not on the chin,[144] the evolution of the type may have been as follows:

VIIbB1 pellet on chin
VIIbB2 pellets on chin and in curls
VIIbB3 pellets in curls

Otherwise the presence or absence of pellets in the curls cannot have a chronological significance. The dies of Simund have been classified according to this sequence (Catalogue 157–177), but there remain two pairs of Bury dies which are distinctive (Catalogue 155–156). They portray a plumpish, square face with pellets on the chin and in the curls which are, unusually, two in number on either side of the bust instead of three. This group has been designated VIIbBx, and should possibly be placed between VIIbB1 and 2, owing to its affinity with the last obverse catalogued under VIIbB1, apparently without pellets in the curls.

The variety designated by North as VIIbC has no pellets on the chin or in the curls. It is clearly followed by a variety with similar lettering but annulet eyes, designated by North as VIIbD. No dating can safely be given to VIIbC[145] or VIIbD, but the latter must have been in issue when the Canterbury moneyer Robert of Canterbury succeeded the deceased Thomas of Valentina in November 1235,[146] since North has identified coins of both moneyers in class VIIbD.[147]

Class VIIc has been divided into three main varieties which appear to be chronological: VIIcA with annulet eyes and (unlike VIIbD) large lettering, VIIcB with large lettering and a distinctive oblong bust, and VIIcC approaching the crude workmanship of class VIII. Again no dating can safely be given to these varieties. The earliest type (VIIcA) is, however, known of the moneyer Ioan Turte at

141 Designated as class 7bB or C; see North 1988, pp. 27, 30.
142 Designated as class 7bD; see North 1988, pp. 27, 30.
143 North 1988, pp. 27, 30.
144 Catalogue 154 and 174–177.
145 North 1998, p. 34.
146 *CR 1234–1237*, p. 144; PRO, E 159/14 [KR 19 Henry III], m. 5; *CR 1234–1237*, p. 270.
147 North 1988, pp. 32, 34.

Canterbury who was dead by 5 March 1237, and was thus possibly in issue at that date.[148] Coins of VIIcB are also known of Ioan FR (Fitz Robert) at Canterbury, who is recorded as having been succeeded by Edward Fitz Odo of Westminster by 14 February 1241.[149] It was during this variety that Simund was replaced at Bury by Ioan, showing that his tenure continued long after the farm of the mint had come to an end. Finally, as will be seen below, class VIIc (and hence VIIcC) appears to have come to an end in 1242. In summary, therefore, the following dates can be pencilled in:

VIIa	ended in *c.* 1222 or later
VIIbA	ended 1223 or later
VIIbB	continued until at least April 1230
VIIbC	?
VIIbD	in issue November 1235
VIIcA	in issue 5 March 1237
VIIcB	in issue 1240/1
VIIcC	ended in 1242

Table 39 summarises the pairs of dies known of Simund and Ioan in greater detail than Table 38. Each obverse is found with a single and unique reverse die, except possibly reverse x in class VIIcA (Catalogue 202A).

Table 39. Classification of known pairs of dies of Simund and Ioan

Moneyer	*Class*	*No. of dies*	*No. of coins*	*No. of singletons*
Simund				
	VIIbBx	2	9	–
	VIIbB1	7	31	2
	VIIbB2	10	52	–
	VIIbB3	4	11	2
	VIIbC	12	35	4
	VIIbD	12	45	6
	VIIcA	3	19	–
	VIIcB	5	15	1
		55	217	15
Ioan				
	VIIcB	13	24	6
	VIIcC	3	5	1
		16	29	7

148 *CR 1234–1237*, p. 421; see also n. 155 below.

149 *CPR 1232–1247*, p. 245.

The surviving coins of Simund are not as completely representative of the number of dies used as those of Norman. As shown in Table 38, using the figures set out in Table 39, it would seem that at least five sets of dies are missing. This is possibly because coins of class VIIb in particular, being less distinctive and variable than other Short Cross classes, have not received the same attention or found their way so readily into notable public and private collections. The length of Simund's tenure at Bury, possibly as much as eighteen years, is also numismatically unfortunate. It limits the possibility of identifying the evolution of class VII at Bury from changes in moneyer. It also provides no help in interpreting the features of individual dies in a series represented by so many badly struck and/or worn coins. The coins of Simund's successor, Ioan, suffer the same physical defects and are also scarcer.

To conclude this section Table 40 shows the mint readings found in class VII. There is notably less variation than in classes V, VI and VIII. This reflects the greater standardisation of design found in class VII.

Table 40. Bury mint readings in Short Cross class VII

Class	*Moneyer*	*Mint reading (no. of dies)*					
		SANT	*SAN*	*SA*	*SANTE*	*SAT*	*Uncertain*
VIIa	Willelm	4	2				
VIIa	Norman	7	11*				
VIIbA				1			
VIIbB			1				
VIIbB	Simund	16	1		4	1	1
VIIbC		10	1		1		
VIIbD		9	1		1?		1
VIIcA		3					
VIIcB		4					1
VIIcB	Ioan				11+1?		1
VIIcC		1			2		
Total		54	17	1	<20	1	4

Note
* Including one die reading CAN.

Short Cross coinage at Bury (1242–1247)

Traditionally the introduction of Short Cross class VIII has been placed at or soon after 1242, when Nicholas of St Albans was 'appointed to some high office'[150] or, as another writer put it, received 'an exceptional

150 Lawrence 1915b, p. 75.

appointment'[151] resulting in his becoming sole moneyer at both London and Canterbury. Both writers were aware, however, that coins of class VIII existed from moneyers other than Nicholas at Canterbury and, questionably, at London.[152]

The career of Nicholas was in fact very complex, making it difficult to associate the change of type with a particular and, as it seems, curiously nebulous event. As early as 30 June 1237 he swore fealty to the barons of the exchequer for keeping the mints of London and Canterbury.[153] He was required to pay 15 marks (£10) yearly in compensation to William the Tailor and Robert of Canterbury, who had become moneyers in 1230 and 1235 respectively.[154] At the time of Nicholas' appointment four dies from Canterbury and nine from London were returned to the exchequer.[155] From this moment his name (as Nichole) began to appear on coins from both mints, and by the end of class VII he had become sole moneyer at London.[156] Later, in November 1240, he was summoned before the exchequer with his workmen and clients (Flemish merchants with their silver), presumably to answer some charge of irregularity.[157] The following January he was further accused of farming the mints of London and Canterbury without due authority.[158] He seems to have surmounted these difficulties, because in 1242 the founderies of the two mints were confirmed to him.[159]

The task of identifying the change of type to class VIII with the career of Nicholas may not only be impossible but also inappropriate. There is no evidence that he had any control over the production of dies or supervised the replacement of existing coin in circulation by the coin he produced. It is far more logical to expect a change of type to have resulted from a change in the person responsible for cutting the dies under the authority of the Fitz Otto family. In fact Richard Abel was presented as a die cutter in 1242,[160] showing that earlier writers had probably lighted upon the correct date for introduction of Class VIII, but for the wrong reason.

At Bury the moneyer Io(ha)n was active from late in class VII, throughout class VIII and in the early stages of the Long Cross coinage. His career enabled

151 Brooke 1950, p. 106.

152 Lawrence 1915b, pp. 93–5; Brooke 1950, p. 113. No coins are at present known of the London mint in class VIII other than in the name of Nichole (see Table 41).

153 PRO, E 159/15 [KR 20–21 Henry III], m. 24d.

154 See previous section.

155 Since North has not identified coins of Robert of Canterbury beyond class VIIcA it would appear to have been the type in issue when he left office on 30 June 1237.

156 North 1988, p. 34.

157 PRO, E 368/13 [LTR 1240], m. 3.

158 PRO, E 368/13 [LTR 1241], m. 4d.

159 *CR 1237–1242*, p. 421.

160 PRO, E 368/14 [LTR 1242], m. 4. This reasoning formed the basis of Brand's dating of class VIII to 1242 (see Brand 1964, p. 69).

Lawrence first to link the end of the Short Cross series and the beginning of the Long Cross.[161]

The generally accepted basic classification of class VIII was made by Elmore Jones in 1948,[162] according to which the activity of London, Canterbury and Bury may be summarised as follows:

Table 41. Mint and moneyer activity in Short Cross class VIII[163]

Class	*Mints*	*Moneyers*	*No.of known Bury dies*	*No. of known Bury coins (and singletons)*
VIIIa	London	Nichole	–	
VIIIb1	London	Nichole		
	Bury	Io(h)an	1	5(–)
VIIIb2	London	Nichole		
	Bury	Iohan	15	33(8)
	Canterbury	Nichole		
		Iohan		
		Willelm		
VIIIb3	London	Nichole		
	Bury	Iohan	9	14(6)
	Canterbury	Nichole		
		Iohan		
		Willelm		
Total			25	52(14)

Thus the reduction to three mints was matched by an unprecedented pruning of the authorised moneyers.

The number of singletons (dies represented by a single surviving specimen) shows clearly that our knowledge of the dies used at Bury in class VIII is somewhat incomplete. Twenty-five pairs of dies are listed in the Catalogue against an estimated usage of at least thirty-five sets. This difference is not surprising since the latest coins in the Short Cross series are less likely to have survived melting when the Long Cross issue was introduced than earlier coins in the series. The great Colchester and Eccles hoards were also concealed before class VIII came into use. Indeed, the knowledge we have from surviving coins arises substantially from

161 Lawrence 1915b, p. 76.

162 Elmore Jones 1945–8, pp. 286–90.

163 Mass 2001, pp. 58–62, following a comment by North 1988, p. 36, adopted a revised classification whereby VIIIa and VIIIb1 of Elmore Jones' classification became VIIIa1 and 2, and VIIIb2 and 3 became VIIIb and c respectively. The activity of the moneyers in Table 41 is derived from Mass (although his summary table on p. 64 is incorrect), but retains the Elmore Jones classification.

foreign hoards, where the coins were outside the net of recoinage. The implication from the estimated number of dies is that coinage at Bury surged markedly in the period 1242–7. There was also a similar increase in activity at London, but not Canterbury, as Table 42 shows:

Table 42. Mint output at Canterbury and London, 1237–1247[164]

	£'000s minted		
Period	*Canterbury*	*London*	*Total*
July 1237–Feb. 1242 (4 years 8 months)	133.2	81.2	214.4
Feb. 1242–Nov. 1247 (5 years 9 months)	126.9	153.4	280.3

To conclude this section, Table 43 shows the variant mint readings appearing on surviving coins of class VIII (see the Catalogue for details).

Table 43. Bury mint readings in Short Cross class VIII

	VIIIb1	*VIIIb2*	*VIIIb3*
SANTE	1		
[ ]E?		1	
SANT·ED		6	
SANT·ED		4	1
SAN[ ]ED		1	
SANT⁝ED		1	
SANTEED		1	
SANTED		1	
SANED (or SANTED)*			1
S]ANED			1
SANED			1
SAN·ED			1
SANE			1
SAN:E			1
SA[ ]			1
]ANED			1

Note
* 'N' retrograde.

164 Derived from Blunt and Brand 1970, Table 1.

Short Cross hoards[165]

Although a number of Short Cross hoards have come to light, including Eccles (1864) and Colchester (1902), between them containing some 15,000 specimens from class V onwards, the descriptive record is often insufficient for the purposes of a detailed mint study, and rarely provides information on dies. The available information on the Eccles and Colchester hoards, moreover, apart from coins which can be specifically identified as coming from these hoards, suffers the further disadvantage of having been classified according to Evans' system, which Lawrence subsequently amended and elaborated.[166] Frustratingly, nine well-recorded Short Cross hoards found in England between 1973 and 1991, containing 814 coins, yielded none struck at Bury.[167]

Despite these drawbacks, Tables 44–47 below summarise the number of coins found in ten lesser hoards by type, in total and identifiable to the mints of Bury,

Table 44. Short Cross hoard summaries: class V

Hoard[a]	*Classes present*	*Total coins*	*Total in class V*	*Bury*		*Canterbury*		*London*	
				No.[b]	*%*	*No.*	*%*	*No.*	*%*
York Minster (1829)	V–VII	71 (74)	16	–	–	5	31.3	11	68.7
Ribe I (1911)	I–VIII	1,169	192	2 (2)	1.0	26	13.5	103	53.6
Ribe II (1958)	II–VIII	165	25	–	–	9	36.0	9	36.0
Wrexham (1926)	I–VIII	67	6	–	–	2	33.3	3	50.0
Rotenfels (1936)	I–VII	107	32	–	–	7	21.9	16	50.0
Kilmaine (1946)	I–VII	231	41	–	–	10	24.4	21	51.2
Clifton (1947)	I–VII	61	26	–	–	4	15.0	13	50.0
Naxos (1969?)	I–VIII	1,293	178	2 (2)	1.1	35	19.7	92	51.7
Gisors (1970)	I–VIII	824	114	–	–	26	22.8	53	46.5
Leconfield (2000)	I–VIII	452	50	– (1)[c]	–	13	26.0	18	36.0
Total		4,440	680	4 (5)	–	137	20.1	339	49.9

Notes

(a) A Bury coin is also recorded ex Barnsley hoard (1856), Catalogue 85 (1).

(b) Figures in parentheses indicate the number of coins identified from the relevant hoard in the Catalogue.

(c) See Catalogue 87 (7) for the Bury cut halfpenny in the Leconfield hoard (2000).

165 The data included in Tables 44–49 are drawn from the following sources: York Minster: Brand and Dolley 1963; Ribe I (1911) and II (1958): Stewart and Brand 1971; Wrexham: Lewis 1970 and Boon 1986, pp. 105–9; Rotenfels: Gittoes and Mayhew 1983; Kilmaine: Kenny 1989–90; Clifton: Carson 1947; Naxos: Stewartby 1994; Gisors: Dumas and Brand 1971; Leconfield: *NC* (2002), Coin Hoards, p. 254 (no. 81), and personal communication with Dr Barrie Cook; Eccles: Vaux 1865, Stewartby 1993 and Sir John Evans MS in Ashmolean Museum, Oxford; 'France': Lawrence 1897; Colchester (1902): Grueber 1903. A comprehensive listing of Short Cross hoards is made by Allen 2001c.

166 Lawrence 1915b, pp. 62–6.

167 Archibald and Cook 2001, pp. 17–52.

Table 45. Short Cross hoard summaries: class VI

Hoard[a]	*Classes present*	*Total coins*	*Total in class VI*	*Bury*		*Canterbury*		*London*	
				No.[b]	*%*	*No.*	*%*	*No.*	*%*
York Minster (1829)	V–VII	71 (74)	10	–	–	2	20.0	8	80.0
Ribe I (1911)	I–VIII	1,169	84	1 (1)	1.2	27	32.1	56	66.7
Ribe II (1958)	II–VIII	165	16	1 (1)	6.3	4	25.0	11	68.8
Wrexham (1926)	I–VIII	67	1	–	–	1	100.0	–	–
Rotenfels (1936)	I–VII	107	31	2 (2)	6.5	6	19.4	22	71.0
Kilmaine (1946)	I–VII	231	36	3 (3)	8.3	8	22.2	24	66.6
Clifton (1947)	I–VII	61	11	1	9.1	2	18.2	8	72.7
Naxos (1969?)	I–VIII	1,293	112	4 (3)	3.6	16	14.3	91	81.2
Gisors (1970)	I–VIII	824	92	1 (1)	1.1	20	21.7	71	77.2
Leconfield (2000)	I–VIII	452	37	–	–	2	5.4	35	94.6
Total		4,440	430	13 (11)	3.0	88	20.5	326	75.8

Notes

(a) One coin also recorded ex Tiree hoard (1787), Catalogue 114 (3).

(b) Figures in parentheses indicate the number of coins identified from the relevant hoard in the Catalogue.

Table 46. Short Cross hoard summaries: class VII

Hoard[a]	*Classes present*	*Total coins*	*Total in class VII*	*Bury*		*Canterbury*		*London*	
				No.[b]	*%*	*No.*	*%*	*No.*	*%*
York Minster (1829)	V–VII	71 (74)	37	1 (1)	2.7	18	48.6	18	48.6
Ribe I (1911)	I–VIII	1,169	810	35 (35)	4.3	467	57.7	307	38.0
Ribe II (1958)	II–VIII	165	96	4 (3)	4.2	52	54.2	40	42.0
Wrexham (1926)	I–VIII	67	51	4 (5)	7.8	19	37.3	24	47.1
Rotenfels (1936)	I–VII	107	7	1 (1)	14.3	4	57.1	2	28.6
Kilmaine (1946)	I–VII	231	115	9 (9)	7.8	59	51.3	47	40.9
Clifton (1947)	I–VII	61	8	–	–	5	62.5	3	37.5
Naxos (1969?)	I–VIII	1,293	672	33 (12)	4.9	377	56.0	257	38.4
Gisors (1970)	I–VIII	824	503	27 (7)	5.4	261	51.9	200	39.8
Leconfield (2000)	I–VIII	452	219	8 (7)	3.7	124	56.6	84	38.4
Total		4,440	2,518	122 (90)	4.8	1,386	55.0	982	39.0

Notes

(a) Bury coins also recorded in the Montpellier hoard (1934) (one coin) and Tiree hoard (1787) (one coin); Catalogue 139 (9), 147 (6).

(b) Figures in parentheses indicate the number of coins identified from the relevant hoard in the Catalogue.

Table 47. Short Cross hoard summaries: class VIII

Hoard	*Classes present*	*Total coins*	*Total in class VIII*	*Bury*		*Canterbury*		*London*	
				No.[a]	*%*	*No.*	*%*	*No.*	*%*
Ribe I (1911)	I–VIII	1,169	49	1 (1)	2.0	19	38.8	28	57.1
Ribe II (1958)	II–VIII	165	25	–	–	11	44.0	14	56.0
Wrexham (1926)	I–VIII	67	1	–	–	1	100.0	–	–
Naxos (1969?)	I–VIII	1,293	274	16 (17)[b]	5.8	106	38.7	141	51.5
Gisors (1970)	I–VIII	824	31	1 (1)	3.2	16	51.6	11	35.5
Leconfield (2000)	I–VIII	452	119	5 (3)	4.2	42	35.4	72	60.5
Total		3,970	499	23 (22)	4.6	195	39.1	266	53.3

Notes

(a) Figures in parentheses indicate the number of coins identified from the relevant hoards in the Catalogue.

(b) The number of Bury coins actually described as ex Naxos exceeds the total listed by Stewartby 1994.

Table 48. Short Cross hoard summaries: Evans classes III and IV

Hoard(s)	*Total coins*	*Bury*		*Canterbury*		*London*	
		No.	*%*	*No.*	*%*	*No.*	*%*
Eccles (1864)	2,503	45[a]	1.8	513	20.5	1,506	60.2
France (1897)	181	4	2.2	54	29.8	103	56.9
Colchester (1902)	3,153	55	1.7	745	23.6	1,818	57.7
Total	5,837	104	1.8	1,312	22.5	3,427	58.7
Other hoards (Tables 44–5)[b]	1,110	17	1.5	225	20.3	665	59.9

Notes

(a) Excluding BM acquisitions: Evans + BM = Fulke 16 + 5; Rauf 29 + 4.

(b) Evans classes III and IV together correspond with Lawrence classes V and VI.

Table 49. Short Cross hoard summaries: Evans class V

Hoard(s)	*Total coins*	*Bury*		*Canterbury*		*London*	
		No.	*%*	*No.*	*%*	*No.*	*%*
Eccles (1864)	2,729	142[a]	5.2	1,663	60.9	920	33.7
France (1897)	327	24	7.3	156	47.7	147	45.0
Colchester (1902)	6,173	402	6.5	3,085	50.0	2,685	43.5
Total	9,229	568	6.2	4,904	53.1	3,752	40.7
Other hoards (Tables 44–5)	2,518	122	4.8	1,386	55.0	982	39.0

Notes

(a) Excluding BM acquisitions: Evans + BM = 142 + 7.

(b) Evans class V corresponds with Lawrence class VII.

Canterbury and London. Tables 48–49 group the information from these hoards according to the Evans classification, to see how far the results are comparable with the recorded details of the Eccles, Colchester and 'France' (1897) hoards. The percentage representation of each of the three mints will be seen to be broadly comparable between the two groups of hoards.

The ratio of the outputs at Canterbury and London (45:55), derived from the figures quoted in Table 42 between February 1242 and November 1247, is close to the ratio of surviving coins in class VIII for those mints (42:58), as summarized in Table 47. Since the Table suggests that Bury may have approached 5 per cent of class VIII output, it could be inferred that Bury minted coin to the value of about £13,500 in the period from 1242 to 1247. Although the Bury sample is very small (23 coins), it happens to correspond closely to the percentage calculated in Table 46 for class VII from the larger sample of 122 Bury coins.

It would be valuable if this sum could be married to estimated die usage to produce an average output for each pair of dies at Bury in this period. However, whilst the time-span (1242–7) embraces the whole of class VIII, it probably also takes in class VIIcC and possibly the very latest dies of VIIcB.[168] A total of 28 pairs of dies are recorded in the Catalogue for classes VIIcC and VIII, giving an 'equivalent' die calculation of 39. This, in turn, would result in an incredible average output of £360 or 86,400 pence from each pair of dies. Applying a more sophisticated formula (Formula (3)) and '95% confidence limits' calculations to the known coins, Stewart Lyon has kindly provided the theoretical range of output set out in Table 50:[169]

Table 50. Theoretical output (pence) per set of dies

Confidence limit	*No. of dies*	*Output*		
		£8,000	*£14,000*	*£21,000*
Lower	37	52,000	91,000	136,000
Mid	46	42,000	73,000	110,000
Upper	60	32,000	56,000	84,000

The mid-point in the range at 73,000 pence is still far higher than would be expected. This suggests in particular that a participation by Bury to overall output of 5 per cent may be unsustainable and that, possibly, some class VIIcB dies may have contributed to its output between 1242 and 1247. Because the class VIII coins in Table 47 derive almost totally from foreign hoards it cannot be argued that the Bury percentage may have been exaggerated by a smaller proportion of coins finding their way abroad than from Canterbury and London.

168 Allen 2001a, p. 12.

169 Private correspondence. See also Lyon 1989, pp. 5, 7. The raw data for Table 50 is drawn from the Catalogue, classes VIIcC and VIII (222–249).

The non-English element in all of the hoards dealt with in Tables 44–47, other than Rotenfels, was insignificant compared with the Short Cross coins present. This is as true of the seven hoards found outside England as of those found within, illustrating the ready acceptance enjoyed by English coins outside their country of origin at this period.

CHAPTER 9

LONG CROSS COINAGE

Introduction

The *Chronicle of Bury St Edmunds* records both the beginning of the Long Cross coinage in 1247[1] and its replacement in 1279.[2] For the new design the limbs of the cross were extended to the circumference of the coin to discourage the fraudulent practice of clipping silver from the edge, an offence frequently levelled at Jews.[3] This was a simpler and thus more common practice than forgery.[4] The new design failed in its objective in that clipping was not eliminated,[5] and the incidence of forgery appears to have increased.[6] The end of the Long Cross series has been taken as the culmination of this Chapter rather than the end of Henry III's reign in 1272 since it is not certain which late variety of the Long Cross coinage was in issue when Henry III died.[7]

The abbey to 1279

Shortly after introduction of the new coinage, on 19 June 1248, Abbot Henry died,[8] and the king appointed Robert Passelew as keeper of the abbey during the vacancy.[9] He was instructed to pay for the funeral expenses out of the profits he accrued,[10] and to meet bequests of 100 and 40 shillings, using the silver of an alms dish forwarded to the king.[11] This detail suggests that the dish was sent to London for melting down because the mint was no longer operating. The sub-sacrist,[12] Edmund of Walpole, a doctor of laws but a monk of less than two years' standing,[13]

1 *The Chronicle of Bury St Edmunds*, p. 14.
2 *The Chronicle of Bury St Edmunds*, p. 70.
3 *The Chronicle of Bury St Edmunds*, p. 67 (*s. a.* 1279); Lawrence 1912, p. 145.
4 In the Close Rolls during the two years to the end of 1247 there is one reference to forgery (*CR 1242–1247*, p. 464), but five to clipping, the first of which involved Jews (*CR 1242–1247*, pp. 433, 541, 545; *CR 1247–1251*, pp. 8–9, 102).
5 *CR 1247–1251*, pp. 63; *CLR 1245–1251*, p. 168; *CR 1247–1251*, p. 298; *CPR 1247–1258*, p. 114.
6 *CR 1247–1251*, p. 61; *CLR 1245–1251*, p. 219; *CR 1247–1251*, pp. 268–9; *CPR 1247–1258*, p. 114.
7 Lawrence 1912, pp. 167–8; Fox and Fox 1910, p. 94.
8 *The Chronicle of Bury St Edmunds*, p. 15; Battely 1745, p. 96.
9 *CR 1247–1251*, p. 64.
10 *CLR 1245–1251*, p. 191.
11 *CLR 1245–1251*, p. 200.
12 *CR 1247–1251*, p. 101.
13 Battely 1745, p. 96. In *Monasticon*, III, p. 106, n. 'b', it is stated without authority that Edmund was admitted as a monk on 20 November 1245. Like Henry of Rushbrook before him he appears to have been an East Anglian by birth.

was elected by the convent to succeed Henry on 7 July and blessed by Hugh, bishop of Ely and formerly abbot of Bury, on 27 September 1248.[14] The king had already assented to the election, and on 17 September instructed Robert Passelew to step down.[15] As the requirement of the Fourth Lateran Council (1215) requiring abbots elect of exempt houses to present themselves for confirmation by the Pope was still not being rigorously enforced,[16] three monks were sent to Rome in Edmund's stead. After initial refusal Innocent IV approved the election against the liquidation of a papal debt of 800 marks (£533 6*s* 8*d*.) to a merchant.[17] The king had also obtained a bond from the prior and convent to the value of 600 marks (£400), payable in two instalments, to secure specified income arising during the vacancy.[18]

Edmund in turn died on 31 December 1256.[19] The king thereupon appointed Robert of Walerand as keeper,[20] but later allowed Robert's brother John to take his place.[21] They abused their position,[22] and John was instructed to return to the abbey silver vessels and cooking utensils belonging to the deceased abbot, as well as horses of the prior and sacrist, and a large cart (*longa caretta*) and carthorses which the sacrist claimed to be his by customary right. He was also instructed to keep the abbot's lands cultivated and sown and not to lay waste or sell his woodlands without the king's permission.[23] He had still failed to account for his keepership at Bury and elsewhere as late as 1260.[24]

On 8 January 1257 the king gave his licence to Roger, the almoner at Bury, and Robert, the chamberlain, for a new abbot to be appointed.[25]

Only six days later the monks elected their prior, Simon of Luton, to succeed Edmund.[26] On this occasion the messengers sent to the Pope would not suffice, and Simon himself was obliged to set out for Rome on 30 July, to be blessed

14 *The Chronicle of Bury St Edmunds*, p. 15; *Memorials*, III, p. 29.

15 *CR 1247–1251*, p. 87. Royal assent had been signified to the Pope on 14 July 1248 (*CPR 1247–1258*, p. 21).

16 Bury had become permanently exempt from all but visitations by papal legates *a latere* in the time of Samson (*Jocelin*, p. 83), a privilege also enjoyed by the other major houses of St Albans, St Augustine's Canterbury, Battle, Evesham, Malmesbury and Westminster (Knowles 1966, p. 591). Neither Richard de Insula (1229–34) nor Henry of Rusbrook (1234–48) had been required to present themselves at Rome; see *The Chronicle of Bury St Edmunds*, p. 21, n. 6.

17 Battely 1745, pp. 96–7.

18 *CPR 1247–1258*, p. 31.

19 *The Chronicle of Bury St Edmunds*, p. 21; *Memorials*, III, p. 30. *Monasticon*, III, p. 106, gives the death of Edmund as '11th kalends of January, 1256', namely 22 December.

20 *CR 1256–1259*, p. 43

21 *CLR 1251–1260*, p. 361; *CR 1259–1261*, p. 85.

22 *CPR 1258–1266*, p. 48.

23 *CR 1256–1259*, p. 118.

24 *CR 1259–1261*, pp. 85, 214.

25 *CPR 1247–1258*, p. 536.

26 *The Chronicle of Bury St Edmunds*, p. 21; *Memorials*, III, p. 30.

eventually by Alexander IV at Viterbo on 22 October 1257.[27] Entries in the Patent Rolls show that the king was presenting incumbents to churches otherwise in the gift of the abbot as late as 18 November 1257,[28] and on 6 December 1257 a direction was given to 'Robert de Walerand, or John his brother' to purchase a gold buckle worth 8 marks out of the profits of the vacancy, to be fastened to the feretory of St Edmund.[29] Restoration to the abbot of his temporalities, however, was confirmed by a writ addressed to the tenants of the abbey on 12 January 1258,[30] one year after the death of Edmund. Simon, in turn, presided over the abbey until his death on 9 April 1279.[31] His successor, John of Northwold, received his temporalities on the following 5 November,[32] by which time the Long Cross coinage was at an end.[33]

In 1255, towards the end of Edmund's abbacy, the scope of the Liberty of St Edmund and its relationship to the king's rights appears to have been challenged, perhaps prompted by the king's advisers. The barons of the exchequer were nevertheless instructed to respect the privileges claimed by the abbot provisionally until 14 October that year[34] and, owing to more pressing calls upon the king, further extensions were granted until 19 April 1260,[35] thus carrying uncertainty forward into the abbacy of Simon.

During this period the abbey encountered serious financial difficulties. On 9 March 1256 the abbot was authorised to tax the burgesses and freemen of Bury to relieve his debts.[36] At the end of 1259 the abbot and the prior and convent levied an aid from their tenants to discharge sums owing to various merchants,[37] and on 2 February 1260 the liabilities of the abbot and convent were assessed at 5,000 marks (£3,333 6*s.* 8*d.*) and divided equally between them.[38] In November of the same year the abbot and convent were authorised to levy a tallage on the

27 Battely 1745, p. 101; *The Chronicle of Bury St Edmunds*, pp. 21–2. The cost of confirmation is given in Arundel MS 30 (used by Gransden, see *The Chronicle of Bury St Edmunds*, p. xlv) as '*duobus milibus sterlingorum*' which Gransden translates as '£2,000 sterling'. Strictly it should be 2,000 pennies, hardly a noteworthy sum. In BL Cotton MS Julius Ai the word '*marcarum*' appears after '*milibus*'; a reference to 2,000 marks (£666 13s. 4d.) may thus have been intended. The costs incurred by his successor, John of Northwold, in 1279 were 1,675 marks ten shillings and nine pence (*The Chronicle of Bury St Edmunds*, p. 70).

28 *CPR 1247–1258*, pp. 602, 604, 606.

29 *CLR 1251–1260*, p. 412.

30 *CPR 1247–1258*, p. 612.

31 *The Chronicle of Bury St Edmunds*, p. 68.

32 *CPR 1272–1281*, p. 331.

33 Fox and Fox 1910, p. 100.

34 *CR 1254–1256*, p. 83. Minting rights were also provisionally reaffirmed (see PRO, E 368/30 [LTR 38–39 Henry III], m. 16).

35 *CR 1254–1256*, p. 257 (to 1 May 1256); *CR 1254–1256*, p. 289 (from 1 May 1256 to 26 June 1256); *CR 1256–1259*, p. 204 (to 29 September 1258); *CR 1259–1261*, pp. 137–8 (to 19 April 1260).

36 *CPR 1247–1258*, p. 465.

37 *CPR 1258–1266*, p. 109.

38 *The Chronicle of Bury St Edmunds*, p. 25.

burgesses and tenants of Bury to relieve indebtedness, occasioned by 'pleas and manifold persecutions'.[39] These exactions were obviously damaging to relations between St Edmunds and the townspeople and tenants called upon to meet them. On top of these difficulties and the expense of Simon's investiture, the burden of taxation upon St Edmunds itself must also have added to the abbey's distress. The *Chronicle of Bury St Edmunds* becomes increasingly absorbed from 1253 onwards with taxation imposed on the abbot and convent, in the form of aids,[40] tenths[41] and scutages.[42]

These demands, at a time of financial crisis for the abbey, must have helped turn the sympathies of St Edmunds away from the king and towards his baronial opponents. The tone of the *Chronicle of Bury St Edmunds*, in common with most monastic records of the time, reveals the critical attitude of the convent towards the king.[43] How far the abbot was of a different view is hard to judge. His relationship as an ecclesiastical tenant-in-chief of the king placed him in a delicate position and Gransden has argued that Simon of Luton, who was in office at the height of the baronial opposition, was a royalist.[44] This, as will be seen below, did not save him on occasion from the king's displeasure. Although the basic sympathy of the abbot and majority of monks may have been at variance, the difference was not over kingship but the way it was exercised.[45] Moreover, the attitude of both parties was not static in the swell of unfolding events, as witnessed by the evidence about to be discussed.

Support by St Edmunds for Simon de Montfort and his cause may have been the main reason for Henry's move, on 7 March 1262, to take the Liberty into his own hands and appoint Robert of Fulham as keeper 'in levying the king's debts *as in other things*'.[46] Unsurprisingly, the ascendancy of the baronial party after the Battle of Lewes on 14 May 1264[47] did not lead to restoration of the Liberty. In spite of St Edmunds being 'at that time . . . exceedingly precious in the eyes

39 *CPR 1258–1266*, pp. 129–30. On 8 November 1259 a dispute with Richard, earl of Gloucester, over lands at Mildenhall and other matters had been settled after more than nine years (*The Chronicle of Bury St Edmunds*, p. 24).

40 *The Chronicle of Bury St Edmunds*, p. 18.

41 *The Chronicle of Bury St Edmunds*, pp. 18, 20; *CPR 1247–1258*, p. 516, recording an assessment of 700 marks (£466 13s. 4d.) imposed on Bury.

42 *The Chronicle of Bury St Edmunds*, p. 24; the scutage in 1258 being levied at the rate of 40 shillings.

43 Gransden 1991a, p. 74.

44 Gransden 1991a, p. 75.

45 Gransden 1991a, p. 86.

46 *CPR 1258–1266*, p. 204. The king's assertiveness appears to have originated from Urban IV's confirmation, on 25 February 1262, of the bull issued by his predecessor absolving Henry from his oath to observe the Provisions of Oxford (Powicke 1947, II, p. 427; Tout 1905, pp. 109–10). The abbey nevertheless seems to have received a temporary remission (*replegianda*) until the end of Easter that year (*CR 1261–1264*, p. 37), subsequently, on 3 November 1262, extended pending the king's return to England (*CR 1261–1264*, p. 163), which occurred on 20 December 1262 (Fryde, Greenaway, Porter and Roy 1986, p. 38).

47 *The Chronicle of Bury St Edmunds*, p. 28.

of the barons'[48] this had to wait until the king was once more a free agent, after defeat of the rebel barons at the Battle of Evesham on 4 August 1265.[49] Shortly afterwards, on 24 September, the king instructed that the abbot and convent be restored to their barony and possessions,[50] confirmed by remission of the king's rancour (and restoration of their coin die) on the 27 October.[51]

The troubles of the abbot, however, were not yet at an end. On 5 December an aid was authorised from the knights and freemen of the abbey to discharge debts arising during the Barons' War and (darkly) 'for other reasons of which the king is silent for the present'.[52] The innuendo behind these words is revealed the next day when a payment of 400 marks (£266 13*s.* 4*d.*) was recorded as due from the abbot to the king's wardrobe, to purchase his goodwill.[53] This was the abbot's share of an 800 mark fine imposed by the parliament at Winchester on 8 September 1265. The chronicler at Bury complained, somewhat speciously, that although the abbot alone had been accused of guarding the coasts against invasion threatened by the queen to rescue Henry from the hands of the barons, the fine was divided equally because both the abbot's and the convent's men had taken part.[54] This incident shows how difficult it is to characterize the attitude of the abbot towards the king's cause.

In the disturbances that continued after the death of Simon de Montfort the loyalty of the abbey clearly remained uncertain, at least in the eyes of the king. A number of Simon's supporters, the so-called Disinherited, had hidden away in Bury and used the town as a base for invading the adjoining marshes and Kings Lynn, and as an outlet for selling their spoils. However, at an enquiry held on behalf of the king by John de Warenne and William de Valence on 27 May 1266, the abbot and convent were absolved, and the burgesses were blamed for these irregularities.[55] Subsequently, on 2 August 1266, 'simple protection' was granted to the abbot and convent for one year, provided that they did not receive the king's enemies in the meantime.[56]

After the Disinherited had seized Norwich at the end of the year,[57] on 25 January following, Henry summoned to Bury those owing military service,[58] and arrived

48 *The Chronicle of Bury St Edmunds*, pp. 26–7. This passage clearly shows the sympathy of the abbey to the baronial cause and the belief that Henry was under the sway of his queen and alien advisers.

49 *The Chronicle of Bury St Edmunds*, p. 31.

50 *CR 1264–1268*, p. 134.

51 *CPR 1258–1266*, p. 471.

52 *CPR 1258–1266*, pp. 518–19.

53 *CPR 1258–1266*, p. 525.

54 *The Chronicle of Bury St Edmunds*, pp. 31–2.

55 *The Chronicle of Bury St Edmunds*, pp. 34–5. Payment on behalf of the burgesses of the resultant fine of 200 marks (£133 6s. 8d.) was accepted as not constituting a precedent (*CPR 1258–1266*, p. 604).

56 *CPR 1258–1266*, p. 634.

57 *The Chronicle of Bury St Edmunds*, p. 37.

58 *CPR 1266–1272*, p. 128. The bishop of Winchester, the abbot of Hyde and the abbot of Ramsey were excused to enable them to maintain peace in their own areas, and Richard Munfichet purchased a remission of service for 20 shillings (*CPR 1266–1272*, pp. 32–3, 128).

there himself on 6 February, followed by the legate Ottobuono who immediately excommunicated the rebels.[59] On 21 February and 9 March commissions were set up to investigate various robberies and trespasses committed during the civil commotion.[60] On 25 April the king appointed guardians to protect the Liberty against disturbers of the peace,[61] and the cause of the Disinherited was finally ended by their defeat at the hands of Edward, the king's son, in the Isle of Ely on 11 July 1267.[62]

During this period the abbey was troubled both by growing restiveness amongst the townspeople and by attempts by the Friars Minor to establish themselves within the town. Briefly in 1264 a so-called Guild of Youth was established and, relying on the support of de Montfort's party, tried unsuccessfully to take over control of the town,[63] and in 1266 a dispute came to a head, decided in favour of the abbot, on whether he or the townsmen should appoint the aldermen and gatekeepers of the town.[64] The Friars Minor had first tried to enter Bury during the vacancy caused by the death of Edmund of Walpole, and after fluctuating fortunes,[65] were eventually in 1263 accommodated upon a plot of land at Babwell, just outside the town.[66]

The burden of taxation continued with a tenth being granted to the king for three years in 1266.[67] Two years later the abbey agreed, somewhat riskily, to be assessed by men of the bishop of Norwich rather than of the king, expecting a greater delay and possibly other advantages to ensue. The convent also paid 20 marks to the bishop's officials in the vain hope of avoiding the town being assessed.[68]

To relieve the financial difficulties oppressing him and his convent the abbot was given licence on 19 June 1268 to stay abroad with a moderate household until Christmas.[69] From the autumn of 1271 the abbot appears again to have been absent from England for many months but this time ostensibly for the

59 *The Chronicle of Bury St Edmunds*, p. 37.

60 *CPR 1266–1272*, pp. 45, 131. The Close Rolls have an entry requesting part payment of a fine of 200 marks for the abbot to have the king's goodwill (*CR 1264–1268*, p. 298) . The balance of this fine is noted in the Liberate Rolls on 27 February 1267 (*CLR 1260–1267*, p. 263). These entries show that the king still entertained real or pretended doubts about the loyalty of St Edmunds at this time.

61 *CPR 1266–1272*, p. 56.

62 *The Chronicle of Bury St Edmunds*, p. 39.

63 *The Pinchbeck Register*, I, pp. 53–7; Lobel 1935, pp. 126–9; Knowles 1948, p. 265. Gransden (*The Chronicle of Bury St Edmunds*, p. xxiv) suggests that the abbey may have pleaded loss of control over the townspeople to avoid responsibility for the activities of the Disinherited.

64 *CR 1264–1268*, p. 197; *The Chronicle of Bury St Edmunds*, p. xxiv.

65 *CPR 1247–1258*, p. 623; *CPR 1258–1266*, pp. 33, 50, 736; Battely 1745, pp. 101–13; *Monasticon*, III, p. 106; *Memorials*, II, pp. 263–85.

66 *Monasticon*, III, p. 106.

67 *The Chronicle of Bury St Edmunds*, p. 36.

68 *The Chronicle of Bury St Edmunds*, pp. 40–5; *CPR 1266–1272*, pp. 354, 410.

69 *CPR 1266–1272*, pp. 238–9.

purpose of pilgrimage rather than limiting his expenses.[70] One entry in the Calendar of Patent Rolls dated 25 October 1270, however, states that the abbey was void.[71] This is perplexing since Simon of Luton did not die until 1279 and there is no indication that he was even abroad late in 1270. It is also inconceivable that the abbot's financial problems would have been overcome if, during a stay overseas brought about by economic necessity, he had ceased to be entitled to the revenues flowing from his temporalities.

In spite of all its troubles, the impression remains that the underlying prosperity of St Edmunds and its eminent status remained intact in the latter years of Henry's reign. The king continued to visit the abbey,[72] and a parliament was held there early in 1267,[73] and again shortly before his death in 1272.[74] Henry instructed his agents to purchase many commodities at the town fairs including cloth,[75] furs,[76] cords,[77] napkins and towels,[78] wax[79] and spices,[80] and even horses.[81] The Rolls also record many and varied gifts by the king to the abbey including oaks for building and repair work,[82] gold coin and ornaments,[83] other donations of money,[84] tapers and wax,[85] buckles,[86] copes,[87] silver candlesticks,

70 *CPR 1266–1272*, p. 511 (approval dated 28 January 1271); *CPR 1266–1272*, pp. 574, 599 (from 10 September or 12 October 1271 to Easter 1272); *CPR 1266–1272*, pp. 642–3 (granting prolonged leave of absence until Midsummer 1272).

71 *CPR 1266–1272*, p. 469.

72 The following visits by Henry III to Bury are mentioned in the Rolls:
7–11 March 1248 (*CR 1247–1251*, pp. 33–4, 108–9; *CLR 1245–1251*, p. 171); 20 November 1248 (*CR 1247–1251*, p. 127); 14–17 March 1251 (*CR 1247–1251*, p. 423; *CLR 1245–1251*, p. 342; *CPR 1247–1258*, p. 90); 2–15 September 1252 (*CR 1251–1253*, pp. 153–7, 245–7, 249–56; *CLR 1251–1260*, pp. 69–71); 5–9 March 1256 (*CR 1254–1256*, pp. 284, 402; *CLR 1251–1260*, pp. 275–6; *CPR 1247–1258*, p. 465); 29 November – 3 December 1258 (*CR 1256–1259*, pp. 347, 349, 464; *CLR 1251–1260*, p. 442; *CPR 1258–1266*, p. 6); 6–21 February 1267 (*CR 1264–1268*, pp. 290–4, 360, 363–6; *CPR 1266–1272*, pp. 32–40, 129–30; *CLR 1260–1267*, pp. 260–2, 264); 2–10 September 1272 (*CR 1268–1272*, pp. 521–4, 570, 572; *CPR 1266–1272*, pp. 674–6). *The Chronicle of Bury St Edmunds*, p. 52, records the date of Henry's arrival as 1 September 1272.

73 *The Chronicle of Bury St Edmunds*, p. 37.

74 *The Chronicle of Bury St Edmunds*, p. 52.

75 *CLR 1245–1251*, pp. 261, 316, 331, 337, 340, 352, 385; *CLR 1251–1260*, pp. 2 ('gold-wrought'), 192, 438, 449; *CLR 1260–1267*, p. 20; *CPR 1258–1266*, pp. 251, 303, 304; *CLR 1260–1267*, pp.164, 206; *CLR 1267–1272*, p. 91 (no. 802).

76 *CLR 1245–1251*, p. 317; *CLR 1251–1260*, p. 58; *CLR 1260–1267*, p. 20; *CLR 1267–1272*, pp. 60 (no. 559), 91 (no. 802).

77 *CLR 1245–1251*, p. 317.

78 *CLR 1245–1251*, p. 316; *CLR 1251–1260*, p. 193.

79 *CLR 1260–1267*, p. 20; *CLR 1267–1272*, p. 60 (no. 559).

80 *CLR 1267–1272*, p. 60 (no. 559).

81 *CR 1242–1247*, p. 506; *CLR 1245–1251*, p. 113.

82 *CR 1247–1251*, pp. 311, 423; *CR 1254–1256*, p. 287.

83 *CLR 1240–1245*, p. 106 (gold cup); *CR 1251–1253*, pp. 427, 465; *CLR 1251–1260*, p. 428.

84 *CR 1247–1251*, p. 544; *CLR 1251–1260*, p. 275 (20 shillings to complete a picture in front of the high altar); *CR 1256–1259*, pp. 161–2.

85 *CLR 1245–1251*, p. 151; *CLR 1251–1260*, p. 68.

86 *CLR 1251–1260*, pp. 194, 412 (out of the profits of the abbey).

87 *CLR 1251–1260*, pp. 297, 337, 383.

cups and an altar front,[88] stags,[89] and a donation to the school at Bury.[90] The eminence of the abbey was in no way better demonstrated, however, than in its continued right to mint coins, a right enjoyed for much of the Long Cross period alone with London and Canterbury.

Long Cross coinage

No major advances in the study of the Long Cross series have been published since the important article by Lawrence, appearing in the *British Numismatic Journal* in three parts between 1912 and 1915.[91] For his work he had access to at least some of the rarer coins from the vast hoard auctioned in Brussels in October 1909. At the sale the dealer, A. H. Baldwin, purchased some 80,000 Long Cross pennies.[92] At the time of writing most of this enormous quantity of coins remains intact but as yet unpublished.[93] A smaller but highly important hoard found at Colchester in 1969 has been recorded in some depth in a British Museum Occasional Paper published in 2001.[94] Happily, for detailed future studies, a photographic record of the hoard was also made by the British Museum before those coins not selected for the national collection were dispersed.

Lawrence established the basic classification and sequence of the coins and, using information collected by Earle Fox (but again largely unpublished),[95] he suggested dates for some of the varieties he had identified. In his study the numismatic and documentary evidence from the mint at Bury was crucial.[96] A summary of Lawrence's findings is set out at Table 51, showing the main classes, the mints operating in each, the number of moneyers known to him and the readings (not dies) he had found. This information naturally cannot claim to represent a comprehensive cross-section of the Long Cross coinage. Nevertheless, it is likely to be sufficiently representative not to be significantly misleading. This conclusion is supported by Figure 10 below, where the histogram for the mint output at Canterbury and London is shown to correspond reasonably closely with that plotted from the reverse readings of those types reckoned to be in issue at the time. Table 51 illustrates clearly that:

88 *CLR 1245–1251*, pp. 343–4.

89 *CR 1261–1264*, p. 227. The other gifts, apart from this one, were made before the abbey became disaffected in the late 1250s. The king himself is not recorded as visiting the abbey between 1258 and 1267 (see n. 72 above).

90 *CR 1254–1256*, p. 46.

91 Lawrence 1912, 1913, 1915a. The earliest years of the new coinage have, however, been analysed in greater depth than Lawrence by three later writers: Wells 1934–7a; Brand 1971; and Davis 1977.

92 Information from P. D. Mitchell.

93 For progress towards publication, see p. 182 below.

94 See n. 158 below. A summary of the English content also appears in an editorial note to Clark *et al.* 1974, pp. 39–40.

95 Lawrence 1912, p. 146; Lawrence 1915a, p. 103.

96 Lawrence 1912, p. 163; Lawrence 1913, p. 89.

Table 51. Number of Long Cross moneyers and reverse readings recorded by Lawrence

Mint	*Class*[a] *I**[b]	*I*[c]	*II*	*III* *a*	*b*	*c*	*IV*	*V* *a*	*b*	*c*	*d*	*e*	*f*	*g*	*h*	*i*[d]	*VI*	*VII*
London	2	9	9^{2}	6^{2}	6^{3}	13^{4}	7^{4}	10^{4}	9^{4}	26^{7}	8^{6}	6^{5}	17^{6}	22^{8}	2^{1}	?		6^{2}
Canterbury		2	9^{3}	4^{3}	9^{3}	7^{3}	4^{4}	10^{4}	11^{4}	22^{6}	17^{5}	4^{3}	11^{6}	35^{8}	4^{3}	?		
Bury St Edmunds		1	3^{1}	2^{1}	2^{1}	3^{1}	1^{1}	7^{1}	2^{1}	2^{1}	1^{1}		1^{1}	3^{3}	2^{1}	1^{1}	1^{1}	2^{2}
Durham								1^{1}	2^{1}	1^{1}				1^{1}			1^{1}	
Sub-total (i)	2	12	21	12	17	23	12	28	24	51	26	10	29	61	8	?	2	8
Bristol				5^{4}	6^{5}	4^{4}												
Carlisle				3^{3}	6^{4}													
Exeter			4^{3}	4^{3}	8^{4}	3^{3}												
Gloucester			4^{4}	8^{4}	5^{4}	4^{4}												
Hereford				5^{4}	5^{4}	3^{3}												
Ilchester				3^{3}	3^{3}	3^{3}												
Lincoln			7^{4}	5^{4}	7^{4}	7^{4}												
Newcastle				6^{4}	5^{4}	4^{4}												
Northampton			12^{4}	12^{4}	10^{4}	4^{4}												
Norwich			1^{1}	9^{4}	8^{4}	3^{3}												
Oxford			5^{4}	6^{4}	7^{4}	4^{4}												
Shrewsbury				4^{2}	5^{4}	4^{4}												
Wallingford				3^{3}	3^{3}													
Wilton					6^{3}	4^{3}												
Winchester			7^{4}	6^{4}	6^{4}	7^{4}												
York			7^{4}	6^{4}	11^{5}	4^{4}												
Sub-total (ii)	–	–	47	85	101	58	–	–	–	–	–	–	–	–	–	–	–	–
Total (i) + (ii)	2	12	68	97	118	81	12	28	24	51	26	10	29	61	8	?	2	8

Notes:
(a) Number of reverse readings, with number of moneyers in superscript.
(b) No moneyer or mint names in class I*.
(c) No moneyer's name in class I.
(d) No details given by Lawrence for Canterbury and London in class Vi.

- Bury was only one of three mints operating virtually throughout the Long Cross period although its output, as a single-moneyer mint, was small;
- the complement of moneyers at each mint was kept low, with four being the most usual at the provincial mints;
- the provincial mints were only employed for the main thrust of the recoinage (classes II–IIIc);
- Winchester and York were restricted to a role in the recoinage alongside other provincial centres;
- activity at the three regular mints appears (as would be expected), after an initial dip, to have expanded following the closure of the provincial mints;
- the number of readings found in class Vg implies an upsurge in mint activity but, as set out below, may be partly explained by the type remaining in use for a number of years.

The most complete summary of refinements to Lawrence's classification is set out in the third edition of North's *English Hammered Coinage*, Volume I, incorporating unpublished work by Archibald and Davis.[97] This elaborated classification has been adopted in the Catalogue for the recording of the Long Cross dies bearing the Bury mint signature, with certain additions. First, Davis's subdivision of class IIIab, with its rounder face than IIIa, into IIIab1, with a straight-sided X, and IIIab2, with an ornamental X, has been applied. Secondly, Archibald's class IIIac, with a straight-sided X followed by a colon instead of a single pellet, included by North in his second edition,[98] but excluded from his third, has been adopted. Further subdivisions in class III could be suggested from variations in the treatment of the bust, although these may reflect the hand of different die cutters rather than chronological succession, and variations in the lettering – particularly R and S. As noted in the Catalogue, the Bury dies of class IIIb even appear to employ two forms of the letter R on the same obverse. Thirdly, in class Vc a new subdivision has been introduced in the Catalogue as Vc(x), for coins bearing the letter R with an upturned rather that wedge-shaped tail. Of the resulting classification only classes IVa, IVb, Va1, Vb1, all unique to London, and Ve have so far not come to light from Bury.

In Table 52 the numbers of reverse dies identified in the Long Cross period bearing the Bury mint signature are compared with the numbers of readings found by Lawrence. Details of the dies are set out in the Catalogue. From the Table it will be seen that Lawrence's readings represent approximately one third of the dies in use at Bury. The Long Cross coinage is, however, considered in greater detail in the next section with reference to mint activity at Bury. Although the mint gives valuable insights into the coinage, die linking is not available to trace subtle changes in the design of the coinage. This is because throughout the Long Cross period Bury was invariably issued with pairs of dies consisting of one obverse and one reverse, with new dies being supplied upon return of the old.

97 North 1994, pp. 225–7.

98 North 1980, p. 182.

Table 52. Bury Long Cross reverses: Lawrence readings and reverse dies known

Class	*No. of Lawrence reverse readings*	*No. of reverse dies identified*
I	1	1
II	3	5[a]
IIIa	2	9[b]
b	2	5[c]
c	3	17
IV	1	1[d]
Va	7	18[e]
b	2	10[f]
c	2	6
d	1	1
e	–	–
f	1	2
g	3	19
h	2	4
i	1	1
VI	1	1
VII	2	4
Total	34	104

Notes
(a) IIa + IIb.
(b) IIIa + IIIabl + IIIab2 + IIIac.
(c) IIIb + IIIbc.
(d) IVab.
(e) Va2 + Va3.
(f) Vb2.

Long Cross coinage at Bury

On 18 June 1247 the king's brother, Richard earl of Cornwall, was granted the right to issue a new coinage in the name of the king. The profits from the exchange, after meeting mint expenses, were to be shared equally by the two brothers and their heirs or assigns. The original grant was initially for five years.[99] On 27 July it was extended to seven years from 1 November 1247, in recognition of a loan from the earl to the king of 10,000 marks, with a proviso that if the king defaulted in his repayments or died the earl could recover his dues from the king's share in the profits.[100] Since the loan was to be used for the 'utility' of the realm, Oman must be correct that it constituted the resources of silver needed to start the recoinage.[101] The earl enjoyed the further concession

99 *CPR 1232–1247*, p. 503.

100 *CPR 1232–1247*, pp. 505 and 511, where the text is amended from seven to twelve. The following year this extension of the grant was formally recorded (*CPR 1247–1258*, p. 12).

101 Oman 1931, p. 145.

to receive back by tale the same quantity of new coin as he had used of old to prime the minting process before calculating the profit to be shared.[102]

St Edmunds must have been concerned how these new arrangements might affect their privilege of coinage. Accordingly, after the end of September 1247 Edmund of Walpole, then the sub-sacrist, and Thomas, a monk of Bury, appeared before the barons of the exchequer to claim the abbot's right to a mint and exchange.[103] This was confirmed by royal mandate on 6 December 1247.[104] On 26 December a further mandate instructed that a die for the new coinage be handed to Edmund and Simon, the almoner at Bury. This was to be against the surrender of the die used to strike the old coinage, thus following already established practice.[105]

It may be assumed that the mint was active from the beginning of the following year until the death of Abbot Henry on 19 June 1248. The earliest known Long Cross coins of Bury consist of one set of dies (represented by one obverse and one reverse) in class Ib, four in class IIa and one in class IIb.[106] These dies were probably all in use before the death of Abbot Henry. The next coins, of class IIIa with five known sets of dies,[107] would on this hypothesis have been issued after installation of Edmund of Walpole as abbot on 17 September 1248, but before the second group of provincial mints, listed below, came into production.

It has been suggested,[108] based partly on a writ of 16 July 1248 authorising the recruitment of foreign experts in minting and exchanging,[109] that the first group of provincial mints, striking in class IIa and/or b, did not open until the 'summer' of 1248,[110] presumably after the recruitment had taken place. However, a

102 *CPR 1232–1247*, p. 505.

103 PRO, E 368/20 [LTR 32 Henry III, Michaelmas 1247], m. 4d. Edmund probably stood in for the sacrist, Nicholas of Warwick, who was described as 'infirm' for some years before he was succeeded by Simon of Luton in 1252 (*Memorials*, II, p. 294). A similar record is found in the King's Remembrancer's Memoranda Rolls (reproduced by Wells 1934–7a, pp. 102–3). This entry contains one apparent inaccuracy in stating that the abbot received confirmation of his moneyer as freely as in the past (*ita libere*) on 30 January 1227. At that date the mint was still farmed back to the king. It is to be wondered how far, on this evidence, the claimed confirmation of minting rights by William Rufus and Richard I, recited on the same occasion by Edmund and Thomas, can be relied upon as true.

104 *CR 1247–1251*, p. 12; see also mandate dated 28 December 1247 in BL Harl. MS 645, fol. 79v.

105 *CR 1247–1251*, p. 101. Wells 1934–7a, pp. 79–84, believed that the writs of 6 and 26 December 1247 referred to two separate sets of dies issued to the abbot's representatives. This enticed him into various bizarre conclusions.

106 See Catalogue 251–255 and Table 59 below.

107 See Catalogue 256–260 and Table 59 below.

108 Davis 1977, p. 140, following Wells 1934–7a, p. 87.

109 *CPR 1247–1258*, p. 21.

110 Davis 1977, p. 140. Different phasing for the introduction of classes IIa and b between Canterbury and London and the provincial mints seems very improbable from a practical point of view, suggesting – implausibly – that dies were extensively cut in various moneyers' names ahead of their required use.

similar writ was issued on 28 August 1247.[111] Foreign officials were thus apparently – and understandably – sought for both the first group of provincial mints and the second group, active from class IIIa or b. The detailed evidence bears out this hypothesis. After London, followed by Canterbury and Bury, alone issuing class I, the earliest provincial mints were Winchester, granted the right to an exchange on 11 December 1247,[112] Exeter, Lincoln and Northampton, granted four moneyers each on 26 February 1248,[113] all active in class IIa,[114] Norwich granted four moneyers at the same time,[115] but apparently not active until class IIb,[116] and Gloucester, Oxford and York,[117] also active in IIb. The mandate of 26 February 1248 shows that the mints were intended to begin operating without delay because the nominated officials were to be presented at the exchequer only fifteen days later, on 12 March. All of these mints were mentioned in connection with the examination of the old and new coinage conducted at London on 11 March 1248, resulting in the issue of trial-plates (*assaia*), by which the standard of the coinage would be measured at London and elsewhere.[118] It is likely that class IIIa, having the distinctive obverse inscription hENRICVS REX III, in place of hENRICVS REX TERCI, followed within months and before the extension of minting rights early in November 1248 to the second group of provincial mints. These were Bristol, Carlisle, Hereford, Ilchester, Newcastle-upon-Tyne, Shrewsbury, Wallingford and Wilton in class IIIab1.[119] The mandate of 6 December 1247 in favour of Bury had granted a die provisionally (*ad*

111 *CPR 1232–1247*, p. 508.

112 *CR 1247–1251*, p. 98. Although the word *cambium* is here used it may be intended to embrace the mint as well as exchange. The phrase '*monetarius cambii*' appears in the Close Rolls (*CR 1268–1272*, p. 371). See also *The De Moneta of Nicholas Oresme*, p. xxii.

113 *CR 1247–1251*, pp. 107–8. Winchester is also mentioned in these mandates.

114 Davis 1977, p. 139.

115 *CR 1247–1251*, p. 107. Norwich was also granted an exchange at the same time as Winchester (*CR 1247–1251*, p. 98). It is not clear why the mint was slow to enter into production.

116 Davis 1977, p. 139.

117 Custody of the 'exchange' (see n. 112 above) at York was granted on 31 March 1248 (*CR 1247–1251*, p. 37), but various problems beset the appointment of the archbishop's moneyer(s) (see *CR 1247–1251*, p. 67; Wells 1934–7a, pp. 88–9), and Lawrence 1912, pp. 156, 178, identified only one moneyer (Tomas) as the archbishop's, in classes IIIb and c. It is, however, even conceivable that Tomas was a replacement for the royal moneyer, Alain. Mandates for the mints of Gloucester and Oxford have so far not been found.

118 BL Hargrave MS 313, fol. 96 v, reproduced in *Chronica Johannis de Oxenedes*, pp. 315–25, *The Red Book of the Exchequer*, pp. 1072–81 (erroneously giving the year of the examination as 1243) and (with translation) in *The De Moneta of Nicholas Oresme*, pp. 53–5. The account is clearly incorrect in stating that instructions were sent to the provincial centres to appoint moneyers after (*postmodum*) 11 March 1248. An earlier instance of such central control occurred in 1236 (PRO, E 159/14 [KR 20 Henry III, Easter 1236], m. 11; PRO, E 159/14 [KR 20 Henry III, Trinity 1236], m. 13), when the abbot at Bury was given until 7 October to submit to the assay of money struck from his die (*ad respondendum de assaye monete cunei sui*).

119 See North 1994, pp. 227–8, and compare Table 51. Entries in the Lord Treasurer's Remembrancer's Memoranda Rolls on 10 October 1248 (reproduced by Wells 1934–7a, pp. 104–5) required nominated officials for these mints to be presented at the exchequer between 1 and 8 November 1248. Nottingham, for which no coins are known (Wells 1934–7a, p.87; Brand 1971, pp. 148–9, n. 3) was also on the list of provincial centres notified.

fabricandum interim argentum suum). This may be because it had already been decided to have a second, wider phase of recoinage with a distinctive obverse, after the old and initial output of the new coinage had been examined.

By 1250 all of the provincial mints closed, with only London, Canterbury, to a modest extent Bury and, fitfully, Durham supplying the needs of the country for new coin during the rest of the Long Cross issue. Since none of the provincial mints struck coins after class IIIc,[120] the closure appears to have been marked by the addition of a sceptre to the obverse design,[121] a feature henceforward retained throughout the coinage.

Martin Allen has estimated mint output between 1247 and 1250 at mints for which actual figures are not recorded by relating known output to the number of coins by mint from ten named hoards.[122] This produced an output of about £84 for each hoard coin in the study. The 197 Bury coins thus resulted in an estimated output of *c.* £17,000. Since, as Table 59 below shows, 37 pairs of dies have been identified from 760 coins from classes I to IIIc, this would result in an average of at least 100,000 coins being struck from each pair. It is hard to believe that the average would have reached anywhere near that figure. The discrepancy may be partly explained because the locally biased Colchester hoard accounted for 164 (83%) of the 197 Bury coins used in the calculation.

Despite the increased references in official records to mint activities at this period the detailed dating of the Long Cross coinage from classes IVa to VII has still not been very clearly settled. Table 53 shows the dates suggested by Lawrence[123] and Brooke.[124] Hopefully, publication of R. C. Churchill's researches into the mint records of the Long Cross period will throw fuller light on the chronology beyond the glosses offered below.

Class IV appears to have superseded class IIIc by the second half of 1250. Steps were taken early that year to close the provincial mints, the officials being requested to appear in three groups on 10, 17 and 24 April 1250 to account for the coin issued.[125] It may be that the closure was less neatly arranged than these mandates suggest, because repairs to the mint building at Newcastle were ordered on 12 May,[126] and on 24 June instructions were repeated to shut the mint at Bristol.[127] Meanwhile, during the Easter term of 1250 Richard

120 Lawrence 1915a, pp. 103–19. Brand 1971, pp. 140–1, adduces evidence that class IIIc dies were in use at Shrewsbury in October 1249.

121 Class IVa et seq.

122 Allen 1999b, p. 209.

123 Lawrence 1912, pp. 166–8 and Lawrence 1913, p. 71, where he advanced the date for class Vc from *c.* 1255 or 1256 to 1252 but did not address the consequential implications for the dating of adjacent types.

124 Brooke 1950, p. 112.

125 PRO, E 368/23 [LTR 34 Henry III, Hilary 1250], m. 8; Wells 1934–7a, pp. 92–3, 106.

126 *CLR 1245–1251*, p. 287.

127 *CR 1247–1251*, p. 297.

Table 53. Long Cross dating by Lawrence and Brooke

Class	*Lawrence*	*Brooke*
IV	*c.* 1250–	1250–1
Va	*c.* 1251–	*c.* 1251–3
Vb	1251 (or 1252)	
Vc	*c.* 1255/6 (revised to 1252–)	*c.* 1253–1258/60
Vd	?	
Ve	1255 or 1256–	
Vf	?	
Vg	*c.* 1258 or 1260–	*c.* 1258/60–1272
Vh	–*c.* 1267–	not listed by Brooke
Vi	?	
VI	–*c.* 1274–	*c.* 1272–1278
VII	–1278–	

Bonaventure and David of Enfield were appointed moneyers at London, both of whom struck coins of class IIIc.[128] If class III dies were used at Bury from late in 1248 until approximately two years later this would represent 31 pairs over the period, a level of activity consistent with a recoinage. Class IV is rare, even from Canterbury and London, suggesting it was of short duration.[129] At Bury, only one pair of IVab dies is known in the type. This is not surprising because the call for coinage at Bury in particular would doubtless have plummeted in the immediate wake of the recoinage.

The next event of chronological importance at Bury is the presentation by Simon, the sacrist, of Randulf le Blund to the barons of the exchequer in the Easter term of 1252 to replace the longstanding moneyer Ion.[130] Since the earliest coins of Randulf are class Vb2/a3 mules, the introduction of class Vb can be dated to no later than the first quarter of 1252. This mule is interesting in that it leap-frogs the rare class Vb1 found in London. Table 54 shows the number of reverse dies so far found bearing his name:

128 PRO, E 368/23 [LTR 34 Henry III, Hilary 1250], m. 14; Lawrence 1912, pp. 159, 179.

129 See Table 51.

130 PRO, E 368/26 [LTR 36 Henry III, Easter 1252], m. 8. Lawrence 1912 gives this date variously as '1252' (p. 164), '1251' (p. 167) and 'before Easter 1251' (p. 179).

Table 54. Reverse dies of Randulf

Class	*No. of dies*
Vb2/a3	1
Vb2	10
Vc/Vc(x)	6
Vd	1
Ve	–
Vf	2
Vg	–

In the first part of his study Lawrence dated class Vc to between January 1255 and Easter 1256, but later brought the date forward to 1252,[131] owing to a reference drawn to his attention in the Rolls for 1252/3 to executors of Nicholas of St Albans.[132] Lawrence was nevertheless puzzled by what had happened to the London die of Nicole between that time and the transfer of its entitlement to William of Gloucester in 1255.[133] This may not have been the originating grant of William's rights, however, because the grant is stated as being 'conferred for life'. This revised dating in fact fits with the increased number of reverse readings noted by Lawrence for class Vc and the upsurge in mint output at Canterbury and London from May 1252 (see Fig. 10 below). The view of Lawrence that Vc only lasted a short time because it was muled with Vd obverses and reverses thus appears to be unjustified.[134] The total readings given by him in classes Va-Vd, as set out in Table 55, tend (in spite of their limitations) to reinforce this view:

Table 55. Reverse readings recorded by Lawrence

Class	*No. of reverse readings*
Va	27
Vb	22
Vc	46*
Vd	25*

Note
*Including mules between Vc and Vd.

In contrast with Canterbury and London, a slackening of activity can be observed from the surviving dies of Bury in class Vc (see Table 52 above), leading to an altogether lower output for the rest of the Long Cross series.

The beginning of Vd can be approximately dated from the evidence of the Bury mint. Table 56 shows the total number of reverse readings in Lawrence, the

131 See n. 123 above.
132 Lawrence 1913, p. 71.
133 On 8 May 1255 (*CPR 1247–1258*, p. 409).
134 Lawrence 1912, p. 167.

number of Bury reverse readings in Lawrence, and the number of dies identified from Bury coins between classes Vc to Vg inclusive.

Table 56. Lawrence readings compared with reverse dies

Class	*Lawrence: total reverse readings*	*Lawrence: total Bury readings*	*Total Bury dies identified*	*Moneyer*
Vc	51	2	6	Randulf
Vd	26	1	1	
Ve	10	–	–	
Vf	29	1	2	
Vg	62	3	6	Renaud
			5	Stephane
			8	Ion

Only one pair of Vd dies has come to light so far from Bury, with the unusual mint signature of BERI, and none of Ve. Since Abbot Edmund of Walpole died on 31 December 1256 and his successor, Simon of Luton, did not receive his temporalities until 12 January 1258, it is likely that the Vd dies were issued to Randulf some weeks, or even months, before the abbot's death. This suggests that the missing class Ve was current during the vacancy of 1257 at Bury and class Vf was already in use when new dies were issued to Randulf after Abbot Simon had been installed. Such chronology fits with the lower number of reverse readings at Canterbury and London in class Ve, which may have been used for the output recorded between June and October 1257, as suggested in Figure 10 below.

In Trinity term 1258 Roger of Neketon presented Reginald Fitz Henry (Renaud of the coins) to replace Randulf.[135] The presence of the abbot was excused owing to illness but the barons of the exchequer stated, incorrectly according to precedent, that he should have otherwise been there in person. It follows that Randulf must have used his two pairs of Vf dies between Simon's confirmation in January 1258 and his ceasing to be abbot's moneyer towards the middle of that year.

The Kempe Register, compiled at Bury in the fourteenth and fifteenth centuries, but incorporating material from the thirteenth century, includes a problematical account relating to the sacrist, for the period from 11 April 1256 to 19 April 1258.[136] This records various payments, including 100 shillings per annum to the moneyer Randulf, for two years service, and 18 shillings to the keepers of the dies. For over half this period from the end of 1256, however, the abbey was vacant. This implies that either the payments to mint personnel were partly *ex gratia*, in the expectation that the mint would shortly be revived, or the rapacious

135 PRO, E 159/31 [KR 42 Henry III, Trinity 1258], m. 15; Madox 1711, p. 604.
136 Harl. MS 645, fol. 261v.

keepers during the vacancy, the Walerand brothers, contrived to operate the mint *sede vacante*, as happened on several occasions at Durham.[137] In fact, there is no direct evidence of this practice being adopted at Bury and, as suggested above, the mint appears to have been relatively inactive in the later 1250s. The sacrist's provisional accounts record a 'profit' of £47 9*s.* 0*d.* over the two year period. Allen has extrapolated this figure to represent an output of 'about £1,000 per annum', based on the 6*d.*/£ profit on bullion purchases.[138] This would imply usage of up to twenty pairs of dies over the two year period, whereas only three sets of dies of Randulf in classes Vd and Vf are known. The discrepancy remains even if, as occurred at the royal mints, a 6*d.*/£ minting fee was also charged to inflate the sacrist's profit. As noted below, a notional profit of £3 was allowed for tax purposes to the sacrist in 1268, in two other Bury manuscripts, raising questions on the composition of the stated profit of £47 9*s.* 0*d.*

The date when the moneyer Stephane replaced Renaud at Bury is not known, but according to the records he in turn was superseded by John de Burnedisse (Ion or, later, Iohs of the coins) on 29 January 1265.[139] Since, as shown above, the Liberty was in the king's hands between 7 March 1262 and 24 September 1265, and the right to dies was only specifically restored on 27 October that year, it is very strange that the sacrist should have presented Ion as the new moneyer and John of Shuldham as the keeper of the dies at a time when the abbot's mint was inoperative. It would have been more logical to take such a step in January following the restoration. It nevertheless appears that Stephane's output must have ended in 1262. If so, Renaud and Stephane between them would have used only eleven pairs of dies over a period of about four years.

The numismatic evidence for the rest of the Long Cross issue is more sketchy. The surviving coins in particular suffer from the usual drawback of being less representative than earlier in the series owing to coins being melted for the recoinage of Edward I in 1279 before preservation as hoarded wealth. As shown by Table 59 below, the majority of surviving dies of Bury from this period are represented by single specimens. It is nevertheless clear that Ion (Iohs) continued to strike coins at Bury from class Vg through to class VII. Class Vh, a crude version of Vg, was according to Lawrence in issue between 1267 and 1271.[140] The following class Vi, distinguished by even greater crudity of execution, can only have existed very briefly owing to its excessive rarity.[141]

---

137 Allen 2003, pp. 30–2. Allen 1999a, p. 210 and n. 6, supported his conclusion that the mint remained open as owing to a charter of Edward I, confirming mint revenues to the sacrist, which he interpreted as allowing the prior and convent to operate the mint during a vacancy. On the author's construction of this charter, see Chapter 8 and n. 77.

138 Allen 1999a, p. 212.

139 PRO, E 368/40 [LTR 49 Henry III, Hilary 1266], m. 6d.

140 Lawrence 1912, p. 161, relied on the evidence of Richard le Specer (or l'Espece) the Canterbury moneyer, whom he considered replaced Gilebert in 1268, and was described as 'lately' a moneyer on 20 May 1271 (see *CR 1268–1272*, p. 371).

141 Doubts have been entertained by numismatists about whether class Vi merits separate classification, or if it is even an official issue. It is so treated in this work.

The introductions of the following classes (VI and VII) were respectively given by Lawrence, following the Fox brothers, to 'approximately' 1274 and 'certainly' 1278.[142] In fact, the brothers were less emphatic, giving the introduction of class VII as 'after the end of 1274, but before the spring of 1278'.[143] The brothers associated class VI – known to them from one coin of Bury and one of Durham – to the period immediately following the receipt of temporalities by Robert de Insula, bishop of Durham on 11 November 1274.[144] More cautiously, an editorial note in the preliminary report on the Colchester (1969) hoard, containing 1,916 specimens struck from the same dies as the hitherto unique coin from Bury, dated the class to 1268 x 1278.[145] The argument that class VI represented the type issued after Bishop Robert de Insula received his temporalities on 11 November 1274 because it was the first type following a gap in issues at Durham mint has lost its force, since class Vg is also known to exist from the mint.[146] An ingenious alternative theory has been suggested that classes VI and VII, showing the king's bust with realistic hair, were the result of the appointment of a new die engraver, Ralph le Blund in 1269.[147]

The Foxes cited in support of 1278 for the beginning of class VII the presentation of Philip de Cambio in the spring of that year to the barons of the exchequer to replace the London moneyer Reginald of Canterbury.[148] Of the readings noted by Lawrence, only one occurs for Renaud in class VII but five for Philip.[149] On the other hand, Joceus the Goldsmith was presented by Simon of Kingston, sacrist at Bury, to replace John de Burnedisse in the spring of 1278,[150] and both moneyers are known in class VII by two sets of dies. This may nevertheless reflect a revival of activity at Bury, as there clearly was at London, between June 1275 and November 1278.[151] It is accordingly not possible to suggest other than that class VII was in issue before 1278. If Ion had carried out his low level of activity on a fairly consistent basis, his pair of class VI dies would have been in use in 1276. The discovery of further dies would naturally, on this hypothesis, nudge the date forward or backwards.

The registers of Bury provide one specific insight into the coinage during the later part of the reign.[152] In 1268 a listing of the sacrist's revenues for taxation purposes included a sum of £3 from the mint. On the basis of a conventional minting profit of 6*d.* in the pound,[153] this would imply an annual output of

142 Lawrence 1912, p. 168.
143 Fox and Fox 1910, p. 94.
144 Fox and Fox 1910, p. 94.
145 Clarke *et al.* 1974, p. 39.
146 See Lawrence 1913, p. 92 and Allen 2003, pp. 171, 202–3.
147 See J.D. Brand, 'Date of Part 2,' in Archibald and Cook 2001, p. 87.
148 PRO, E 159/51 [KR 6 Edward I, Easter 1278], m. 5, transcribed by Fox and Fox 1910, p. 129.
149 Lawrence 1913, p. 82.
150 PRO, E 159/51 [KR 6 Edward I, 1278], m. 3d, m. 5d, transcribed by Fox and Fox 1910, p. 129.
151 Fox and Fox 1910, p. 93; see also Crump and Johnson 1913, pp. 204–5.
152 BL Harl. MS 638 fol. 240b; BL Harl. MS 3977, fol. 56b.
153 *CPR 1247–1258*, p. 13.

28,800 pence, equivalent to about one set of dies per annum.[154] From the admission of John de Burnedisse in 1265 to the end of the Long Cross series, a period of approximately thirteen years, so far sixteen sets have been found to exist from Bury. It may appear strange that since the right to mint coins at Bury was obviously inalienably attached to the abbot's barony, the sacrist should have enjoyed the profits of its exercise. However, the abbot would have been free to make such an arrangement with the convent without affecting his own relationship with the king, and may have done so when the abbey was wrestling with its financial problems in the 1250s and 1260s. Owing to changes, not to say confusion, between the revenues due to the abbot and convent, an agreement had been made between the parties by 1234,[155] and subsequently a customary was compiled defining these and other rights of the abbot and the obedientiaries.[156]

To conclude this section, Figure 10 below shows the total reverse readings at London and Canterbury by class listed by Lawrence superimposed, according to the dating scheme suggested above, over the statistics for output at those mints between November 1247 and 1266.[157]

Long Cross hoard evidence

As already intimated, no Long Cross hoard has so far been published in sufficient detail to be exploited fully using the tools of modern numismatic research. One drawback is a preoccupation with obverse and reverse legends rather than dies, a lead taken by Lawrence. The early hoards in particular are sadly deficient in details. Although Colchester (1969) has received close attention in a British Museum Occasional Paper,[158] and the Museum holds photographs and weights of all the coins, the daunting Brussels (1908) hoard at the time of writing remains substantially unpublished. However, following earlier work by R. L. Davis and by C. Wren, R. C. Churchill and R. I. Thomas are well advanced towards completing a study of the latter hoard. Unfortunately, its sheer scale militates against their carrying out a comprehensive die study for the main mints of London and Canterbury. Table 57 below shows the proportion of Bury coins in six major hoards, and three from more recent but modest hoards, in comparison with the total, London and Canterbury coins. The last three hoards show the relative lack of utility of small hoards at this period in illuminating mint activity at Bury.

154 This calculation is not out of line with die output estimates for the reigns of Edward I and II, and especially since one (rather than a pair) of less durable reverses was issued to Bury with each obverse; cf, however, Chapter 8, pp. 148, 160.

155 Gransden 1975, pp. 29–30.

156 *The Customary of the Benedictine Abbey of Bury St Edmunds in Suffolk*, p. xxxiii and *passim*.

157 Lawrence 1913, pp. 75–89; Blunt and Brand 1970, Table I, opposite p. 64.

158 Archibald and Cook 2001. A helpful die study of Bury coins by Mark Walpole is included (p. 101, Table 2), and has been used (with revisions) in the present work.

Figure 10

Mint Output at London and Canterbury:
November 1247–1266

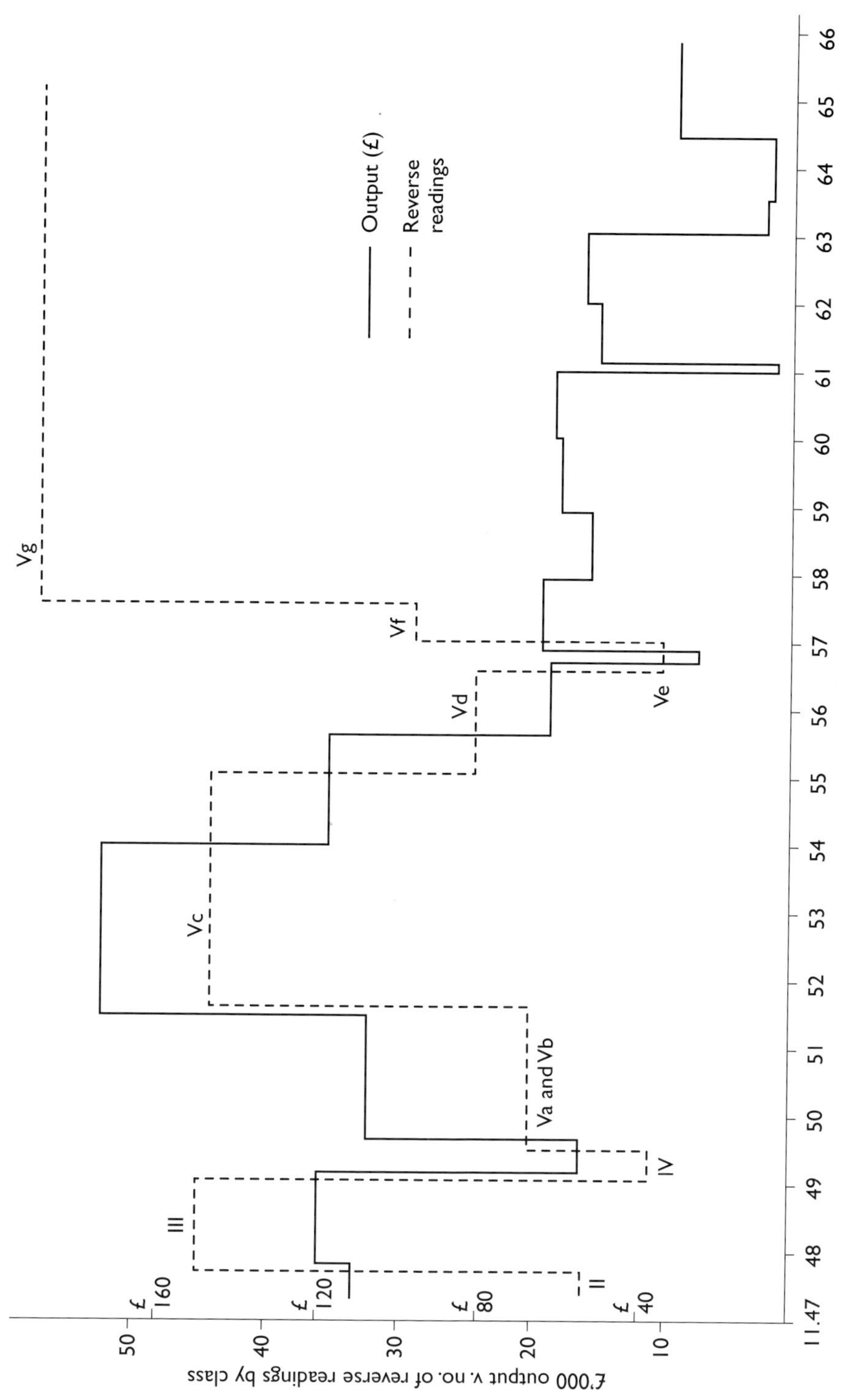

Table 57. Summary of Long Cross hoards

Hoard		*Total*	*London*	*Canterbury*	*Bury*
Bantry Bay (1834)[159]		702	235	222	14
Tower Hill (1869)[160]		201	75	79	6
Palmer's Green (1911)[161]		208	112	70	7
Steppingley (1912)[162]		455	249	149	13
Slype (1914)[163]		1,312	521	499	31
Hornchurch (1938)[164]		409	165	157	11
Total		3,287	1,357	1,176	82
	%	(100)	(41)	(36)	(2.5)
Sporle (1995, 1997–9)[165]		29	12	5	7
Welwyn Garden City (1992)[166]		44	20	14	0
Greywell (1988, 1995)[167]		102	47	36	1
Total		175	79	55	8
	%	(100)	(45)	(31)	(0.5)

Overall numbers by class published for the Colchester (1969) hoard are set out and totalled in Table 58, omitting the large group of 1,916 coins of Bury class VI from the same pair of dies.[168] The Bury content from this hoard represents 3.9% (excluding class VI). If the provincial mints and Durham are excluded the percentage rises to 5.3%.

Although the Colchester hoard contained a significant number of Long Cross coins, its importance is dwarfed by the great Brussels find of 1908, containing Short Cross coins and approximately 80,000 Long Cross pence stretching from class I to Vg, ending at Bury with Stephane. For various reasons, including dispersal before auctioning, melting of inferior specimens, theft and limited disposals, about 55,000 from the original total remain in the hands of A. H. Baldwin and Sons Ltd, who acquired the bulk of the hoard at auction in 1909. Fortunately it has been possible to carry out a die study of the Bury content of both hoards: for Colchester from photographs in the British Museum, and for Brussels from the

159 Sainthill 1844, pp. 124–7; *Inventory*, pp. 10–11 (no. 33).
160 Evans 1869; *Inventory*, pp. 91–2 (no. 254).
161 Grueber 1912; *Inventory*, pp. 88–9 (no. 247).
162 Lawrence and Brooke 1914; *Inventory*, pp. 129–30 (no. 342).
163 Brooke 1914, pp. 256–9.
164 Allen 1938–41; *Inventory*, pp. 70–1 (no. 193).
165 Archibald and Cook 2001, pp. 99–100.
166 Archibald and Cook 2001, p. 55.
167 Archibald and Cook 2001, p. 60.
168 Archibald and Cook 2001, p. 64.

Table 58. The Colchester (1969) hoard

	Classes					
Mint(s)	*I*	*II*	*III*	*IV*	*Va-c*	*Total*
London	41	208	1,820	24	3,024	5,117
Canterbury	21	80	903	9	2,125	3,138
Bury	2	14	148	4	270	438
Durham	0	0	0	0	21	21
Provincial	0	121	2,480	0	0	2,601
Total*	64	423	5,351	37	5,440	11,315

Note
* Excluding 10 coins of uncertain mint.

coins owned by, or traceably dispersed by, Baldwin. No imitations purporting to hail from Bury have been identified in either hoard.[169]

The results of the study are set out in Table 59, in which examples from other sources are also noted. Although the residue of the Brussels hoard is approximately five times larger than Colchester, the 1,317 Bury coins traced represent a markedly lower percentage (2.4%) than in the Colchester hoard. This may be because the Bury content of the Colchester hoard was exaggerated by its closeness to Colchester. The latter hoard also contained a separate group of 1,916 Bury coins, all of class VI and struck from the same pair of dies. This group is interesting in that it converts one of the greatest rarities of the Long Cross series into the commonest Bury coin of all. Numismatically, its importance is in illustrating how poorly struck a coin could be when it left the mint and before it suffered the vagaries of circulation. Such an intact group of coins can only have undergone minimal usage and yet all have a relatively inferior appearance. It is conceivable that the coins were struck from dies in poor condition.

Table 59 shows that Colchester gave a very full picture of coinage at Bury over the period spanned by the hoard, only four pairs of dies between class I and Vb inclusive out of sixty-four identified in Brussels not being present.[170] It is also clear that the Brussels hoard gives a virtually complete picture of coinage at the mint up to at least the early period of office of Stephane in Vg, with only two pairs of dies (Ion, Va3, Ll and Mm), apparently not being represented in the hoard.[171]

169 On Long Cross imitations, generally, see North 1995. Questions have been informally voiced to the author on the authenticity of the class Vd coins with the reverse reading RAND ON BERI (see Catalogue 322). See also n. 171 below.

170 Two sets of dies are also absent from class Vc but this was the latest type to be represented in the Colchester (1969) hoard.

171 Class Va3 of Ion, dies Ll, see Catalogue [303], with a reverse circle composed of bold pellets, could conceivably be imitative.

Table 59. Bury dies from the Brussels (BRU) and Colchester (COL) hoards and other sources

Class/moneyer		*Dies O. + R.*	*No. of coins*			
			BRU	*COL*	*OTHER*	*Total*
Ib		A	1+1?	2	3	6+
	S/T	1	1+1?	2	3	6+
ION						
IIa		A	4	–	6	10
		B	11	–	4	15
		C	14	5	4	23
		D	5	2	8	15
IIb		A	16	7	5	28
	S/T	5	50	14	27	91
IIIa		A	7	2	4	13
		B	19	5	1	25
		C	8	2	2	12
		D	7	4	1	12
		E	4	1	2	7
IIIab1		A	8	1	3	12
		B	15	3	7	25
IIIab2		A	9	4	2	15
IIIac		A	10	2	4	16
IIIb		A	14	7	1	22
		B	24	3	3	30
		C	21	6	6	33
IIIbc		A	17	6	–	23
		B	13	5	1	19
IIIc		A	13	5	3	21
		B	14	3	3	20
		C	22	14	4	40
		D	12	3	2	17
		E	10	7	3	20
		F	25	12	4	41
		G	8	2	3	13
		H	23	8	5	36
		I	13	5	–	18
		J	10	5	1	16
		K	12	2	4	18
		L	21	4	1	26
		M	14	6	1	21
		N	6	4	3	13
		O	21	8	1	30
		P	10	4	4	18
		Q	22	5	4	31
	S/T	31	432	148	83	663
IVab		A	7	4	12	23
	S/T	1	7	4	12	23

Class/moneyer	*Dies O. + R.*	*No. of coins*			
		BRU	*COL*	*OTHER*	*Total*
Va2	A	12	3	3	18
	B	13	4	2	19
	C	10	4	2	16
	D	16	4	2	22
Va3	A	19	9	4	32
	B	15	3	7	25
	C	19	11	8	38
	D	12	3	1	16
	E	13	4	4	21
	F	20	7	3	30
	G	16	6	1	23
	H	21	5	3	29
	I	14	3	2	19
	J	14	–	9	23
	K	3	–	–	3
	L	–	–	1	1
	M	–	–	1	1
S/T	17	217	66	53	336
RANDULF					
Vb2/a3	A	18	3	1	22
Vb2	A	45	16	6	67
	B	30	14	2	46
	C	44	12	5	61
	D	25	32	–	57
	E	14	8	–	22
	F	16	9	2	27
	G	31	13	4	48
	H	26	27	3	56
	I	48	12	7	67
	J	8	7	3	18
S/T	11	305	153	33	491
Vc	A	35	4	6	45
	B	34	10	5	49
	C	40	25	6	71
	D	16	–	2	18
	E	30	–	6	36
Vc(x)	A	29	12	7	48
S/T	6	184	51	32	267
Vd	A	9	–	8	17
S/T	1	9	–	8	17
Ve	–	–	–	–	–
S/T	–	–	–	–	–

Table 59. Bury dies from the Brussels (BRU) and Colchester (COL) hoards and other sources (continued)

Class/moneyer	*Dies O. + R.*	*No. of coins*			
		BRU	*COL*	*OTHER*	*Total*
Vf	A	2	–	–	2
	B	19	–	7	26
S/T	2	21	–	7	28
RENAUD					
Vg	A	24	–	2	26
	B	12	–	5	17
	C	20	–	4	24
	D	13	–	5	18
	E	12	–	–	12
	F	3	–	–	3
STEPHANE					
	A	4	–	3	7
	B	2	–	1	3
	C	–	–	2	2
	D	–	–	3	3
	E	–	–	3	3
ION					
	A	–	–	9	9
	B	–	–	1	1
	C	–	–	5	5
	D	–	–	3	3
	E	–	–	1	1
	F	–	–	1	1
	G	–	–	2	2
	H	–	–	1	1
S/T	19	90	–	51	141
Vh	A	–	–	2	2
	B	–	–	1	1
	C	–	–	2	2
	D	–	–	1	1
S/T	4	–	–	6	6
Vi	A	–	–	1	1
S/T	1	–	–	1	1
VI	A	–	1,916*	1*	1,917*
S/T	1	–	–	–	–
VII	A	–	–	2	2
	B	–	–	1	1
IOCE					
	A	–	–	1	1
	B	–	–	2	2
S/T	4	–	–	6	6

Class/moneyer	*Dies O. + R.*	*No. of coins*			
		BRU	*COL*	*OTHER*	*Total*
ACCUMULATED SUB-TOTALS					
I	1	1+1?	2	3	6+
II	5	50	14	27	91
III	31	432	148	83	663
IV	1	7	4	12	23
Va	17	217	66	53	336
Vb	11	305	153	33	491
Vc	6	184	51	32	267
Vd	1	9	–	8	17
Ve	–	–	–	–	–
Vf	2	21	–	7	28
Vg	19	90	–	51	141
Vh	4	–	–	6	6
Vi	1	–	–	1	1
VI	1	–	–	–	*
VII	4	–	–	6	6
Total	104	1,317+1?	438	321	2,076+

Note
* Not included in totals: 1 + 1,916.

Figure 11 shows the number of coins of each set of dies known from the two hoards. On average each set of dies is represented by seventeen coins in the Brussels Hoard and five coins in Colchester. Archibald and Cook calculated the average weight of coins in the main Colchester hoard (excluding class VI) at 1.43 g, compared with a standard, using 242 pence to the pound, of 1.45 g.[172] Class VI from Bury was also calculated at 1.43 g, with a spread from 1.62 g down to 1.11 g.[173] Table 60 below shows the average weight of Bury coins for each main type represented in the Brussels and Colchester hoards, from which it is apparent that the former, with a far larger sample, consistently shows a lower weight than the latter. In Figures 12 and 13, this difference is plotted for the two classes most fully represented in both hoards, namely, IIc and Vb. Figure 12 suggests that heavier coins were selected in class IIIc in the Colchester hoard, and there is little doubt that Brussels was more representative of weights used in the initial phase of the Long Cross coinage. Figure 13, in contrast, shows a closer connection between the two hoards. Ignoring the odd maverick weight, a wider weight span (as would be expected) is found as the size of sample increases.

172 Archibald and Cook 2001, pp. 87–8.
173 Archibald and Cook 2001, pp. 104, 111.

Figure 11

Number of Bury coins per set of dies from Brussels and Colchester hoards

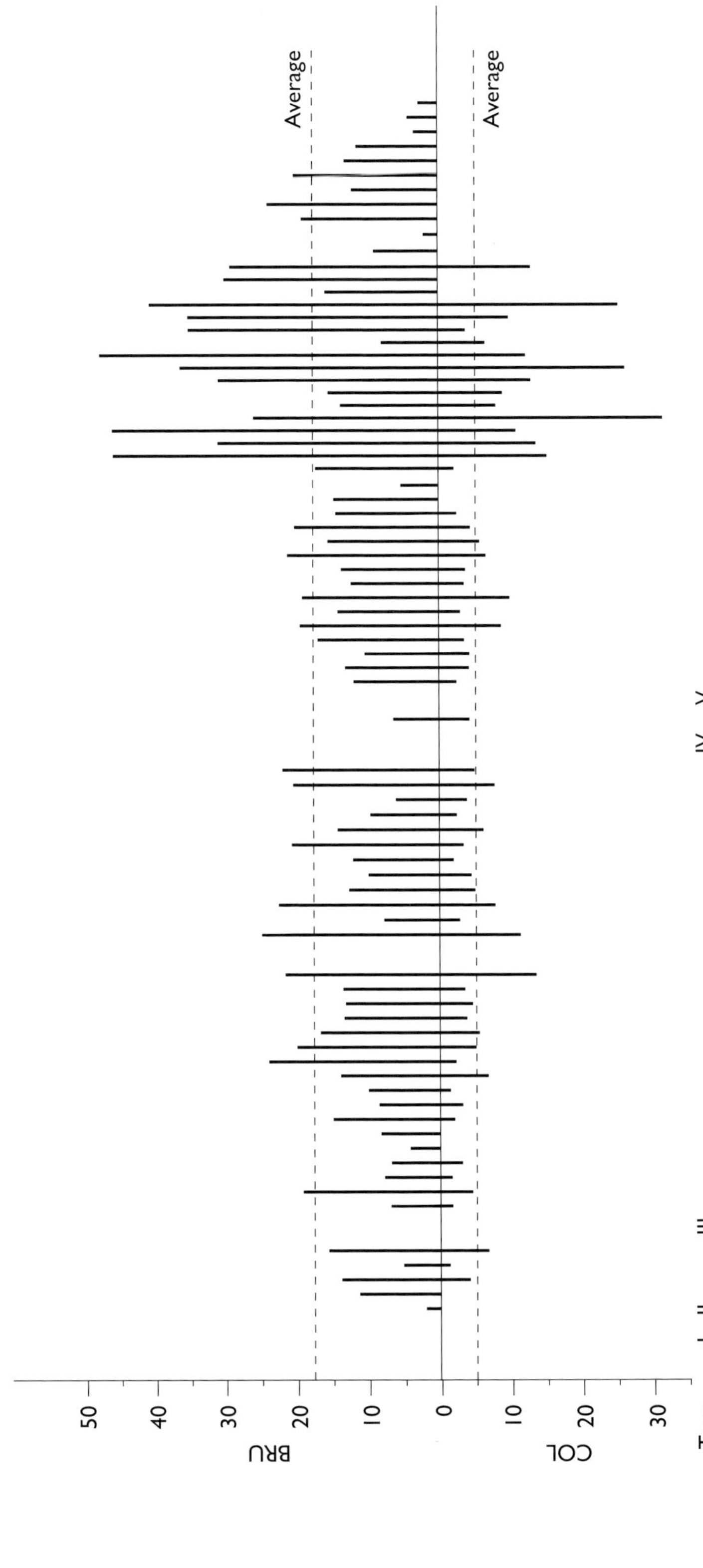

Table 60. Average weights of Bury coins in the Brussels (BRU) and Colchester (COL) hoards

	BRU		*COL*	
Class	*No. of coins*	*Average weight (g)*	*No. of coins*	*Average weight (g)*
II	92	1.39	14	1.42
IIIa	39	1.41	15	1.42
IIIb	87	1.40	32	1.44
IIIc	250	1.40	101	1.43
IV	7	1.41	4	1.44
Va	213	1.41	66	1.44
Vb	296	1.42	152	1.43
Vc	184	1.40	52	1.45
Total	1,168		436	

Figure 12

Comparison of average, maximum and minimum weights of Bury Coins in the Brussels (BRU) and Colchester (COL) hoards by die pairings in class IIIc

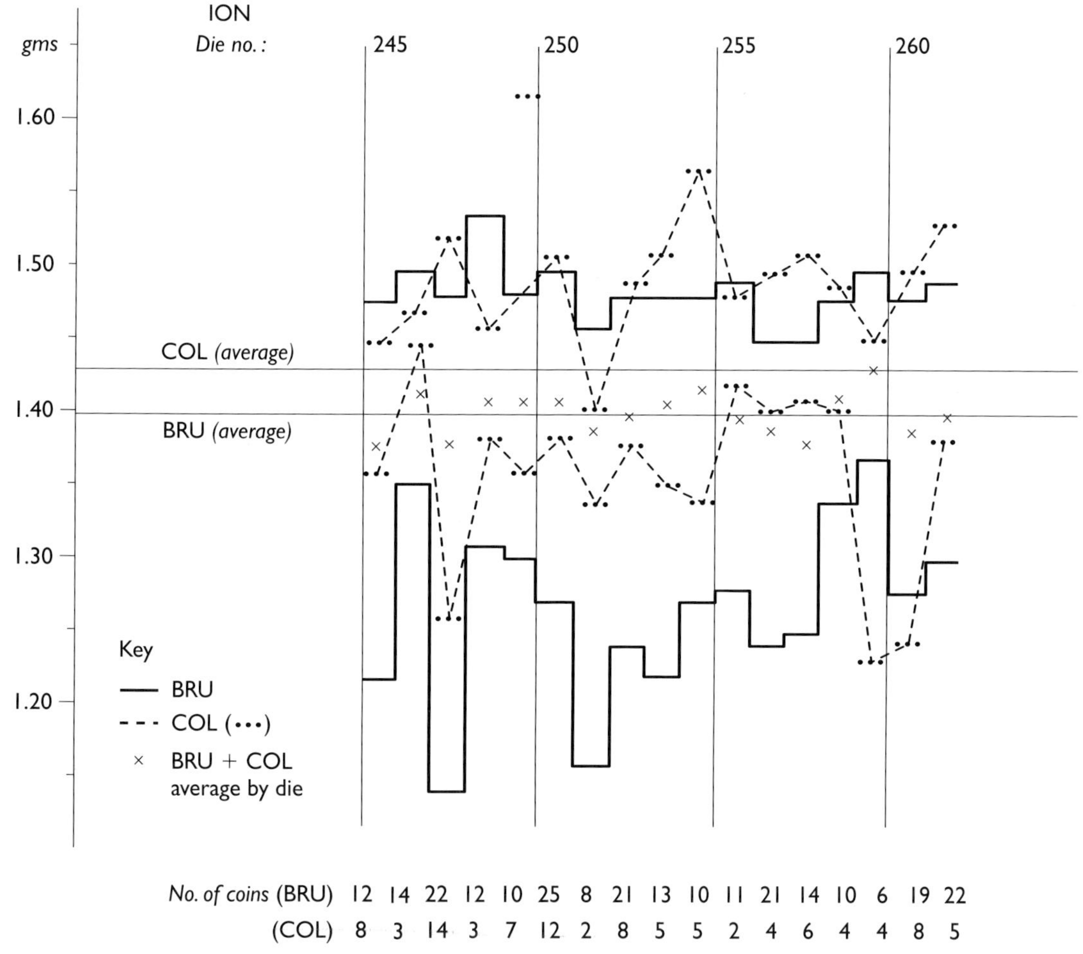

Figure 13

Comparison of average, maximum and minimum weights of Bury coins in the Brussels (BRU) and Colchester (COL) hoards by die pairings in class Vb

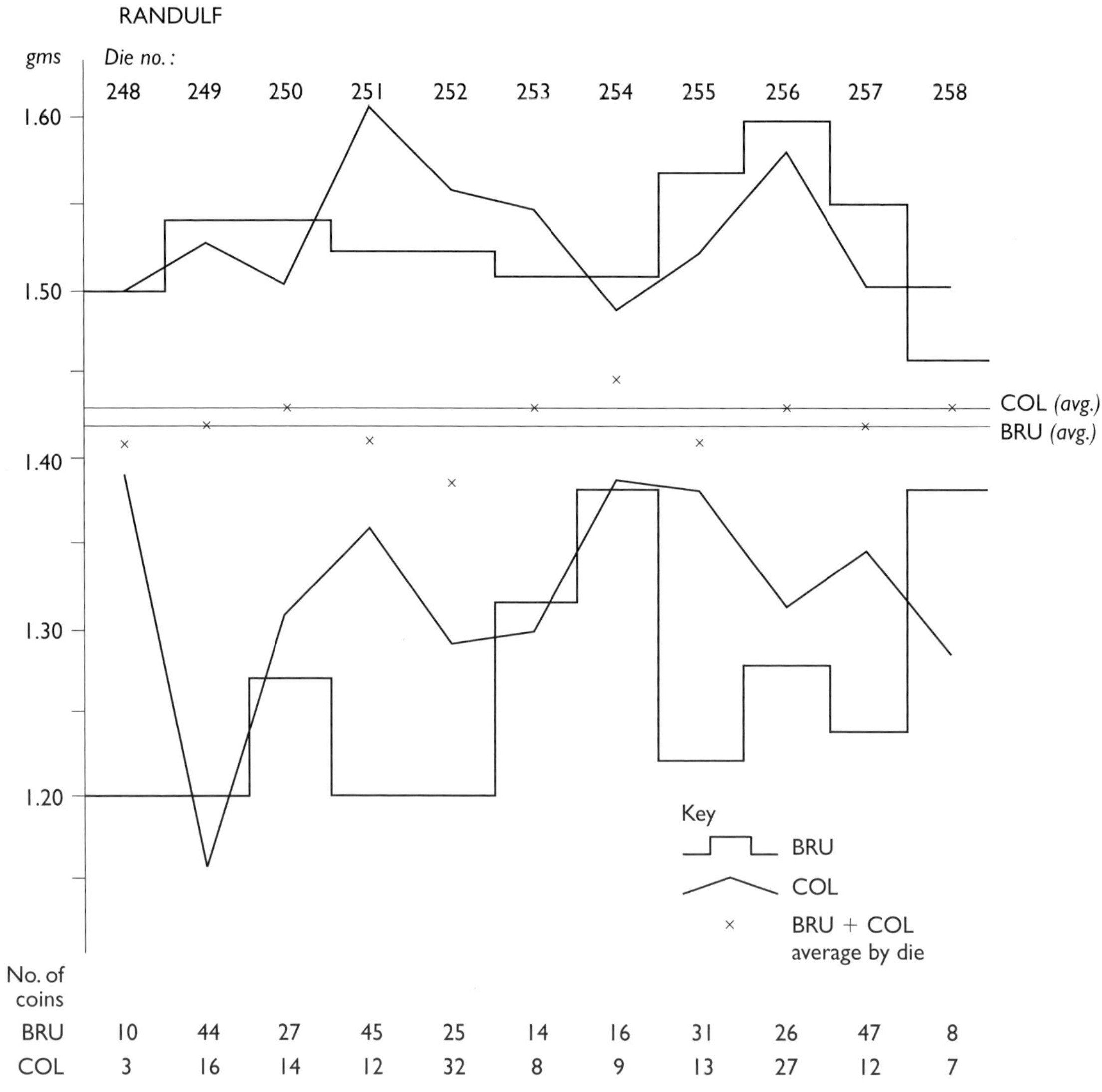

To conclude this chapter, the dating scheme outlined above is related to the number of known die sets used at Bury in Figure 14, and mint readings used during the Long Cross series, ignoring ligulations and punctuation, are summarised in Table 61.

Figure 14

Output at Bury and estimated dates of issue

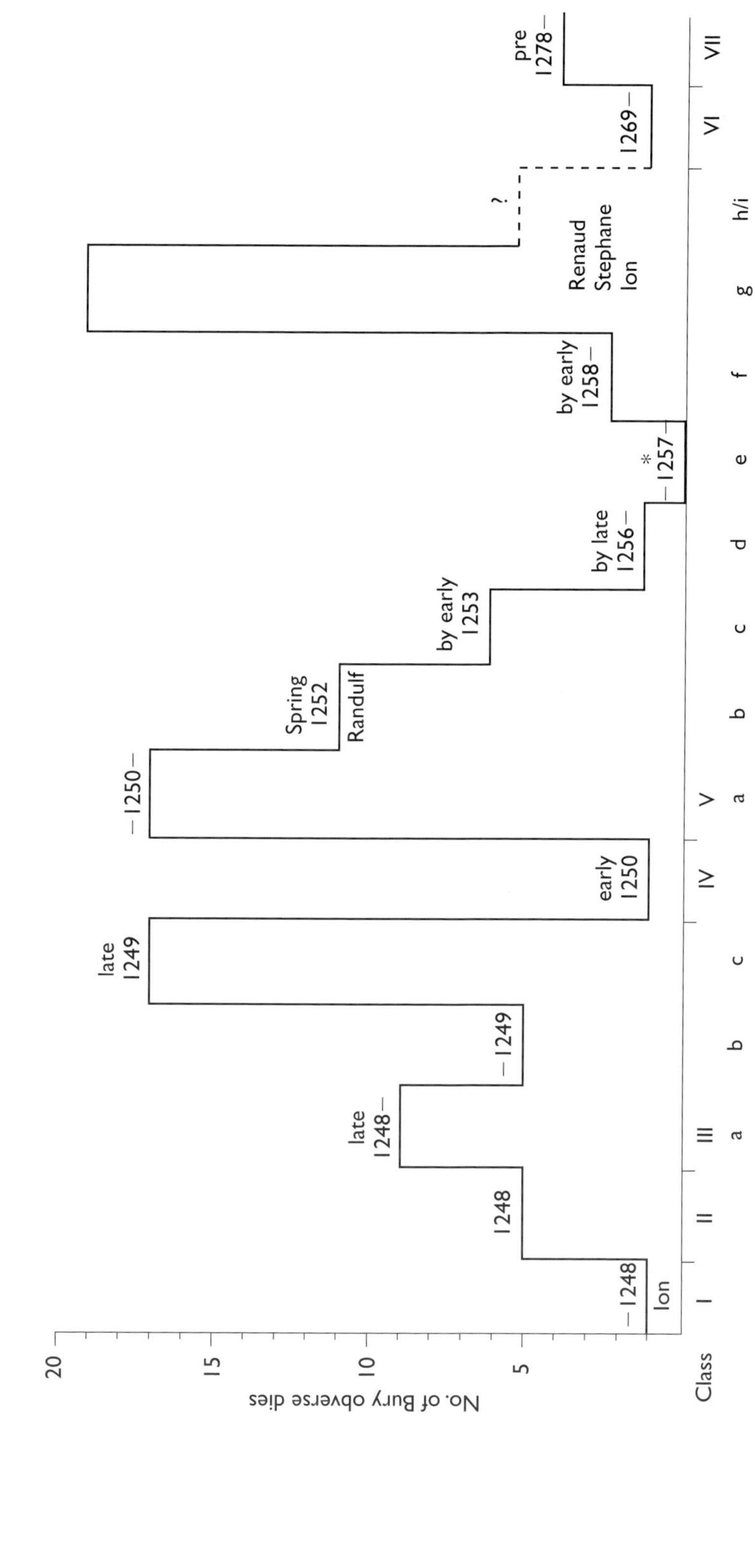

* Abbey vacant between 31 December 1256–12 January 1258

Table 61. Bury mint readings recorded in the Long Cross coinage

	No. of dies																
Mint reading	*I*	*II*	*III*			*IV*	*V*									*VI*	*VII*
			a	*b*	*c*		*a*	*b*	*c*	*d*	*e*	*f*	*g*	*h*	*i*		
AED	1																
SEINTED		1	1				8						3	1		1	
SEDMVND		4	8	5	17	1	6										
SEINED							1										
SENTED							1						3	1	1		
SED							1	10	6			2	4				
BERI										1							
SEDM													6				
SE													1				
SEITED													1	1			
SEITEDT																	1
S ENTEDM													1				1
?							1							1	1		2
	1	5	9	5	17	1	18	10	6	1	0	2	19	4	2	1	4

CHAPTER 10

CONCLUSION[1]

The foundation of Bury's importance was laid when the remains of St Edmund were moved to the settlement of Beadericesworth within a few decades of his death. Although at that time the fame of the saint was so widespread that a Memorial coinage was struck in his name, the history of the shrine is shrouded in obscurity until more reliable information becomes available for the reign of Cnut. It appears that in his reign, possibly resulting from reawakened interest in the saint, the remains were placed in the charge of an organised Benedictine community. This revival resulted in St Edmunds ousting the old Saxon name of Beadericesworth.

The greatest impetus, however, to the prestige and influence of the abbey and embryonic town was afforded by Edward the Confessor. He made extensive grants to the abbey and community, including jurisdiction over the hundreds of West Suffolk and – of primary significance to this work – the right to strike coins.

The close interest taken by Edward the Confessor was mirrored by his successors. They not only consistently confirmed privileges already conferred[2] but also added to them, with the grant of markets and fairs, and in various other ways. Royal support was especially important in avoiding St Edmunds' subjection to the bishops of East Anglia. Royal visits are recorded from all the kings except Harold II and William I and II. Even Richard I managed to make journeys to Bury during his two brief spells in the country after his accession.

Mostly, the abbey remained closely identified with the king's interests. This was nowhere more apparent than during the reign of Stephen when the abbot was the king's watchdog over his enemies in East Anglia. Loyalty was only briefly strained to breaking point in the 1260s when the king's financial demands on the Church, possibly exacerbating already existing economic difficulties at Bury, turned St Edmunds towards the cause of Simon de Montfort. The breach was gradually repaired, but the king did not thereafter show the same generosity in gifts to the abbey as previously.

The physical development of the abbey and town appears to have taken place very rapidly between the Conquest and about 1100, although building work,

1 In this Chapter cross references to Chapters 1–9 have been omitted and references included only to material not hitherto mentioned in the text.

2 An exception was Henry II's non-confirmation of certain rights granted by Stephen.

especially to repair or replace existing structures, naturally continued throughout the Middle Ages. Domesday Book provides an unusually full (but still tantalisingly incomplete) picture of Bury before 1066 and again in 1086. The evidence shows that the town was largely reconstructed in that period, with the abbey precincts encroaching on areas hitherto inhabited by the townspeople. These measures were necessitated by the scale of the new monastic church, rededicated to the saint in 1095, and the complex of ancillary buildings to accommodate the monks, other abbey inmates and visitors.

The population of the town, possibly amounting to 1,500 in 1086, was closely dependent upon the abbey for its prosperity. This is evident from the list of occupations mentioned in Domesday Book and, although Bury was located in a wealthy area of sheep rearing and wool production,[3] regular commerce in the town probably never lost its dependent link with the abbey. However, the markets and fairs obviously attracted trade to Bury unconnected with the abbey and shrine as such. This is clearly evident from the extensive purchases made by Henry III's agents at Bury and by the presence there of merchants from continental Europe.[4] But, despite this commercial development, as the twelfth century progressed the relationship between the abbey and the town became more strained. The protection of the abbey had given the growing urban population a favoured environment into which to settle, but as the inhabitants of other urban centres won the right to control their own affairs the abbey and convent came to be regarded as an obstacle to progress and the obedientiaries as oppressors. This was to lead to riots at Bury after the period covered by this volume.

Four examples will serve to demonstrate the enormous wealth and influence of the abbey in the two centuries after the Conquest. Firstly, that (according to calculations made by Knowles from Domesday Book) Bury was the fourth Benedictine house in revenues after Glastonbury, Ely and Christchurch, Canterbury; secondly, that the abbatial church was larger in size than, for example, Norwich cathedral; thirdly, that Bury was one of the select few houses to obtain exemption from papal visitations at the end of the twelfth century and, lastly, that dies for striking coins were issued more regularly and consistently to the abbot of Bury than to any other ecclesiastic who enjoyed such rights between 1042 and 1279. Most extraordinarily, the latter right continued to be enjoyed, as Figure 15 below shows, against the progressive eradication of minting at other urban centres as the period progressed.

Bury was particularly fortunate in having an eminent abbot, Baldwin, at the Conquest. During his long tenure he was able, through his Norman origins and continuation as royal physician to both the Conqueror and William Rufus, to consolidate the advantages gained by the abbey under the Confessor. Baldwin's

3 Ely abbey had 13,400 sheep in six counties in 1086 (Power 1941, pp. 32–3). Figures are not available for Bury, although the freemen were obliged to send their sheep into the abbot's folds (Vinogradoff 1908, p. 424 and n. 3).

4 Moore 1985, p. 21 n. 61.

immediate successors were all men elected from without the convent, until the appointment of Ording in the reign of Stephen. Thereafter until 1279, with the exception of Hugh I, the abbot was invariably an appointee from within. It did not follow that they were men of second-rate standing. Samson clearly justifies his reputation not merely through having the advantage of a readable biographer. His successor, Hugh of Northwold, later became bishop of Ely, and Edmund of Walpole undoubtedly gained rapid promotion to the abbacy because of his abilities.

The increasing role played by the convent and later by the Pope, as compared with the king, in the appointment of abbots can readily be traced at Bury in the period to 1279. It is also clear that abbots chosen from within the community itself had invariably served in the office of (sub) cellarer or (sub) sacrist.[5] These positions were the best training ground for the considerable administrative and financial skills expected of a competent abbot.

Of these powerful obedientiaries it was the sacrist who came to have overall control of the mint at Bury. He recruited lay personnel for its actual operations and, by the reign of Henry III at least, presented them to the barons of the exchequer for vetting and approval. The precise make-up of the mint organisation probably varied from time to time, but after the moneyer the most important officials were the assayer and custodians of the dies. It appears that sometimes (possibly always?) there were two custodians, presumably one to retain the obverse die when not in use and the other the reverse(s). The assayers and custodians were likely to gain promotion to the position of moneyer,[6] and as such to enjoy a privileged tax status.

Despite the role assumed by the sacrist, the right of coinage remained firmly attached to the abbot in person, as part of his temporalities. This was so both before and after separation of the abbot's and convent's property at the beginning of the twelfth century. Consequently, when the abbot died, the right of coinage fell into abeyance until his successor was appointed. This was of some importance during the Norman period, when the longest vacancy was of seven years duration, affording the prospect for the numismatist of matching vacancies to gaps in mint output at Bury. At present, however, the dearth of surviving coins from the period frustrates this possibility. It was, of course, always open to the king and his advisers to keep the mint in operation during such vacancies, but there is no persuasive evidence that this ever happened. It is, indeed, hard to see what advantage the crown would have gained from doing so. At the other extreme, the Calendar of Patent Rolls even recorded that the abbey was vacant in 1270, implying a cessation of mint activity, when it patently was not. The arrangement under which the mint was farmed back to the crown during Henry III's minority, on the other hand, was clearly exceptional and, vitally, made with

5 See Thompson 1981–4, pp. 91–7. Thompson omits Edmund of Walpole from his list of sub-sacrists.

6 *The Pinchbeck Register*, II, pp. 15–18.

the abbot's consent. He and the convent might nevertheless have felt it prudent to acquiesce in the arrangement at a time when the franchise was coming under threat.

A distinction has to be drawn between the right to operate the mint and exchange, attaching to the abbot, and the benefit, or profits, to be derived from its exercise. Doubtless, the abbot was both franchisee and beneficiary in the early days of the mint, but during the reign of Henry III, possibly from the 1250s or 1260s, profits were credited to the sacrist's account. This made sense as he had entire management of the activity.

The volume of coinage issuing from Bury was never great. In the earlier stages of its history, it would be surprising if the mint produced anything remotely approaching 1 per cent of the total coinage. However, as the number of mints in operation declined, not surprisingly the percentage contribution from Bury tended to increase. Evidence from the Short Cross period when surviving coins are plentiful is regrettably defective, mainly because important hoards are so inadequately recorded. Various calculations produce estimates between 0.7 and 4.8 per cent of the total coinage. The percentage of Bury Long Cross coins in the local Colchester (1969) hoard (3.9 per cent) may well exaggerate its mint output at that period, since the percentage in the vast Brussels hoard was approximately 2.4 per cent.

The number of Bury dies and coins in this study, by reign, type (or class) and moneyer, is summarised in Table 62, below. This shows that, after a steady but low level of activity in the reign of the Confessor, the reigns of William I and II produce only one surviving coin. Time alone may tell how far this results from the accidents of survival and discovery, as opposed to inactivity. The coins of Henry I and Stephen are in turn of such scarcity as to give an incomplete picture of coinage at Bury (as elsewhere) between 1100 and 1154, but sufficient specimens are recorded to show that the mint was active enough to support a complement of two and even three moneyers within that period. In the next reign the ability of Bury to withstand the closure of lesser mints becomes clearly evident. In the first Tealby issue of Henry II Bury was one of twenty-nine mints; by the sixth and last type, one of only fourteen.

The operation of the Bury mint during the Short Cross period displays a number of peculiarities, not least its total absence from 1180 until the recoinage of John in 1205. Given its resilience during the Tealby issue and its later reappearance, the most plausible explanation is that the role of Bury could not be accommodated within the measures to centralise the coinage through the exchanges at Canterbury and London. In this situation the abbot may well have continued to be entitled to strike coin for his own use, but did not consider it worthwhile to maintain a mint establishment if he could not employ it also to strike from silver belonging to others. Further peculiarities from this period are the extensive die linking found at Bury between 1205 and 1208, and the farm of the mint back to the king between 1223 and 1229.

Table 62. Summary of Bury dies and coins by reign, type and moneyer to 1279

Reign/type (class)	*Moneyer*	*No. of dies*		*No. of coins*
		O.	*R.*	
Edward the Confessor				
ii (Small Flan)	Morcere	1	1	3
v (Expanding Cross)		1	1	6
vii (Helmet)		1	1	6
ix (Sovereign-Eagles)		1	1	1
xi (Hammer Cross)		2	2	10
xiii (Facing Bust)		1	1	4
xv (Pyramids)		–	–	–
	S/T	7	7	30
Harold II		–	–	–
William I				
III (Canopy)	Godinc	1	1	1
	S/T	1	1	1
Henry I				
VII (Quatrefoil and Stars)	Unknown	1	1	1
XIII (Stars in Lozenge Fleury)	Godric	1	2	4
	Oddo	1	1	1
XIV (Pellets in Quatrefoil)	Godric	1	1	5
	Oddo	4	4	7
XV (Quadrilateral on Cross Fleury)	Gilebert	6	6	19
	S/T	14	15	37
Stephen				
I (Watford)	Gilebert	9	9	46
	Acelin	3	3	7
	Hunfrei	1	1	1
	Henri	1	1	1
II (Cross Voided and Mullets)	Acelin	1	1	4
	Hunfrei	1	1	2
VI (Profile/Cross and Piles)	Acelin	1	1	2
	Hunfrei	1	1	3
	]ric	1	1	1
	?	1	1	1
VII (Awbridge)	Acelin	1	1	3
	Gilebert?	1	1	1
	Willem	2	2	4
	S/T	24	24	76

Table 62. Summary of Bury dies and coins by reign, type and moneyer to 1279 (continued)

Reign/type (class)	*Moneyer*	*No. of dies*		*No. of coins*
		O.	*R.*	
Henry II: Tealby				
A1	Willem	2	2[a]	17
A2		2	1(+1)	20
C1		2[b]	2	22
	Henri	1	3	18
C2		1	1	2
B1		1	1	26
D1		2	2[c]	11
D3		2	1	12
E2/3		1	1	11
F	Raul	11	13	48
	S/T	25	27	187

Notes
(a) One reverse die also used with A2 obverse (5 coins).
(b) One obverse die shared also with Henri.
(c) One reverse die shared with a D1 and D3 obverse.

Reign/type (class)	*Moneyer*	*O.*	*R.*	*No. of coins*
*Short Cross: John/Henry III**				
Vb1	Fulke	1	3	35
Vb2/1		(1)	(1)	7
Vb2		4	7	53
Vc		1	1(+2)	12
	S/T	6	11	107
VIc1	Rauf	2	2	} 105
VIc2		5	14	} 105
VIc3		3	8	} 105
	S/T	10	24	105

Note
*In class V the classification is by obverse die, ignoring any die links between varieties. In class VI obverse and reverse dies are separately classified.

Reign/type (class)	*Moneyer*	*O.*	*R.*	*No. of coins*
Short Cross: Henry III				
VId		1	1	12
	S/T	1	1	12

Reign/type (class)	*Moneyer*	*No. of dies*		*No. of coins*
		O.	*R.*	
VIIa	Rauf	2	2	5
	Willelm	6	6	70
	Norman	17	18	169
VIIbA		1	1	2
VIIbB		1	1	4
VIIbBx	Simund	2	2	9
VIIbB1		7	7	31
VIIbB2		10	10	52
VIIbB3		4	4	11
VIIbC		12	12	35
VIIbD		12	12	45
VIIcA		3	4?	19
VIIcB		5	5	15
	Ioan	13	13	24
VIIcC		3	3	5
	S/T	98	<100	496
VIIIa		–	–	–
VIIIb1		1	1	5
VIIIb2		15	15	33
VIIIb3		9	9	14
	S/T	25	25	52
	Short Cross sub-total	140	161	772
Long Cross				
I	Ion	1	1	6
IIa		4	4	63
IIb		1	1	28
IIIa		5	5	69
IIIab1		2	2	37
IIIab2		1	1	15
IIIac		1	1	16
IIIb		3	3	85
IIIbc		2	2	42
IIIc		17	17	399
	S/T	37	37	760

Table 62. Summary of Bury dies and coins by reign, type and moneyer to 1279 (continued)

Reign/type (class)	*Moneyer*	*No. of dies*		*No. of coins*
		O.	*R.*	
Long Cross (continued)				
IVab		1	1	23
Va2		4	4	75
Va3		13	13	261
Vb2/a3	Randulf	1	1	22
Vb2		10	10	469
Vc		5	5	219
Vc (x)		1	1	48
Vd		1	1	17
Ve		–	–	–
Vf		2	2	28
Vg	Renaud	6	6	100
	Stephane	5	5	18
	Ion	8	8	23
Vh		4	4	6
Vi		1	1	1
	S/T	62	62	1310
VI		1	1	(1,917)*
VII		2	2	3
	Ioce	2	2	3
	S/T	5	5	(1,917)*+6
	Long Cross sub-total	104	104	2,076
	Total	315	339	3,179
Summary				
Edward the Confessor		7	7	30
William I		1	1	1
Henry I		14	15	37
Stephen		24	24	76
Henry II (Tealby)		25	27	187
Short Cross V		6	11	107
VIc		10	24	105
VId–VIII		124	125	560
Long Cross I–III		37	37	760
IV–V		62	62	1,310
VI–VII		5	5	(1,917)* +6
	Total	315	339	3,179

Note
* Excluded from totals.

The number of reverse dies issued with each obverse shows some variation over the period of this study. In the early days of the mint normally one obverse appears to have been issued with one reverse. In the Short Cross issue, before about 1216, this was changed to one obverse with two reverses, and exceptionally three and even four. After 1216 for the rest of the issue and throughout the Long Cross coinage a set of dies again consisted of one obverse with one reverse,[7] but sets of one obverse with two reverses were reinstated when Bury participated in the new coinage of Edward I from 1280.[8] The lack of die linking in the early history of the mint could arise from the low level of demand for dies between each change of type, but after some linking in the Tealby and early Short Cross issues, its absence is clearly attributable to the rule – apparently rigorously applied by those in charge of the exchange at London – that obsolete or worn out sets of dies had to be surrendered against the supply of new.

The extent to which Bury increasingly operated alongside a dwindling number of major mints, and in particular London and Canterbury, is shown in Figure 15.[9]

English coinage during the whole of the period from 1042 to 1279 found its way not only to other parts of the country through the impetus of taxation and other monetary transactions but, particularly after the introduction of the immobilised Short and Long Cross issues, also abroad. Figures 16 and 17 show the location of the main finds (1) in England and (2) abroad referred to above containing coins of Edward the Confessor (E), Henry I (H), Stephen (S), Henry II (T), and the Short Cross (x) and Long Cross (X) issues.

From the weight variation demonstrated in the Catalogue, not just in times of civil unrest, as under Stephen, or as a result of clipping or wear, it is clear that the acceptability of English coin abroad must have been based on its purity rather than its weight. The weight variation in the Long Cross coins from the Brussels hoard is particularly striking.

The vexed question of type changes in the late Anglo-Saxon and Norman period cannot yet be claimed to have been satisfactorily resolved. It is still uncertain how frequently and regularly and with what actual or intended effect one type succeeded another. Without raking over the arguments set out in Chapters 3 to 5, however, some regularity in the pattern of change should be expected, if only to minimise the inconvenience of an already irksome arrangement. Taking this into account a tentative periodicity is set out in Table 63 below for the substantive types.

7 An isolated reference to the issue of one obverse with two reverse dies occurs in 1231 but cannot be associated with any surviving coins (see *The Pinchbeck Register*, II, pp. 5–6).

8 Die studies (unpublished) by the author.

9 Fig. 15 is based on North 1994, *passim*.

Figure 15

Number of mints operating in England, 1042–1279

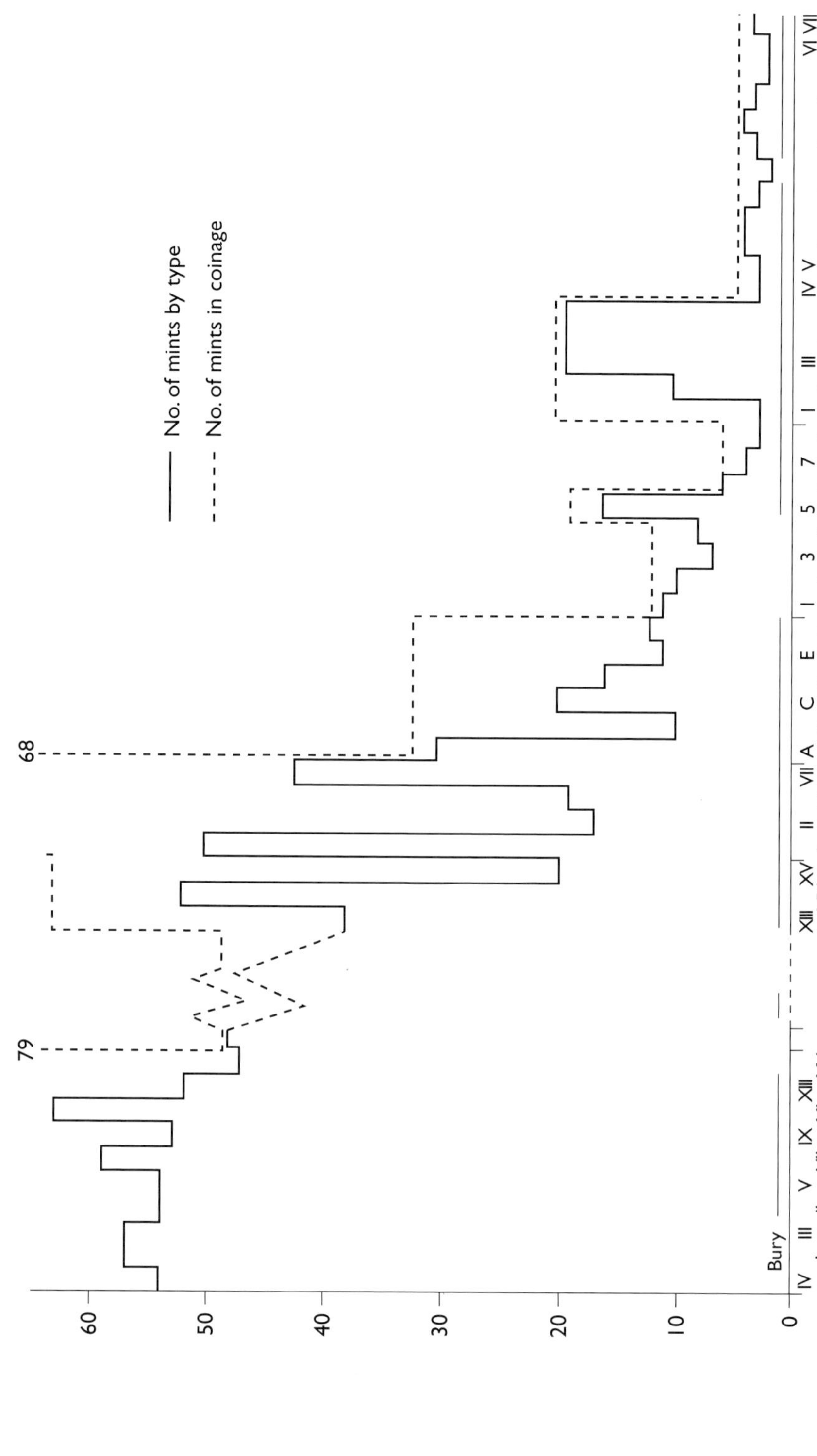

Figure 16

Location of hoards containing Bury coins (1): England

Table 63. Tentative duration of types, 1066–1135

Dates	*No. of types issued*	*No. of years of issue*	*Total years*
1066–1087	7	3	21
1087–1100	2	3	13*
	4	2	
1100–1135	14	2	35
	1	7	

Note
* On this hypothesis William II would have died midway through the currency of his last type.

Figure 17

Location of hoards containing Bury coins (2): abroad

To conclude, brief reference is made to the history of the mint after 1279 and of the mint establishment's physical whereabouts. It is hoped that these will be explored fully in a subsequent volume.

After the introduction of the new coinage of Edward I in 1279, the abbot at Bury began to strike coins of the new design from 26 June 1280.[10] The moneyer at the time was Robert of Hadley, usually referred to as Robert de Hadeleie. He is numismatically notable because his name, without that of the mint, appeared on his coins whereas at other mints operating by that time the mint name alone was included. After class IVc of the new coinage at Bury, however, the reverses bore the inscription (initially with minor variations in spelling) VILL SCIE DMV NDI, set between the limbs of the reverse cross. The mint remained active through the remainder of Edward I's reign, through that of Edward II, whose coins closely resembled those of his father, and into the reign of Edward III. By that time shortage of silver and inflation had rendered the minting of sterlings uneconomic.[11] Although the abbot was granted further dies[12] the mint closed, never to open again.

It is not known where the mint workshops or exchange were located during the period from 1042 to 1279, but various conjectures have been made. A map in Tymm's *Handbook of Bury St Edmunds* (1891) shows the sacrist's house at the south-westerly corner of the Great Court.[13] M. R. James, whose knowledge of the abbey was profound, appeared to agree with this general location when he wrote: 'Passing through [the Great Gate] . . . you find yourself in the gardens which represent the great court of the Abbey. Immediately on the right the Guest Hall is conjectured; beyond it the Mint.'[14] Whittington in his HMSO guide to Bury St Edmunds does not mention the mint,[15] but Pevsner's map, reproduced by courtesy of Whittingham from an article in the *Archaeological Journal*, shows the mint adjoining the sacristy, near the south-east corner of the abbey church.[16] The only contemporary documentary evidence of its whereabouts is from the very close of the mint's activity. A writ of 1329 states it at that time not to have been in the abbey precincts, but in a street in the town called Le Mustow.[17] The locations mentioned are indicated in Figure 18.

10 Fox and Fox 1910, p. 117.
11 Fox and Shirley-Fox 1913, p. 110.
12 Fox and Shirley-Fox 1913, p. 108.
13 Tymms 1891, map opposite p. 15.
14 James 1930, p. 39.
15 Whittingham 1971, based on Whittingham 1952.
16 Pevsner 1974, p. 134. The plan reproduced by Pevsner appears opposite p. 192 in Whittingham 1952; the mint location is referred to at p. 182.
17 *CPR 1327–1330*, p. 411.

Figure 18

Putative location of the Bury mint workshops (and exchange)

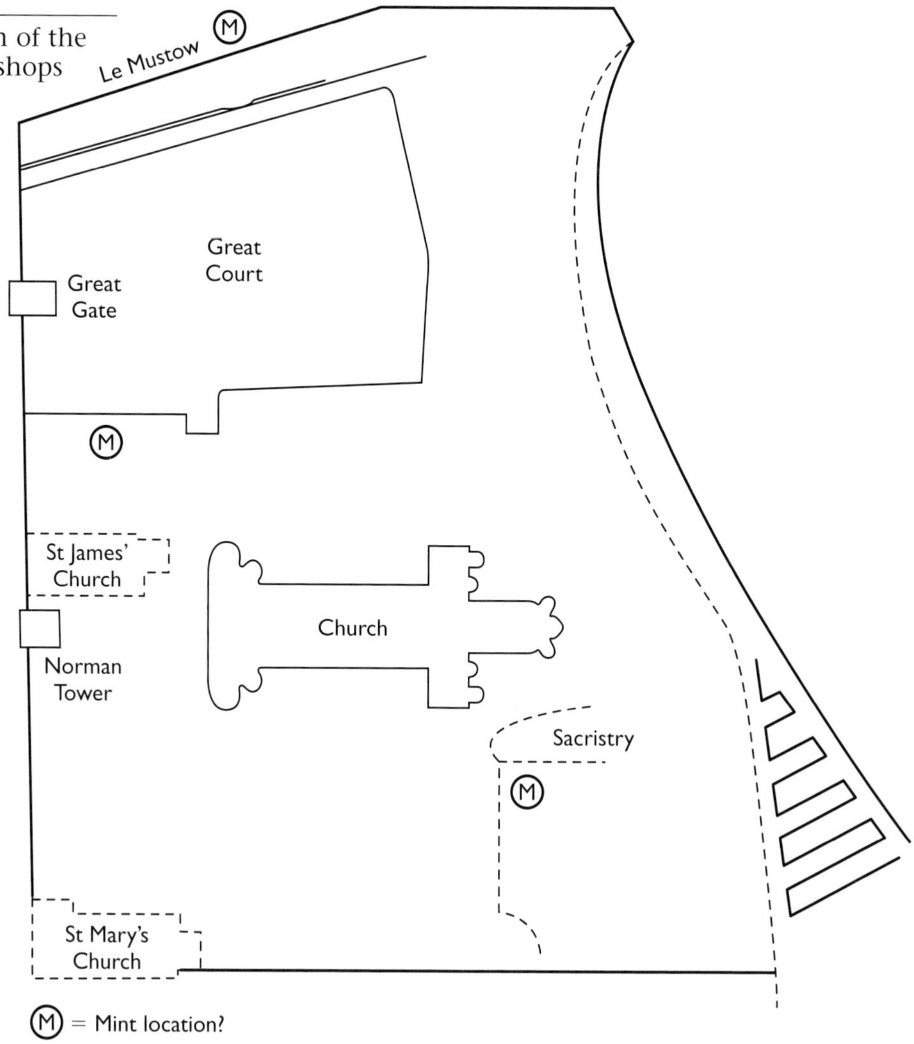

Without the unexpected help of archaeology it is unlikely the location of the mint workshops will ever be established. This lack of knowledge is, however, a small loss compared with the benefits derived from the survival of so much numismatic material, in documentary evidence and coins, from the mint of Bury St Edmunds.

THE CATALOGUE OF COINS

Explanatory notes

The Catalogue was finalised in December 2004 and makes no pretence to be a complete record of the known coins of Bury at that date. Nevertheless, the main likely sources of material have, as far as practicable, been trawled up to and including the Tealby issue. In the Short and Long Cross series many Bury coins will have eluded the author's net but, because of the large number that have been traced and the tendency for rarer coins to reach publication, the adverse impact should be minimised.

No coin has been included in the Catalogue unless the author possesses it or has adequate photographic or other illustrations to enable the dies to be identified and to ensure that it is not recorded more than once. Descriptions of coins for which no concrete image could be found are recorded under 'Other references'.

Catalogue numbers have been given to each die combination identified. When the attribution to Bury of a moneyer is uncertain, the numbers given to the relevant die pairings are shown in brackets. Such coins are illustrated in the Plates to help resolve the uncertainty if further relevant coins come to light. Where, in the author's opinion, a die pairing is doubtfully attributable to Bury, no catalogue numbers are given and the moneyer's name is placed in parentheses. These die pairings are likewise illustrated. Where, in the author's opinion, the Bury origin of a coin should be rejected, the coin is not illustrated.

The obverse (O.) and reverse (R.) readings are represented as closely as the limitations of the chosen font permit. For example, the square forms of the letters A and C are not shown. Ligulations are indicated by closing the space between the relevant letters. Illegible or obscure portions of the legends are shown within brackets by a blank space or putative letters. Special features of an obverse or reverse die are described immediately below the transcription of the legend.

Each coin struck from the same pair of dies is given an Arabic number in parentheses, except for the large number of Long Cross coins from the Brussels (1908) and Colchester (1969) hoards. The coin chosen to illustrate that die combination in the Plates is marked by an asterisk. The illustrations have been chosen for their capability to show the salient features of the dies rather than to publish previously unillustrated coins.

In the Catalogue the initial reference for each coin states the most recently known owner or documentary evidence. This is followed, when ascertainable, by the hoard or find to which the coin relates and the year of discovery. The reader unfamiliar with the hoards cited should refer, for hoards deposited in Britain, to Thompson's *Inventory* (Thompson 1956), as updated by Allen 2002. Further information is also included in the footnotes relating to hoards discussed in the text. The ownership pedigree and any illustrations are then briefly referenced in chronological sequence. When a coin is published in an accessible source, the pedigree is given to the extent needed to guard the reader against mistaking such references for evidence of separate coins. To this end, Catalogue references to collectors and notable auctions (e.g. Elmore Jones) are elaborated under Ownership Pedigrees below. Accordingly, references in the Catalogue to coins sold by auction consist of the name of the auction house, the date or dates of sale and the lot number, and coins sold by Seaby in *SCMB* or Spink in *NCirc* are cited by the month and year of the publication and the reference number of the coin offered for sale.

The die axis (in degrees), up to and including the reign of Stephen, and the weight (in grams) is given for each coin, where known. The author has in many instances not been able to verify this information and, in particular, certain of the irregular die axes may be suspect. Where a coin has been cut into fractions, or is obviously damaged, corroded or worn, the weight is shown within brackets and all such coins have been excluded from any weight analysis in the main text.

In the Long Cross series, coins from the same pair of dies are grouped together under three headings: those from the Brussels hoard (1908), from the Colchester hoard (1969) and from other sources, identified respectively as BRU, COL and OTHER, suffixed by the number of coins occurring under each heading in parentheses.

OWNERSHIP PEDIGREES

Allen	Dr M. R. Allen, (former) collector, Cambridge.
Armitage	E. F. P. Armitage, collector (deceased).
Argyll	N. D. Campbell, 15th Duke of Argyll, collector (d. 1949). Anglo-Saxon and Norman coins purchased by Spink in 1949, a proportion being offered without attribution in *NCirc* from Nov. 1952 onwards.
Ashmolean Museum	Ashmolean Museum, Oxford.
'Astronomer'	F. McClean, collector (d. 1904). Sotheby, 11–12 June 1906, lots 1–242.

Baldwin	A. H. Baldwin & Sons Ltd., London coin dealers and auctioneers.
Baldwin, A. H. F.	A. H. F. Baldwin, of A. H. Baldwin & Sons Ltd., dealer and collector (d. 1970). Many of his coins selected from the Brussels hoard are still in the company's stocks.
Banes	A. A. Banes, collector (deceased). Sotheby, 30–31 Oct. 1922, lots 1–392.
Banks, Lady	Lady Dorothea Banks, wife of Sir Joseph Banks and sister-in-law of (Miss S. S.) Banks (*qv*).
Banks	Miss S. S. Banks, collector (d. 1818). Collection donated to the British Museum in 1818 by Lady Banks (*qv*).
Bascombe	R. E. Bascombe, collector (deceased), of Bury St Edmunds. Sotheby, 4–5 Feb. 1908.
Bertram	Mlle S. Bertram, France. Part owner of the Gisors hoard (1970).
Bird	Dr B. Bird, collector (d.1993). Glendining/Spink, 20 Nov. 1974, lots 1–300.
Blunt	C. E. Blunt, collector (d. 1987). Collection acquired by the Fitzwilliam Museum in 1990, including the collection formed by J. S. Shirley-Fox (*qv*) and his brother H. B. Earle Fox, previously bequeathed to Blunt.
Brand	Dr J. D. Brand, collector (d. 1990). Collection sold by Baldwin and by Glendining, 2 May 1984, lots 82–111. Bury coins acquired by Eaglen (*qv*) in 1983.
Briggs	A. Briggs, collector (deceased). Sotheby, 23 March 1893, lots 172–379.
BM	British Museum coin not published in *BMC*, with the year of acquisition in parentheses.
BMC	*British Museum Catalogue* (when followed by a number this refers to the coin as listed in the relevant catalogue): C. F. Keary, *Anglo-Saxon Series*, 2 vols (London, 1887). G. C. Brooke, *The Norman Kings*, 2 vols (London, 1916). D. F. Allen, *The Cross-and-Crosslets ('Tealby') Type of Henry II* (London, 1951).
Bruun	L. E. Bruun, collector (d. 1923). Sotheby, 18–22 May 1925, lots 1–965.

Burkinshaw	S. Birkinshaw, coin dealer.
Burstal	Dr E. Burstal, collector (d. 1967). Glendining, 15 Oct. 1984, lots 1–340.
Carlyon-Britton	Major P. W. P. Carlyon-Britton (d. 1938). Sotheby, 17–21 Nov. 1913, lots 1–783 (part I); 20–24 Nov. 1916, lots 784–1531 (part II); 11–13 Nov. 1918, lots 1532–1975 (part III).
Carlyon-Britton, R.	R. C. Carlyon-Britton, collector (d. 1960), son of P. W. P. Carlyon-Britton (*qv*).
Conte	Dr W. J. Conte, collector, Connecticut, USA. Part of collection acquired by the Fitzwilliam Museum in 2001, part auctioned by Classical Numismatic Group, 19 Sept. 2001, lots 1729–1989 (part I); 22 May 2002, lots 2159–2360 (part II), and part bought privately by Mass.
Crafter	T. C. R. Crafter, collector, Hertfordshire.
Cuff	A. Cuff, collector (d. 1853).
Davis	R. L. Davis, collector, Berkshire.
Dawson	A. M. Dawson, collector, Lancashire.
Dolphin	Dolphin Coins and Medals Ltd., coin dealers, Hampstead (London) and Leighton Buzzard.
Doubleday	G. V. Doubleday, collector (d. 1993). Glendining/ Baldwin, Anglo-Saxon coins, 6 Oct. 1987, lots 1–637; Norman and Plantagenet coins, 8 June 1988, lots 1–457.
Drabble	G. C. Drabble, collector (d. 1939). Glendining, 4–6 July 1939, lots 1–801 (part I); 13–14 Dec. 1943, lots 802–1219 (part II).
Duart-Smith	F. W. Duart-Smith, collector (d. 1945). Glendining, 27–28 Nov. 1945, lots 1–406.
Dupree	(T. W. J.) D. Dupree, collector. Coins acquired by Spink in the late 1980s.
Durrant	Lt. Col. W. Durrant, collector (d. 1846). Sotheby, 19–24 and 26–28 April 1847, lots 1–1158.
Eaglen	Dr R. J. Eaglen, collector, Berkshire (followed by collection reference of B and three or four digits in parentheses).
Ebsworth	N. J. Ebsworth, collector, Warwickshire.

Elmore Jones	F. Elmore Jones, collector (d. 1982). Glendining, Anglo-Saxon coins, 12–13 May 1971, lots 1–1016; Norman and Plantagenet coins, 13 April 1983, lots 1017–1291 (part I), 10 April 1984, lots 1292–1601 (part II) and 7 Oct. 1986, lots 1602–1911 (part III).
Evans	Sir John Evans, collector (d. 1908). Collection acquired by Spink and sold to John Pierpoint Morgan, P. W. P. Carlyon-Britton (*qv*) and via *NCirc* from June 1910 onwards.
Finn	P. Finn, dealer (d. 2000).
Fitzwilliam Museum	Fitzwilliam Museum, Cambridge.
Frost	H. G. Frost, collector (deceased). Bury coins bequeathed to the Moyses Hall Museum, Bury St Edmunds in 1976.
Gardner	T. C. Gardner, collector (deceased). Coins photographed in 1980s by Tatler (*qv*).
Gittoes	G. P. Gittoes, collector, Middlesex.
Grainger	Rev. Canon J. Grainger, collector (deceased).
Grantley	Lord John R. B. N. Grantley, 5th Baron, collector (d. 1943). Glendining, 20–21 April 1944, lots 1241–1670 (part IV).
Hanham	Sir John L. Hanham, collector (d. 1955).
Harkness	F. W. Harkness, collector (d. 1933).
Harris	Dr E. J. Harris, collector, Middlesex.
Hasluck	F. W. Hasluck, collector (d. 1920).
Hild.	Hildebrand (followed by the number of a coin in the systematic collection at Stockholm, as listed in Hildebrand 1881).
Higgs	W. S. Higgs, collector (deceased). Sotheby, 29 April 1830.
Jacob	K. A. Jacob, collector (d. 1995).
Jarmin	K. W. Jarmin, collector. Coins photographed by Osborne (*qv*) before 1983.
King	H. H. King, collector (d. 1976).
Lainchbury	A. W. Lainchbury, collector (d. 1978). Glendining, 15 March 1973, lots 361–798.
Lawrence	Dr L. A. Lawrence, collector (d. 1949). Glendining, 14 March 1951, lots 178–572 (part II); 28 Nov. 1951, lots

	988–1429 (part IV). Selections of his coins were acquired by the British Museum in 1935 and 1947.
Lincoln	W. S. Lincoln & Son, former London coin dealers.
Lockett	R. C. Lockett, collector (d. 1950). Glendining, 6–9 June 1955, lots 1–1222 (English part I); 4–6 Nov. 1958, lots 2628–3545 (English part III); 26–27 April 1960, lots 3546–4249 (English part IV).
Lubbock	R. M. Lubbock, London coin dealer.
Mack	Cdr. R. P. Mack, collector (d. 1974). Most of collection published in *SCBI* 20 . Glendining/Spink, 18 Nov. 1975, lots 1–290 (part I) and 23 March 1977, lots 1–270 (part II).
Mangakis	D. (Bersi-)Mangakis, collector (d. 1999). Collection acquired by Spink in 1969.
Martin, C. J.	C. J. Martin (Coins) Ltd., dealer in coins and antiquities, Southgate (London).
Martin	Rev. J. W. Martin, collector (deceased). Sotheby, 23–27 May 1859, lots 1–574.
Mass	Prof. J. P. Mass, collector (d. 2001). Short Cross coins published in *SCBI* 56, being progressively auctioned by Dix, Noonan, Webb, as from 17 March 2004, lots 1–442 (part I).
Montagu	H. Montagu, collector (d. 1895). Sotheby, 11–16 May 1896, lots 1–857 (part II); 16–20 Nov. 1897, lots 1–737 (part V).
Mossop	H. R. Mossop, collector (d. 1988).
Murdoch	J. G. Murdoch, collector (d. 1902). Sotheby, 31 March and 1–4 April 1903, lots 1–772 (part I).
Murrell	R. J. Murrell, collector (deceased). Sotheby, 13–17 July 1886, lots 1–948.
National Museum of Wales	National Museum of Wales, Cardiff.
North	J. J. North, collector, Sussex. Plantagenet collection sold to Conte (*qv*) in 1997.
Olroyd	'Olroyd' collection bequeathed to the British Museum in 1946.
Osborne	B. R. Osborne, collector (d. 1990). Bury coins acquired by Eaglen (*qv*) in 1983.

Palmer	D. J. Palmer, collector, Suffolk (followed by collection reference of SED and up to three digits in parentheses).
Parsons	H. A. Parsons, collector (d. 1952). Glendining, 28 Oct.–1 Nov. 1929, lots 1–906 (part I); 11–13 May 1954, lots 1–1060 (part II).
Pheatt	W. H. Pheatt, collector, Arizona, USA. Buckland, Dix & Wood, 21 March 1995, lots 401–875.
Rashleigh	J. Rashleigh, collector (d. 1905). Sotheby, 21 June–1 July 1909, lots 1–1185, as property of E. W. Rashleigh. A number of his coins from the Watford hoard (1818) were given to the British Museum in 1849.
Reynolds	H. M. Reynolds, collector (d. 1948).
Rogers	Very Rev. E. Rogers, collector (d. 1961).
Rostron	S. Rostron, collector (deceased). Sotheby, 16–20 May 1892, lots 1–654.
Roth	B. M. S. Roth, collector (d. 1915). Sotheby, 19–20 July 1917, lots 1–379.
Royal Mint Museum	Royal Mint Museum, Llantrisant.
Seaby	B. A. Seaby Ltd., former London coin dealers, and publishers of *SCMB*.
Shepherd	Rev. E. J. Shepherd, collector (d. 1874). Sotheby, 22–25 July 1885, lots 1–534.
Shirley-Fox	J. S. Shirley-Fox, previously J. Shirley Fox, collector (d. 1939). Collection bequeathed to Blunt (*qv*).
Shuttlewood	R. A. Shuttlewood, collector (d. 2000).
Smith	H. P. Smith, collector (deceased). Sotheby, 17–18 and 20–21 Dec. 1886, lots 1–921.
Southgate	Rev. R. Southgate, collector (d. 1795). Sotheby sale planned over eight days in May 1795, but collection acquired by Tyssen (*qv*).
Spink	Spink & Son Ltd., London coin dealers and auctioneers, publishers of *NCirc*.
Spink, P.	P. Spink of Spink & Son Ltd., dealer and collector (d. 1980).
Spink, S. M.	S. M. Spink of Spink & Son Ltd., dealer and collector (d. 1947).

Stewartby	Right Hon. Baron Stewartby, previously (Sir) B. H. I(an) H. Stewart, collector, London.
Taffs	H. W. Taffs, collector (d. 1955). Glendining, 21–23 Nov. 1956, lots 1–927.
Talbot Ready	W. T. Ready, dealer and collector (d. 1914).
Tatler	Dr G. L. V. Tatler, collector (d. 1998).
Thomsen	C. J. Thomsen, collector, Denmark (deceased). After his death his coins were acquired by the Royal Collection, Copenhagen, in 1868.
Thomas	R. I. Thomas, collector, Essex.
Trenerry	Michael Trenerry, dealer and collector, Cornwall.
Tyssen	S. Tyssen, collector (d. 1800). Sotheby, 12 April–31 May 1802, lots 1–3128.
Wells	W. C. Wells, dealer and collector (d. 1949).
Woodhead	P. Woodhead, collector, Gloucestershire.
Youde	Maj. W. J. C. Youde, collector (d. 1964). Coins acquired by Spink (*qv*) after his death.

EDWARD THE CONFESSOR (1042–66)

Small Flan type (*BMC* ii, Hild. B)

Morcere

1	Aa	O.	+EDPE/RD RE	
		R.	+HORCEP ON ED	
			Pellet in third quarter	
		(1)	*SCBI* Estonian Collections, ED 1065. Edise hoard (1903)? 270°	1.15
		(2)*	Palmer (SED 27). Reputedly found in Thetford area, *c.* 1980. 180°	1.14
		(3)	*BMC* 1561. Listed under uncertain mints, but see *BNJ* 28 (1955–7), p. 55. Purchased from Cuff (1939). Possibly from the Thwaite hoard (1832), see *BNJ* 28 (1955–7), p. 36. 270°	0.97

Expanding Cross type (*BMC* v, Hild. E). Heavy issue

Morcere

2	Aa	O.	+EDPER/.D RECX: Bust 'd' (*BNJ* 28 (1955–7), p. 138, Fig. 13)	
		R.	+MORCEREE ON EDHVN	
		(1)	*BMC* 203. City of London hoard (1872). Presented by E. H. Willett (1876), see *BNJ* 28 (1955–7), p. 55. 0°	1.62
		(2)	*SCBI* Copenhagen IV, 801. Lyngby hoard (1861). 0°	1.62
		(3)	Palmer (SED 872). R. gilded. 0°	1.62
		(4)*	Eaglen (B071). Ex Lockett 3804; Bird 200, illustrated. Reverse partly double-struck. 0°	1.59
		(5)	Carlyon-Britton, I (1913) 599, Pl. XV; Parsons, I (1929) 197(a). Die axis?	–
		(6)	Palmer (SED 870). Ex Elmore Jones 123, illustrated. Cut halfpenny. 270°	[0.80]

Other references: Briggs (1893) 223 and W. Talbot Ready, see *BNJ* 47 (1977), p. 73.

Three coins of this type and moneyer are recorded for Bury in the City of London hoard (1872), see *Inventory*, no. 255, p. 93. *Coin Hoards* 5 (1979), p. 103, refers to dispersal of a hitherto unrecorded parcel containing one Bury coin of this type.

Edward the Confessor (*cont.*)

Pointed Helmet type (*BMC* vii, Hild. F)

Morcere

3	Aa	O.	+EDPER/D RE Sceptre with lis head.	
		R.	+MORCERE ON EDM	
		(1)	*SCBI* South-Eastern Museums (Museum of London) 1249/MOL. Gracechurch Street hoard (mid 19th century)? Corroded with metal adhering to surface. 90°	[1.43]
		(2)	*SCBI* Museums in East Anglia (Bury) 1303. Ex *SCMB*, Jan. 1965, H. 2609, illustrated; Frost collection. 90°	1.35
		(3)*	Eaglen (B010). Ex Carlyon-Britton, I (1913) 607, Pl. XVI; Lockett 828, Pl. XIX; Elmore Jones 124, illustrated. See also *NC* (1905), Pl. VII, 12 (this coin). 90°	1.32
		(4)	Palmer (SED 62). Ex Duke of Argyll collection; Doubleday 28, Pl. I. 90°	1.30
		(5)	*SCBI* South-Eastern Museums (Museum of London) 1337/MOL. Gracechurch Street hoard (mid 19th century)? Corroded. 180°	[1.15]
		(6)	Glendining, 26 Nov. 1970, 897. Die axis?	–

3(1) and (5) are listed by the Museum of London as from the City of London hoard (1872), but Dolley (*BNJ* 27 (1952–4), p. 213) attributed them to the Gracechurch Street hoard. Thompson (*Inventory*, no. 244, p. 87) agrees. The City of London hoard is recorded as containing three coins of *BMC* vii (*Inventory*, no. 255, p. 94) but no known provenance exists for 3(2)–(4) or (6).

Other references: Roth (1917) 87, stated to be 'from the City hoard'; Parsons, I (1929) 201; Taffs (1956) 96; *SCMB*, June 1957, 5170, 'MORCERE ON EDM', stated incorrectly to be illustrated in Pl. III; C. J. Martin, Jan. 1983, cut farthing, said to be from 'same dies as Lockett (1955) 828'.

Sovereign-Eagles type (*BMC* ix, Hild. H)

Morcere

4	Aa	O.	EΛDPΛRD REX ΛNGLOV No cross on orb?	
		R.	+MORCΛR[E] [O]N EΛDM:	
		(1)*	Eaglen (B226). Ex Elmore Jones 125. 90°	1.29

Other references: Parsons I (1929) 203. Probably same coin as above.

Hammer Cross type (*BMC* xi, Hild. G)

Morcere

5 Aa O. +EΛDPΛRD/ RD RE
R. MORCRE ON EΛDMVN

(1)	*SCBI* Ashmolean Museum 938. 180°	1.28
(2)	*BMC* 204. City of London hoard (1872). Presented by E. H. Willett (1876), see *BNJ* 28 (1955–7), p. 55. See also *Inventory*, no. 244, p. 88. 180°	1.26
(3)	Glendining, 23 April 1991, 1. Ex Elmore Jones 126; Osborne collection. 45°	1.23
(4)*	Eaglen (B016). Ex Baldwin (1976); King collection. 270°	1.22
(5)	Doubleday 29, Pl. I, 'blistered in a fire'. 270°	[1.18]
(6)	Palmer (SED 353). Ex Lockett 846; Glendining, 14 March 1973, 277; Glendining, 11 July 1984, 186, read as MOCRE; Pheatt 610 (Buckland, Dix & Wood, 21 March 1995). 270°	1.05
(7)	*SCMB*, Jan. 1964, H2014, Pl. 4. Die axis?	–
(8)	*BNJ* 58 (1988), Coin Register 188, p. 157. Cut farthing. Found near Marham, Norfolk in 1987. 180°	[0.22]

Other references: Montagu (1896) 147, 'in fair condition'; Carlyon-Britton, III (1918) 1806, 'a fragment'; Drabble, II (1943) 887; Taffs (1956) 99, read as MORCRE ON EADMVND [*sic*]; Glendining, 24 May 1972, 641, not illustrated.

6 Bb O. +EΛDPΛR·/RD RE
R. +MORCRE ON EΛDMVN
Cross saltire in first and fourth quarters.

(1)	*SCBI* South-Eastern Museums (Museum of London) 1429/MOL, where described as 'probably ex City Hoard, 1872'. Cf *BNJ* 27 (1952–4), p. 213, where Dolley concurs with the Museum of London's attribution to the Gracechurch Street hoard (mid 19th century)? Broken in half. 180°	[1.17]
(2)*	Eaglen (B227). Ex Lockett 846; Elmore Jones 127; possibly also Roth (1917) 87, where described as from the City of London hoard (1872). Chipped, broken and rejoined. 0°	[1.06]

Other references: *Inventory*, no. 255, p. 94, lists seven coins of this type for Morcere from the City of London hoard (1872), but designates them erroneously as *BMC* ix instead of xi (*BNJ* 27 (1952–4), p. 66.) A supplementary list, *Inventory*, no. 255, p. 98, adds one further coin, described as *BMC* xi.

Edward the Confessor (*cont.*)

Facing Bust type (*BMC* xiii, Hild. Ac)

Morcere

7	Aa1	O.	EADPARD REX·	
		R.	+MARCERE ON EAD:	
		(1)	*BMC* 205. City of London hoard (1872). Presented by E. H. Willett (1876), see *BNJ* 27 (1952–4), p. 55. 0°	1.14
		(2)*	Eaglen (B024), Ex Wells? 90°	1.03
		(3)	Palmer (SED 631). Ex Elmore Jones 128. 0°	1.00
7A	Aa2	O.	As above	
		R.	As above, but with two vertical lines added, connecting the central cross and inner circle.	
		(1)*	*SCBI* South-Eastern Museums (Museum of London) 1569/MOL. City of London hoard (1872). [?]. 180°	0.99

Inventory, no. 255, p. 95 gives one coin of this type to Bury from the City of London hoard (1872), listed incorrectly as *BMC* xv for xiii (*BNJ* 27 (1952–4), p. 66). However, two coins are attributed above to the hoard. Since the British Museum would doubtless have selected the coin of dies Aa2, if afforded the opportunity to do so, the provenance of this coin may be questionable.

Other references: Montagu (1896) 128.

Pyramids type (*BMC* xv, Hild. I)

No coins known of this type.

HAROLD II (1066)

No coins known of this reign.

WILLIAM I (1066–87)

In this reign the only known coin is as follows:

Canopy type (*BMC* III)

Godinc

8 Aa O. +PILLEMIIS RE
R. +GODINC ON EIIDMII
(1)* BM (1960). Ex Spink. 45° 1.03

WILLIAM II (1087–1100)

No coins known of this reign.

HENRY I (1100–35)

Annulets type (*BMC* I)

References:

Moneyer unknown

– – – Andrew 1901, pp. 388, 392, referring to Southgate (1795, 8th day) 109 and Tyssen (1802) 1003. These references are ignored by Brooke in *Norman Kings*.

Quatrefoil and Piles type (*BMC* VII)

Moneyer unknown

9 Aa O.]ENR[
R.]S(supine) : ED[
(1)* Eaglen (B803). Found near Southwark Bridge, London (1988?). Cut farthing. 180° (?) [0.24]

(Adalbot)

– – O. +hENRIC REX
R. +ADALBOT : ON SAN
(1) Lockett 1057, illustrated. Ex Smith (1886) sale; Reynolds. See also Andrew 1901, p. 390 and Pl. VIII,

Henry I, Quatrefoil and Piles type (*BMC* VII) (*cont.*)

3 and *SCMB*, Dec. 1986, p. 374. Attributed to Sandwich.

(2) *SCBI* Stockholm 275. 180°, 1.20g.

(3) *NC* (1901), p.390:
'+ΛDΛLBOT ON SAN. Murrell sale, 1886 [16 (4/5)].'

Cross in Quatrefoil type (*BMC* IX)

(Wulfwart)

– – O. '+hENRI REX
R. +PVLFPART : ON : SAN'

Andrew 1901, p. 392 with following comment: 'Bury St Edmunds Museum. Found at Whepstead within five miles of Bury St Edmunds.' The undocumented collection was stolen from the museum at Moyses Hall in 1965 and not subsequently recovered (see *SCBI* East Anglian Museums, p. 103). There is no indication whether this is the coin with the same O. and R. legends now in the BM, ex Wells (see *Norman Kings* I, p.ccxxxv and Pl. XLI, 8), Armitage and Mack (*SCBI* 1529 and Glendining, 23 March 1977, 253) and given to Sandwich.

Full Face/Cross Fleury type (*BMC* X)

(Godric)

– – O. +hENRICVS[:] REX:

R. +CVODRI[C : O]H : SAH

(1)* BM (1973). Lincoln hoard (1971/2). 270° 1.23

Described in *Coin Hoards* 1 (1975), p. 90, as Bury, but is possibly of Sandwich. See Chapter 5 above.

(Gilebert)

– – O. '+hE. . . .EX:
R. +GILEBERT : ON..N'

Andrew 1901, p.391, with following comment: 'L. A. Lawrence. This spelling of the moneyer's name does not occur elsewhere in Henry's reign'. It is now known to occur on several reverse dies of Gilebert at Bury in *BMC* XV, but no coins of Gilebert before *BMC* XV have come to light with an unambiguously Bury inscription.

Double Inscription type (*BMC* XI)

(Wulfstan)

–	–	O.	[ ]hEN[	
		R.	[ ]VLSTA[ ]ON SAN[P]	
		(1)*	*SCBI* Ashmolean Museum 218. Ex Magdalen College (Driver collection). 0°	1.28

Described as 'Bury St Edmunds or Sandwich', but reverse appears to read SANP for Sandwich.

Smaller Profile/Cross and Annulets (*BMC* XII)

Other references:

NCirc, May 1989, 2535 (illustrated). Small, irregular flan (0.87g), purportedly reading '[G]ODRICVS ON SA'.

Star in Lozenge Fleury type (*BMC* XIII)

Godric

10	Aa	O.	+hENRICVS R·	
		R.	+GODRIC : ON : S : EDM:	
	(1)*	Eaglen (B388). Ex Tyssen (1802) 1020 (4/4); Durrant (1847) 187; Shepherd (1885) 122; Montagu, II (1896) 298, illustrated; Murdoch (1903) 238 and Pl. III; Lockett 3910, illustrated. See also Ruding 1840, III, Pl. II, 5 (this coin) and Andrew 1901, p. 391 and Pl. VII, 1. Casts of the coin are in the British Museum with the query 'genuine?'. 90°		1.33
	(2)	Lincoln Museum. Lincoln hoard (1971/2). Die axis?		1.29
	(3)	*NCirc*, Dec. 1991, 7989, illustrated. Metal detector find. Die axis?		1.24

Other references: Brooke 1950, p. 89, lists Godric as a moneyer under types XII and XIV. Since the coin described at Catalogue 10(1) must have been known to him but is not mentioned, 'XII' is probably a typographical error for 'XIII'.

11	Ab	O.	As above	
		R.	+GODRIC.ON.SAN[	
		(1)*	Eaglen (B1017). Ex Baldwin (1990). Corroded. 180°	[1.16]

[Odd]o

12	Aa	O.	+hE[ ]ICVS R [ ]
		R.	]O[:] N SANEEDMV:

Henry I, Star in Lozenge Fleury type (*BMC* XIII) (*cont.*)

		(1)*	BM (1973). Lincoln hoard (1971/2). Bent. 120°	0.98

Other references:

Coin Hoards 1 (1975), p. 90 (no. 359), refers to two Bury coins of type XIII in the Lincoln hoard (see Catalogue 10 (2) and 12 (1) above).

Pellets in Quatrefoil type (*BMC* XIV)

Godric

13	Aa	O.	+hENRICVS RE:	
		R.	+GODRICVS:OH:SA'E: NB. Latinised name of moneyer.	
		(1)*	Eaglen (B031). Ex Carlyon-Britton, II (1916) 1397, Pl. XXXII; Parsons, II (1954) 247; Mack, II (1977) 257, illustrated; and *SCBI* Mack 1549. See also *Norman Kings*, I, p. 301 and II, Pl. XLIV, 6. 45°	1.33
		(2)	*BMC* 112, Pl. XLIV, 5. Bournemouth/Canterbury hoard (1901)? See P. W. P Carlyon-Britton 1927–8, p. 101, and Stewart 1977. Ex Mrs Stern, 1911. 225°	1.23
		(3)	Lincoln Museum. Lincoln hoard (1971/2). Die axis?	1.21
		(4)	Lincoln Museum. Lincoln hoard (1971/2). 315°	1.12
		(5)	Lincoln Museum. Lincoln hoard (1971/2). Die axis?	0.93

Other references:

Coin Hoards 1 (1975), p. 90 (no. 359) refers to three Bury coins of type XIV in the Lincoln hoard. There were, in fact, four: Catalogue 13 (3)–(5) and 15 (3) below.

–	–	O.	+hENRICVS[ ]
		R.	+GODRIC:ON:SAN[ ]
		*	*BMC* 111, Pl. XLIV, 4. Watford hoard (1818). Ex Rashleigh (1909) 457, Pl. VII. See also Andrew 1901, p. 392, where the coin is transcribed as +hENRICVS R .GODRIC:ON:SANT
		*	Brooke, in *Norman Kings*, II, p. 301, places the coin under Bury. Archibald, however, has found an obverse die link with a coin from the Lincoln hoard (1971/2), the reverse of which reads +GODRIC:ON:SAHD:. *BMC* 111 has accordingly been transferred to Sandwich. Both coins are illustrated in the Catalogue.

Andrew 1901, p. 391, cites a coin from the Simpson Rostron (1892) sale and

Reynolds collection, purportedly reading
'+hEN. . . S R
+[GOD]RIC:ON:SANTIE:'

Oddo

14 Aa O. +hEN[ ]S REX
Bust of unusual style.
R. +OD[DO:ON:SA]NCADM

(1)* Eaglen (B579). Ex Elmore Jones 1655, noting that coin had previously been illustrated in error as lot 1079. Possibly from Bournemouth/Canterbury hoard (1901). See also Biddle 1976, p. 409, n. 1. 225° — 1.34

(2) Conte collection (a coin not acquired by the Fitzwilliam Museum). 'Beauvais' (Paris region?) hoard (*c.* 1987). See introduction to Glendining, 4 Nov. 1987, coin no. 10 from parcel of twenty coins not offered. Die axis? — 1.09

15 Bb O. hENRICVS RE[ ]
No initial cross or inner circle. See North 1994, p. 198.
R. +O[ ]DO DE SANC EDMVN
No punctuation in legend.

(1)* Eaglen (B275). Bournemouth/Canterbury hoard (1901). Ex Carlyon-Britton, III (1918) 1934 (1/2), acquired from Baldwin, April 1902 (*BNJ* 19 (1927–8), p. 101); Elmore Jones 1079, where subsequent lot 1655 (see Catalogue 14 (1) above) was erroneously illustrated. 225° — 1.33

(2) Palmer (SED 604). South Kyme hoard (1922). Ex Osborne collection; Eaglen (B228). Fragmented. 270° — [1.15]

(3) BM (1973). Lincoln hoard (1971/2). 135° — 1.12

16 Cc O. +hE N (retrograde)R[
R. +ODDO .ON [ ]ANE [ ]

(1)* Eaglen (B603). 'Beauvais' (Paris region?) hoard (*c.* 1987). Ex Glendining, 4 Nov. 1987, 17. 0° — 1.09

[Odd]a?

17 Dd O.]SR: — 0.96
R.]A[:]ON[:] SANTIED[

(1)* *BMC* 113. Ex Lincoln (1894); H. P. Smith (1886) 468(?). Andrew 1901, p. 392, cites
'. . . . . . .AR ON SANTIEDM'
from the Smith sale, 1886. 0°

Henry I, Pellets in Quatrefoil type (*BMC* XIV) (*cont.*)

Other references:

Coin Hoards 4 (1978), p. 107, records three coins of *BMC* XIV from Bury in the Bournmouth/Canterbury hoard (1901). Apart from Catalogue 13 (2), possibly 14 (1) and 15 (1), *BNJ* 19 (1927–8), p. 101, records a coin construed as
'hENRICVS REX
+ODDO : ON : SAN[--]M'
(acquired by P. W. P.Carlyon-Britton in April 1902 from Baldwin) as emanating from the hoard. Curiously, the recorded legible letters make a connection with either Catalogue 14 (1) or 15 (1) improbable.

Andrew 1901, p. 392, lists
'hEN. . . . .
+ODDE ON[S]ANTIED·'
from P. W. P. Carlyon-Britton collection, described as 'recently found at Bury St Edmunds.' Whereabouts unknown. See *Norman Kings*, I, p. cci, where Brooke refers to 'Odde (Henry I, type XIV). Num. Chron., 1901, p.392 = P.W.P.Carlyon-Britton coll. (moneyer's name doubtful).' Oddo was not otherwise listed by Brooke, and it is remarkable he omitted the Carlyon-Britton coin described in Catalogue 15 (1).

Grantley, IV (1944) 1274 (1/3)
'+h[ENRICV]S REX
]OD[ ]ON EADM'

Od(d)e was a moneyer at Thetford in Henry I, type XV (*BMC* 289) and Stephen type I (*BMC* 108–9).

Murdoch, I (1903) 226
'ALDRED (?) ON SANTIE (?)'
See *Norman Kings*, I, p. cci, 'probably Shaftesbury', based on *BMC* 165–6:
+ALDRED:ON:SAFTE:
(*Norman Kings*, II, pp. 311–12).

Quadrilateral on Cross Fleury type (*BMC* XV)

Gilebert

18	Aa	O.	+hENRICVS[:]	
		R.	GILLEBERT ON [S]A S reclines?	
		(1)	BM (1921), South Kyme hoard (pre 1922). See *Inventory*, no. 337, p. 126. 225°	1.36
		(2)	*NCirc*, Dec. 2004, HS1881. Pimprez hoard (2002). 135°(?)	1.35
		(3)*	Eaglen (B129B/263). Ex Seaby (1980). 315°	1.20

19 Bb O.]ENR[
R. +GILEBERT : ON : SAN

(1) *SCBI* Museums in East Anglia (Bury) 1432. R. partly double struck. 225° — 1.43

(2) Spink. Pimprez hoard (2002). 315° — 1.42

(3) Eaglen (B1040). Ex Dolphin (1994). 270° — 1.37

(4) Eaglen (B1028). Ex *NCirc*, Sept. 1991, 5530. Probably Rashleigh (1909) 456 (2/2), transcribed as reading '[+G]ILEBERT:O--- '. 270° — 1.36

(5)* Eaglen (B604). 'Beauvais' (Paris region?) hoard (*c.* 1987). Glendining, 4 Nov. 1987, 34. Irregular flan. 90° — 1.34

(6) Dolphin list 6 (1995) 112. Die axis? — –

Other references:

Andrew 1901, p. 391:
'hENRIC:
+GILEBERT ON SAN'
'Watford find. A.A. Banes'.

Rashleigh (1909) 456 (1/2):
'+GILEBERT: [ON:]SAN'

Parsons, I (1929) 302 (1/3):
'+GILBERT [*sic*]:ON:SAN'

Drabble (1939) 677 (1/5):
'GILEBERT:ON:SAN'

20 Cc O. +hENRI[CV][

R. +GIL[L]EBERT[ ]ON[ ]EDM[ ]N
Possibly colons either side of ON.
Brooke read *BMC* 201 (Catalogue 20 (1)) as having one L in the moneyer's name but the inscription is unclear.

(1)* *BMC* 201, Pl. XLVII, 3. Watford hoard (1818). Ex Rashleigh (1909) 455. See also Andrew 1901, p. 391. 225° — 1.40

(2) Fitzwilliam Museum. Ex Conte collection. 225° — 1.42

21 Dd O. +hENRICVS·

S reclines.

R. +GILEBERD:ON EDMV.

(1) *SCBI* Northern Museums (Manchester) 1140/Ma. Prestwich hoard (1972). 60° [?] — 1.45

Henry I, Quadrilateral on Cross Fleury type (*BMC* XV) (*cont.*)

		(2)	Palmer (SED 881). Pimprez hoard (2002). Ex Spink, 6–7 Oct. 2004, 418. 135°	1.43
		(3)	Spink, Pimprez hoard (2002). 315°	1.41
		(4)	Spink, Pimprez hoard (2002). 315°	1.40
		(5)*	Eaglen (B1041). Ex Baldwin (1995). 0°	1.37
		(6)	Palmer (SED 666). 45°	1.03
22	Ee	O. R.	+hENRICV[S] +GIL[ ]EDM:	
		(1)*	*SCBI* Northern Museums (Blackburn) 1139/Bl. Prestwich hoard (1972). 0° [?]	1.32
23	Ff	O. R.	+[ ]RICVS +GIL[R]D ON [ ]DM	
		(1)*	Eaglen (B1113). Pimprez hoard (2002). Ex Spink (2004). 135°	1.38

Other references:

Inventory, no. 372, p. 143: Watford hoard (1818), 'Gilebert, 2' (coins). See Catalogue 20 (1), for one of them.

Andrew 1901, p. 391, cites three additional coins of type XV in the name of Gilebert to those referred to in Catalogue 19 (Other references) and 20 (1), all purportedly from the Watford hoard:
'+. . . . .
. .ILEBERT. . . . .' '2 specimens', see Catalogue 19 (1) and *SCMB*, Feb. 1961, 4544 (reading '[G]ILEBERT. . . . . .') and
'+hENRI[. .
+GILLEBER. . . . . .' (third specimen).

Lawrence, II (1951) 340 (1/6):
'+GILEB–'

Andrew 1901, p. 391:
'+hENRIC:
+GILEBERT ON EDM'
'Lincoln & Son'.

Coin Hoards 1 (1975), no. 360, p. 92: Prestwich hoard, 'Bury 2' (coins). See Catalogue 21 (1) and 22 (1).

STEPHEN (1135–54)

Watford type (*BMC* I)

Gilebert

24	Aa	O.	+STI [ ]NE REX: Unusual style of bust. Crude workmanship.	
		R.	+GILLEBERT:ON:SA: Pellets towards cross ends and at base of fleurs-de-lys.	
		(1)	Palmer (SED 780). 270°	1.42
		(2)	Spink. Pimprez hoard (2002). 0°	1.42
		(3)	*BMC* 7. Watford hoard (1818). Ex J. Rashleigh (1849). Irregular flan. 0°	1.41
		(4)	BM (1921). South Kyme hoard (pre-1922). Flat areas. 135°	1.39
		(5)	*BMC* 8. Pl. XLIX, 3. Watford hoard (1818). Ex (E. W.) Rashleigh (1909) 554. Although double struck, appears to be from same dies as *BMC* 7, etc. 180°	1.38
		(6)	Fitzwilliam Museum. Ex Conte collection. Surfaces hammered? 45°	1.34
		(7)*	Eaglen (B044). Prestwich hoard (1972). Ex Glendining, 26 May 1977, 71. Small diameter flan. 45°	1.18
		(8)	*SCBI* Scottish Museums (Glasgow) 273. Cut halfpenny. 180°	[0.65]
25	Bb	O.	+SI·EFNE RE:	
		R.	+GILEBERT:ON:ED: Annulets at cross ends (filled in on some coins).	
		(1)	Prestwich hoard (1972). Ex Glendining, 13–14 Nov. 1974, 13? Struck off-centre. Die axis?	1.42
		(2)	Prestwich hoard (1972). Die axis?	1.42
		(3)	*SCBI* Northern Museums (Huddersfield) 1168/Hud. Die axis?	1.42
		(4)	*SCBI* Northern Museums (Manchester) 1169/Ma. 180°	1.40
		(5)	Moscow Museum of Fine Arts. See Elmore Jones and Blunt 1967, p. 88, no. 10 and Pl. III. 45°	1.40
		(6)	Eaglen (B605). 'Beauvais' (Paris Region?) hoard (*c.* 1987). Glendining, 4 Nov. 1987, 101 (2/2). 180°	1.39
		(7)	Spink. Pimprez hoard (2002). 225° [*sic*]	1.39

Stephen, Watford type (*BMC* I) (*cont.*)

		(8)	*BNJ* 64 (1994), Coin Register 259, p. 155 and Pl. 21. Metal detector find at Cranwich, Norfolk (1994). 315° [*sic*]	1.38
		(9)	Palmer (SED 24). Found in East Anglia (1994). 270°	1.37
		(10)	*BMC* 6. Ex Sotheby, 25 July 1910, 103. 270°	1.36
		(11)	*SCMB*, June 1984, E195, illustrated. Ex Elmore Jones 1378. Die axis?	1.36
		(12)	Spink, 6–7 Oct. 2004, 462. Pimprez hoard (2002). 90°	1.34
		(13)	Prestwich hoard (1972). Struck off-centre. Die axis?	1.33
		(14)	Dix, Noonan, Webb, 11 Dec. 2002, 113 (1/3). Ragged and worn. 90°	[1.32]
		(15)*	Eaglen (B059). Prestwich hoard (1972). 270°	1.24
		(16)	Whereabouts unknown. Probably ex Rashleigh (1909) 555c. Irregular flan; struck off-centre. Die axis?	–
		(17)	Ex Osborne collection. Ex C. J. Martin (1973). Die axis?	–
26	Cb	O.	+STIEFNE:	
		R.	As above	
		(1)*	Royal Mint Museum. 90°	1.41
	NB. Only example so far found of die-links between pairs of dies at Bury in reign (Bb, Cb, Cc).			
27	Cc	O.	As above	
		R.	+GILEBERT:ON:EDM	
		(1)	Eaglen (B013). Prestwich hoard (1972). Glendining, 3 Sept. 1975, 233. 90°	1.41
		(2)	*BMC* 4. Ex Sotheby, 25 July 1910, 103. R. struck off-centre. 180°	1.39
		(3)	Palmer (SED 22). Ex Lockett 1109; Doubleday 646. 270°	1.39
		(4)	*BMC* 5. Watford hoard (1818). Ex J. Rashleigh (1849). Very irregular flan. 135°	1.38
		(5)*	Eaglen (B025). Watford hoard (1818)[?]. Ex (E. W.) Rashleigh (1909) 552, Pl. VIII; S. M. Spink and Hanham collections. 0°	1.37
		(6)	Fitzwilliam Museum. Ex Roth (1917) 161; Drabble, I (1939) 678; P. Spink and Conte collections. 180°	1.33

		(7)	Palmer (SED 513). Square flan. 0°	1.27
		(8)	*SCBI* Northern Museums (Preston)1170/Pr. Prestwich hoard (1972). 100° [*sic*]	1.26
		(9)	Lawrence 115 (BM cast). South Kyme hoard (pre-1922)? Ex Montagu, V (1897) 110 (1/2). See *NC*^{5} 2 (1922), p. 21, nos 63–4. Die axis?	–
		(10)	*SCMB*, Nov. 1986, E459, illustrated. Die axis?	–
		(11)	Jarmin collection (ex?). Die axis?	–
28	Dd	O. R.	]NE RE[:]]ERT:ON:SAN[Annulets at cross ends.	
		(1)*	*BNJ* 64 (1994), Coin Register 260, p. 156 and Pl. 21. *BNJ* states, 'Last three letters of moneyer's name partially visible but not in doubt'. Find spot uncertain but finder resident in Poole, Dorset. 0°	1.15
29	Ee	O. R.	+STIEFNE: +GILEBERT:ON:SAN Annulets in upper and lateral cross ends.	
		(1)	Moscow Museum of Fine Arts. See Elmore Jones and Blunt 1967, p. 88, no. 11 and Pl. III. 45°	1.28
		(2)	Palmer (SED 395). South Lancs metal detector find (1994). See *BNJ* 64 (1994), Coin Register 261, p. 156 and Pl. 21, where double-struck O. is construed as ending in RE and R. as reading GILBERT. 90°	1.24
		(3)*	BM (1974). Prestwich hoard (1972). 90°	1.08
30	Ff	O.	]EFN[Large lettering. Inner circle weak or absent. +GIL[ ]ERT [ ]N S[Annulets at cross ends. Unusual orientation of cross.	
		(1)*	*SCBI* Midlands Museums (Nottingham) 739. Nottingham hoard (1880). 270°	1.17
31	Gg	O. R.	]T[ ]FNE[.] Crude bust. Large thin lettering. +GILEB[ ]A Large lettering.	
		(1)*	Eaglen (B1032). Nicked. 0°	[0.93]

Other references: *Inventory*, no. 372, p. 144. Watford hoard (1818): 'Gilebert, 9.'

Murdoch, I (1903) 252:
'+STIEFNE: [R]
+GILEBERT [ON] S[AN]EDM'

Stephen, Watford type (*BMC* I) (*cont.*)

Rashleigh (1909) 553. Watford hoard (1818)?

Probably same coin as Grantley, IV (1944) 1295:
'+STIEFNE
+G[IL]EBERT:ON:EDM' (Dies Cc).

Rashleigh (1909) 555a. Watford hoard (1818)?
'+GILLEBE[RT]—' (Dies – a?).

Rashleigh (1909) 555b. Watford hoard (1818)?
'+[GILEB]ERT[:O]N:ED' (Dies Bb?)

Rashleigh (1909) 555c.
'+------[O]N:ED' (Dies Bb?), see 25 (16) above.

BNJ 7 (1910), p. 36. Sheldon hoard (1867), no. 50:
'ST[IEF]NE RE: 1.36
+GILEBER[T:]ON:ED:' (Dies Bb?) –°
See also *Inventory*, no. 329, p. 123.

Lawrence 1922, p. 21. South Kyme hoard (pre-1922) nos 63–6:

63 '+STIEFNE:
+GILEBERT:ON:EDM' (Dies Cc?) 1.36

64 '+STIEFNE: 1.39
+GILEBERT:ON:EDM' (Dies Cc?)

65 '+ST [1.30
+GILEB[(Dies –?)

66 ']REX: 1.38
]LEBERT [ ]SA' (Dies Aa?)

Drabble, II (1943) 978:
'+GILEBERT:ON:EDM' (Dies Cc?)

Lawrence, II (1951) 346 (1/3):
'+G[IL]EBERT:ON:['

32 Hh O. +STIEFNE
Large lettering. No inner circle.
R. +GILEBERT:ON:SA[
Unusual orientation of cross. Roundel in centre of cross and annulets on cross ends. Pellet at bases of fleurs-de-lis.

(1)* *SCBI* Midlands Museums (Nottingham) 833. Nottingham Hoard (1880). 45° 1.03

(2) Fitzwilliam Museum. Ex Conte collection. 0° 1.03

[33] Ii O. ST[ALDE] FE (reading uncertain)[1]
Large, grotesque bust.
R.]BERT[ ]ON[

Roundels in centre of cross and on four limbs, pellets at bases of fleurs-de-lis and annulets at limb ends.

(1)* BM (1985). Ex Elmore Jones collection. See *BNJ* 41 (1972), p. 206. 90° 1.22

[1] See *Norman Kings* I, Pl. LVIII, 16 for similar R. design reading +BALDWI:ON:T. Elmore Jones considered (from annotation on a coin envelope) that the O. of 33 (1) could have been struck over a R. of the moneyer Baldwin.

– O.]EF[ ]E
Erased die.
R. +GILE[ ]ERT:ON[ ]EI
Annulets at cross ends.

(1) BM (1974). Prestwich hoard (1972). Chipped. 0° See Seaby 1980, p. 52, and Alliss and Seaby 1984, where this coin and that described under 'Other references' immediately below are attributed to Eye (Suffolk) owing to the existence of a cut halfpenny of type *BMC* VI, reading D(or H)V[N]:EIE (illustration A, p. 182) and found about two miles from Bury, possibly at Kentford. [0.76]

Other references: Alliss and Seaby 1984, ill. D, p. 182, construed as

'+[. . .]IEF[. . .]'
Erased die.

'[..]ILL[. . . . .O]N[E?..]'
No colon stops after N.

Found in two halves at Gosbeck, Suffolk, in 1980.
Die axis? [0.99g].

Fitzwilliam Museum. Ex Conte collection:
O.]EF[
R. +G[ ]:EI. 30° [1.05g]

Fitzwilliam Museum. Ex Conte collection:
O. STIEFNE
Bust left, local die
R. +[ ]LELM:ON[ ]EI[. 150° [0.96g]

Acelin

[34] Aa O.]EX:
R. +A[C][ ]:[

Unusual orientation of cross. Annulets at sinister cross ends.

(1)* Eaglen (B606). 'Beauvais' (Paris region?) hoard (*c.* 1987). Ex Glendining, 14 Nov. 1987, 101 (1/2). Irregular flan. 90° 1.13

Stephen, Watford type (*BMC* I) (*cont.*)

No obvious alternative mint candidature. The rounded back of the second (illegible) letter of the moneyer's name discounts it as a D. The last letters on the R. could read . . EA.

35	Bb	O.	+STIEFNE RE	
		R.	+A[ ]ELIN:ON:SANT	
		(1)	*BMC* 3. Watford hoard (1818). Ex J. Rashleigh (1849). 180°	1.41
		(2)	Glendining, 5 Oct. 1987, 442. Prestwich hoard (1972). Ex Sotheby, 6 Dec. 1974, 4. Struck off-centre. Die axis?	1.39
		(3)*	*BM* 137A. Evans at BM construed R. reading as ABELIN [ON CA]NT. See *Norman Kings*, II, p. 335, n. 3. Uneven flan. 270°	1.34
		(4)	Prestwich hoard (1972). 0°	1.30
		(5)	Eaglen (B312). Very irregular flan. 90°	1.26
[36]	Cc	O.	+STIE[	
		R.	+AC[ ]N'E:	
		(1)*	*BMC* 138. Ex Higgs (1830) 56. Included by Brooke under 'Uncertain mints (Bury St. Edmunds?)', *Norman Kings*, II, p.356. 90°	1.41

Other references: Watford hoard (1818). *Inventory*, no.372, p.144: 'Stephen: BMC. . .i. . .Canterbury, Abelin, 2'; Duart-Smith (1945) 143 (1/3): 'ACE. . .·ANT', pierced; Mack 1966, p. 41: '+ACEL:ON:SANT'.

Hunfrei

37	Aa	O.	]TIFNENE R [(reading unclear; double struck?)	
		R.	+hVNF[ ]ED Large lettering.	
		(1)*	Shown to BM (1986). Struck off-centre. Die axis?	–

Other references: *SCMB* June 1983, p. 149: 'a variety with a star in the legend now in the BM' (not found in trays).

Henri

38	Aa	O.	]EFNE:	
		R.	+h[EN]RI:ON:EDMVN	
		(1)*	Found at Saffron Walden, Essex (1988). Die axis?	–

(Iun)

– O. Not recorded
R. IVN:ON:[ ]MV

– Taffs (1956) 137 (6/6). See Mack 1966, p. 41; Brooke 1950, p. 256. Coin not traced.

Oddo?

– O. [ ]NE[
R.][O][ ]ONS:[
Oddo is not (otherwise) known at Bury after type XIV of Henry I.

(1)* Palmer (SED 611). 270° 1.29

Unknown moneyers

[39] Aa O. +S[
R.]DM[

Annulets at cross ends. Appears to be insufficient space for Gilebert's name.

(1)* BM (1946). Olroyd bequest. 180° 1.40

– O.]NE REX:
R.]:ON:SA[

Roundels in cross ends.

Moscow Museum of Fine Arts. See Elmore Jones and Blunt 1967, p. 89, no. 19 and Pl. III, 19, described as 'probably Bury St. Edmunds'.

Cross Voided and Mullets (*BMC* II)

Acelin

40 Aa O. +STIE N E:
R. +ACE:ON:S:EDMVND
Straight-backed C.

(1) *BMC* 146, Pl. LIII, 3. Linton hoard (1883). See Wakeford 1883, p. 114, no. 33, Pl. VII, 4; Mack 1966, p. 49. 270° 1.41

(2) Eaglen (B343). Ex Elmore Jones 1392. 180° 1.36

(3)* Eaglen (B410). Ex Glendining, 2 Oct. 1985, 91 (1/3). Broken and repaired. 180° [1.17]

Stephen, Cross Voided and Mullets type (*BMC* II) (*cont.*)

		(4)	Palmer (SED 97). Wicklewood hoard (1989). Ex Christie, 15 May 1990, 299. Cut halfpenny. 270°	[0.64]

Other references: Golding 1868, p. 5, records a coin reading
'+STIEFNE.R [*sic*]
. . . . . .ON.S.EDMVND'
said to be in the collection of the Museum at Bury, whose coins were stolen in 1965 and not recovered.

Hunfrei

41	Aa	O.	+ STEFN E:	
		R.	+hVNFREI:ON: S:ED	
			'S' on O. and R. reclining.	
		(1)*	Eaglen (B057). Ex Carlyon-Britton, II (1916) 1469, Drabble (1939) 703. See Mack 1966, p. 49. 315°	1.37
		(2)	Palmer (SED 505). 180°	1.34

Gilebert?

–		O.	+STIEF[	
		R.	+GILEBERT:[	
		(1)	Lawrence (1951) 361 (1/2), illustrated at Pl. II, 361 (2). Not referred to by Mack 1966. Possibly Sudbury, see Elmore Jones 1955–7, p. 546, referring to *BMC* 183 (SV) and 211 (SVB), apparently struck in the name of Gilebert in type VII.	

Profile/Cross and Piles (BMC VI)

Acelin

42	Aa	O.	+STIEFN[ ]E:	
		R.	+ACE:ON: S :EDMV	
			Straight-backed C; reclining S.	
		(1)	BM (1990). Wicklewood hoard (1989), 62. Bent. 90°	1.40
		(2)*	Shown to BM (1986) and said to have been found at Bognor Regis. See *BNJ* 57 (1987), Coin Register 198, p. 145 and Pl. VII. 270°	1.36

Hunfrei

43	Aa	O.	+STIEFNE:	
		R.	+hVNFREI:ON:S:ED	

		(1)	BM (1990). Wicklewood hoard (1989). Bent. 180°	1.44
		(2)*	Eaglen (B1006). Wicklewood hoard (1989). Ex Christie, 15 May 1990, 75. 0°	1.42
		(3)	*BNJ* 64 (1994), Coin Register 282. Metal detector find at Newmarket, Suffolk (1994). R. transcribed as '+hV[ ]FRI[ ]·S·ED'. 160° [*sic*]	1.41

Other references: Alliss and Seaby 1984, illustration A at p. 182; cut halfpenny reading
]FN E:'
+D (or h) V[ ]:EIE 270°, 0.56g
attributed to Eye, Suffolk.

[ ]ric

44	Aa	O.	+STIEFN E:	
		R.	+[ ]RIC:ON:[ ]:[ ]D[Letter before R on R. appears to be D or O. Probably reads S:ED[. In BM trays moneyer is hazarded as Ælfric.	
		(1)*	BM (1990). Wicklewood hoard (1990). Bent. 180°	1.32

Unknown Moneyer

45	Aa	O.	[ ]	
		R.	+[ ]:S[ ]DM·	
		(1)*	Palmer (SED 689). Cut halfpenny. 180°	[0.56]

Awbridge (*BMC* VII)

This type was not superceded until 1158, by the Tealby (or Cross and Crosslets) issue of Henry II.

Acelin

46A	A1a	O.	+STIEFN E	
		R.	+ACE:ON:S:EDMV:	
		(1)*	Eaglen (B276). Ex Elmore Jones 1104. See also Ruding 1840, III, Pl. II, 18; Golding 1868, p. 5; Elmore Jones 1966b; Elmore Jones 1975, Pl. 42A, same R. as Pl. 42B. O. tooled. Small flan. 160°	[1.15]
46B	A2a	(2)*	Eaglen (B411). Ex *SCMB* Oct. 1985, no. E379, illustrated. The faint illustration in *BNJ* 58 (1988) Coin Register 231 is of this coin. Off-centre. 45°	1.36

Stephen, Awbridge type (*BMC* VII) (*cont.*)

46C	A3a	(3)*	Elmore Jones 1975, Pl. 42B. Die axis?	–

Although the three above coins share the same reverse die, Obverse A1 (even allowing for tooling) appears to be different from A2/3.

Other references: Martin (1859), 71.

[Gilebe?]rt

47	Aa	O.	]N E	
		R.	+[ ]RT:ON:S:E[Round-backed E	
		(1)*	Eaglen (B1043). Portsdown Hill hoard (1995). Ex Buckland, Dix & Wood, 28 June 1995, 171. Partly Flat. 0°	[1.16]

Willem

48	Aa	O.	]EFNE	
		R.	+P[ ]M:ON: :ED	
		(1)*	Dresden, *NCirc*, March 1982, p. 49 and Fig. 12.	1.44
49	Bb	O.	+STIEF N E	
		R.	+PILLEM:ON: S :ED Reclining S (on R.).	
		(1)*	BM (1990). Wicklewood hoard (1989). 45°	1.37
		(2)	Eaglen (B1007). Wicklewood hoard (1989). Ex Christie, 15 May 1990, 134. Cut halfpenny. 45°	[0.62]
		(3)	Elmore Jones 1955–7, p. 548 and Pl. XXXI, 3. Thetford excavations (*c.* 1953). See also Mack 1966, p.56. Die axis? The R. of this coin is from the same die as 49(1) and (2); the O., however, is too faintly struck and off-centre to be categorically identified with die B.	–

Other references: *BMC* 183, reading ']LEBE[ ]:ON:S[', extended by a die duplicate to read SV (Elmore Jones 1955–7, p. 546), is accordingly now assigned by the BM to Sudbury.

HENRY II (1154–89)

TEALBY (CROSS-AND-CROSSLETS) COINAGE (1158–80)

Willem

A1 (*BMC* 42–43)

50	Aa	O.	+hENRI REX ANGL Die flaw develops above sceptre.**	
		R.	+PILLEM:ON:SC:EDM	
			Inscription begins at 11 o'clock.	
		(1)	Eaglen (B072). Ex Glendining, 13 March 1974, 208; Baldwin (1978).	1.43
		(2)	*BMC*42, Pl. I, 3. Awbridge hoard (*c.* 1902).	1.43
		(3)	Eaglen (B277). Ex Elmore Jones 1117 (1/3).	1.38
		(4)*	*SCBI* Norweb 321. Ex A. H. F. Baldwin (private collection); Spink, 17 June 1987, 1290, illustrated (1/4).	1.17
		(5)	*SCBI* Museums in East Anglia (Bury) 1473. Ex Frost collection.	1.14
		(6)	Doubleday 897 (1/4). Fragment. Corroded reverse.	[1.00]
		(7)	Palmer (SED 533). Ex Lawrence. Irregular flan (clipped ?).	[0.89]

Other references: Lawrence 372 (3/6), '*BMC*42'.

** The light coins occur both with, 50(5), and without, 50 (4), O. flaw.

51	Bb	O.	+hENRI REX ANGL	
		R.	+WILLEM:SC:ON:ED: Inscription begins beyond 12 o'clock.	
		(1)	Doubleday 897 (2/4). Ex Lawrence, IV (1951) 989 (part).	1.45
		(2)	*BMC* 43, Pl. I., 4. Tealby Hoard (1807). Ex Banks collection (1818).	1.43
		(3)	Winchester Museum. West Meon hoard (1992), 7. See Archibald and Cook 2001, p. 4. Not illustrated.	1.43

Henry II, Tealby Cross-and-Crosslets (Tealby) Type, Willem (*cont.*)

		(4)	*SCBI* Norweb 322. Ex A. H. F. Baldwin (private collection); Spink, 17 June 1987, 1290 (2/4). Coin referred to in *BMC*, p. 9, footnote to *BMC* 43.	1.42
		(5)	Palmer (SED 29). Ex Lawrence, IV (1951) 989 (part) and Doubleday 898 (1/3).	1.41
		(6)	Fitzwilliam Museum. Ex Shirley-Fox and Blunt collections.	1.40
		(7)*	Woodhead collection. Ex Ebsworth (1966).	1.39
		(8)	Eaglen (B278). Ex Elmore Jones 1117 (2/3).	1.33
		(9)	Doubleday 897 (3/4). Ex Lawrence, IV (1951) 989 (part). Irregular flan.	1.30
		(10)	Palmer (SED 694). Cut halfpenny.	[0.53]

Other references: Lawrence, II (1951) 372 (4/6), '*BMC* 43'.

A2 (*BMC* 44)

52	Cb	O.	hENRI REX ΛNGL	
		R.	As above.	
		(1)	*BMC* 44, p.9 and footnote: 'cf. similar coin at A. H. Baldwin & Sons, 1946 [see (4) below], also coin illustrated by Heywood in *BNJ*, I, pl. no.18 [see (5) below].'	1.45
		(2)*	Eaglen (B279). Ex Elmore Jones 1117 (3/3).	1.41
		(3)	Palmer (SED 85). Ex Doubleday collection (not in sales)?	1.41
		(4)	*SCBI* Norweb 323. Ex A. H. F. Baldwin (private collection); sold Spink, 17 June 1987, 1290 (3/4).	1.22
		(5)	Heywood 1903–4, p.107 and Pl. 18. Stated to be in 'Mr. Carlyon Britton's collection'.	–

Other references: Lawrence, IV (1951) 989 (8 and 9/10).

A2 (*BMC* 45–48)

53	Dd	O.	+hENRI REX ΛNGL	
		R.	+WILLEM:ON:SC:ED: Inscription begins at 12 o'clock. Some specimens show features of design (e.g. sceptre) more skimpily struck up than others.	
		(1)	Royal Mint Museum. Hocking catalogue, 328.	1.45
		(2)	Reading University.	1.45
		(3)	*BMC* 45, p.9, footnote: 'cf. coins from the same dies in Royal Mint Museum, no. 328 [see (1) above] and	1.44

in R.C.Lockett, D.Mangakis and F.Elmore Jones [see (10) below] collections; also in Carlyon-Britton sale, 1916, Lot 1525, illustrated by Heywood in *BNJ*, I, Pl. no.17' [see (15) below].

(4) Palmer (SED 465). 1.42

(5)* Eaglen (B073). Ex Sir John Evans collection; Lockett 1181, (2/4) and Baldwin (1978). 1.41

(6) *BMC* 46. Leicester hoard (1927), 3. Irregular flan. 1.41

(7) Palmer (SED 28). Ex Lawrence; Doubleday 898 (2/3). 1.40

(8) Dawson collection. Ex Lainchbury and Doubleday collections. 1.40

(9) *BMC* 48. Ex Baldwin (1946). Chipped. [1.38]

(10) Elmore Jones, 1410. Offered in *SCMB*, June 1984, E201 (illustrated). 1.38

(11) *BMC* 47. Leicester hoard (1927), 4. Irregular flan. 1.37

(12) *BNJ* 72 (2002), Coin register 227, p.210 and Pl. 23, 227. Penkridge, Staffordshire, metal detector find (2002). 1.35

(13) Crafter collection. 1.28

(14) Osborne collection (ex). Ex Spink (1965). Chipped. –

(15) Carlyon-Britton 1525, Pl. cxxxv, and Heywood 1903–4, Pl. no. 17. –

Other references: Lawrence, II (1951) 372 (5/6), 'BMC 45/8'.

C1 (*BMC* 49–51)

54 Ee O. +hENRI:R:AN
R. +PILLELM:ON:S :EDM
With curvilinear 'M's, and retrograde S.

(1) *BMC* 50. Tealby hoard (1807). Ex Banks collection (1818). Irregular flan. 1.47

(2) *BMC* 51, Pl. XI.16. Tealby hoard (1807). Ex Banks collection (1818). Irregular flan. 1.46

(3) Palmer (SED 19). Ex Lawrence, IV (1951) 989 (10/10); Doubleday 898 (3/3). 1.44

(4)* *BMC* 49. Awbridge hoard (*c.* 1902). *BMC* p. 10, n.: 'cf. coins from same dies in Fitzwilliam Museum, Cambridge, from Hasluck Collection, in F. Elmore Jones [see (8) below] and D. Mangakis Collections; and in Astronomer Sale, 1906, Lot 222 [see (13) below]; and Bascombe sale, 1908, Lot 87.' The Fitzwilliam Museum coin is of dies Ff (*BMC* 52–53). 1.43

Henry II, Tealby Cross-and-Crosslets (Tealby) Type, Willem (*cont.*)

See Blackburn 1987, p. 113 and Catalogue 55(2) below.

(5)	*SCBI* Museums in East Anglia (Bury) 1474. Ex Frost collection. Square flan.	1.42
(6)	Christie, 15 May 1990, 143 (414). Wicklewood hoard (1989).	1.41
(7)	Palmer (SED 742). Ex Burstal (1984) 72. Irregular flan.	1.41
(8)	Eaglen (B584). Ex Elmore Jones 1681 (2/2).	1.39
(9)	Palmer (SED 582). 'Ex Essex find'.	1.28
(10)	Doubleday 897 (4/4). Fragment.	[1.25]
(11)	Palmer (SED 816). Irregular flan.	1.24
(12)	Seaby stock (1975). Ex Davis collection.	–
(13)	'Astronomer' (1906) 222, Pl. III. Ex Martin and Rostron collections.	–

Other references:

'PILL[EL]M:ON:S:EDM. . . nearly square, F[ine].' Described as type 'B'; *SCMB,* July 1949, 8193.

Lawrence, II (1951) 372 (6/6), '49/51'.

Bascombe (1908) 153 (2/86). 'Penny of St. Edmundsbury' (cf. *BMC* 49, p. 10 n., 54 (4) above).

'+PILLEL(M):ON:S:E[DMD]' with retrograde S, and O. reading 'HENRI REX', *SCMB* Feb. 1956, H5016.

Lockett 2975 (1/6), '*BMC* 49/51'.

C1 (*BMC* 52–53)

55 Ff O. +hENRI:R:AG:
R. +PILLAM:S:EDMVH
with curvilinear 'M's.

(1)*	*BMC* 52. Illustrated by Brooke 1927, Pl. XIV, 7. Mantle stated to be 'edged with pellets'. *BMC,* p.10 '. . . another illustrated by Lawrence, *B.N.J.* xiv, pl. no. 6; cf, two coins from the same dies in Royal Mint Museum, nos. 329 and 330' (see 55(3) and (4) below).	1.46
(2)	Fitzwilliam Museum. Ex Hasluck bequest (1920). Coin Recorded in *BMC* as *BMC 49* (see also Blackburn 1987, p. 113). Irregular flan.	1.44

		(3)	Royal Mint Museum. Hocking catalogue, 330.	1.44
		(4)	Royal Mint Museum. Hocking catalogue, 329.	1.42
		(5)	*BMC* 53. Lark Hill hoard (1854).	1.39
		(6)	Palmer (SED 726). Cracked.	1.34
		(7)	Palmer (SED 355). Ex Pheatt (1995), 726 (2/2). Cracked.	1.33
		(8)	Eaglen (B288). Ex Trenerry (1983).	1.16
		(9)	Eaglen (B585). Ex Elmore Jones 1681 (1/2). This coin not illustrated. Small flan.	1.05

Other references:

'+HENRI·R·AN
+PILLA·ON·S·EDMVN'
Golding 1868, p. 5. Although said to be 'perfect' and 'in the best preservation', possibly from Ff dies. Also stated to have been found at Tealby.

Henri

C1 (*BMC* 16)

56	Fg	O.	As above.	
		R.	+h E N R I :[O]N : S: ED˙ Moneyer's name widely spaced and D. F. Allen (*BMC*, p. 4) suggests it may have been engraved over an erased name, possibly that of Willem (p. cxvii). At p. cix he wrongly states that the obverse die (F) passed from Henri to Raul, not Willem to Henri.	
		(1)*	*BMC* 16. Lark Hill hoard (1854), Pl. XII, 5: 'cf. coin from same dies in F. Elmore Jones collection' [see 56 (4) below].	1.43
		(2)	Winchester Museum. West Meon hoard (1992), 6. Archibald and Cook 2001, p. 4. Not illustrated. Irregular flan.	1.41
		(3)	Eaglen (B169). Ex C. J. Martin (1981).	1.39
		(4)	Elmore Jones 1116 (1/4). See Plates taken before sale, 13/18.	1.36

C1 (*BMC* 17–18)

57	Fh	O.	As above.	
		R.	+hENRI:ON:S:EDMV: Legend begins after 12 o'clock.	
		(1)	*BMC* 17, Pl. XII, 6: 'cf. similar coin in R. C. Lockett Collection,' (see Other references below). Ex Lawrence (1947). Irregular flan.	1.42

Henry II, Tealby Cross-and-Crosslets (Tealby) Type, Henri (*cont.*)

(2) Christie, 15 May 1990, 143 (1/4). Wicklewood hoard (1989). 1.41

(3) Winchester Museum. West Meon hoard (1992), 5. Archibald and Cook 2001, p. 4 and Pl. 8, 5. 1.41

(4) Eaglen (B058). Ex Baldwin (1978). 1.40

(5) *BMC* 18. Lark Hill hoard (1854). Square flan. 1.39

(6)* Eaglen (B168). Ex C. J. Martin (1981). 1.34

(7) Elmore Jones 116 (2/4). See Elmore Jones Pl. 13/19. 1.31

(8) Ashmolean Museum. Gayton hoard (1998), 128. 1.21

(9) Eaglen (B723). Ex Doubleday 894 (1/4), where incorrectly catalogued as B1 (*BMC* 19). Small flan. 1.20

(10) Palmer (SED 20). Ex Doubleday 893 (1/2). Irregular flan. 1.08

Other references:

Lockett 1181 (3/4), '17/18'.

SCMB, Nov. 1974, H4598: 'hEN[RI]:ON:S:EDMV: .

Very weak in places but for issue good VF.'

BNJ 29 (1958–9), p.83.
'+hENRI:R:AG:
–ENRI:ON:S:EDM–
16· 22gr' [1.05g].
Tealby hoard (1807).

C1 (*BMC* –)

This die set is designated by T. C. R. Crafter as C3; see Crafter 1998. pp. 45, 62, and 58(2) below.

58 Ii O. +hENR[ ]R[
R. +hENRI:ON:S.E D

Letters ED widely spaced, with die flaw running through. Crosslets of unusual execution.

(1) Palmer (SED 115). Wicklewood hoard (1989). Ex Christie, 15 May 1990, 143 (2/4). 1.42

(2) Crafter collection. See Crafter 1998, p. 62 and Pl. 6, 21. 1.40

(3)* Eaglen (B229). Ex Spink (1965) and Osborne collection. Irregular flan. 1.36

(4) Elmore Jones1116 (4/4). See Elmore Jones Pl. 13/21. 1.31

C2 (*BMC* –)

59 Jj O. [+hE]NRI:RE
Row of pellets in lower folds of mantle. Cf. *BMC* 298, Pl. X, 11.

R. [+]h E N R I : ON·S·E[D][
Moneyer's name widely spaced.

(1)* Eaglen (B580). Ex Elmore Jones 1678, illustrated. Irregular flan. 1.44

(2) BM (1953). Ex Elmore Jones (1953). 1.31

Other references: Lawrence 989 (2/10), 'C2 (unpublished)'.

B1 (*BMC* 19–23)

60 Kk O. +hENRI REX ΛN
On most specimens the pellets are unclear.

R. +hEN R I : O N:S:EDM:
Letters R I : O well spread. Retrograde S.

(1) Eaglen (B1046). Ex Birkbeck College; Baldwin (1995). 1.47

(2)* *BMC* 19, Pl. X, 4: 'cf. coins from the same dies in Royal Mint Museum, no. 331 [see 60 (14) below]; Ashmolean Museum [see 60 (6) below]; Copenhagen Museum, from Thomas Collection, no. 9576 [see 60 (15) below]; in F. Elmore Jones [see 60(7) below] and D. Mangakis [see 60(24) below] Collections and at A. H. Baldwin and Sons (2), 1946'. 1.44

(3) *BMC* 22. Leicester hoard (1927), 5. 1.44

(4) Palmer (SED 21). Ex Doubleday 893 (2/2). 1.44

(5) *BMC* 21. Leicester hoard (1927), 6. Irregular flan. 1.41

(6) *SCBI* Ashmolean Museum 324. Ellesborough hoard (1777). Given by Sir J. Russell, Bt. (1777). 1.40

(7) Elmore Jones 1116 (3/4). See Elmore Jones Pl. 13/20. 1.40

(8) Eaglen (B722). Ex Doubleday 894 (2/4). 1.40

(9) *SCBI* Scottish Museums (Glasgow) 335. 1.40

(10) Ashmolean Museum. Gayton hoard (1998), 24. 1.40

(11) *SCBI* Museums in East Anglia (Norwich) 1471. Ex T. Southwell. 1.39

(12) *BMC* 20. Lark Hill hoard (1854). 1.38

(13) Eaglen (B046). Ex Glendining, 16 June 1977, 294 (1/2). Struck off-centre. 1.37

(14) Royal Mint Museum. Hocking catalogue, 331. Two straight sides to flan. 1.33

Henry II, Tealby Cross-and-Crosslets (Tealby) Type, Henri (*cont.*)

(15) Copenhagen, Nationalmuseet. Thomsen 9576. Broken. [1.30]

(16) Crafter collection. Ex Seaby (1979) and Palmer. 1.28

(17) Jacob collection (ex). Ex Spink (1949). Irregular chipped flan. [1.26]

(18) Palmer (SED 317). East Anglian metal detector find. Two incomplete fragments. [1.26]

(19) *SCBI* Norweb 324. Ex A. H. F. Baldwin (private collection); Spink, 17 June 1987, 1290 (4/4). Irregular flan. 1.21

(20) Eaglen (B721). Ex Doubleday 894 (3/4). 1.20

(21) *BMC* 23. Ex Lawrence (1935). Clipped? 1.17

(22) Dorman Memorial Museum, Middlesborough. Thewles, Cleveland hoard. (1932). [1.14]

(23) Christie, 15 May 1990, 143 (3/4). Wicklewood hoard (1989). Cut halfpenny. [0.72]

(24) Osborne collection. Ex Mangakis; Baldwin (1973). –

(25) *NCirc*, April 2000, HS039, illustrated. Ex Shuttlewood collection. –

(26) Private collection. –

Other references:

Lawrence, IV (1951) 989 (1/10), '19/23'.

Taffs (1955) 140 (no reading given).

BNJ 29 (1958–9), p. 83:
'+h-NRI REX AN
+hE-RI:ON:2:EDM-
Unusually round striking'.
22.28gr [= 1.44g], from Tealby hoard (1807).

SCMB, June 1971, H942. 'BMC 19. VF, unusually good specimen'.

SCMB, May 1973, H3535. 'hENRI ON S EDM, nearly VF for issue'.

D1 (*BMC* –)

61 Ll O. +hENRI:REX
R. +hENRI:ON:S:EDMV
Reclining S.

(1) BM (1962). Presented by Elmore Jones. Irregular flan and cracked. 1.44

(2)* Eaglen (B582). Ex Elmore Jones 1679 (2/3). Stated in auction catalogue to weigh 29.2gr = 1.91g. 1.42

(3) Palmer (SED 43). 1.38

(4) Eaglen (B725). Ex Lawrence, IV (1951) 989 (3 or 4/10); Doubleday 895 (1/4). 1.35

(5) Palmer (SED 724). Flat sided flan. 1.27

(6) Eaglen (B724). Ex Lawrence, IV (1951) 989 (part)?; Doubleday 894 (4/4). 1.25

(7) Ashmolean Museum. Gayton hoard (1990), 38. Small flan. Bent. 1.11

(8) Harris collection. –

Other references: *SCMB*, July 1960, 6610.
'D. . .hENRI ON S EDM [*sic*]'.

D1 (?) (*BMC* 27)

62 Mm O. +hENRI[
R. +hENRI:ON:S:EDMV
Legend begins before 12 o'clock. Slightly tilted 'S'.

(1)* *BMC* 27, Pl. XIX, 13. 'Possibly from' Tealby hoard (1807). 1.43

(2) *BNJ* 55 (1985), p. 60, illustrated at p. 76, Pl. I, 22. Found 'nr. Chelmsford' (1984–5). Irregular flan. 1.35

(3) Palmer (SED 632). Cut halfpenny. [0.61]

D3 (*BMC* 24–26)

63 N1/N2m O. +hEN REX AN
Appears to exist in two states, with sceptre handle (N1) retooled more thickly (N2).
R. As above.

(1) *SCBI* Museums in East Anglia (Bury) 1472. Ex Frost collection. Thick sceptre. Irregular flan. 1.44

(2) Palmer (SED 704).Thick sceptre. 1.44

(3)* Eaglen (B581). Ex Elmore Jones 1679 (1/3). Thick sceptre (N2). 1.40

(4) *BMC* 26, Pl. XX, 22. Chinon hoard (*c.* 1913). Ex Lawrence (1935). Thick sceptre. Irregular flan. 1.39

(5)* Palmer (SED 305). Thin sceptre (N1). 1.39

(6) Palmer (SED 741). Thick sceptre. Irregular flan. 1.38

(7) Eaglen (B726). Ex Doubleday 895 (2/4). Thick sceptre. Irregular flan. 1.38

Henry II, Tealby Cross-and-Crosslets (Tealby) Type, Henri (*cont.*)

(8) Palmer (SED 491). Thin sceptre. Irregular flan. 1.35

(9) *BNJ* 66 (1996), Coin Register 311, p. 169 and Pl. 22, 311. Pentlow, Suffolk, metal detector find (1996). Thin sceptre. Irregular flan. 1.31

(10) *BMC* 25. Lark Hill hoard (1854). Thin sceptre. Wedge -shaped split. [1.30]

(11) *BMC* 24. Ex Olroyd bequest (1946). Thick sceptre. 1.26

Other references:

Taffs (1956) 140 (no reading given).

BNJ 29 (1958–9), p. 83:
'-hEN REX AN
+hENR-:S:ED-'
21.08 gr. [=1.35 g], from Tealby hoard (1807).

D3(?) (BMC –)

64 Oo O. +hENRIR[
R. +hENR[ ]ON S[.]ED.

Crudely executed dies.

(1)* Eaglen (B727). Ex Lawrence, IV (1951) 989 (3 or 4/10); Doubleday 895 (3/4). 1.35

E2–3 (BMC 28–30)

65 Pp O. +hENRI REX
Two pellets in dexter shoulder fold, instead of three (E2) or one (E3).
R. +hENRI:ON:S:EDM:
Reclining S. *BMC* gives mint name as ending in 'M (or N)'.

(1) *BMC* 29, Pl. XXII, 3. Lark Hill hoard (1854). 'Square flan with angles turned over.' 1.47

(2) *BMC* 30. Leicester hoard (1927), 9. 'Square flan with edges turned over'. 1.46

(3)* Eaglen (B583). Tealby hoard (1807). Ex Elmore Jones 1679 (3/3). See *BNJ* 29 (1958–9), p. 83, 7, this coin. Irregular flan. 1.41

(4) Eaglen (B1102). Corné, Loire hoard (*c.* 1930), see *NCirc*, May 1966, pp.125–6, illustrated. Ex Spink (with Elmore Jones ticket). 1.41

(5) Eaglen (B728). Ex Lawrence, IV (1951) 989 (5/10); Doubleday 895 (4/4). 1.40

(6) Ashmolean Museum. Gayton hoard (1998), 8. 1.40

(7) *BMC* 28. Lark Hill hoard (1854): 'cf. similar coin in R.C. Lockett collection [see 65 (8) below]'.

(8) Eaglen (B074). Ex Talbot Ready; Lockett 1181 (4/4). Irregular flan. 1.35

(9) Palmer (SED 41). Found at Hockwood-cum-Wilton (1985). 1.33

(10) Fitzwilliam Museum. Ex Shirley-Fox and Blunt collections. Ragged. [1.29]

(11) Private collection. –

Other references:

SCBI South Eastern Museums (Letchworth) 1998. Mile Ditches (nr. Royston, Cambs) Hoard (1978), 2. See Archibald and Cook 2001, pp.10–11, Pl. 9, where catalogued as 'Bust D or E' reading somewhat speculatively
[hEN] R REX
[ ]:ON:EDM (1.14).

Raul

F1 (*BMC* 31)

66 QIq O. +hEN REX AN
Ringlets (type F)
Appears to exist in two forms with sceptre handle (QI) retooled more thickly (Q2), see 67 (1) and (3) below.
+RAVL:ON:S[ ]EDM:
Legend begins at 1 o'clock. Reclining S.

(1) *BMC* 31. Leicester hoard (1927), 143: 'cf. coin from same dies in F. Elmore Jones Collection', see 66 (2) below. 1.43

(2)* Eaglen (B345). Ex Elmore Jones 1409 (1/5). 1.43

(3) Palmer (SED 442), Irregular flan and undersize. 1.08

FI (*BMC* 32)

67 QI/ O. As above
Q2r R. +RA[ ]ON:S:EDMV
Legend begins after 12 o'clock. Reclining S.

(1)* Eaglen (B346). Ex Elmore Jones 1409 (3/5). Thin sceptre (QI). Irregular flan. 1.42

(2) Eaglen (B344). Ex Elmore Jones 1409 (2/5). Thick sceptre. Irregular flan. 1.39

(3)* *BMC* 32, Pl. XXIII, 17. Ex Lawrence (1935). Thick Sceptre (Q2). Irregular flan. 1.37

(4) Ashmolean Museum. Gayton hoard (1998), 51. Thin sceptre. 1.37

Henry II, Tealby Cross-and-Crosslets (Tealby) Type, Raul (*cont.*)

FI? (*BMC* 33)

68	Rr	O.	+hENRI REX	
		R.	As above	
		(1)	*SCBI* Scottish Museums (Glasgow) 336.	1.47
		(2)	Eaglen (B075). Ex Parsons, II, 263 (1/6), recorded as '– ON EDMV'.	1.45
		(3)*	*BMC* 33. Ex Lawrence (1947): 'cf. coin from same dies in Hunterian Museum, Glasgow (Coates Collection, no. 529) [see 68 (1) above] and similar coin in Copenhagen Museum, from Thomsen Collection, no. 9574 [see 68 (7) below].'	1.41
		(4)	Eaglen (B576). Ex Birkenshaw (1986).	1.39
		(5)	Eaglen (B730). Ex Lawrence, IV (1951) 989 (6 or 7/10); Doubleday 896 (2/2). Finger nail shaped.	1.38
		(6)	Eaglen (B347). Ex Elmore Jones 1409 (4/5). Irregular flan.	1.35
		(7)	Copenhagen, Nationalmuseet, Thomsen 9574.	1.33

Other references:

Lawrence, II (1951) 372 (1/6). '33'.

F1 (*BMC* 33A)

69	Ss	O.	+hENRI REX: Flaw developing from chin through to hand.	
		R.	+RAVL:ON:S:EDMV: Reclining S.	
		(1)	Eaglen (B076). *SCMB*, Dec. 1974, H4653 (illustrated); Baldwin (1978).	1.48
		(2)	Ashmolean Museum. Gayton hoard (1998), 48. Irregular flan.	1.33
		(3)	*BMC* 33A, Pl. XX, 19. Fitzwilliam Museum. See Blackburn 1987, p. 113. Chipped.	[1.32]
		(4)*	Eaglen (B143). Ex Seaby (1981).	1.30
		(5)	*SCBI* South-Eastern Museums (Letchworth) 1963. Mile Ditches, nr. Royston hoard (1978). See Archibald and Cook 2001, p. 11, not illustrated.	1.27
		(6)	BM (1985). Ex executors of Elmore Jones.	1.21

Other references: Lockett 3956 (1/7), '33a'.

FI (*BMC* 34–35)

70 Tt O.]ENRI:REX
R. +RAVL:ON:S:EDM:
Reclining S.

(1) *BMC* 34. Leicester hoard (1927), 7. Irregular flan. 1.46

(2) *BMC* 35. Leicester hoard (1927), 8. Irregular flan. 1.46

(3) Palmer (SED 33). Ex Elmore Jones 1680 (1/2); Trenerry (1986). 1.42

(4)* Eaglen (B077). Ex Baldwin (1978). 1.39

(5) Eaglen (B1029). *SCMB*, Sept. 1991, E3 (illustrated). 1.38

Other references: Lawrence, II (1951) 372 (2/6); '34/5'.

FI (*BMC* 36)

71 Tu O. As above
R. +RAVL:ON:S:EDM:
Legend begins at 1 o'clock. Reclining S.

(1) Ashmolean Museum. Gayton hoard (1998), 49. 1.35

(2)* *BMC* 36. Leicester hoard (1927), 10. Irregular flan. 1.31

(3) Ashmolean Museum. Gayton hoard (1998), 103. Irregular flan. 1.26

(4) Palmer (SED 391). Ex A. M. Dawson. Small, irregular flan. Worn. [1.07]

FI (*BMC* –)

72 Vv O.]RI REX A
R.]ON:S:EDMV
The moneyer may safely be assumed to be Rauf.
Tilted S.

(1) Eaglen (B729). Ex Lawrence, IV (1951) 989 (6 or 7/10); Doubleday 896 (1/2). 1.40

(2)* BM (1985). Ex executors of Elmore Jones. Lozenge shaped but not clipped. 1.18

FI (*BMC* –)

73 Ww O. +h[ ]REX
R.]:ON:S:EDM
The moneyer may be safely assumed to be Rauf.
Reclining S.

(1)* Eaglen (B348). Ex Elmore Jones 1409 (5/5). 1.20

FI (*BMC* 36A)

74 Xx O.]EX ANG
R. +RAVL:[ ]N[ ]:ED[ ]V

Henry II, Tealby Cross-and-Crosslets (Tealby) Type, Raul (*cont.*)

		(1)*	*BMC* 36A, Pl. XXIII, 16. Ashmolean Museum. Ex Lawrence. See *SCBI* Ashmolean Museum 348.	1.41
			F2 (*BMC* 37–39)	
75	Yy	O.	+hENRI:REX	
		R.	+RAVL:ON:S:EDMV Reclining S.	
		(1)*	*BMC* 37, Pl. XXIV, 6.	1.42
			F2 (*BMC* 38–39)	
76	Yz	O.	As above	
		R.	+ROVLF:ON:S:EDM˙ Reclining S.	
		(1)	Palmer (SED 354). Ex Elmore Jones 1680 (2/2); Pheatt (1995) 726 (1/2).	1.48
		(2)	Ashmolean Museum. Gayton hoard (1998), 27. Irregular flan.	1.48
		(3)	*BMC* 38. Tealby hoard (1807). Ex Banks collection (1818). 'Cf. similar coin in Copenhagen from Thomsen Collection, no. 9573 [see 76 (7) below]'. Irregular flan.	1.47
		(4)	*BMC* 39, Pl. XXIV, 7. Irregular flan.	1.46
		(5)	A. M. Dawson collection. Found near Brussels, pre (?) 1984. See Blackburn 1987, where the coin is illustrated (p. 117) and described (p. 118) as 'F3. . . RALVL:]ON:S:ED[MV]'. The coin, besides being of type F2, reads]F:ON:S:ED[, with reclining S. Irregular flan.	1.45
		(6)	Eaglen (B172). Ex C. J. Martin (1981). Irregular flan.	1.43
		(7)	Copenhagen, Nationalmuseet, Thomsen 9573.	1.39
		(8)*	Eaglen (B230). Ex Spink (1965) and Osborne collection. Irregular flan.	1.35
		(9)	Ashmolean Museum. Gayton hoard (1998), 54.	1.31
		(10)	Palmer (SED 817). Small flan.	1.17
			F.. (***BMC*** 40)	
77	AA/aa	O.	]hENRI REX No pellets on drapery folds, but on sceptre.	
		R.	+RAVL:ON·S[ ]ED: Reclining S.	
		(1)*	*BMC* 40, Pl. XXIII, 15. Tealby hoard (1807). Ex Banks collection (1818). Irregular flan.	1.46

		(2)	Ashmolean Museum. Gayton hoard (1998), 67.	1.40
			F.. (*BMC* 41)	
78	BB/bb	O.	+hENRI[	
		R.	]VL:ON:S:EDM	
			Retrograde S. Uncertain if M is straight-sided or curvilinear. *BMC* p. 8: 'Large lettering of unusual type; cf. no. 117a of the moneyer Ricard of Canterbury'.	
		(1)*	*BMC* 41, Pl. XXV, 19. Ex Carlyon-Britton 1525 (1/2) and Lawrence (1947).	1.44
			F. . (*BMC* -)	
[79]	CC/cc	O.	+hE[	
		R.	]AVL:ON:[S][	
			Reclining S. Probably a Bury reading.	
		(1)*	Ashmolean Museum. Gayton hoard (1998), 100.	1.33

SHORT CROSS COINAGE (1180–1247)

In *SCBI* J. P. Mass Collection , references to Eaglen die combination numbers are taken from the present author's PhD thesis (1989), and do not correspond with the Catalogue numbers appearing below.

JOHN (1199–1216)

The die identities for John's reign are an extension of those recorded by Brand 1964, pp. 61–2.

Fulke

			Class Vb1	
80	Ax	O.	hENRICVS R./EX	
		R.	+FVLKE·ON·SADMV	
			Minute third curl under two main curls.	
		(1)	Royal Mint Museum. Hocking catalogue 404.	1.44
		(2)	Palmer (SED 90). Ex Mangakis and Woodhead collections; Spink, 29 March 1990, (1/9); Eaglen (B993).	1.35

John, Short Cross, Class Vb1, Fulke (*cont.*)

		(3)*	Eaglen (B221). Ex Brand collection; Baldwin (1983).	1.20
		(4)	*SCBI* J. P. Mass Collection 1456. Cut halfpenny.	[0.49]
81	Aa	O. R.	As above +FVLKE·ON·SADMV	
		(1)	BM. Ex Banks (1818).	1.40
		(2)	BM. Colchester hoard (1902), 1006.	1.38
		(3)*	Eaglen (B387). Ex Spink (1985).	1.36
		(4)	*SCBI* J. P. Mass Collection 1455. Ex Woodhead collection.	1.35
		(5)	Eaglen (B224). Ex Brand collection; Baldwin (1983).	1.33
		(6)	Gittoes collection. Phillips, 17 Nov. 1990. Cut halfpenny.	[0.61]
82	Ab	O. R.	As above +FVLKE·ON·S·EDM	
		(1)	Fitzwilliam Museum. Ex Hasluck bequest.	1.47
		(2)*	Gittoes collection. Eccles hoard (1864). Ex Evans and Lockett collections; Glendining, 23 June 1982, 174.	1.45
		(3)	BM. Colchester hoard (1902), 999.	1.44
		(4)	*SCBI* Scottish Museums (Glasgow) 384.	1.42
		(5)	Palmer (SED 743). Ex Eaglen (B056), North and Conte (?) collections.	1.39
		(6)	Colchester Museums. Colchester hoard (1902).	1.38
		(7)	BM. 'GIHR'.	1.37
		(8)	Eaglen (B289). Ex Trenerry (1983).	1.35
		(9)	Palmer (SED 18). Found in Diss area.	1.15
		(10)	Palmer (SED 314). Cut halfpenny.	[0.74]
		(11)	Gittoes collection. Cut halfpenny.	[0.62]
83	Ac	O. R.	As above +FVLKE·NN·S·EDM	
		(1)	Birmingham Museum and Art Gallery	1.50
		(2)	Colchester Museums. Colchester hoard (1902).	1.49
		(3)	Gittoes collection. Ex Eaglen (B567).	1.48
		(4)	Eaglen (B992). Ex Woodhead collection; Spink, 29 March 1990, 1 (1/9).	1.43

(5)* Palmer (SED 350). 1.41

(6) Fitzwilliam Museum. Ex Shirley-Fox and Blunt collections. 1.39

(7) Baldwin (1988). Ex Brand collection; Eaglen (B223). 1.39

(8) Gittoes collection. 1.38

(9) *SCBI* J. P. Mass Collection, 1457. See Dix, Noonan, Webb, 17 March 2004, 282. 1.34

(10) Gittoes collection. Bent and worn. [1.29]

(11) Mass collection (not in *SCBI*). Ex Eaglen (B194). Worn. [1.05]

(12) Palmer. (SED 298). Cut halfpenny. [0.64]

(13) 'Formerly belonging to Mr Ebsworth'. –

(14) Gardner collection (1988). –

Class Vb2/1

84 Bc O. hENRICVS R/EX
R. +FVLKE·NN·S·EDM

(1) Eaglen (B732). Ex Doubleday 950 (1/10). 1.48

(2) *SCBI* J. P. Mass collection, 1458. Ex Harris collection. 1.45

(3) Gittoes collection. Eccles hoard (1864). Ex Evans; Lockett; Glendining, 23 June 1982, 174. 1.44

(4) BM. Colchester hoard (1902), 1007. 1.44

(5) Royal Mint Museum. Hocking catalogue 388. 1.41

(6) Palmer (SED 410). 1.33

(7)* Eaglen (B430). 1.30

Class Vb2

85 Bd O. As above
R. +FVLKE·ON·S·AD

(1) *SCBI* Yorkshire Museums (York) 1270. Barnsley find (1856). 1.50

(2) Birmingham Museum and Art Gallery. 1.47

(3)* Eaglen (B460). Naxos hoard (1969?). Ex Baldwin (1986). 1.38

(4) BM. Colchester hoard (1902), 997. 1.37

(5) *SCBI* Scottish Museums (Edinburgh) 385. 1.17

(6) Eaglen (B234). Ex Osborne collection (1983). 1.08

(7) Palmer (SED 677). Cut halfpenny. [0.59]

John, Short Cross, Class Vb2, Fulke (*cont.*)

		(8)	Coin Market Values (illustration).	–
86	Cd	O. R.	hENRICVS R/EX as above	
		(1)	BM. Eccles hoard (1864), 412.	1.47
		(2)	Palmer (SED 912).	1.43
		(3)*	Eaglen (B283). Ex Elmore Jones collection; Spink (1983).	1.40
		(4)	Ulster Museum. Ex Canon Grainger collection (1890).	1.37
		(5)	Gittoes collection. R. off centre.	1.32
		(6)	*SCBI* J. P. Mass Collection 1460. See Dix, Noonan, Webb, 17 March, 2004, 312. R. off centre.	1.26
		(7)	Palmer (SED 245). Cut halfpenny.	[0.59]
		(8)	Ex Lockett collection.	–
87	Ce	O. R.	As above +FVKE·ON·S·ADMV	
		(1)*	Palmer (SED 782). East Anglian metal detector find. Gilded, probably shortly after issue.	1.44
		(2)	BM. Colchester hoard (1902), 1000.	1.43
		(3)	Copenhagen. Ribe hoard, I (1911) 110.	1.43
		(4)	BM. Eccles hoard (1864), 411.	1.37.
		(5)	*SCBI* J. P. Mass Collection 1459.	1.30
		(6)	Eaglen (B008). Ex Seaby (1975).	1.20
		(7)	Gittoes collection. Leconfield hoard (2000). Cut halfpenny. This piece is not recorded in the summary of the hoard in *NC* 160 (2000), pp. 354–5.	[0.57]
		(8)	Palmer (SED 365). Cut halfpenny.	[0.49]
88	Cf	O. R.	As above +FOLKE·ON·SADM	
		(1)	Gittoes collection	1.47
		(2)*	BM. Colchester hoard (1902), 996.	1.43
		(3)	Eaglen (B222). Ex Lockett and Brand collections; Baldwin (1983).	1.31
		(4)	Stewartby collection.	1.27
89	Df	O. R.	hENRICVS R/EX As above	

		(1)*	BM. Eccles hoard (1864), 410.	1.38
		(2)	Palmer (SED 695).	1.22
90	Dg	O. R.	As above +FVLKE·ON·S·ADM	
		(1)	Palmer (SED 600).	1.46
		(2)	BM. Eccles hoard (1864), 409.	1.44
		(3)	Eaglen (B426). Ex Osborne collection (1985).	1.42
		(4)	Copenhagen. Ribe hoard, I (1911) 109.	1.42
		(5)*	Ex Lockett collection.	–
91	Dh	O. R.	As above +FVLKE·ON·S·ADM	
		(1)*	BM. Colchester hoard (1902), 998.	1.43
		(2)	Eaglen (B056 EX). Ex North collection (1985).	1.38
92	Xf	O. R.	hENRICVS R/EX As above	
		(1)	Eaglen (B1031). Ex Spink, 16 March 1992, 155.	1.48
		(2)	Fitzwilliam Museum. Colchester hoard (1902).	1.47
		(3)	Gittoes collection. Ex Spink, 16 March 1992, 156. Part flat.	1.46
		(4)*	Birmingham Museum and Art Gallery.	1.45
		(5)	Palmer (SED 392). Cut halfpenny.	[0.76]
		(6)	Palmer (SED 526). Cut halfpenny.	[0.71]
		(7)	Ex Lubbock. Off centre.	–
93	Xg	O. R.	As above As above	
		(1)	Palmer (SED 129). Ex Gittoes collection.	1.53
		(2)	Colchester Museums. Colchester hoard (1902).	1.49
		(3)	Gittoes collection. Ex Youde and Dupree collections. R. off centre.	1.48
		(4)	Archibald and Cook 2001, p. 42 and Pl.12, 1. From hoard of unknown date and location of discovery.	1.45
		(5)*	Eaglen (B362). Ex C. J. Martin (1984).	1.44
		(6)	*SCBI* Polish Museums 396.	1.28
94	Xi	O. R.	As above +FVLKE·ON·SAND	
		(1)	Eaglen (B1020).	1.45

John, Short Cross, Class Vb2, Fulke (*cont.*)

		(2)*	Eaglen (B461). Naxos hoard (1969?). Ex Baldwin (1986).	1.32
		(3)	Gittoes collection. Irregular flan; bent.	[1.29]
			Class Vc	
95	Ef	O. R.	hENRICVS R/EX As above	
		(1)	Gittoes collection. Ex Palmer (SED 284).	1.36
		(2)	Palmer (SED 220). Found near Chichester (1992?).	1.32
		(3)*	Eaglen (B235). Ex Osborne collection (1983).	1.33
		(4)	Palmer (SED 819). Cut halfpenny.	[0.64]
		(5)	*SCBI* J. P. Mass Collection 1705. Cut halfpenny.	[0.63]
96	Ei	O. R.	As above As above	
		(1)	BM. Eccles hoard (1864), 408.	1.47
		(2)*	Eaglen (B225). Eccles hoard (1864). Ex Lockett and Brand collections; Baldwin (1983).	1.35
97	Ej	O. R.	As above +FVLKE·ON·S·AD	
		(1)	BM. Hasluck bequest (1920), 1074.	1.44
		(2)*	Eaglen (B014). Ex Seaby (1975).	1.35
		(3)	Palmer (SED 87). Ex Lawrence, IV (1951), 1014; Mangakis and Woodhead collections; Spink, 29 March 1990, 1 (3/9).	1.33
		(4)	Gittoes collection. Worn.	[1.28]
		(5)	*SCBI* J. P. Mass Collection 1705A. Cut halfpenny.	[0.59]

JOHN/HENRY III

The variety of class VIc in use at the accession of Henry III in 1216 is likely to have been VIc3 (see Chapter 8).

N.B. Ornamental letters (principally on coins of Class VIc2) are indicated by underlining.

Class VIc1

Rauf

98	Aa	O.	hENRICVS R/EX Pellets either side of nose. Cf. Class VIx (Canterbury), Stewart 1979, p. 30.	
		R.	+RAVF·ON·SANT˙AD:	
		(1)*	BM. Eccles hoard (1864), 1485.	1.39
		(2)	BM. Colchester hoard (1902), 1002.	1.26
		(3)	Eaglen (B315). Ex Brand collection. Cracked.	1.22
		(4)	Gittoes collection. Spink (1992). Cut farthing.	[0.33]
99	Ab	O.	As above	
		R.	+RAVF·ON·SA[ ]AD˙	
		(1)*	*SCBI* J. P. Mass Collection 1871, where construed as dies Aa. See Dix, Noonan, Webb, 17 March 2004, 364.	1.34
			Class VIc1-2 transitional/VIc2	
100	Bc	O.	hENRICVS R/EX Pellets either side of nose and on chin. Ornamental R (not always clear) and S with serifs and pellet (see also R. f below).	
		R.	+RAVF·ON·SANTAD	
		(1)*	BM. Colchester hoard (1902), 1010. R. double struck.	1.44
		(2)	Gittoes collection. Worn.	[1.27]
101	Bd	O.	As above	
		R.	+RAVF·ON·SANTAD	
		(1)	Colchester Museums. Colchester hoard (1902).	1.46
		(2)*	BM. Colchester hoard (1902), 1005.	1.43
		(3)	*SCBI* J. P. Mass Collection 1872. Ex North and Conte collections. Plugged.	[1.32]
		(4)	Palmer (SED 200). Lozenge shaped.	[1.00]
102	Be	O.	As above, but possibly flaw between I and C.	
		R.	+RAVF·ON·SANTAD	
		(1)	Palmer (SED 143). Reputedly found near Bury St Edmunds (1991).	1.42
		(2)*	Fitzwilliam Museum. Colchester hoard (1902).	1.41
103	Bf	O.	As above, possibly with flaw between I and C.	
		R.	+RAVF.ON·SANTAD	

John/Henry III, Short Cross, Class VIc1, Rauf (*cont.*)

			Ornamental S with serifs and pellet. Mass had not encountered such an S (see *SCBI* J. P. Mass Collection, pp. 45–6).	
		(1)	Colchester Museums. Colchester hoard (1902).	1.46
		(2)	*SCBI* Merseyside County Museums 923.	1.42
		(3)*	Gittoes collection.	1.33
		(4)	Gittoes collection. Cut halfpenny.	[0.64]
		(5)	Palmer (SED 373). Cut halfpenny.	[0.60]
			Class VIc2	
104	Cg	O. R.	hENRICVS R/EX +RAVF ·ON·SANTAD	
		(1)*	BM. Eccles hoard (1864), 1481.	1.48
		(2)	Birmingham Museum and Art Gallery.	1.39
		(3)	Fitzwilliam Museum. Ex Shirley-Fox and Blunt collections.	1.27
		(4)	BM. Eccles hoard (1864), 1482.	1.26
		(5)	Palmer (SED 135). Cut halfpenny. Reputedly found near Ipswich (1991).	[0.68]
105	Ch	O. R.	As above +RAVF·ON·SANTAD	
		(1)	*SCBI* Ashmolean Museum 372.	1.46
		(2)	*SCBI* J. P. Mass Collection 1873. Corné hoard (*c.* 1930). Ex North and Conte collections.	1.42
		(3)	Eaglen (B231). Ex Osborne collection. Pierced.	[1.33]
		(4)	*SCBI* Northern Museums (Blackburn) 1381. Colchester hoard (1902).	1.32
		(5)	Gittoes collection.	1.32
		(6)*	Eaglen (B355). Ex Elmore Jones 1522 (pt).	1.17
106	Di	O. R.	hENRICVS R/EX +RAVF·ON·SANTE:	
		(1)*	BM. Eccles hoard (1864), 1484.	1.45
		(2)	Stewartby collection.	1.36
		(3)	Gittoes collection.	1.33
		(4)	Rotenfels hoard (1936). See *BNJ* 53 (1983), p. 25, Wieland 98.	–

107	Dj	O. R.	As above +RAVF·ON·SANTEA	
		(1)	BM. Eccles hoard (1894). Presented by King George V (1920).	1.45
		(2)*	Gittoes collection. Ex Elmore Jones 1522 (pt).	1.44
		(3)	Eaglen (B111).	1.43
		(4)	Palmer (SED 413).	1.40
		(5)	*SCBI* Scottish Museums (Edinburgh) 387.	1.37
		(6)	*SCBI* Museums in East Anglia (Bury) 1507. Ex Frost collection.	1.36
		(7)	*SCBI* J. P. Mass Collection 1875.	1.35
108	Ek	O. R.	hENRICVS R/EX +RAVF·ON·SANTAD	
		(1)	BM. Colchester hoard (1902), 1009.	1.53
		(2)	Gittoes collection.	1.47
		(3)	Palmer (SED 318). Worn.	[1.30]
		(4)*	Ex Lockett collection.	–
109	El	O. R.	As above +RAVF[ ] ON[ ]SANTAD	
		(1)	*SCBI* East Anglian Museums (Ipswich) 1506.	1.49
		(2)*	Palmer (SED 374). Irregular flan.	1.44
		(3)	Colchester Museums. Colchester hoard (1902).	1.37
110	Fm	O. R.	hENRICVS R/EX +RAVF·ON·SANTEA	
		(1)	BM Colchester hoard (1902), 1004.	1.48
		(2)*	Copenhagen. Ribe hoard, I (1911).	1.40
		(3)	BM Colchester hoard (1902), 1013.	1.37
		(4)	Gittoes collection.	1.36
		(5)	*SCBI* Museums in East Anglia (Bury) 1507.	1.36
		(6)	Palmer (SED 621). Worn.	[1.32]
		(7)	Stewartby collection. Naxos hoard (1969?).	1.30
		(8)	Dublin Museum. Kilmaine hoard (1946).	1.18
		(9)	*SCBI* J. P. Mass Collection 1874A. Cut halfpenny.	[0.54]
111	Fn	O. R.	As above +RAVF·ON·SANTEA	
		(1)*	Ulster Museum. Ex Canon Grainger collection (1890).	1.39

John/Henry III, Short Cross, Class VIc1, Rauf (*cont.*)

		(2)	Gittoes collection. Ex Youde and Dupree collections. Irregular flan. R. off-centre.	[1.37]
		(3)	Eaglen (B374). Ex Lawrence, IV (1951) 1022; Doubleday 950 (3/10).	1.22
112	Go	O. R.	hENRICVS R/EX +RAVF[ ]ON·SANTAD	
		(1)*	Eaglen (B232). Ex Osborne collection.	1.36
			Class VIc 2/3	
113	Ep	O. R.	As above +RAVF[ ]ON·SANTAD	
		(1)*	Gittoes collection. Struck off-centre.	1.43
		(2)	Rotenfels hoard (1936). See *BNJ* 53 (1983), p. 25, where the coin is classified as VIc3.	–
114	Fq	O. R.	As above +RAVF·ON·S'ANTEA	
		(1)	Colchester Museums. Colchester hoard (1902).	1.40
		(2)	Dublin Museum. Kilmaine hoard (1946).	1.39
		(3)	BM. Tiree hoard (1787). ('E 2004').	1.38
		(4)	*SCBI* J. P. Mass Collection 1874, where attributed to dies Fn. Ex Woodhead, North and Conte collections.	1.26
		(5)	Fitzwilliam Museum.	1.22
		(6)*	Ex Lockett collection.	–
		(7)	Palmer (SED 310). Cut halfpenny.	[0.53]
115	Gr	O. R.	As above +RAVF.ON·SANTAD	
		(1)	BM. Eccles hoard (1864), 416.	1.61
		(2)	Gittoes collection. Ex Elmore Jones 1522 (pt).	1.43
		(3)*	Eaglen (B316). Ex Lockett and Brand collections.	1.42
		(4)	BM. Eccles hoard (1864), 417.	1.42
		(5)	Gittoes collection. Ex Spink, 16 March, 1992, 156. Chipped.	[1.13]
116	Gs	O. R.	As above +RAVF·ON·SANTA	
		(1)*	BM Eccles hoard (1864), 1486.	1.42

Class VIc 3

117 Hs O. hENRICVS R/EX
R. As above

(1) BM. Colchester hoard (1902), 1008. 1.42

(2) BM. Eccles hoard (1864), 1480. 1.41

(3) Dublin Museum. Kilmaine hoard (1946). 1.40

(4) Eaglen (B066). Ex Seaby (1978). 1.36

(5) Stewartby collection. 1.34

(6)* Palmer (SED 603). Naxos hoard (1969?). Ex Spink (1987) and Mass collection (not in *SCBI*). 1.31

(7) *SCBI* J. P. Mass Collection 1876. Ex Mangakis, North and Conte collections. See Dix, Noonan, Webb, 17 March 2004, 372. Recorded by Eaglen as 1.18 g. 1.25

(8) BM. 'E2003'. 1.18

118 Ht O. As above
R. +RAVF·ON·SANTA
This R. is very similar to s above but, pending clearer examples coming to light, is treated as distinctive.

(1) Eaglen (B995). Ex Mangakis and Woodhead collections; Spink, 29 March 1990, 1 (4/9). 1.40

(2)* Birmingham Museum and Art Gallery. 1.40

Class VIc 3/2

119 Iu O. hENRICVS. R/EX
R. RAVF·ON·SANTAD

(1) Palmer (SED 11). Clipped? [1.37]

(2) Palmer (SED 821). Buckled and clipped. [1.35]

(3) *SCBI* Scottish Museums (Glasgow) 388. 1.27

(4) Eaglen (B594). Pierced. [1.22]

(5)* BM. Colchester hoard (1902), 1014. 1.21

(6) Eaglen (B233). Ex Osborne collection (1983). 1.19

(7) Glendining, 23 April 1991, 341 (1/3). –

(8) American Numismatic Society. –

(9) Ex Doubleday 950 (2/10), Eaglen (B733) and North. –

120 Iv O. As above
R. +RAVF'ONSANTAD

John/Henry III, Short Cross, Class VIc 3/2, Rauf (*cont.*)

		(1)*	BM. Eccles hoard (1864), 1483. Uneven flan.	1.47
		(2)	Eaglen (B1005). Ex Harris collection. Uneven flan.	1.42
		(3)	*SCBI* J. P. Mass Collection 1877. Badly worn.	[1.28]
		(4)	Palmer (SED 140). Lozenge-shaped flan; worn.	[1.28]
		Class VIc 3		
121	Iw	O. R.	As above. +RAVF·ON·SANTA	
		(1)*	BM. Colchester hoard (1902), 1001.	1.36
		(2)	Gittoes collection.	1.32
		(3)	Colchester Museums. Colchester hoard (1902). Partly flat; creased.	[1.15]
122	Jx	O. R.	hENRICVS R/EX +RAVF·ON·SANTE No second R. is known with O. 'J'. The issue of single reverses at Bury with each obverse may have begun in this or the next sub-class (VId).	
		(1)	Colchester Museums. Colchester hoard (1902).	1.48
		(2)*	BM. Colchester hoard (1902), 1003.	1.42
		(3)	Copenhagen. Ribe hoard, I (1911)164. Nicked.	[1.22]
		(4)	Palmer (SED 148). Cut farthing.	[0.30]

HENRY III (1216–72)

			Class VId	
123	Aa	O. R.	hE<u>N</u>RICVS R/EX +RAVF·O<u>N</u>·SA<u>N</u>TE Pellet under + and on cross-bar of 'N's.	
		(1)	BM. Eccles hoard (1864), 415.	1.47
		(2)	BM. Eccles hoard (1864), 418.	1.45
		(3)*	Gisors hoard (1970).	1.40
		(4)	BM. Colchester hoard (1902), 1011.	1.39
		(5)	*SCBI* J. P. Mass Collection 1896. See Dix, Noonan, Webb, 17 March 2004, 379.	1.38
		(6)	Gittoes collection. Ex Elmore Jones 1522 (pt).	1.36

		(7)	Eaglen (B195). Ex Lockett collection.	1.33
		(8)	Stewartby collection. Naxos hoard (1969?).	1.32
		(9)	Eaglen (B1045).	1.31
		(10)	*SCBI* J.P. Mass Collection 1896A. Worn.	[1.24]
		(11)	Palmer (SED 535). Ex North and Mass collections.	1.04
		(12)	Palmer (SED 178). East-Anglian find (1992). Cut halfpenny.	[0.68]

Class VIIaA

The classification used for class VII broadly reflects that described in *SCBI* J. P. Mass Collection, pp. 49–58, in turn substantially based on earlier work by Stewart (1979), pp. 26–41, and North (1988), pp. 25–39.

124	Aa	O.	hENRI[ ]S R/EX Bust with affinities to class VId, but no pellet at chin. R. +RAVF ON SANTE	
		(1)*	BM. Eccles hoard (1864), 1487.	1.50
		(2)	Colchester Museums. Colchester hoard (1902).	1.48

Class VIIaB

125	Aa	O. R.	hENRICVS R/EX +RAVF ON SANTE	
		(1)	BM. Colchester hoard (1902), 1012. See *BNJ* 49 (1979) Pl. V, 91.	1.40
		(2)*	*SCBI* J. P. Mass Collection 1967. Ex North and Conte collections. This coin is described by Mass as having 'S with long crescent serifs', but this characteristic is not obvious on the O. or R. of 125 (1) or (2).	1.18
		(3)	Gittoes collection. Cut farthing.	[0.45]

Class VIIaB-C
Group 1 (well proportioned bust).

Willem

126	Aa	O. R.	hENRICVS R/EX Pellets in curls. +WILLELM ON SAN	
		(1)	BM. Colchester hoard (1902), 1030.	1.51
		(2)*	BM. Eccles hoard (1864), 120.	1.47
		(3)	Colchester Museums. Colchester hoard (1902).	1.39
		(4)	Copenhagen. Ribe hoard, I (1911).	1.36

Henry III, Short Cross, Class VIIaB–C1, *Willem* (*cont.*)

127 Bb O. hENRICVS R/EX
Pellets in sinister curls.
R. +WILLELM·ON·SANT

(1)*	Birmingham Museum and Art Gallery, 181. Ex Harkness collection.	1.50
(2)	*SCBI* J. P. Mass Collection 1970. Ex North and Conte collections.	1.47
(3)	Palmer (SED 434). R. struck off-centre.	1.46
(4)	Gittoes collection.	1.46
(5)	Stewartby collection. Ex Lawrence collection.	1.43
(6)	Gittoes collection.	1.43
(7)	Colchester Museums. Colchester hoard (1902).	1.41
(8)	Colchester Museums. Colchester hoard (1902).	1.40
(9)	Eaglen (B735). Ex Lawrence, IV (1951) 1031; Doubleday 950 (4/10).	1.38
(10)	Palmer (SED 164). Spink, 16 March 1992, 157 (pt).	1.38
(11)	Colchester Museums. Colchester hoard (1902). Uneven flan.	1.36
(12)	Colchester Museums. Colchester hoard (1902).	1.36
(13)	Eaglen (B339 EX). Ex Gittoes collection.	1.36
(14)	Palmer (SED 692).	1.36
(15)	Gittoes collection. Uneven flan thickness.	1.36
(16)	Eaglen (B386).	1.31
(17)	Colchester Museums. Colchester hoard (1902). Worn.	[1.28]
(18)	American Numismatic Society.	–
(19)	Ex Mass collection. Photographed in 1990.	–
(20)	Rotenfels hoard (1936). See *BNJ* 53 (1983), p. 25, where the obverse of this coin is said, doubtfully, to be identical with a coin of Rauf in the BM (Catalogue 125 (1)).	–
(21)	Gisors hoard (1970).	–
(22)	Gittoes collection. Found in Dorset (1991?). Cut halfpenny.	[0.63]

128 Cc O. hENRICVS R/EX
No pellets in curls.
R. +WILLELM ON SANT
Markedly thick initial cross. Short, chubby lettering.

		(1)	Colchester Museums. Colchester hoard (1902).	1.50
		(2)*	BM. Eccles hoard (1864), 420.	1.47
		(3)	Palmer (SED 165). Spink, 16 March 1992, 157 (pt).	1.46
		(4)	*SCBI* J. P. Mass Collection 1969 ('VIIa 3'). Ex North and Conte collections.	1.45
		(5)	Fitzwilliam Museum. Ex Shirley-Fox and Blunt collections.	1.42
		(6)	Eaglen (B999). Ex Woodhead collection; Spink, 29 March 1990, 1 (8/9).	1.41
		(7)	Colchester Museums. Colchester hoard (1902).	1.41
		(8)	BM. Colchester hoard (1902), 1031.	1.40
		(9)	Gittoes collection. Ex Brand and Eaglen (B339) collections.	1.40
		(10)	Eaglen (B102). Ex Osborne collection.	1.39
		(11)	Colchester Museums. Colchester hoard (1902).	1.38
		(12)	Palmer (SED 702). R. struck off-centre.	1.38
		(13)	Gittoes collection.	1.37
		(14)	Eaglen (B339 EX). Ex Gittoes collection.	1.36
		(15)	BM. Colchester hoard (1902), 1027.	1.35
		(16)	Gittoes collection. Worn.	[1.28]
		(17)	*SCBI* Museums in East Anglia (Bury) 1511. Ex Frost collection.	1.25
		(18)	Dublin Museum. Kilmaine hoard (1946).	1.03
		(19)	Palmer (SED 181). Cut halfpenny.	[0.58]
			Group 2 ('Hapsburg' chin, with elongated, bearded jaw).	
129	Dd	O.	hENRICVS R/EX Pellets in curls.	
		R.	+WILLELN ON·SANT	
		(1)	*SCBI* Ashmolean Museum 373.	1.50
		(2)*	Eaglen (B167).	1.46
		(3)	*SCBI* J. P. Mass Collection 1968 ('VIIa 2'). Ex Eaglen (B021). See Dix, Noonan, Webb, 17 March 2004, 385.	1.44
		(4)	Palmer (SED 319).	1.40
		(5)	Ex North collection. R. struck off-centre.	1.37

Henry III, Short Cross, Class VIIaB–C2, *Willem* (*cont.*)

130	Ee	O.	hENRICVS R/EX Pellets in curls.	
		R.	+WILLELM ON SAN	
		(1)	BM. Hasluck bequest (1920), 1075. See Stewart 1979, Pl. V, 92.	1.45
		(2)	Dublin Museum. Kilmaine hoard (1946). Irregular flan.	1.38
		(3)	BM. 'E2006'.	1.36
		(4)	Palmer (SED 820).	1.34
		(5)*	BM. Eccles hoard (1864), 1490.	1.29
		(6)	Palmer (SED 911).	1.17
131	Ff	O.	hENRICVS R/EX Pellets in curls.	
		R.	+WILLELM ON SANT	
		(1)	BM. Eccles hoard (1864), 421.	1.49
		(2)	Copenhagen. Ribe hoard, I (1911).	1.49
		(3)	Eaglen (B237). Ex Osborne collection (1983).	1.48
		(4)	BM. Colchester hoard (1902), 1029.	1.46
		(5)	Lawrence 1915b, Pl. IV, 44.	1.46
		(6)	*SCBI* South-Eastern Museums (Maidstone) 2009/Ma. Eccles hoard (1864).	1.46
		(7)	BM. Eccles hoard (1864), 1488.	1.45
		(8)	Colchester Museums. Colchester hoard (1902). Ragged edge.	1.45
		(9)	BM. Eccles hoard (1864), 1489.	1.44
		(10)	Stewartby collection. Colchester hoard (1902).	1.41
		(11)	BM. Colchester hoard (1902), 1028.	1.38
		(12)	Eaglen (B340). Ex Brand collection.	1.38
		(13)*	Ex Lockett collection (Lot 1195 or 2980?).	–
		(14)	Palmer (SED 169). Cut farthing.	[0.36]

Class VIIaC

SCBI J. P. Mass Collection, Pl. 73, classified all of Norman's class VIIa dies as VIIa 3 (= C), regrettably abandoning North's classification of coins with a crude bust ('7a D') as a distinctive variety (p. 53).

Norman

132	Aa	O.	hENRICVS R/EX 'Hapsburg' chin.	
		R.	+NOR[M]AN ON SANT	
		(1)	Palmer (SED 44).	1.52
		(2)	Colchester Museums. Colchester hoard (1902). Irregular flan.	1.45
		(3)*	Eaglen (B1101). Naxos hoard (1969?). Ex North and Mass (*SCBI* J. P. Mass Collection, 1974) collections.	1.34
		(4)	Colchester Museums. Colchester hoard (1902).	1.29
		(5)	Colchester Museums. Colchester hoard (1902).	1.28
133	Ab	O.	As above	
		R.	+NORMAN ON SANT	
		(1)	BM. Eccles hoard (1864), 413.	1.56
		(2)	Copenhagen. Ribe hoard, I (1911), '395'. Overstruck on both sides R. on O. and vice versa.	1.50
		(3)*	BM. Eccles hoard (1864), 1493.	1.49
		(4)	Gittoes collection.	1.46
		(5)	Royal Mint Museum. Hocking catalogue 417.	1.45
		(6)	Palmer (SED 26).	1.44
		(7)	BM (1915), 1491.	1.43
		(8)	Gittoes collection. Irregular flan.	1.42
		(9)	Eaglen (B236). Ex Osborne collection.	1.42
		(10)	Gittoes collection. Ex Brand and Eaglen (B328) collections.	1.38
		(11)	*SCBI* Ashmolean Museum 371.	1.37
		(12)	Gittoes collection. Pheatt, 21 March 1995, 758 (1/4). Cracked. Chipped (?).	[1.36]
134	Bb	O.	hENRICVS R/EX Pellet touching lower lip?	
		R.	As above	
		(1)	*SCBI* J. P. Mass Collection 1973.	1.45
		(2)*	Eaglen (B318). Ex Brand collection. Struck off-centre. Clipped?	1.40
135	Bc	O.	As above	
		R.	+NORMAN ON SAN	
		(1)*	*SCBI* Museums in East Anglia (Ipswich) 1505.	1.38

Henry III, Short Cross, Class VIIaC, *Norman* (*cont.*)

136	Cc	O.	hENRICVS R/EX Pellet on chin.	
		R.	As above	
		(1)	Copenhagen. Ribe hoard, I (1911).	1.49
		(2)	Gittoes collection.	1.45
		(3)	Gittoes collection.	1.44
		(4)*	Birmingham Museum and Art Gallery. Ex Harkness.	1.44
		(5)	Fitzwilliam Museum. Ex Shirley-Fox and Blunt collections.	1.42
		(6)	Eaglen (B737). Ex Doubleday 950 (6/10).	1.39
		(7)	Eaglen (B328 EX). Colchester hoard (1902). Ex Gittoes collection.	1.38
		(8)	*SCBI* Northern Museums (Manchester) 1379. Eccles hoard (1864).	1.25
		(9)	Colchester Museums. Colchester hoard (1902).	–
		(10)	Palmer (SED 207). Cut halfpenny.	[0.73]
		(11)	Palmer (SED 443). Cut halfpenny.	[0.54]
137	Bd	O.	As above	
		R.	+NORMAN ON SANT	
		(1)	*SCBI* Museums in East Anglia (Bury) 1504. Ex Frost collection.	1.51
		(2)*	Colchester Museums. Colchester hoard (1902). Irregular flan.	1.50
		(3)	Eaglen (B166).	1.47
		(4)	*SCBI* Yorkshire Collections 1271. York Minster find (1829).	1.42
		(5)	*SCBI* Scottish Museums (Edinburgh) 386.	1.36
		(6)	Eaglen (B996). Ex Woodhead collection. Spink, 29 March 1990, 1 (5/9).	1.35
		(7)	Lawrence 1915b, Pl. IV, 43.	–
138	Be	O.	As above	
		R.	+NOR[M]AN ON SAN Large lettering.	
		(1)*	BM (1920). Eccles hoard (1864). Gift of King George V.	1.48
139	Ee	O.	hENRICVS R/EX	
		R.	As above	

		(1)	Eaglen (B395). Ex Baldwin (1985).	1.46
		(2)*	Fitzwilliam Museum 172. Colchester hoard (1902).	1.45
		(3)	Palmer (SED 623).	1.45
		(4)	Palmer (SED 63).	1.43
		(5)	Colchester Museums. Colchester hoard (1902). Irregular flan. R. off-centre. Worn.	1.41
		(6)	Eaglen (B325). Ex Brand collection.	1.38
		(7)	Gittoes collection.	1.38
		(8)	Copenhagen. Ribe hoard, I (1911), '162'.	1.37
		(9)	Gittoes collection. Montpellier hoard (1934). R. struck off-centre.	1.36
		(10)	National Museum of Wales. Wrexham hoard (1926).	1.20
		(11)	Gittoes collection. Clipped?	[1.13]
		(12)	Trenerry collection. Irregular flan/clipped.	–
140	Ff	O. R.	hENRI[ ]/E[ ] Pellet on chin.]NOR[ ]N O[ ]NT	
		(1)*	Colchester Museums. Colchester hoard (1902).	1.37
		(2)	Palmer (SED 630). Clipped?	[1.24]
141	Gg	O. R.	hENRICVS R/EX +NORMAN ON SANT Retrograde N in place of M.	
		(1)	Copenhagen. Ribe hoard, I (1911).	1.54
		(2)	Colchester Museums. Colchester hoard (1902).	1.42
		(3)	Colchester Museums. Colchester hoard (1902).	1.40
		(4)*	Eaglen (B101 EX). Ex Gittoes collection.	1.36
		(5)	Dublin Museum. Kilmaine hoard (1946). Worn.	[1.31]
142	Hh	O. R.	hENRICVS R/EX Pellet on chin. +NORMAN ON SANT	
		(1)	*SCBI* Northern Museums (Blackburn) 1376/Bl. Colchester hoard (1902).	1.48
		(2)	*SCBI* South-Eastern Museums (Maidstone) 2007/Ma. Catalogued as 'VIIbi'. Eccles hoard (1864).	1.46
		(3)	Eaglen (B375). Ex Baldwin (1985).	1.45
		(4)*	Birmingham Museum and Art Gallery. Ex Harkness. Nicked at edge.	[1.44]

Henry III, Short Cross, Class VIIaC, *Norman* (*cont.*)

		(5)	*SCBI* Northern Museums (Huddersfield) 1377/Hud.	1.39
		(6)	BM. Colchester hoard (1902), 1015.	1.36
		(7)	Gittoes collection. Ex Eaglen (B101).	1.31
		(8)	Copenhagen. Ribe hoard, I (1911).	1.28
		(9)	Palmer (SED 799). Partly flat.	[1.27]
		(10)	Palmer (SED 309).	1.25
		(11)	Ex Osborne collection (1.43 g?).	–
143	Ii	O. R.	hENRICVS R/EX +NORMAN ON SANT	
		(1)	Gittoes collection.	1.55
		(2)	Colchester Museums. Colchester hoard (1902).	1.43
		(3)*	Eaglen (B319). Ex Brand collection. Cracked.	[1.40]
		(4)	Colchester Museums. Colchester hoard (1902).	1.39
		(5)	Palmer (SED 545).	1.38
		(6)	Palmer (SED 649). Worn.	[1.35]
		(7)	Palmer (SED 500). Worn.	[1.24]
		(8)	Palmer (SED 301). Cut halfpenny.	[0.67]
144	Jj	O. R.	hENRICVS R/EX +NORMAN ON SAN	
		(1)	Colchester Museums. Colchester hoard (1902).	1.50
		(2)	Gittoes collection. Glendining, 21 Sept. 1983, 136.	1.50
		(3)	*SCBI* Merseyside County Museums 922. R. reading stated as '.AN'.	1.49
		(4)	Eaglen (B1007). Ex Harris collection.	1.48
		(5)	Colchester Museums. Colchester hoard (1902). Irregular flan.	1.48
		(6)	Palmer (SED 671). R. struck off-centre.	1.46
		(7)	*SCBI* J. P. Mass Collection 1971.	1.43
		(8)	Eaglen (B736). Doubleday 950 (5/10).	1.43
		(9)	Colchester Museums. Colchester hoard (1902).	1.41
		(10)	Colchester Museums. Colchester hoard (1902).	1.39
		(11)	BM. Eccles hoard (1864), 414.	1.38

		(12)	Palmer (SED 166). Ex Brand; Spink 16 March 1992, 157(pt). R. struck off-centre.	1.38
		(13)	Dublin Museum. Kilmaine hoard (1946).	1.36
		(14)	Eaglen (B906).	1.36
		(15)	Palmer (SED 512). R. struck off-centre.	1.35
		(16)	Ex Palmer (SED 244). Worn.	[1.33]
		(17)	Gittoes collection. Found nr. Harlow, Essex (1992?). Worn.	[1.32]
		(18)	Palmer (SED 37).	1.31
		(19)	*SCBI* Ashmolean Museum 368.	1.30
		(20)	Palmer (SED 651). Worn.	[1.18]
		(21)	Eaglen (B327). Ex Brand collection.	1.13
		(22)	Eaglen (B309). Ex C. J. Martin (1983).	1.11
		(23)*	Ex Lockett collection.	–
		(24)	Mlle. S. Bertram collection. Gisors hoard (1970).	–
		(25)	Palmer (SED 596). Cut halfpenny.	[0.73]
145	Kk	O. R.	hENRICVS R/EX +NORMAN ON CAN Mint signature reading CAN for SAN.	
		(1)	BM. Eccles hoard (1864), 1693.	1.49
		(2)	BM. Colchester hoard (1902), 296.	1.47
		(3)*	BM. Eccles hoard (1864), 1694.	1.45
		(4)	Gittoes collection.	1.41
		(5)	BM. Colchester hoard (1902), 295.	1.37
		(6)	*SCBI* J. P. Mass Collection 1976.	1.32
		(7)	Palmer (SED 577).	1.29
		(8)	BM. Eccles hoard (1864), 57.	1.25
		(9)	National Museum of Wales. Wrexham hoard (1926). Worn.	[1.15]
146	Ll	O. R.	hENRICVS R/EX +N[:]ORMAN ON·SAN	
		(1)	BM. Colchester hoard (1902), 1017.	1.47
		(2)*	*SCBI* Ashmolean Museum 370.	1.45
		(3)	Palmer (SED 531).	1.33
147	Mm	O. R.	hENRICVS R/EX +NORMAN ON SAN	

Henry III, Short Cross, Class VIIaC, *Norman* (*cont.*)

		(1)	Copenhagen. Ribe hoard, I (1911).	1.48
		(2)	BM. Eccles hoard (1846), 1493.	1.46
		(3)	Eaglen (B020).	1.42
		(4)*	BM. Eccles hoard (1902), 1492.	1.41
		(5)	Gittoes collection. O. struck off-centre.	1.41
		(6)	BM. Tiree hoard (1787).	1.37
		(7)	Palmer (SED 210). Ex Gittoes collection.	1.33
		(8)	Gittoes collection. Ex Brand and Eaglen (B324) collections.	1.32
		(9)	Palmer (SED 527).	1.30
		(10)	Copenhagen. Ribe hoard, I (1911).	1.25
		(11)	Dublin Museums. Kilmaine hoard (1946). Small flan. Worn.	[1.16]
		(12)	Palmer (SED 366).	–
148	Nn	O. R.	hENRICVS R/EX +NORMAN·ON·SAN	
		(1)	Palmer (SED 88). Ex Woodhead and Eaglen (B998) collections.	1.44
		(2)	Eaglen (B320). Colchester hoard (1902). Ex Brand collection.	1.41
		(3)*	Eaglen (B326). Ex Brand collection. Cracked.	[1.33]
		(4)	American Numismatic Society.	–
149	Oo	O. R.	hENRICVS R/EX +NORMAN ON SAN	
		(1)	Colchester Museums. Colchester hoard (1902).	1.43
		(2)	Palmer (SED 167). Spink, 16 March 1992, 157 (pt).	1.42
		(3)	*SCBI* Yorkshire Collections (Leeds) 1272/LM 276.	1.39
		(4)	Palmer (SED 650).	1.38
		(5)	Colchester Museums. Colchester hoard (1902).	1.36
		(6)	*SCBI* J. P. Mass Collection 1972.	1.32
		(7)	Palmer (SED 476). Impression of R. cross on O. Chipped.	[1.29]
		(8)	National Museum of Wales.	1.26
		(9)*	Eaglen (B322). Ex Brand collection.	1.25
		(10)	Eaglen (B323).Ex Brand collection.	1.24

150	Pp	O.	hENRICVS R/EX Large bust	
		R.	·+·NOR·MAN·ON·SAN	
		(1)	Palmer (SED 378). R. struck off-centre. Ex Mass (1994).	1.52
		(2)	Royal Mint Museum. Gift ex Lady Banks (1818).	
			Hocking catalogue 418.	1.49
		(3)	*SCBI* South-Eastern Museums (Maidstone) 2006/Ma. Eccles hoard (1864).	1.49
		(4)	Palmer (SED 86). Ex Harris and Eaglen (B1006) collections.	1.48
		(5)	*SCBI* South-Eastern Museums (Maidstone) 2005/Ma. Eccles hoard (1864).	1.47
		(6)	Eaglen (B997). With Elmore Jones ticket. Ex Woodhead collection, Spink, 29 March 1990, 1 (6/9).	1.46
		(7)	Stewartby collection. Ex Lawrence collection.	1.43
		(8)	Colchester Museums. Colchester hoard (1902).	1.43
		(9)	Colchester Museums. Colchester hoard (1902).	1.43
		(10)	Colchester Museums. Colchester hoard (1902).	1.42
		(11)	Copenhagen. Ex Thomsen collection.	1.41
		(12)	Eaglen (B317). Ex Brand collection.	1.40
		(13)	BM. Hasluck bequest (1920).	1.38
		(14)	Gittoes collection. Worn, bent.	[1.33]
		(15)	Gittoes collection. Ex Woodhead and Palmer collections. Clipped.	[1.32]
		(16)	Colchester Museums. Colchester hoard (1902). Irregular flan.	[1.31]
		(17)*	*SCBI* J. P. Mass Collection 1975. Ex North and Conte collections.	1.29
		(18)	Ex Davis collection.	–
		(19)	Palmer (SED 168). Cut halfpenny. Spink, 16 March 1992,157 (pt).	[0.63]
			Class VIIaD (with crude bust = North 7aD)	
151	Qq	O.	hENRICVS R/EX	
		R.	+NORMAN ON SAN	
		(1)*	Eaglen (B321). Ex Brand collection.	1.41
		(2)	Colchester Museums. Colchester hoard (1902). Irregular flan.	1.41

Henry III, Short Cross, Class VIIaD, *Norman* (*cont.*)

		(3)	Palmer (SED 46).	1.35
		(4)	Palmer (SED 441). Irregular flan. R. struck off-centre.	[1.31]
		(5)	Private owner (photographs ex Osborne, 1983).	–
152	Rr	O. R.	hENRICVS R/EX +NORMAN ON SAN	
		(1)	Copenhagen. Ribe hoard, I (1911), '396'.	1.40
		(2)	Eaglen (B324 EX). Ex Glendining, 17 Oct. 1979, 76(pt); Gittoes collection.	1.32
		(3)	Gittoes collection. Worn.	[1.19]
		(4)*	Ex Lockett collection.	–
		(5)	Eaglen (B287). Cut halfpenny.	[0.55]
			Class VIIbA	
153	Aa	O. R.	hENRICVS R/EX +NORMAN ON·SA	
		(1)*	Copenhagen. Ribe hoard, I (1911).	1.43
		(2)	Eaglen (B595).	1.35
			Class VIIbB1 (pellet on chin)	
154	Aa	O. R.	hENRICVS R/EX Pellet on chin. +NORHAN ON SAN H for M on R.	
		(1)	Stewartby collection. Naxos hoard (1969?).	1.38
		(2)	Palmer (SED 467).	1.36
		(3)	*SCBI* Ashmolean Museum 369.	1.34
		(4)*	Copenhagen Ribe hoard, I (1911).	1.16

Simund

Class VIIbBx

The obverses show a plump face, with pellets on the chin and in curls. This sub-class should possibly be placed between the VIIbB1 and VIIbB2 dies (see below) of Simund.

155	Aa	O. R.	hENRICVS R/EX Two curls each side. +SIHVND ON SANT	

		(1)	Colchester Museums. Colchester hoard (1902).	1.48
		(2)	BM. Colchester hoard (1902), 1020.	1.44
		(3)*	Eaglen (B1008). Ex Harris collection.	1.43
		(4)	Eaglen (B740). Ex Doubleday 950 (10/10).	1.41
		(5)	Gittoes collection. Ex Eaglen (B002).	1.19
156	Bb	O.	hENRICVS R/EX Two curls each side.	
		R.	+SIHVND ON SAN	
		(1)	Eaglen (B389).	1.46
		(2)	Copenhagen. Ribe hoard, I (1911).	1.40
		(3)*	Copenhagen. Ribe hoard, II (1958), '165'.	1.32
		(4)	Dublin Museum. Kilmaine hoard (1946).	1.29
			Class VIIbB1 (pellet on chin) (continued)	
157	Aa	O. R.	hENRICVS R/EX +SIHVND ON SAT	
		(1)	Colchester Museums. Colchester hoard (1902).	1.46
		(2)	Colchester Museums. Colchester hoard (1902).	1.44
		(3)	BM. Colchester hoard (1902), 1024.	1.43
		(4)	Eaglen (B332). Colchester hoard (1902). Ex Brand collection.	1.43
		(5)*	BM. Colchester hoard (1902), 1023.	1.41
		(6)	Colchester Museums. Colchester hoard (1902).	1.39
		(7)	Palmer (SED 504).	1.36
		(8)	Colchester Museums. Colchester hoard (1902).	–
		(9)	Mlle. S. Bertram. Gisors hoard (1970).	–
158	Bb	O. R.	hENRICVS R/EX +SIHVND'ON·SANT	
		(1)	Colchester Museums. Colchester hoard (1902).	1.48
		(2)	Palmer (SED 293).	1.44
		(3)	Eaglen (B334). Ex Brand collection.	1.41
		(4)	Palmer (SED 721). Ragged flan. O. struck off-centre.	1.34
		(5)*	Eaglen (B738). Ex Doubleday 950 (8/10).	1.27
		(6)	American Numismatic Society.	–
		(7)	Palmer (SED 444). Cut halfpenny.	[0.70]

Henry III, Short Cross, Class VIIbB1, *Simund* (*cont.*)

159	Cc	O. R.	hENRICVS R/EX +SIHVND ON SANT˙	
		(1)	Eaglen (B061). Ex Spink (1978).	1.49
		(2)	Gittoes collection. Colchester hoard (1902).	1.49
		(3)	Palmer (SED 629).	1.42
		(4)	*SCBI* J. P. Mass Collection 2048. Ex Doubleday 950 (7/10); Eaglen (B739EX).	1.41
		(5)	Colchester Museums. Colchester hoard (1902).	1.41
		(6)	Colchester Museums. Colchester hoard (1902).	1.37
		(7)*	Copenhagen. Ex Thomsen collection.	1.22
		(8)	Dublin Museum. Kilmaine hoard (1946).	1.21
		(9)	Ex North collection. Ex Eaglen (B144).	–
160	Dd	O. R.	hENRICVS R/EX Flaw (?) across dexter cheek. +SIHVND ON SANT	
		(1)*	Ex Lockett collection.	–
161	Ee	O. R.	hENRICVS R/EX +SIHVND ON SANT	
		(1)*	Eaglen (B768). Ex Spink (1988).	1.46
		(2)	Palmer. (SED 333). Lozenge shaped flan. O. struck off-centre.	[1.31]
162	Ff	O. R.	hE[+SIHVND ON SANT	
		(1)*	Eaglen (B397). Ex Baldwin (1985).	1.38
163	Gg	O. R.	+hE[ ]VS R/EX +SIHVND ON SAN[	
		(1)	Colchester Museums, 1483 (1903).	1.45
		(2)*	Palmer (SED 120).	1.39
			Class VIIbB2 (pellets on chin and in curls)	
164	Aa	O. R.	hENRICVS R/EX SIHVND ON SANT (NB: abnormalities of lettering, not evident on all examples).	
		(1)	Copenhagen. Ribe hoard, I (1911).	1.44
		(2)*	Eaglen (B711). Gisors hoard (1970). Gift ex Mlle. S. Bertram.	1.35

		(3)	Dublin Museum. Kilmaine hoard (1946).	1.12
		(4)	Trenerry collection.	–
165	Bb	O. R.	hENRICVS R/[+SIHVN[']D ON SANT	
		(1)*	BM. Eccles hoard (1864), 419.	1.52
		(2)	Eaglen (B238). Ex Osborne collection.	1.44
166	Cc	O. R.	hENRICVS R/EX +SIHVNDE ON SANT	
		(1)	Colchester Museums. Colchester hoard (1902).	1.47
		(2)	Gittoes collection. Glendining, 21 Sept. 1983, 136 (pt).	1.43
		(3)*	BM. Colchester hoard (1902), 1026.	1.43
		(4)	BM. Colchester hoard (1902), 1025.	1.41
		(5)	Palmer (SED 950). Worn.	[1.34]
167	Dd	O. R.	hENRICVS R/EX +SIHVND ON SANT	
		(1)	BM. Colchester hoard (1902), 1021.	1.50
		(2)	Colchester Museums. Colchester hoard (1902).	1.42
		(3)*	BM. Colchester hoard (1902), 1018.	1.39
		(4)	Eaglen (B400). Naxos hoard (1969?). Ex Baldwin (1985).	1.28
		(5)	Palmer (SED 376). Small flan. R. struck off-centre.	1.27
168	Ee	O. R.	hENRICVS R/EX +S·IHVND ON SANT Flaw or pellet before I.	
		(1)	Colchester Museums. Colchester hoard (1902).	1.48
		(2)	Palmer (SED 407).	1.48
		(3)*	Gittoes collection. Ex Eaglen (B062) collection.	1.45
		(4)	Eaglen (B363). Ex C. J. Martin (1984).	1.40
		(5)	Gittoes collection. Worn.	[1.34]
		(6)	Gittoes collection. Worn.	[1.31]
		(7)	Copenhagen. Ribe hoard, I (1911), '400'. Struck off-centre.	1.28
		(8)	Palmer (SED 49). Small flan. R. off-centre.	[1.03]
169	Ff	O. R.	hENRICVS R/EX +SIHVND ON SANTE	

Henry III, Short Cross, Class VIIbB2, *Simund* (*cont.*)

		(1)	Colchester Museums. Colchester hoard (1902).	1.51
		(2)	Colchester Museums. Colchester hoard (1902).	1.51
		(3)	Copenhagen. Ribe hoard, I (1911).	1.47
		(4)	Gittoes collection. Glendining, 21 Sept. 1983, 136 (pt). Partly flat.	[1.30]
		(5)	Eaglen (B081 EX). Ex Gittoes collection. Glendining, 21 Sept. 1983, 136 (pt).	1.30
		(6)	Palmer (SED 308). Nicked edge. Worn.	[1.26]
		(7)*	Eaglen (B335). Ex Brand collection.	1.03
		(8)	National Museum of Wales. Wrexham hoard (1926).	1.01
170	Gg	O. R.	hENRICVS R/EX +SIHVND ON SANTE	
		(1)	Gittoes collection. Glendining, 21 Sept. 1983, 136 (pt). Struck off-centre.	1.50
		(2)	Gittoes collection.	1.48
		(3)	Palmer (SED 42).	1.45
		(4)	Gittoes collection. Found at London Bridge (1988). Ragged edge.	[1.45]
		(5)*	Copenhagen. Ribe hoard, I (1911).	1.40
		(6)	Eaglen (B001). Ex Baldwin (1958). Irregular flan.	[1.40]
		(7)	Stewartby collection. Naxos hoard (1969?).	1.39
		(8)	Palmer (SED 23).	1.24
171	Hh	O. R.	hENRICVS R/EX +SIHVND ON SANT	
		(1)	Colchester Museums. Colchester hoard (1902).	1.49
		(2)	Gittoes collection. Ex Eaglen (B170).	1.47
		(3)*	Eaglen (B062 EX). Ex Gittoes collection.	1.43
		(4)	*SCBI* Museums in East Anglia (Ipswich) 1510. Colchester hoard (1902).	1.40
172	Ii	O. R.	hENRICVS R/EX +SIHVND ON SANT	
		(1)	Colchester Museums. Colchester hoard (1902).	1.47
		(2)*	Eaglen (B052). Ex Seaby (1977).	1.43
		(3)	Colchester Museums. Colchester hoard (1902).	1.32

		(4)	Gittoes collection.	1.30
		(5)	Ex North Collection. Colchester hoard (1902).	1.17
		(6)	Palmer (SED 377). Small, lozenge-shaped flan. O. struck off-centre.	[1.02]
173	Jj	O. R.	E]NRICVS R/[ ]ND ON SANT	
		(1)	Gittoes collection. Ex C. J. Martin (1987). Irregular flan. Buckled. Struck off-centre.	1.45
		(2)*	Palmer (SED 45).	1.37
			Class VIIbB3 (pellets in curls)	
174	Aa	O. R.	hENRICVS R/EX +SIHVND ON SANT	
		(1)	Copenhagen. Ribe hoard, I (1911).	1.47
		(2)	Copenhagen. Ribe hoard, I (1911).	1.42
		(3)	Gittoes collection. Leconfield hoard (2000), 151.	1.40
		(4)	Gittoes collection.	1.39
		(5)*	Ex North collection.	1.35
		(6)	Palmer (SED 483). Irregular flan. Struck off-centre.	[1.23]
		(7)	Private collection (photographed by R. Osborne).	–
175	Bb	O. R.	hENRICVS R/EX +SIHVND·ON·SANT	
		(1)*	Colchester Museums. Colchester hoard (1902).	1.37
176	Cc	O. R.	hE[ ]/EX +SIHVN ON SANTE	
		(1)*	Ex Woodhead collection.	–
177	Dd	O. R.	hENRICVS R/EX +SIHVND ON SANTE	
		(1)*	Palmer (SED 145).	1.51
		(2)	Palmer (SED 53). Irregular flan.	1.51
			Class VIIbC (no pellets; 'broken', i.e. flawed, non annulet-shaped, eyes).	
178	Aa	O. R.	hENRICVS R/EX +SIHVND ON SANTE	
		(1)	BM. Colchester hoard (1902).	1.51
		(2)	Palmer (SED 796). Irregular flan.	1.51
		(3)	Fitzwilliam Museum. Colchester hoard (1902).	1.45

Henry III, Short Cross, Class VIIbC, *Simund* (*cont.*)

		(4)	Eaglen (B741). Doubleday 950 (9/10).	1.44
		(5)	Copenhagen. Ribe hoard, I (1911).	1.41
		(6)*	Copenhagen. Ribe hoard, I (1911).	1.39
		(7)	Eaglen (B767). Ex Spink (1988).	1.38
		(8)	Mlle. S. Bertram collection. Gisors hoard (1970).	–
179	Bb	O. R.	hENRICVS R/EX +SIHVND ON SAN·	
		(1)*	Eaglen (B1102). Ex North, Conte and Mass (*SCBI* 2049) collections.	1.46
		(2)	Colchester Museums. Colchester hoard (1902).	1.40
		(3)	Palmer (SED 530).	1.33
180	Cc	O. R.	hENRICVS R/EX +SIHVND ON SANT	
		(1)	Eaglen (B358). Ex C. J. Martin (1984).	1.44
		(2)	Gittoes collection. R. struck off-centre.	1.38
		(3)*	Dawson collection.	1.25
181	Dd	O. R.	]ICVS R/EX +SIHVND ON SANT	
		(1)*	Colchester Museums. Colchester hoard (1902).	1.34
182	Ee	O. R.	hENRICVS R/EX +SIHVND ON SANT	
		(1)	Colchester Museums. Colchester hoard (1902).	1.49
		(2)*	Eaglen (B337). Ex Brand collection.	1.35
		(3)	Gittoes collection. Leconfield hoard (2000), 218. Flat, bent.	[1.28]
183	Ff	O. R.	hENRICVS R/EX +SIHVND ON SANT	
		(1)	*SCBI* Museums in East Anglia (Bury) 1509. Ex Frost collection.	1.50
		(2)	Colchester Museums. Colchester hoard (1902).	1.46
		(3)*	BM. 'E2005'. Cracked and chipped.	[1.46]
		(4)	*SCBI* Northern Museums (Blackburn)1382/BL. Colchester hoard (1902).	1.45
		(5)	Colchester Museums. Colchester hoard (1902).	1.43

		(6)	Palmer (SED 173).	1.40
		(7)	Fitzwilliam Museum.	1.32
184	Gg	O. R.	hENRICVS R/EX +SIHVND ON SANT	
		(1)*	Colchester Museums. Colchester hoard (1902).	1.45
		(2)	Copenhagen. Ribe hoard, I (1911).	1.38
185	Hh	O. R.	hENRICVS R/EX +SIHVND ON SANT	
		(1)*	Eaglen (B567 EX). Ex Gittoes collection; Glendining, 21 Sept. 1983, 136 (pt).	1.34
186	Ii	O. R.	hENRICVS R/EX +SIHVND[·]ON·SANT	
		(1)*	Eaglen (B1044).	1.42
187	Jj	O. R.	hENRICVS R/EX SIHVND ON SANT	
		(1)*	Gittoes collection. Creased.	1.35
		(2)	Palmer (SED 320). O. struck off-centre.	1.29
		(3)	Palmer (SED 294). Lozenge-shaped flan. O. struck off-centre.	[1.20]
188	Kk	O. R.	hENRICVS R/EX +SIHVND ON SANT	
		(1)	Gittoes collection. Leconfield hoard (2000), 224. Irregular flan. Bent.	1.44
		(2)*	Gitoes collection. Irregular flan. Creased.	1.43
189	Ll	O. R.	hENRICVS R/EX +SIHVND ON SANT	
		(1)*	Palmer (SED 624).	1.52
			Class VIIbD (annulet eyes)	
190	Aa	O. R.	hENRICVS R/EX Eyes imperfect annulets; could be late VIIb C. +SIHVND ON SANT Flaw at base of V on some coins.	
		(1)	Gittoes collection. Glendining, 21 Sept. 1983, 136 (pt).	1.49
		(2)	*SCBI* J. P. Mass Collection 2050. Ex Brand and North collections.	1.44
		(3)*	Eaglen (B336). Ex Brand collection.	1.42
		(4)	Copenhagen. Ribe hoard, I (1911).	1.41

Henry III, Short Cross, Class VIIbD, *Simund* (*cont.*)

		(5)	Copenhagen. Ribe hoard, I (1911).	1.41
		(6)	Palmer (SED 302). R. struck off-centre.	1.41
		(7)	Colchester Museums. Colchester hoard (1902). R. struck off-centre.	1.41
191	Bb	O. R.	hENRICVS R/EX +SIHVND ON SANT	
		(1)	Eaglen (B053). Ex Seaby (1977).	1.47
		(2)	Gittoes collection. Ex Eaglen (B081) collection.	1.43
		(3)*	Eaglen (B1000). Ex Woodhead collection. Spink, 29 March 1990, 1 (9/9).	1.43
		(4)	Eaglen (B333 EX). Ex Gittoes collection.	1.42
		(5)	Colchester Museums. Colchester hoard (1902).	1.42
		(6)	BM. Leconfield hoard (2000). R. struck off-centre. Small flan.	[1.19]
192	Cc	O. R.	hENRICVS R/EX +SIHVND [ ]ANT	
		(1)*	Copenhagen. Ribe hoard, I (1911).	1.45
193	Dd	O. R.	hENRICVS R/EX +SIHVND ON SANT	
		(1)	Colchester Museums. Colchester hoard (1902).	1.58
		(2)	Palmer (SED 174).	1.46
		(3)	Colchester Museums. Colchester hoard (1902).	1.43
		(4)*	Eaglen (B170 EX). Ex Gittoes collection.	1.38
		(5)	Palmer (SED 234). R. off-centre.	1.38
		(6)	Dublin Museum. Kilmaine hoard (1946). O. and R. partly flat. R. off-centre.	1.37
		(7)	Eaglen (B127).	1.35
		(8)	Fitzwilliam Museum. Ex Shirley-Fox and Blunt collections.	1.32
		(9)	Gittoes collection. Small, irregular flan. Clipped?	[1.13]
194	Ee	O. R.	h[ ]VS R/EX +SIHVN[ ]ANT	
		(1)*	Copenhagen. Ribe hoard, I (1911).	1.31
195	Ff	O. R.	hENRICVS R/EX +S·IMVND ON S·A·NT	

		(1)	Colchester Museums. Colchester hoard (1902).	1.49
		(2)	Eaglen (B002 EX). Ex Gittoes collection. Split.	1.49
		(3)	Gittoes collection.	1.44
		(4)*	Eaglen (B300).	1.36
		(5)	Colchester hoard (1902). Ex North and Conte collections. See Dix, Noonan, Webb, 17 March 2004, 395 (1/2).	1.30
196	Gg	O. R.	hENRICVS R/EX +SIMVND ON SANT	
		(1)*	Eaglen (B338). Ex Brand collection.	1.42
197	Hh	O. R.	·hENRICVS[+SIHVND ON SANT	
		(1)	*SCBI* Museums in East Anglia (Norwich) 1508. Colchester hoard (1902).	1.45
		(2)	Gittoes collection. Glendining, 21 Sept. 1983, 136 (pt).	1.39
		(3)*	Copenhagen. Ribe hoard, I (1911).	1.35
		(4)	Palmer (SED 691). O. and R. partly flat.	1.35
198	Ii	O. R.	]CVS R/EX]SIHVND ON S[	
		(1)*	Eaglen (B126). Ex C. J. Martin (1980). Damaged.	[1.43]
199	Jj	O. R.	hENRICVS R/EX +SIHVND ON SANT	
		(1)*	Eaglen (B422).	1.45
200	Kk	O. R.	hENRICVS R/EX h appears to be superimposed on E. +SIHVND ON SAN	
		(1)	Palmer (SED 436).	1.53
		(2)	Ex Jacob collection.	1.52
		(3)*	BM. Colchester hoard (1902), 1019.	1.49
		(4)	Gittoes collection. Glendining, 21 Sept. 1983, 136 (pt).	1.48
		(5)	Palmer (SED 2).	1.44
		(6)	Stewartby collection.	1.37
		(7)	Eaglen (B171). Ex C. J. Martin (1981).	1.36
		(8)	*SCBI* Northern Museums (Pontefract)1383/Po.	1.23

Henry III, Short Cross, Class VIIbD, *Simund* (*cont.*)

201	Ll	O.	hENRICVS R/EX Shape of eyes not clear.	
		R.	SIHVND [ ]N SANT[ ] Last letter probably E.	
		(1)*	BM. Leconfield hoard (2000).	1.40
			Class VIIcA (large lettering)	
202	Aa	O.	hENRICVS R/EX	
		R.	+SIHVND ON SANT	
		(1)	Colchester Museums. Colchester hoard (1902).	1.50
		(2)	Gittoes collection.	1.49
		(3)	Colchester Museums. Colchester hoard (1902).	1.48
		(4)	Palmer (SED 414). Damaged edge.	[1.44]
		(5)	*SCBI* Scottish Museums (Edinburgh) 390. Classified as VIIbD.	1.43
		(6)*	Stewartby Collection. Naxos hoard (1969?).	1.41
		(7)	*SCBI* J. P. Mass Collection 2102. Ex Lawrence, IV (1951) 1024 and North and Conte collections.	1.39
		(8)	Colchester Museums. Colchester hoard (1902).	1.39
202A	Ax	O.	As above	
		R.	+SIHVND ON SANT O. of die A. but R. appears to be otherwise unrecorded (x).	
		(1)*	Mlle. S. Bertram. Gisors hoard (1970).	–
203	Bb	O.	hENRICVS R/EX	
		R.	+SIHVND ON SANT Chevron barred A.	
		(1)*	Eaglen (B329). Ex Brand collection.	1.46
		(2)	Ex North Collection.	1.38
		(3)	Palmer (SED 23). Irregular flan. Damaged. R. struck off-centre.	[1.24]
		(4)	Eaglen (B396). Corroded.	[1.04]
204	Cc	O.	hENRICVS R/EX	
		R.	+SIHVND ON SANT	
		(1)*	Copenhagen. Ribe hoard, I (1911). Irregular flan.	1.47
		(2)	Eaglen (B293). Ex Allen. Irregular flan.	[1.44]
		(3)	Colchester Museums. Colchester hoard (1902).	1.44
		(4)	Copenhagen. Ribe hoard, I (1911).	1.44

		(5)	Eaglen (B330). Ex Brand collection. Struck off-centre.	1.40
		(6)	Copenhagen. Ribe hoard, I (1911).	1.39
			Class VIIcB (oblong face)	
205	Aa	O. R.	hENRICVS R/EX +SIHVND ON SANT	
		(1)	Colchester Museums. Colchester hoard (1902).	1.51
		(2)	Gittoes collection. Ex Brand and Eaglen (B333) collections.	1.44
		(3)	Palmer (SED 42). Struck off-centre.	1.44
		(4)*	Eaglen (B373). Ex Baldwin (1985).	1.40
		(5)	Palmer (SED 408).	1.40
206	Bb	O. R.	hENRICVS R/EX Two curls each side. +SIHVND ON SANT	
		(1)	Colchester Museums. Colchester hoard (1902).	1.48
		(2)	*SCBI* Scottish Museums (Edinburgh) 389. Classified as VIIbA3.	1.47
		(3)	Palmer (SED 176). Irregular flan. Cracked.	1.44
		(4)*	Eaglen (B125).	1.33
206A	Cc	O. R.	hENRI[ ]/EX +SIHVND O[	
		(1)*	*SCBI* J. P. Mass Collection 2103. Ex North and Conte collections. Identified by Mass as from same dies 206 (Bb) above.	1.43
207	Dd	O. R.	hENRICVS R/EX +SIHVND O⁝N SANT	
		(1)	Colchester Museums. Colchester hoard (1902).	1.47
		(2)	Copenhagen. Ribe hoard, I (1911).	1.46
		(3)*	Eaglen (B331). Ex Brand collection.	1.39
208	Ee	O. R.	hEN[ ]/EX +SIHVND ON SANT	
		(1)	Colchester Museums. Colchester hoard (1902).	1.51
		(2)*	Palmer (SED 177). O. struck off-centre.	1.44

Ioan

209	Aa	O. R.	hENRICVS R/EX +IOAN ON SANTE·	
		(1)*	Stewartby collection. Naxos hoard (1969?).	1.38

Henry III, Short Cross, Class VIIcB, *Ioan* (*cont.*)

210	Bb	O. R.	hENRICVS R/E[+IOAN ON SANTE	
		(1)*	Copenhagen. Ribe hoard, I (1911).	1.35
		(2)	Stewartby collection. Naxos hoard (1969?).	1.32
211	Cc	O. R.	hENRICVS R/E[+IOAN ON SANTE	
		(1)*	Copenhagen. Ribe hoard, I (1911).	1.41
		(2)	*SCBI* J. P. Mass Collection 2104. Ex Woodhead, North and Conte collections. Described in *SCBI* as from 'new dies'.	1.38
212	Dd	O. R.	hENRICVS R/EX +IOAN ON SANTE	
		(1)*	Copenhagen. Ribe hoard, I (1911).	1.45
		(2)	Gittoes collection. Bent, worn.	[1.16]
213	Ee	O. R.	hENRICVS R/EX +IOAN ON SANTE	
		(1)*	Copenhagen. Ribe hoard, I (1911).	1.35
		(2)	*SCBI* J. P. Mass Collection 2105. Ex North and Conte collections.	1.26
		(3)	Ex Jacob collection.	1.26
214	Ff	O. R.	hE[ ]RICVS R/EX +IOAN ON SANTE[	
		(1)*	Stewartby collection. Naxos hoard (1969?).	1.31
215	Gg	O. R.	hENRICVS R/EX +IOAN ON SANTE	
			Pellet on chin. See North 1988, p. 31 and Pl. II, 40.	
		(1)*	Eaglen (B609). Naxos hoard (1969?). Ex Stewartby collection.	1.50
		(2)	Stewartby collection. Naxos hoard (1969?).	1.40
		(3)	Palmer (SED 179). Irregular flan. R. struck off-centre.	1.32
		(4)	Eaglen (B341). Ex Mossop and Brand collections.	1.30
216	Hh	O. R.	hENRICVS R/E[+IOAN ON SANTE	
		(1)*	Stewartby collection. Naxos hoard (1969?).	1.38
		(2)	National Museum of Wales. Wrexham hoard (1926).	1.38
217	Ii	O. R.	hENRICVS R/EX +IOAN ON SANTE	

		(1)*	Copenhagen. Ribe hoard, I (1911).	1.46
218	Jj	O. R.	hENRICVS R/EX +IOAN ON SANTE	
		(1)	Copenhagen. Ribe hoard, I (1911).	1.46
		(2)*	Eaglen (B608). Naxos hoard (1969?). Ex Stewartby collection.	1.37
		(3)	Stewartby collection. Naxos hoard (1969?).	1.34
219	Kk	O.	hENRICVS R/EX	
		R.	+IOAN ON SAN[	
		(1)*	BM. Leconfield hoard (2000). Nicked edge. R. struck off-centre.	[1.25]
220	Ll	O. R.	hENRICVS R/EX +IOAN ON SANTE	
		(1)*	Palmer (SED 547). Nicked edge. Worn.	[1.38]
221	Mm	O. R.	]ENRICVS R/E[+IOAN O[N]E	
		(1)*	Palmer (SED 601). Struck off-centre. Partly flat.	[1.28]
			Class VIIcC	
222	Aa	O. R.	hENRICVS R/EX +IOAN ON SANTE	
		(1)*	*SCBI* J. P. Mass Collection 2107. Naxos hoard (1969?). Ex North and Conte collections. See Dix, Noonan, Webb, 17 March 2004, 395 (2/2).	1.41
223	Bb	O. R.	hENRI[ ]/EX +IOAN ON SANT	
		(1)*	*SCBI* J. P. Mass Collection 2106. Ex North and Conte collections.	1.38
		(2)	Eaglen (B408). Clipped.	[0.96]
224	Cc	O. R.	]CVS R/EX +I[ ]ON SANTE	
		(1)*	BM. Leconfield hoard (2000). This coin is not listed in the summary of the hoard in *NC* 160 (2000), pp. 354–5.	1.47
		(2)	Palmer (SED 745). Small flan. Struck off-centre?	[1.07]
			Class VIIIa	

Class VIII is classified according to the Elmore Jones nomenclature (Elmore Jones 1945–8), rather than that of *SCBI* J. P. Mass Collection, pp. 58–62.

Class VIIIa is known only from coins of Nichole at London.

Henry III, Short Cross, *Ioan* (*cont.*)

Class VIIIb1

225 Aa O. hENRICVS R/EX
R. +IOAN ON SANTE
SCBI J. P. Mass Collection 2114 classified this die combination as an VIIIa1 (= VIIIa)/VIIIa2 (=VIIIb1) mule.

(1) Palmer (SED 578). Recorded in *SCBI* J. P. Mass Collection 2114. 1.36

(2) BM (1927). 1.34

(3)* Eaglen (B280). Ex Elmore Jones 1226. 1.33

(4) Doubleday 951. –

(5) Stewartby collection. –

Class VIIIb2

Ioan (as Iohan)

226 Aa O. h[ ]ICVS R/EX
R. +IOhA[ ]SANT·ED

(1)* Mlle S. Bertram. Gisors hoard (1970). 1.27

227 Bb O. hENRICVS R/EX.
Pellet on end of upper serif of S?
R. +IOhAN⁝ON·SANT·ED

(1) Eaglen (B587). Naxos hoard (1969?). *NCirc*, Feb. 1987, 256. 1.43

(2)* Eaglen (B991). Naxos hoard (1969?). Ex Woodhead collection; Spink, 29 March 1990, 2. 1.38

(3) Gittoes collection. Small flan. [0.95]

228 Cc O. h[ ]:R/EX
R. +IOhAN·ON·SANT·ED (or ED?)

(1)* Eaglen (B464). Naxos hoard (1969?). Ex Baldwin (1986). 1.41

229 Dd O. hENRICVS⁝R/EX
R. +IOhAN⁝ON·SANTEED

(1) Gittoes collection. Leconfield hoard (2000), 324. 1.42

(2) BM. 'E2001'. 1.40

(3)* Eaglen (B462). Naxos hoard (1969?). Baldwin (1986). 1.36

(4) *SCBI* J. P. Mass Collection 2140. Naxos hoard (1969?). 1.34

		(5)	Sporle hoard (1995). See Archibald and Cook 2001, p. 55 and Pl. 14, 3.	1.32
230	Ee	O.	hENRICVS⁝R/EX	
		R.	+IOhAN⁝ON·SANT·ED	
		(1)*	Eaglen (B463). Naxos hoard (1969?).	1.46
231	Ff	O.	hENRICVS⁝R/EX	
		R.	+IOhAN[⁝]ON⁝SANT⁝ED	
		(1)*	Palmer (SED 701).	1.46
		(2)	Sporle hoard (1995). See Archibald and Cook 2001, p. 55 and Pl. 14, 4.	1.43
		(3)	Ex North collection. Naxos hoard (1969?).	1.38
		(4)	*SCBI* Ashmolean Museum. 367.	1.27
		(5)	Palmer (SED 163). Irregular flan	–
232	Gg	O.	hENRICVS R/EX	
		R.	+IOhAN˙ON[ ]SANT·ED	
		(1)*	Gittoes collection. Elmore Jones 1527 (1/2).	1.44
233	Hh	O.	hENRICVS R/EX Flaws developing, obscuring sinister eye and crossing dexter cheek.	
		R.	+IOhAN·ON·SANT·ED	
		(1)*	BM. Ex Lawrence collection. Ragged edge.	[1.38]
		(2)	*SCBI* J. P. Mass Collection 2166. Naxos hoard (1969?). Ex North and Conte collections. See Dix, Noonan, Webb, 17 March 2004, 406, where the dies were correctly identified with 'Eaglen 213', being identical dies to 210 and now renumbered as 233.	1.38
		(3)	Palmer (SED 794). Irregular flan.	1.33
		(4)	Gittoes collection. Crinkled and worn. Struck off-centre.	[1.31]
		(5)	Palmer (SED 654). Small flan. R. struck off-centre.	[1.20]
234	Ii	O.	hENRICV[ ] R/EX	
		R.	+IOhAN.ON[⁝] SANTED No punctuation apparent between T and E.	
		(1)*	Gittoes collection. Leconfield hoard (2000), 323.	0.49
		(2)	*SCBI* J. P. Mass Collection 2139. Naxos hoard (1969?). Ex North and Conte collections.	1.33
235	Jj	O.	hEN[ ]/EX	
		R.	]ON:[ ]NT·ED	
		(1)*	Stewartby collection. Naxos hoard (1969?).	1.34

Henry III, Short Cross, Class VIIIb2, *Ioan* (*cont.*)

236	Kk	O.	hENRI[ ]VS R/EX Lombardic N.	
		R.	+IOhAN ON [⁝]SAN[ ]ED	
		(1)*	*SCBI* J. P. Mass Collection 2115. Ex Mangakis, North and Conte collections. Mass (*SCBI* p. 60) claimed to have detected a curule shaped X on this coin, but this is very uncertain. The style of O., with a pair of triple curls and of R. , with pommée cross, suggest conventional VIIIb2 dies.	1.24
		(2)	Palmer (SED 325). Small flan. Partly flat.	[1.06]
		(3)	Gittoes collection. Small flan. Worn.	[0.96]
237	Ll	O.	hENRICVS:R/EX	
		R.	+IOhAN·ON·SANT·ED	
		(1)*	Palmer (SED 822). Irregular shaped flan. Edge crack.	1.37
		(2)	Gittoes collection. Small, chipped flan. Bent.	[1.13]
238	Mm	O.	hENRICVS⁝R/EX	
		R.	+IOhAN·ON·SANT·ED	
		(1)*	BM. Leconfield hoard (2000). Edge split, with (?) fragment missing.	[1.38]
239	Nn	O.	h[ ]NRICVS[ ]/E[ ]	
		R.	+IOhAN·O[ ]NT·ED	
		(1)*	Stewartby collection. Naxos hoard (1969?). Irregular flan.	1.40
240	Oo	O.	]NRICVS [.][	
		R.	+IOhAN⁝O[ ]E E unclear.	
		(1)*	Stewartby collection. Naxos hoard (1969?). Struck off-centre. Edge crack. Partly flat.	[1.29]
			Class VIIIb3	
241	Aa	O.	]NRICVS R/EX	
		R.	]SAN ED (or SANTED) Retrograde N.	
		(1)*	*SCBI* J. P. Mass Collection 2164. Ex North and Conte collections. R. struck off-centre.	1.28
242	Bb	O.	hENRICVS · R/EX	
		R.	+IOhAN ON'SANED	
		(1)	Stewartby collection. Naxos hoard (1969?).	1.43
		(2)*	Stewartby collection. Naxos hoard (1969?).	1.38

		(3)	BM. Ex Lawrence (1950). Fragment	[1.36]
		(4)	Palmer (SED 330). Chipped.	[1.27]
243	Cc	O. R.	hENRIC[ ] R/[ ]X +IOhAN[ ] SAN:E	
		(1)*	Ex North collection. Naxos hoard (1969?).	1.37
		(2)	Eaglen (B588). Naxos hoard (1969?). Spink (1987).	1.35
244	Dd	O. R.	hENRICVS R/EX +IOhAN·ON[ ]ED	
		(1)*	Eaglen (B356). Elmore Jones 1527 (2/2). Small flan.	1.10
245	Ee	O. R.	hENRICVS R/EX +IOhAN⁝ON SANE	
		(1)*	Copenhagen. Ribe hoard, I (1911).	1.40
246	Ff	O. R.	hENRICVS R/EX +IOhAN·ON·SAN·ED	
		(1)*	Eaglen (B589). Naxos hoard (1969?). Spink (1987).	1.37
		(2)	*SCBI* South-Eastern Museums (Wisbech) 2004/Wis.	[1.19]
247	Gg	O. R.	hENRICVS·R/EX +IOhAN⁝ON·SANT.ED	
		(1)*	Palmer (SED 364). Small flan. Edge crack.	[1.07]
248	Hh	O. R.	hENRICV[ ] R/[ ]IOhAN ON SA[	
		(1)*	Palmer (SED 3).	1.30
249	Ii	O. R.	hE[ ]S R/EX +IO[ ]ANED	
		(1)*	*SCBI* J. P. Mass Collection 2165. Part flat. Irregular flan.	[1.28]

LONG CROSS COINAGE (1247–78)

HENRY III (continued)

In this section of the Catalogue, coins from the 1908 Brussels (BRU) and 1969 Colchester (COL) hoards are grouped together, followed by coins from other sources (OTHER). Coins from both hoards in the Eaglen and Palmer

Henry III, Long Cross (*cont.*)

collections are identified respectively by the letter B followed by three or four digits and by SED followed by up to three digits, shown in parentheses following the relevant weights. Coins selected by the British Museum from the 1969 Colchester hoard are likewise identified by the letters BM alongside the relevant weight. Long Cross coins selected for illustration from the Brussels and Colchester hoards are identified by an asterisk after their relevant weight. The weights of unattributed coins from the 1908 Brussels hoard refer to coins remaining (at the end of 2003) in the hands of A. H. Baldwin & Sons Ltd, and those from the 1969 Colchester hoard are taken from records of the hoard compiled by the British Museum.

Coins without sceptre

Class Ib (no moneyer's name)

250 Aa O. hENRICVS. REX ANG
R. LIE TER CI'. AED

BRU (1 or 2)

(1) BM. Bruun (1925) 248; Lockett 1198, illustrated. Double struck. 1.48

(2) Baldwin. Present whereabouts unknown. –

COL (2)

1.46* BM, 1.37 (die turned in axis)

OTHER (3)

(1) *SCBI* Scottish Museums (Glasgow) 685. Ex Hunter collection. 1.38

(2) Fitzwilliam Museum. Ex Finn; North and Conte collections. 1.35

It is conceivable that this is the missing coin from the Brussels hoard, although Baldwin have no record of having disposed of it.

(3) Found at East Martin, Hants, 1995. *BNJ* 65 (1995), Coin Register 229, p. 248 and Pl. 27. Cut halfpenny. –

Other references:

Ruding 1840, III, Supplement II, Pl. I, 14, reading LIE' TER' CI'. HED [*sic*], but almost certainly drawn from dies Aa. Hawkins 1887, p. 196, believed it to have been a blundered representation of a coin from the Canterbury mint.

Davis 1977, p. 140, n. 19, refers to 'only about five examples known'.

Class IIa (REX TERCI; X with curved limbs)

Ion

251 Aa O. *hEHRICVS·REX·TERCI'
Double barred ligulated H(=N).
R. ION ONS EIN TED

BRU (4)

1.45 (SED 184), 1.45 (B467), 1.44* (B782), 1.42 (B885).

OTHER (6)

(1)	Eaglen (B285). Ex Elmore Jones 1238 (1/2), Seaby (1983).	1.49
(2)	*SCBI* Scottish Museums (Stranraer) 687. Whithorn excavations, 1984–91.	1.45
(3)	Sporle hoard (1995). See Archibald and Cook 2001, p. 57 and Pl. 14, 65 (in error for 85).	1.38
(4)	Ex Woodhead collection.	–
(5)	Birmingham Museum and Art Gallery.	1.33
(6)	*NCirc*, Dec. 1989, 6619.	–

252 Bb O. *hEHRICVS REX TERCI'
R. IOH OHS' EDM VHD

BRU (11)

1.45 (B431), 1.45 (B886), 1.45, 1.42 (B470), 1.41, 1.40, 1.39, 1.39, 1.39, 1.37*, 1.22

OTHER (4)

(1)	Palmer (SED 388).	1.45
(2)	Thomas collection.	1.45
(3)	*SCBI* Scottish Museums (Glasgow) 688.	1.40
(4)	Palmer (SED 31).	1.37

253 Cc O. *hEHRICVS REX TERCI'
Pellets elongated with linear strokes.
R. IOH OHS' EDM VND

BRU (14)

1.50, 1.46, 1.44, 1.43 (B887), 1.43 (SED 183), 1.42, 1.41, 1.40, 1.40, 1.39, 1.38, 1.34, 1.32*, 1.30 (B468).

COL (5)

1.44, 1.44, 1.43 (B240), 1.39, 1.37 BM.

OTHER (4)

Henry III, Long Cross, Class IIa, *Ion* (*cont.*)

		(1)	BM. Steppingley hoard (1912), 41.	1.38
		(2)	Fitzwilliam Museum. Ex Shirley-Fox and Blunt collections. Pierced.	[1.26]
		(3)	*SCBI* Museums in East Anglia (Bury) 1716. Ex Frost collection.	1.23
		(4)	Ex Woodhead collection.	–
254	Dd	O. R.	*hEHRICVS REX TERCI' IOH OHS' EDM VHD	
			BRU (5)	
			1.44* (B469), 1.42, 1.40 (SED 182), 1.39, 1.37.	
			COL (2)	
			1.41, 1.35 BM.	
			OTHER (8)	
		(1)	Palmer (SED 387).	1.42
		(2)	Birmingham Museum and Art Gallery. Ex Lockett 1201 (13/17). Chipped and cracked.	[1.42]
		(3)	Palmer (SED 445).	1.40
		(4)	Eaglen (B067). Ex Spink (1978). Chipped.	[1.40]
		(5)	BM. Hornchurch hoard (1938).	1.39
		(6)	Fitzwilliam Museum. Ex Shirley-Fox and Blunt collections.	1.38
		(7)	Ex Osborne collection.	–
		(8)	Gardner collection (1988).	–
			Class IIb (REX TERCI; X with uniform limbs)	
255	Aa	O. R.	*hEHRICVS REX TERCI IOH OHS' EDM VHD	
			BRU (16)	
			1.48, 1.46, 1.45, 1.44 (B471), 1.44 (B572), 1.42, 1.39, 1.37, 1.37, 1.36, 1.35, 1.31, 1.27, 1.27, 1.21, 1.07* (B573).	
			COL (7)	
			1.47 BM, 1.47, 1.45, 1.44 (B239), 1.43, 1.42, 1.39.	
			OTHER (5)	
		(1)	Palmer (SED 54). Ex Harris collection.	1.39
		(2)	Ex North collection.	1.35

		(3)	Thomas collection.	1.35
		(4)	BM. Ex Banks (1818).	1.32
		(5)	Birmingham Museum and Art Gallery.	1.30

Class IIIa (narrow but less elongated face than type II; REX·III'. R. with wedge shaped or curved tail)

256	Aa	O. R.	*hEHRICVS REX·III' IOH OHS' EDM VHD	
			BRU (7)	
			1.45, 1.43 (B477), 1.43 (SED 195), 1.42* (B888), 1.39, 1.37, 1.31.	
			COL (2)	
			1.45, 1.34.	
			OTHER (4)	
		(1)	BM ('E2138').	1.40
		(2)	Eaglen (B291).	1.31
		(3)	Eaglen (B349). Ex Elmore Jones 1538 (1/3).	1.21
		(4)	Palmer (SED 346). Cut halfpenny.	[0.57]
257	Bb	O. R.	*hENRICVS REX·III' IOH OHS' EDM VHD	
			BRU (19)	
			1.48, 1.46, 1.46, 1.44, 1.44, 1.43, 1.43, 1.41, 1.41, 1.40, 1.40, 1.40, 1.39, 1.37, 1.37* (B474), 1.36, 1.35, 1.33 (B478), 1.32.	
			COL (5)	
			1.51 BM, 1.50 BM, 1.45, 1.42 (B1008) Ex Dupree, *NCirc*, June 1990, 3164, 1.39.	
			OTHER (1)	
		(1)	Palmer (SED 151). Cut farthing.	[0.38]
258	Cc	O. R.	*hEHRICVS REX·III'. ION ONS EDM VND	
			BRU (8)	
			1.42 (B1002), 1.41 (B1003), 1.40, 1.39, 1.38 (B475), 1.37, 1.33*, 1.30.	
			COL (2)	
			1.36 (SED 334), 1.31	
			OTHER (2)	
		(1)	Birmingham Museum and Art Gallery.	1.39
		(2)	Gardner collection (1988).	–

Henry III, Long Cross, Class IIIa, *Ion* (*cont.*)

259 Dd O. *hEHRICVS' REX·III'
R. ION ONS' EDM VND

BRU (7)

1.40, 1.40, 1.39, 1.31, [1.23] chipped, 1.21* (B673), 1.16 small flan.

COL (4)

1.45, 1.42 (B241), 1.42, 1.35 BM.

OTHER (1)

(1) Eaglen (B009). Ex Spink (1975). 1.45

260 Ee O. *hEHRICVS REX·III'
R. ION ONS' EDM VND
Pellets in N's on R.

BRU (4)

1.47* (B889), 1.40 (SED 145), 1.28, 1.23 (B479).

COL (1)

1.38 BM

OTHER (2)

(1) Thomas collection. 1.28

(2) Palmer (SED 121). Cut halfpenny. [0.57]

Class IIIab1 (broader, rounder face; vestigial or no neck showing)

261 Aa O. *hEHRICVS REX·III'
R. ION OHS EIH TED
Pellet in S.

BRU (8)

1.47 (B890), 1.41 (B476), 1.40, 1.39* (B484), 1.37 (B670), 1.37, 1.32, 1.23 (B489) small flan.

COL (1)

1.52 BM

OTHER (3)

(1) Palmer (SED 77). 1.49

(2) *SCBI* Scottish Museums (Edinburgh) 689. Slype hoard (1914). 1.47

(3) BM. Slype hoard (1914), 114. 1.33

262 Bb O. *hEHRICVS REX·III'
R. ION ONS' EDM VND

BRU (15)

1.48, 1.46, 1.44* (B472), 1.44 (B473), 1.43, 1.43, 1.41, 1.40, 1.40, 1.38, 1.37, 1.37 (B485), 1.36, 1.31, 1.30.

COL (3)

1.41 (B242), 1.40 BM, 1.37

OTHER (7)

(1) Palmer (SED 746). 1.46

(2) Palmer (SED 841). 1.37

(3) Palmer (SED 335). 1.36

(4) Thomas collection. Ex Palmer (SED 134). 1.31

(5) BM. Hasluck bequest (1920), 808. 1.22

(6) Ex North collection. 1.11

(7) Ex Woodhead collection. –

Class IIIab2 (X with alternate straight and curved limbs)

263 Aa O. *hEHRICVS REX·III'
R. ION ONS EDM VND

BRU (9)

1.52, 1.45* (B483), 1.43 (SED 65), 1.43, 1.43, 1.40, 1.37 (B432), 1.36, 1.27 (B482).

COL (4)

1.49 BM, 1.45 BM, 1.42, 1.37.

OTHER (2)

(1) Eaglen (B745). Ex Doubleday 1040 (1/8). 1.44

(2) Fitzwilliam Museum. 1.34

Class IIIac (REX:)

264 Aa O. *hENRICVS REX:III'
R. IOH ONS' EDM VHD

BRU (10)

1.53, 1.48 (B498), 1.45 (B499), 1.45, 1.44 (SED 186), 1.42 (SED 37), 1.39 (B527), 1.38, [1.37] chipped, [1.25] worn.

COL (2)

1.48 BM, 1.38*

Henry III, Long Cross, Class IIIac, *Ion* (*cont.*)

OTHER (4)

(1) Fitzwilliam Museum. Ex Shirley-Fox and Blunt collections. 1.43

(2) Stewartby collection. Ex Lawrence collection. 1.35

(3) Palmer (SED 680). 1.32

(4) Unknown owner (1988). –

Class IIIb (round face; no neck; first R with shaped tail, second with wedge)

265 Aa O. *hEHRICVS REX·III'
R. ION ONS' EDM VND

BRU (14)

1.50, 1.47, 1.46, 1.46, 1.45, 1.42, 1.42, 1.41, 1.40 (B490), 1.40, 1.39, 1.38, 1.37, 1.36* (B493).

COL (7)

1.49, 1.48, 1.47, 1.46, 1.43, 1.41, 1.41.

OTHER (1)

(1) BM. Slype hoard (1914), 115. 1.45

266 Bb O. *hEHRICVS REX·III'
R. ION ONS' EDM VND

BRU (24)

1.49#, 1.47, 1.45, 1.45, 1.45, 1.44 (SED 67), 1.43, 1.43, 1.43, 1.41 (B487), 1.41* (B654), 1.41, 1.40, 1.40 (B486), 1.40, 1.39, 1.38, 1.36, 1.35, 1.34 (B492), 1.33, 1.33, 1.29, [1.20] metal flaw.

Thomas collection

COL (3)

1.45, 1.41, 1.36.

OTHER (3)

(1) Dawson collection. 1.45

(2) Fitzwilliam Museum. Ex Shirley-Fox and Blunt collections. 1.44

(3) BM (1909). 1.35

267 Cc O. *hEHRICVS REX·III'
R. ION ONS'EDM VND

BRU (21)

1.51 (SED 492), 1.50, 1.46, 1.46, 1.44, 1.44, [1.43] chipped?, 1.42, 1.41, 1.40* (B488), 1.39, 1.37(B496), 1.37, 1.37, 1.35, 1.33, 1.33, 1.32, 1.32, 1.26, 1.22.

COL (6)

1.52, 1.45, 1.45 (B085), 1.44 BM, 1.44, 1.44.

OTHER (6)

(1) BM. Slype hoard (1914), 113. 1.47

(2) *SCBI* Museums in East Anglia (Bury) 1717. Ex Frost collection. 1.47

(3) Palmer (SED 34). 1.41

(4) Palmer (SED 369). 1.40

(5) Ex North collection. 1.37

(6) Eaglen (B390). Partly flat. [1.28]

Class IIIbc (broad face; ENR of hENRICVS ligulated)

268 Aa O. *hENRICVS REX·III'
R. ION ONS' EDM VND

BRU (17)

1.51, 1.50, 1.48, 1.46, 1.45, 1.43, 1.43, 1.42 (SED 20), 1.42, 1.41 (B491), 1.41, 1.39* (B497), 1.39, 1.38, 1.37, 1.37 (B891), 1.30.

COL (6)

1.47 (B243), 1.45, 1.42, 1.41, 1.39, 1.36.

269 Bb O. *hENRICVS REX·III'
R. ION ONS' EDN VND

BRU (13)

1.50, 1.49, 1.44, 1.43, 1.42, 1.41, 1.40, 1.39, 1.39, 1.38* (B494), 1.36, 1.32, 1.32.

COL (5)

1.46 BM, 1.46, 1.45, 1.40 (B051), 1.38.

OTHER (1)

(1) Eaglen (B1009). Ex Youde, Dupree; *NCirc* June 1990, 3172. 1.44

Class IIIc (shorter face; REX:III'; often pellets between side curls)

270 Aa O. *hEHRICVS REX:III'
No pellets between curls.
R. IOH OHS' EDM VND

Henry III, Long Cross, Class IIIc, *Ion* (*cont.*)

			BRU (13)	
			1.48* (B783), 1.47, 1.43 (B892), 1.42, 1.42, 1.41, 1.40, 1.37, 1.37, 1.31, 1.27, 1.22 (SED 191), –.	
			COL (5)	
			1.45 BM, 1.45, 1.44, 1.43, 1.36.	
			OTHER (3)	
		(1)	Eaglen (B350). Ex Elmore Jones 1538 (2/3).	1.41
		(2)	Eaglen (B743). Ex Doubleday 1040 (2/8).	1.28
		(3)	Palmer (SED 517).	1.23
271	Bb	O.	*hENRICVS REX:III' No pellets between curls.	
			ION ONS' EDM VND	
			BRU (14)	
			1.50, 1.49 (B501), 1.47 (B480), 1.46 (SED 747), 1.43, 1.43 (B481), 1.42 (SED 68), 1.42, 1.41 (B525), 1.40, 1.39, 1.36, 1.36, 1.35 (B495).	
			COL (3)	
			1.47 (SED 736), 1.45, 1.43* BM.	
			OTHER (3)	
		(1)	Eaglen (B011). Ex Spink (1975).	1.35
		(2)	Birmingham Museum and Art Gallery.	1.35
		(3)	Ex Tatler collection.	–
272	Cc	O.	*hENRICVS REX:III' No pellets between curls.	
		R.	ION ONS' EDM VND	
			BRU (22)	
			1.48, 1.47, 1.46* (B511), 1.46 (B893), 1.44, 1.43, 1.43, 1.42, 1.41, 1.40, 1.39, 1.38, 1.38, 1.36, 1.36, 1.36, 1.35, 1.34, 1.33, 1.31 (B570), 1.30, 1.14.	
			COL (14)	
			1.52 (SED 257). Ex Harris collection, 1.47, 1.47, 1.47, 1.46, [1.43] damaged, 1.43 BM, 1.43, 1.42, 1.42, 1.39, 1.38, 1.37, [1.26] worn.	
			OTHER (4)	
		(1)	Palmer (SED 315).	1.53

(2) Eaglen (B712). 1.42

(3) *SCBI* Scottish Museums (Edinburgh) 690. Slype hoard (1914). 1.39

(4) *SCBI* Scottish Museums (Glasgow) 692. 1.26

273 Dd O. *hENRICVS REX:III'
R. ION ONS' EDM VND

BRU (12)

1.53, 1.46 (B531), 1.45, 1.44, 1.43, 1.42, 1.41 (B516), 1.40, 1.38* (B894), 1.37 (B504), 1.36, 1.31.

COL (3)

1.46, 1.39, 1.38.

OTHER (2)

(1) Eaglen (B746). Ex Doubleday 1040 (3/8). 1.37

(2) Palmer (SED 139). 1.28

274 Ee O. *hENRICVS REX:III'
R. IOH OHS' EDM VND

BRU (10)

1.48, 1.45 (B895), 1.45, 1.45, 1.44, 1.44, 1.40 (B515), 1.38 (SED 192), 1.35, 1.30.

COL (7)

1.62 (B1001), 1.47 (B084), 1.47, 1.43, 1.42#, 1.41 (B245), 1.36* BM.

#Thomas collection. Ex Trenerry.

OTHER (3)

(1) Palmer (SED 411). 1.51

(2) Eaglen (B744). Ex Doubleday 1040 (4/8). 1.31

(3) Ex North collection. 1.29

275 Ff O. *hENRICVS REX:III'
R. ION ONS' EDM VND

BRU (25)

1.50, 1.49 (B896), 1.48, 1.47, 1.47, 1.45, 1.45, 1.44, 1.44, 1.43, 1.43, 1.42, 1.42, 1.40* (B503), 1.40, 1.40, 1.40, 1.38 (B500), 1.38 (B684), 1.37, 1.36, 1.36, 1.34, 1.32, 1.27.

COL (12)

1.51, 1.48, 1.46 (B129A), 1.46, 1.46, 1.45, 1.44 BM, 1.43, 1.43, 1.42, 1.38, 1.38.

OTHER (4)

Henry III, Long Cross, Class IIIc, *Ion* (*cont.*)

		(1)	Eaglen (B082). Ex Seaby (1979). Pierced.	[1.39]
		(2)	Palmer (SED 58).	1.38
		(3)	BM (1909).	1.37
		(4)	Museum of London. Great George St., Westminster find. Cut halfpenny.	[0.70]
276	Gg	O. R.	*hENRICVS REX:III' ION ONS' EDM VND	
			BRU (8)	
			1.46 double struck, 1.46, 1.43* (B524), 1.42 (B502), 1.42, 1.40, 1.39, [1.16] worn.	
			COL (2)	
			1.40 *SCBI* Museums in East Anglia (Ipswich) 1719, 1.34 BM.	
			OTHER (3)	
		(1)	Palmer (SED 361). Double struck.	1.46
		(2)	BM. Slype hoard (1914), 116.	1.42
		(3)	Eaglen (B244). Ex Osborne collection.	1.27
277	Hh	O. R.	*hENRICVS REX:III' ION ONS'EDM VND	
			BRU (23)	
			1.48 (SED 189), 1.48 (B512), 1.48 (B680), 1.46, 1.45* (B897), 1.44, 1.43, 1.43, 1.42, 1.42, [1.41] clipped? 1.41, 1.39, 1.39, 1.39, 1.38, 1.35, 1.33, 1.32, 1.31, [1.30] chipped? 1.25,1.24.	
			COL (8)	
			[1.49] clipped? 1.47, 1.45 double struck, irregular flan, 1.41, 1.41, 1.40, 1.39 (B191), 1.38 off-centre.	
			OTHER (5)	
		(1)	Eaglen (B747). Ex Doubleday 1040 (6/8).	1.49
		(2)	Eaglen (B412). Ex C. J. Martin (1985).	1.31
		(3)	Birmingham Museum and Art Gallery.	1.33
		(4)	Eaglen (B742). Ex Doubleday 1040 (5/8).	1.31
		(5)	Ex North collection. Cut halfpenny.	[0.70]
278	Ii	O.	*hENRICVS REX:III'	
		R.	ION ONS' EDM VND	
			BRU(13)	

1.48. 1.47, 1.46, 1.44, 1.44, 1.41, 1.41, 1.40 (B433), 1.40 (B898), 1.40 (SED 69), 1.39*, (B509), 1.39, 1.22 (B514), small flan.

COL (5)

1.51, 1.49, 1.49, 1.45, 1.35.

279 Jj O. *hENRICVS REX:III'
R. ION ONS' EDM VND

BRU (10)

1.48 (B522), 1.46, 1.46, 1.45, 1.44, 1.43, 1.40, 1.40 (B899), 1.38, 1.27.

COL (5)

1.57, 1.49* BM, 1.49, 1.39, 1.34.

OTHER (1)

(1) BM. Slype hoard (1914), 117. 1.47

280 Kk O. *hENRICVS REX:III'
R. ION ONS' EDM VND

BRU (12)

1.49* (B529), 1.46, 1.46 (B519), 1.40, 1.39, 1.39 (B510), 1.39, 1.38, 1.38, 1.38, 1.28, [1.09] (B508) corroded.

COL (2)

1.48, 1.42 BM.

OTHER (4)

(1) Eaglen (B372). 1.32

(2) Palmer (SED 536). Small flan. 1.14

(3) Trenerry collection. –

(4) Ex Tatler collection. –

281 Ll O. *hENRICVS REX:III'
R. ION ONS' EDM VND'
Vestigial first D.

BRU (21)

1.45* (B900), 1.44 (SED 187), 1.44, 1.43, 1.43, 1.42, 1.41 (B571), 1.41, 1.41, 1.41, 1.41 (B506), 1.40, 1.40, 1.39, 1.38, 1.36, 1.35, 1.35, 1.34, 1.25, 1.24.

COL (4)

1.50, 1.44 BM, 1.43, 1.40.

OTHER (1)

Henry III, Long Cross, Class IIIc, *Ion* (*cont.*)

No.	Die		Description	Weight
		(1)	Palmer (SED 332).	1.25
282	Mm	O.	*hENRICVS REX:III'	
		R.	ION ONS' EDM VND	
			BRU (14)	
			1.45, 1.45, 1.43, 1.43, 1.42, 1.39, 1.38* (B612), 1.37, 1.37, 1.35, 1.34, 1.32, 1.29 (B518), 1.25.	
			COL (6)	
			1.51 (B106), 1.49, 1.46, 1.44 BM, 1.41, 1.41.	
			OTHER (1)	
		(1)	Eaglen (B1010). Ex Dupree collection; *NCirc*, June 1990, 3185.	1.40
283	Nn	O.	*hENRICVS REX:III'	
		R.	IOH ONS' EDH VND'	
			BRU (6)	
			1.50, 1.46, 1.43* (B528), 1.42, 1.41, 1.37 (B520).	
			COL (4)	
			1.45, 1.41, [1.34] BM clipped, 1.23.	
			OTHER (3)	
		(1)	BM (1909).	1.42
		(2)	Ex Woodhead collection.	–
		(3)	BM. Tower Subway find. Cut halfpenny.	[0.76]
284	Oo	O.	*hENRICVS REX:III'	
		R.	IOH ONS EDM VND	
			BRU (21)	
			1.49 (SED 188), 1.44, 1.43, 1.42, 1.41, 1.41, 1.41 (B507), 1.41, 1.41, 1.41, 1.40, 1.38 (B530), 1.37, 1.37 (B517), 1.37, [1.36] clipped, 1.34, 1.31, 1.28, 1.27, [1.21] clipped.	
			COL (8)	
			1.50, 1.47 (B192), 1.47, 1.46 * BM, 1.43 BM, 1.39, 1.38, 1.24.	
			OTHER (1)	
		(1)	*SCBI* Scottish Museums (Glasgow) 691. Balmaclellan hoard (1924).	1.39
285	Pp	O.	*hENRICVS REX:III'	
		R.	ION ONS' EDM VND	

BRU (10)

1.48, 1.47 (B628), 1.45*(B901), 1.43, 1.43 (B526), 1.39, 1.39, 1.38 (B521), 1.38 (B505), 1.34 clipped?

COL (4)

1.49 BM, 1.43, 1.40, 1.40.

OTHER (4)

		(1)	Fitzwilliam Museum. Ex Shirley-Fox and Blunt collections.	1.41
		(2)	Palmer (SED 156). Cracked.	1.36
		(3)	Museum of London. Great George St., Westminster find. Pierced and plugged(?).	[1.26]
		(4)	Davis collection.	–

286 Qq O. *hENRICVS REX⁝III'
R. ION ONS' EDM VND

BRU (22)

1.49, 1.47, 1.46, 1.44, 1.44* (B661), 1.43, 1.43 (B513), 1.43 (B523), 1.42, 1.42, 1.41 (B902), 1.41 (SED 193)#, 1.39, 1.38 (B532), 1.38, 1.38, 1.37, 1.36, 1.36 (SED 190), 1.32, 1.31, 1.30.

weighed in hoard at 1.25g

COL (5)

1.53 BM, 1.46, 1.46 Ex North, 1.44 (B086), 1.38.

OTHER (4)

		(1)	*SCBI* Museums in East Anglia (Bury) 1718. Ex Frost collection.	1.41
		(2)	Eaglen (B301). Ex Woodhead collection.	1.38
		(3)	Eaglen (B351). Ex Elmore Jones 1538 (3/3).	1.36
		(4)	Royal Mint Museum. Hocking 425. Ex Banks (1818).	1.43

Coins with sceptre and legend beginning at 12 o'clock

Class IVab (central fleur but 'pellet' ends to crown; wide, shallow 'h')

287 Aa O. *hENRICVS REX:III'
R. ION ONS' EDM VND

BRU (7)

1.50* (B533), 1.48 (B674), 1.44, 1.44 (B664), 1.42, 1.42, 1.19 small flan.

Henry III, Long Cross, Class IVab, *Ion* (*cont.*)

			COL (4)	
			1.49 BM, 1.48, 1.42, 1.36 (B246).	
			OTHER (12)	
		(1)	BM. Palmers Green hoard (1911), 96.	1.43
		(2)	Stewartby collection.	1.40
		(3)	Palmer (SED 609).	1.37
		(4)	Harris collection.	1.35
		(5)	Ex Elmore Jones 1856.	1.33
		(6)	Thomas collection. Ex Palmer (SED 375).	1.33
		(7)	Fitzwilliam Museum. Ex Shirley-Fox and Blunt collections.	1.32
		(8)	Davis collection.	–
		(9)	Ex Woodhead collection. Ex R. Carlyon-Britton. Possibly from Brussels hoard.	–
		(10)	Ex Woodhead collection.	–
		(11)	Ex Lawrence, II (1951) 433 (3/3), illustrated.	–
		(12)	Palmer (SED 137). Cut halfpenny.	[0.59]
			Legend begins at 10 o'clock	
			Class Va2 (very broad face; X with uniform limbs; round eyes)	
288	Aa	O. R.	hENRICVS REX III'. ION ONS' EDM VND	
			BRU (12)	
			1.53, 1.49, 1.48, 1.46, 1.46, 1.45 (B539), 1.44, 1.39, 1.37 (B650), 1.36, 1.36 (B446), 1.35.	
			COL (3)	
			1.42, 1.41, 1.35* BM.	
			OTHER (3)	
		(1)	Birmingham Museum and Art Gallery.	1.49
		(2)	BM. Steppingley hoard (1912), 42.	1.48
		(3)	Palmer (SED 352). Ex Elmore Jones 1858 (1/2).	1.25
289	Bb	O. R.	hENRICVS REX:III'. ION ONS' EDM VND	

BRU (13)

1.49, 1.48, 1.47, 1.46 (B617), 1.45, 1.43, 1.43, 1.42, 1.41* (B682), 1.41, 1.35 (B537), 1.33, 1.32.

COL (4)

1.47, 1.40, 1.39 BM, 1.29 (B107).

OTHER (2)

(1) Palmer (SED 96). Partly flat. 1.49

(2) Palmer (SED 306). Cut halfpenny. [0.80]

290 Cc O. hENRICVS REX III'.
R. IOH ONS' EDM VND

BRU (10)

1.49, 1.47, 1.46 (B653), 1.46, 1.46, 1.44, 1.41, 1.40 (B541), 1.38, 1.32* (B685).

COL (4)

1.51 BM, 1.49, 1.49, 1.33.#

Thomas collection

OTHER (2)

(1) Palmer (SED 35). 1.47

(2) Palmer (SED 511). 1.39

291 Dd O. hENRICVS REX III'.
R. ION ONS EIN TED

BRU (16)

1.51, 1.49, 1.48, 1.47 (B540), 1.45* (B613), 1.44, 1.44, 1.44, 1.43, 1.41, 1.41, 1.37, 1.37, 1.33, 1.30 (B538), 1.21.

COL (4)

1.48, 1.47, 1.47, 1.46 BM.

OTHER (2)

(1) Palmer (SED 371). 1.37

(2) Eaglen (B704). 1.36

Class Va3 (marginally less broad face; X with alternate curved limbs)

292 Aa O. hENRICVS REX III.'
R. ION ONS' EDM VND

BRU (19)

Henry III, Long Cross, Class Va3, *Ion* (*cont.*)

			1.48, 1.47, 1.46 (B675), 1.46, 1.46, 1.45, 1.45, 1.45, 1.45, 1.45, 1.44 clipped?, 1.44, 1.42* (B663), 1.42, 1.42, 1.40 (B439), 1.40, 1.22, –.	
			COL (9)	
			1.53 BM, 1.48, 1.46, 1.43 (B247), 1.43 (B357), 1.41 (SED 338), 1.38, 1.37, 1.29 BM.	
			OTHER (4)	
		(1)	Eaglen (B748). Ex Doubleday 1040 (7/8).	1.45
		(2)	Thomas collection. Ex Harris collection.	1.45
		(3)	Palmer (SED 389).	1.31
		(4)	Palmer (SED 251).	1.29
293	Bb	O. R.	hEHRICVS REX III'. ION ONS' EDM VND	
			BRU (15)	
			1.48* (B649), 1.48, 1.43 (B689), 1.42, 1.41, 1.40 (B436), 1.39, 1.38, 1.38, 1.38, 1.37, 1.37, 1.37, 1.36, 1.31.	
			COL (3)	
			1.48 BM, 1.47, 1.45 BM.	
			OTHER (7)	
		(1)	Harris collection.	1.45
		(2)	BM. Palmers Green hoard (1911) 97.	1.43
		(3)	Eaglen (B1011). Ex Dupree collection; *NCirc*, June 1990, 3193.	1.32
		(4)	Palmer (SED 477).	1.31
		(5)	Eaglen (B186). Ex Spink (1982).	1.30
		(6)	Royal Mint Museum. Steppingley hoard (1912).	1.41
		(7)	Trenerry collection.	–
294	Cc	O. R.	hENRICVS REX III'. ION ON·S EIN ED	
			BRU (19)	
			1.50, 1.49, 1.47, 1.45, 1.45, 1.45 (B686), 1.43, 1.43 bent, 1.42 clipped ?, 1.42, 1.41 (B546), 1.41* (B545), 1.40, 1.40, 1.38, 1.33, [1.32] clipped, 1.19, 1.18 irregular flan.	
			COL (11)	

			1.53, 1.52, 1.52, 1.52, 1.50, 1.48, 1.48, 1.44, 1.41, 1.38, 1.38 BM.	
			OTHER (8)	
		(1)	BM.	1.45
		(2)	Palmer (SED 297).	1.39
		(3)	Eaglen (B196). Ex C. J. Martin (1982). Irregular flan.	1.35
		(4)	Palmer (SED 494).	1.32
		(5)	*SCBI* Scottish Museums (Glasgow) 694. R. construed as S EDMV–.	1.31
		(6)	Fitzwilliam Museum. Ex Shirley-Fox and Blunt collections.	1.15
		(7)	Ex Woodhead collection.	–
		(8)	Gardner collection (1988).	–
295	Dd	O. R.	hENRICVS REX III'. ION ONS EIN TED	
			BRU (12)	
			1.48 (B672), [1.48]* (B544), 1.48, 1.46, 1.45 (B618), 1.42, 1.40, 1.40, 1.37 (B535), 1.36, 1.33, 1.23 (B671).	
			COL (3)	
			1.45 , 1.45 BM, 1.33.	
			OTHER (1)	
		(1)	Jarmin collection (1988).	–
296	Ee	O. R.	hENRICVS REX III'. ION ONS EIN TED	
			BRU (13)	
			1.52, 1.51 (B614), 1.51, 1.51, 1.46, 1.46 (B659), 1.44* (B435), 1.43, 1.42, 1.42, 1.38, 1.31, 1.22 (B660).	
			COL (4)	
			1.46 (SED 36), 1,41, 1.37, 1.37 irregular flan, partly flat.	
			OTHER (4)	
		(1)	BM. Slype hoard (1914), 118.	1.48
		(2)	*SCBI* Museums in East Anglia (Bury) 1720. Ex Frost collection.	1.40
		(3)	Ex Woodhead collection.	–
		(4)	Ex North collection. Cut halfpenny.	[0.71]

Henry III, Long Cross, Class Va3, *Ion* (*cont.*)

297 Ff O. hENRICVS REX III'
R. ION ONS EHT ED

BRU (20)

1.55, 1.52, 1.51, 1.50* (B676), 1.47, 1.47 (B648), 1.44, 1.43, 1.43, 1.43, 1.43, 1.42, 1.41, 1.40, 1.39, 1.39, 1.36, 1.36, 1.30 (B635), 1.25.

COL (7)

1.53 (B015), 1.50, 1.50, 1.49 BM, 1.48, 1.39, 1.31.

OTHER (3)

(1) Palmer (SED 633). 1.40

(2) Museum of London. Great George St., Westminster find. 1.29

(3) Stewartby collection. Ex Lawrence collection. 1.23

298 Gg O. hENRICVS REX III'
R. IOH ONS' EIN TED

BRU (16)

1.53, 1.50, 1.50, 1.50, 1.47, 1.45, 1.42, 1.42, 1.41, 1.39, 1.38 (B687), 1.37* (B690), 1.37, 1.36, 1.36, 1.34.

COL (6)

1.49 BM, 1.49, 1.45, 1.40 (B007), 1.33, [1.32] fragment.

OTHER (1)

(1) Palmer (SED 435). 1.48

299 Hh O. hENRICVS REX III'
R. ION ON·S EIN TED

BRU (21)

1.52, 1.51, 1.50, 1.48 (B542), 1.48, 1 45, 1.45, 1.44, 1.43, 1.43, 1.43, 1.42, 1.40, 1.39, 1.39, 1.38, 1.37, 1.35, 1.34, 1.29, 1.22 (B536).

COL (5)

1.51, 1.49, 1.45, 1.42 * BM, 1.35.

OTHER (3)

(1) Eaglen (B769). Ex Baldwin (1988). 1.41

(2) Elmore Jones 1858 (2/2). 1.27

(3) Eaglen (B360). 1.26

300 Ii O. hENRICVS REX III'
R. ION ON·S EIN TED

BRU (14)

1.51, 1.47, 1.47, 1.47, 1.43, 1.42, 1.42 (B615), 1.42, 1.40, 1.40, 1.38 (B619), 1.37, 1.35* (B434), 1.25 (B543).

COL (3)

1.50, 1.50, 1.32.

OTHER (2)

(1) Eaglen (B574). Ex Baldwin (1986). 1.46

(2) Palmer (SED 349). Cut halfpenny. [0.69]

301 Jj O. hENRICVS REX III'
R. IOH OHS EIH TED

BRU (14)

1.54, 1.47, 1.46, 1.46 (B547), 1.44, 1.43, 1.41, 1.41, 1.40* (B658), 1.40, 1.36, 1.30, [1.27] clipped, 1.21 small flan.

COL (-)

OTHER (9)

(1) *SCBI* Northern Museums (Whitby) 1776. 1.50

(2) Birmingham Museum and Art Gallery. 1.45

(3) BM. Hornchurch hoard (1938). 1.43

(4) BM. Slype hoard (1914), 119. 1.41

(5) Eaglen (B174). Ex Grantley collection; Baldwin (1982). 1.40

(6) Ex Jacob collection. Clipped. [1.38]

(7) *SCBI* Scottish Museums (Edinburgh) 693. Slype hoard (1914). 1.38

(8) BM. Palmers Green hoard (1911). 1.36

(9) Palmer (SED 458). 1.35

302 Kk O. hENRICVS REX III'
R. ION OHS' EDM VND

BRU (3)

1.38* (B438), 1.32 (B437),1.25 (B636).

[303] Ll O. hE[N X] III[
R. IOII[ ][ ]TED
Possibly imitative?

OTHER (1)

Henry III, Long Cross, Class Va3, *Ion* (*cont.*)

(1)* Palmer (SED 447). Cut halfpenny. [0.60]

304 Mm O. hENRICVS REX III'
R. ION ONS EIH T[ED]
Second N retrograde.

OTHER (1)

(1)* *SCBI* Northern Museums (Sheffield) 1775. 1.37

Randulf

Class Vb2/Va3 mule

305 Aa O. hENRICVS REX III'.
Wedge-shaped feet to 'R's.
RAN DVL F:ON S'ED
Ball-shaped foot to 'R'.

BRU (18)

1.50, 1.50, 1.48, 1.47, 1.47, 1.46, 1.46 (SED 196), 1.45, 1.41, 1.41*(B441), 1.40 (B688), 1.38 (B644), 1.38, 1.36, 1.36, 1.35 (B553), 1.35, 1.20.

COL (3)

1.50 BM. 1.45 BM, 1.39.

OTHER (1)

(1) Eaglen (B770). Ex Baldwin (1988). 1.33

Class Vb2 (wedge-shaped feet to R)

306 Aa O. hENRICVS REX III'.
R. RAN DVL F⁝OH S.'ED

BRU (45)

1.54, 1.52 (B634), 1.51, 1.50, 1.50, 1.49, 1.48, 1.48, 1.48, 1.48, 1.48, 1.47, 1.47, 1.47, 1.46, 1.46, 1.46, 1.46, 1.45, 1.44, 1.44 (B550), 1.44, 1 43* (B452), 1,43, 1.43, 1.43, 1.43, 1.43, 1.42, 1.42, 1.41, 1.40, 1.39, 1.38, 1.37, 1.37, 1.36, 1.36, 1.36, 1.31, 1.30, [1.28] chipped, 1.28, 1.20, 1.20 (SED 71) small flan.

COL (16)

1.53 (B128), 1.50, 1.50#, 1.49, 1.49, 1.48, 1.46 BM, 1.43, 1.42, 1.41, 1.39, 1.39, 1.38 (B093), 1.38, 1.21 BM, 1.15.

Dawson collection.

OTHER (6)

		(1)	Birmingham Museum and Art Gallery.	1.57
		(2)	*SCBI* Scottish Museums (Edinburgh) 697. Slype hoard (1914).	1.49
		(3)	BM. Steppingley hoard (1912), 44.	1.41
		(4)	Palmer (SED 474).	1.40
		(5)	Palmer (SED 727).	1.31
		(6)	Fitzwilliam Museum. Ex Shirley-Fox and Blunt collections.	1.17
307	Bb	O. R.	hENRICVS REX III'. RAN DVL FOH S'ED	
			BRU (30)	
			1.54, 1.48, 1.48, 1.48, 1.48, 1.47* (B450), 1.47, 1.46, 1.46, 1.45, 1.45 (B630), 1.45, 1.45 (B620), 1.45, 1.44, 1.43, 1.42, [1.42] (B552) encrusted, 1.41, 1.41, 1.40, 1.40, [1.39] worn? , 1.39 (B616), 1.39, 1.38, 1.38, 1.27, [1.13] (SED 73) fragment, [1.12] fragment.	
			COL (14)	
			1.50, 1.46, 1.45, 1.45, 1.44 BM, 1.44, 1.43 BM, 1.41, [1.41] chipped, 1.40, 1.39, 1.39, 1.37 (B095), 1.31.	
			OTHER (2)	
		(1)	BM. Slype hoard (1914), 120.	1.49
		(2)	Palmer (SED 446).	1.48
308	Cc	O. R.	hENRICVS REX III' RAI DVL FOH S'ED	
			BRU (44)	
			1.52, 1.51, 1.48, 1.47, 1.47, 1.46, 1.45, 1.44, 1.44, 1.44, 1.44, 1.44, 1.44, 1.44, 1.43, 1.43, 1.43, 1.42, 1.42, 1.42, 1.42, 1.42, 1.42 (B657), 1.42, 1.41 (SED 372), 1.41, 1.41, 1.41, 1.41, 1.40 (B449), 1.40, 1.40, 1.39, 1.39, 1.39, 1.39, 1.38, 1.36, 1.36, 1.35 (B555), 1.34* (B442), 1.33, 1.32, 1.20.	
			COL (12)	
			1.72 BM, 1.48, 1.48 (B294), 1.47, 1.45, 1.44, 1.42, 1.42 (B190), 1.40, 1.36, 1.36 BM, 1.36.	
			OTHER (5)	
		(1)	Eaglen (B030). Flan crack.	1.43
		(2)	Palmer (SED 55). Ex Harris collection.	1.37
		(3)	Fitzwilliam Museum, 1201.	1.36

Henry III, Long Cross, Class Vb2, *Randulf* (*cont.*)

		(4)	Palmer (SED 730). Obverse double-struck. Small flan.	1.14
		(5)	Trenerry (Summer 1987 list, H74).	–
309	Dd	O. R.	hENRICVS REX III' RAN DVL F:ON S'ED	
			BRU (25)	
			1.52, 1.49, 1.47, 1.47, 1.46, 1.45, 1.45, 1.43, 1.43, 1.43, 1.43, 1.42 (B451), 1.40, 1.39 * (B637), 1.38, 1.35, 1.35, 1.35, 1.32 (B638), 1.32, 1.30, 1.26, 1.25, 1.23, 1.20.	
			COL (32)	
			1.56 (B087), 1.53 (B088), 1.53 (B248), 1.52, 1.52 (B050), 1.52, 1.51, 1.49, 1.49, 1.47, 1.47, 1.46, 1.46, 1.46, 1.45, 1.45, 1.44 (B402), 1.44, 1.43, 1.42, 1.42, 1.42, 1.42, 1.41, 1.41, 1.40,1.40, 1.37, 1.35, 1.34, 1.32 BM, 1.29.	
310	Ee	O. R.	hENRICVS REX III' RAN DVL FON S'ED	
			BRU (14)	
			1.51, 1.50, 1.48, 1.47, 1.46, 1.46, 1.44, 1.43, 1.43, 1.42, 1.42, 1.37, 1.37* (B643), 1.32.	
			COL (8)	
			1.55 (B189), 1.51, 1.49, (B096), 1.47, 1.47, 1.40, 1.38 BM, 1.30.	
311	Ff	O. R.	hENRICVS REX III'. RAN DVL:F ON S'ED	
			BRU 16)	
			1.51, 1.50, 1.49, 1.48, 1.48, 1.47 (B642), 1.47* (B646), 1.46, 1.46, 1.46 (B645), 1.45 (B692), 1.42, 1.41, 1.39, 1.38, 1.38 (B549).	
			COL (9)	
			1.49, 1.47 (B089), 1.47, 1.47, 1.43 (B090), 1.41 BM, 1.39, 1.39, 1.39 BM irregular flan.	
			OTHER (2)	
		(1)	Stewartby collection.	1.23
		(2)	Palmer (SED 287). Worn.	[1.21]
312	Gg	O. R.	hENRICVS REX III' RAN DVL F·OH S'ED	

BRU (31)

1.57, 1.51, 1.51 (SED 72), 1.50* (B677), 1.50, 1.49, 1.49, 1.48, 1.47, [1.46] cracked and clipped, 1.45, 1.45, 1.45, 1.44, 1.44, 1.42, 1.42, 1.41, 1.41, 1.38, 1.38 (B623), 1.38, 1.36, 1.35, 1.34 (B551), 1.32, 1.32, 1.27, 1.27, 1.24, 1.22.

COL (13)

1.53, 1.51, 1.47, 1.46 (B108), 1.45, 1.44, 1.44, 1.44 BM, 1.44, 1.43, 1.42, 1.42, 1.38.

OTHER (4)

		(1)	Elmore Jones 1860 (1/4).	1.42
		(2)	Palmer (SED 606).	1.34
		(3)	Palmer (SED 329).	1.30
		(4)	Ex Woodhead collection.	–
313	Hh	O. R.	hENRICVS REX III' RAN DVL F:ON S'ED	

BRU (26)

1.60, 1.52, 1.51, 1.50, 1.50, 1.47, 1.46 clipped?, 1.46, 1.44, 1.44, 1.43, 1.43, 1.42, 1.42, 1.41, 1.41, 1.41, 1.41, 1.40 (B548), 1.40. 1.40, 1.39* (B621), 1.37, 1.34, 1.30, 1.28 (B443).

COL (27)

1.59, 1.51, 1.49, 1.48, 1.47 (B091), 1.47 (B094), 1.46, 1.46, 1.45, 1.45, 1.44 (SED 795), 1.44, 1.44 BM, 1.43, 1.43, 1.43, 1.42, 1.41, 1.41, 1.41 cracked, 1.40, 1.40, 1.37, 1.37, 1.33, 1.32, 1.31.

OTHER (3)

		(1)	Palmer (SED 59).	1.62
		(2)	BM. Steppingley hoard (1912), 43.	1.56
		(3)	Eaglen (B465). Ex Baldwin (1986).	1.45
314	Ii	O. R.	hENRICVS REX III' RAN DVL F.ON S'ED	

BRU (48)

1.55, 1.53, 1.53, 1.52, 1.51, 1.50, 1.50, 1.49, 1.49, 1.48, 1.47, 1.47, 1.46, 1.46, 1.46, 1.45, 1.45, 1.45, 1.45, 1.44, 1.44 chipped, 1.44, 1.44, 1.44, 1.43 (B453), 1.43, 1.42, 1.42, 1.42, 1.41, 1.41, 1.41, 1.41, 1.40, 1.40, 1.39, 1.39, 1.39, 1.38* (B668), 1.38, 1.37 (B629), 1.37 (B534), 1.35, 1.33, 1.32 (B610), 1.26, 1.26, 1.24.

Henry III, Long Cross, Class Vb2, *Randulf* (*cont.*)

COL (12)

1.50 BM, 1.49, 1.49, 1.47, 1.46, 1.45 (B092), 1.43, 1.43, 1.43, 1.41, 1.39, 1.35 BM.

OTHER (7)

(1) Fitzwilliam Museum. Ex Shirley-Fox and Blunt collections. Clipped ? 1.53

(2) BM. Hornchurch hoard (1938). 1.44

(3) Palmer (SED 4). 1.42

(4) Ex North collection. 1.38

(5) Thomas collection. 1.32

(6) Jarmin collection (1950). –

(7) Palmer (SED 449). Cut halfpenny. [0.77]

315 Jj O. hENRICVS REX III'
R. RAN DVL FON S'ED

BRU (8)

1.46, 1.45, 1.45 (B647), 1.44, 1.44, 1.43, 1.42 (B1004), 1.38.

COL (7)

1.50*, 1.49, 1.48, 1.47, 1.42, 1.39, 1.23.

OTHER (3)

(1) Royal Mint Museum. Slype hoard (1914). 1.51

(2) BM. Slype hoard (1914), 121. 1.48

(3) Palmer (SED 393). 1.34

Class Vc (almond-shaped eyes)

316 Aa O. hENRICVS REX III'
R. RAN DVL F:ON S'ED

BRU (35)

1.51, 1.50, 1.50, 1.50, 1.47, 1.47, 1.47 (B693), 1.46, 1.45, 1.44, 1.44, 1.44, 1.43, 1.43, 1.42, 1.42, 1.42, 1.41 (B678), 1.41, 1.41, 1.40, 1.39, 1.39, 1.39, 1.38, 1.38, 1.37, 1.36, 1.36* (B454), 1.35, 1.32, 1.32, 1.31 (B445), 1.26, 1.12.

COL (4)

1.52 BM, 1.51, 1.47 (B187), 1.41.

OTHER (6)

		(1)	Royal Mint Museum. Palmers Green hoard (1911).	1.49
		(2)	Eaglen (B749). Ex Doubleday 1040 (8/8).	1.45
		(3)	Eaglen (B342). Gift ex Baldwin (1984).	1.41
		(4)	Eaglen (B176). Ex Grantley.	1.35
		(5)	Ex North collection.	1.34
		(6)	Palmer (SED 448). Cut halfpenny.	[0.67]
317	Bb	O. R.	hENRICVS REX III' RAN DVL FON S'ED	
			BRU (34)	
			1.57* (B559), 1.48, 1.48 (B631), 1.47, 1.46, 1.46, 1.46, 1.45, 1.45, 1.44, 1.44, 1.43, 1.43, 1.42, 1.42 (B691), 1.42, 1.41, 1.41, 1.41(B624), 1.40, 1.40, 1.39 (B558), 1.39, 1.36, 1.36, 1.35, 1.34, 1.34, 1.34, 1.33, 1.32, 1.25, 1.20, 1.18.	
			COL (10)	
			1.51, 1.51, 1.50, 1.48, 1.46 BM, 1.45, 1.45, 1.43, [1.37] clipped, 1.35.	
			OTHER (5)	
		(1)	Royal Mint Museum. Slype hoard (1914).	1.55
		(2)	*NCirc*, June 1990, 3199. Ex Dupree collection.	1.40
		(3)	Palmer (SED 243).	1.32
		(4)	Palmer (SED 714).	1.32
		(5)	Davis collection.	–
318	Cc	O. R.	hENRICVS REX III' RAN DVL FON S'ED	
			BRU (40)	
			1.56, 1.53, 1.52, 1.51, 1.50, 1.49, 1.48, 1.48, 1.48, 1.47, 1.46, 1.46, 1.46, 1.46, 1.45, 1.43 (B652), 1.43, 1.42, (B556), 1.42, 1.41, 1.40, 1.39, 1.39, 1.39, 1.39, 1.39, 1.39, 1.38 (B632), 1.38, 1.37, 1.37, 1.37* (B622), 1.35, 1.34, 1.32, 1.27, 1.27, 1.24, 1.18 small flan, 1.13.	
			COL (25)	
			1.53 irregular flan, 1.51, 1.51, 1.50, 1.49, 1.49, 1.48, 1.47, 1.46, 1.45, 1.45, 1.44 BM, 1.44, 1.44, 1.44, 1.43, 1.43, 1.42, 1.41, 1.41, 1.40, 1.36 (SED 32), 1.33, [1.28] clipped, 1.28.	
			OTHER (6)	

Henry III, Long Cross, Class Vc, *Randulf* (*cont.*)

(1) BM. Steppingley hoard (1912), 45. 1.50

(2) Thomas collection. Ex Harris collection. 1.50

(3) Palmer (SED 412). 1.49

(4) Fitzwilliam Museum. Ex Shirley-Fox and Blunt collections. Clipped? 1.49

(5) *SCBI* Scottish Museums (Glasgow) 698. Slype hoard (1914). 1.49

(6) Palmer (SED 155). Cut halfpenny. [0.62]

319 Dd O. hENRICVS REX III'
R. RAN DVL FON S'ED

BRU (16)

1.51 (B633), 1.47, 1.46, 1.44 (B639), 1.42* (B667), 1.42, 1.41, 1.41, 1.39, 1.37, 1.35, 1.34 (SED 74), 1.33, 1.32, 1.32, 1.25.

OTHER (2)

(1) Royal Mint Museum. Palmers Green hoard (1911). 1.37

(2) *SCBI* Scottish Museums (Edinburgh) 701. 1.17

320 Ee O. hENRICVS REX III'
R. RAN DVL F:ON S'ED

BRU (30)

1.53, 1.51* (B641), 1.50, 1.49, 1.48, 1.47, 1.47, 1.46, 1.46, 1.46, 1.46, 1.45, 1.45, 1.45, 1.44, 1.42, 1.42, 1.42, 1.42, 1.40, 1.40, 1.38, 1.36, 1.35 (B444), 1.32 (B554), 1.29, 1.27, 1.26, 1.07 small flan, 1.05 small flan.

OTHER (6)

(1) BM. 'Grierson 240'. 1.53

(2) Birmingham Museum and Art Gallery. 1.49

(3) Royal Mint Museum. Palmers Green hoard (1911). 1.49

(4) *SCBI* Museums in East Anglia (Bury), 1721. Ex Frost collection. 1.45

(5) Eaglen (B 012). Ex Seaby (1975). 1.25

(6) Ex Woodhead collection. –

Class Vc(x) (R's with upturned rather than wedge-shaped tails).

Position in Vc series uncertain, but possibly not last, since examples occur in the Colchester hoard (1969), whereas dies Dd and Ee are absent, and no later types are represented until the batch of 1,916 coins of class VI.

321 Aa O. hENRICVS REX III
R. RAN DVL F:ON S'ED

BRU (29)

1.54, 1.53, 1.52, 1.52, 1.49, 1.47, 1.47, 1.46 cracked, 1.46, 1.46, 1.45 (B694), 1.45* (B440), 1.44, 1.44, 1.43, 1.42, 1.40, 1.40, 1.40 (B557), 1.40, 1.38, 1.38, 1.36 (B656), 1.34, [1.33] chipped, 1.32, 1.28, 1.26, 1.22 small flan.

COL (12)

1.53 BM, 1.51, 1.50, BM, 1.48, 1.47 (SED 607), 1.46, 1.46, 1.45 BM, 1.45, 1.41, 1.35, 1.32

OTHER (7)

(1)	Eaglen (B175). Ex Grantley.	1.45
(2)	*SCBI* Scottish Museums (Edinburgh) 699. Slype hoard (1914).	1.44
(3)	*SCBI* Scottish Museums (Glasgow) 700. Slype hoard (1914).	1.42
(4)	BM. Palmers Green hoard (1911), 99.	1.39
(5)	Palmer (SED 323).	1.13
(6)	Ex Woodhead collection.	–
(7)	Palmer (SED 521).	[0.62]

Class Vd (crown with tapered fleurs)

322 Aa O. hENRICVS REX · III'
R. RA ND ONB ERI
This pair of dies is unusual in the absence of ligulation between the letters N and R on the O. and in the mint signature.

BRU (9)

1.50#, [1.45] (B679) chipped, 1.45, 1.44 irregular flan, [1.44] clipped, 1.42* (B455), 1.42 (B560), 1.39 cracked, 1.32.

#Thomas collection

OTHER (8)

(1)	BM. Ex Rev. E. Rogers	1.46
(2)	Palmer (SED 475).	1.43
(3)	Stewartby collection. Irregular flan.	1.43
(4)	Palmer (SED 100). Ex Carlyon-Britton, Lawrence, IV (1951)1050 (27/27) and Woodhead collections. Possibly from Brussels hoard.	1.39

Henry III, Long Cross, Class Vd, *Randulf* (*cont.*)

		(5)	Birmingham Museum and Art Gallery. Ex Lawrence, II (1951) 436 (9/9).	1.26
		(6)	Ex Eaglen (B249) and North collections.	–
		(7)	Davis collection (pre-1989).	–
		(8)	Ex Woodhead collection.	–
			Class Ve (crown with pelleted double band)	
			No coins known from Bury.	
			Class Vf (crown with double band)	
323	Aa	O. R.	·hENRICVS REX III.' RAN DVL F.OH ·S·'ED	
			Tiny pellets on O. and R.	
			BRU (2)	
			1.45* (B456), 1.44 (B625).	
324	Bb	O. R.	hENRICVS REX III' RAN DVL F⁝ON S'ED	
			BRU (19)	
			1.50 (B447), 1.50, 1.48, 1.47, 1.47, 1.47* (B651), 1.45 (B611), 1.44, 1.44, 1.44, 1.43, 1.43, 1.43, 1.43, 1.42, 1.42, 1.41, 1.40, 1.33.	
			OTHER (7)	
		(1)	Thomas collection. Ex Woodhead collection.	1.49
		(2)	BM. Ex Lawrence collection.	1.49
		(3)	Palmer (SED 89).	1.48
		(4)	Palmer (SED 356).	1.46
		(5)	Stewartby collection. Ex Lawrence collection.	1.40
		(6)	Birmingham Museum and Art Gallery.	1.31
		(7)	Ex North collection. Small flan.	1.28

Renaud

			Class Vg (solid band to crown with low central fleur)	
325	Aa	O. R.	hENRICVS REX·III'. REN AVD ONS EDM	
			BRU (24)	

1.63, 1.55, 1.54, 1.53, 1.52, 1.51, 1.49, 1.48, 1.48, 1.47, 1.47, 1.47 (B458), 1.43, 1.43, 1.42 (B562), 1.42, 1.41, 1.41* (B666), 1.40, 1.39, 1.37, 1.31, 1.31, 1.25.

OTHER (2)

(1) Palmer (SED 322). Ex Davis collection. 1.36

(2) Palmer (SED 494). Cut halfpenny. –

326 Bb O. hENRICVS REX III'.
R. REN AVD ONS EDM

BRU (12)

1.51, 1.48, 1.47, 1.47* (B669), 1.47, 1.46, 1.45, 1.42, 1.38 (B566), 1.37, 1.29, 1.25.

OTHER (5)

(1) Eaglen (B1024). Ex C. J. Martin (1991). 1.44

(2) Eaglen (B250). Ex Osborne collection. 1.40

(3) Birmingham Museum and Art Gallery. 1.38

(4) *SCBI* Scottish Museums (Edinburgh) 702. 1.37

(5) *NCirc*, Dec. 1989, 6638. –

327 Cc O. ·h.ENRICVS REX III.'
R. REN AVD ONS' EDM

BRU (20)

1.57, 1.54, 1.53, 1.52, 1.51, 1.50* (B640), 1.49, 1.49, 1.47, 1.47, 1.46, 1.44, 1.43, 1.42, 1.40, 1.36 (B457), 1.34, 1.32, 1.29 (B563), 1.20.

OTHER (4)

(1) Fitzwilliam Museum. Ex Shirley-Fox and Blunt collections. 1.40

(2) Thomas collection. Ex Palmer (SED 514). 1.39

(3) Palmer (SED 626). 1.34

(4) Ex North collection. –

328 Dd O. ⁝hENRICVS REX III'
R. REN AVD OIS' EDM

BRU (13)

1.54, 1.51, 1.51, 1.51 (B 683), 1.50, 1.48, 1.47, 1.45, 1.44 (B561), 1.43* (B655), 1.38, 1.34, 1.32.

OTHER (5)

Henry III, Long Cross, Class Vg, *Renaud* (*cont.*)

		(1)	BM. Slype hoard (1914), 122.	1.49
		(2)	BM. Hornchurch hoard (1938).	1.47
		(3)	Palmer (SED 30).	1.46
		(4)	Ex North collection.	1.46
		(5)	Ex Lawrence and Woodhead collections.	–
329	Ee	O. R.	hENRICVS REX III'. REN AVD ONS EDM	
			BRU (12)	
			1.63, 1.53, 1.51 (B564), 1.51, 1.51 (B627), 1.50, 1.47* (B681), 1.46 (B626), 1.42, 1.42, 1.41, 1.29.	
330	Ff	O. R.	hENRICVS REX III.' REN AVD ONS EDM	
			BRU (3)	
			1.50, 1.47* (B565), 1.41.	

Stephane

331	Aa	O. R.	hENRICVS REX III' STE PhA NEO S'ED	
			BRU (4)	
			1.50 (B662), 1.45* (B459), 1.39, 1.19.	
			OTHER (3)	
		(1)	Palmer (SED 368).	1.44
		(2)	BM. Palmers Green hoard (1911), 100. Chipped.	[1.43]
		(3)	Eaglen (B177). Ex Grantley; Baldwin (1982).	1.27
332	Bb	O. R.	hENRICVS REX III' STE PhA NEO S'ED	
			BRU (2)	
			1.35 (B665), 1.34* (B448).	
			OTHER (1)	
		(1)	Eaglen (B909). Possibly from Brussels hoard. Ex Wells and Woodhead collections.	1.47
333	Cc	O. R.	hENRICVS REX III.' STE PhA NEO N'SE	
			OTHER (2)	

		(1)*	Eaglen (B910). Ex Woodhead collection.	1.47
		(2)	Palmer (SED 194). Possibly from Brussels hoard.	1.41
334	Dd	O. R.	hENRICVS RE[ ] III [ ] STE Ph[ ] [ ] S'ED	
			OTHER (3)	
		(1)*	BM. Coventry hoard (1958).	1.39
		(2)	Ex North collection.	1.31
		(3)	Stewartby collection. Cut halfpenny.	–
335	Ee	O. R.	hENRICVS REX III' STE PhA NOH S[ ]ED	
			OTHER (3)	
		(1)	Eaglen (B708). Ex Allen collection.	1.30
		(2)	Whereabouts unknown. Greywell hoard (1988). See Archibald and Cook 2001, p. 64 and Pl. 14, 2.	1.27
		(3)*	Palmer (SED 534).	1.14

Ion

336	Aa	O. R.	hENRICVS REX III'. ION ONS EIH TED	
			OTHER (9)	
		(1)*	BM. Steppingley hoard (1912), 46.	1.49
		(2)	Stewartby collection. Ex Lawrence, IV (1951) 1055 (pt).	1.49
		(3)	Palmer (SED 839). Ex Lawrence, IV (1951) 1055 (pt), North and Conte (?) collections.	1.46
		(4)	Fitzwilliam Museum. Gift of Miss J. Ritchie (1963). Chipped.	[1.40]
		(5)	Palmer (SED 431).	1.39
		(6)	Ex North collection.	1.39
		(7)	Palmer (SED 653).	1.30
		(8)	Fitzwilliam Museum. Ex Shirley-Fox and Blunt collections.	1.27
		(9)	*SCBI* Scottish Museums (Cromarty Courthouse) 695. Cromarty, Castle Gate find (1991?).	1.27
337	Bb	O. R.	hENRICVS REX III' ION ONS EIN TED	
			OTHER (1)	

Henry III, Long Cross, Class Vg, *Ion* (*cont.*)

		(1)*	Birmingham Museum and Art Gallery.	1.33
338	Cc	O.	hENRICVS REX III'.	
		R.	IOH ONS EIN TED	
			OTHER (5)	
		(1)	Birmingham Museum and Art Gallery.	1.39
		(2)	*SCBI* Scottish Museums (Glasgow) 696. Described as Vh.	1.39
		(3)	Palmer (SED 76).	1.34
		(4)*	BM Steppingley hoard (1912), 47.	1.30
		(5)	Palmer (SED 690).	1.20
339	Dd	O.	hENRICVS REX III'	
		R.	IOH ONS ENT. EDM	
			OTHER (3)	
		(1)	Thomas collection.	1.40
		(2)*	Palmer (SED 304).	1.26
		(3)	Palmer (SED 172).	1.16
340	Ee	O.	hENRICVS REX III'	
		R.	IOh SON SEI TED	
			OTHER (1)	
		(1)*	BM. Steppingley hoard (1912), 48.	1.49
341	Ff	O.	hENRICVS REX [	
		R.	IOh [ ] SEN TED	
			OTHER (1)	
		(1)*	BM. Steppingley hoard (1912), 49.	1.55
342	Gg	O.	hENRICVS REX III [ ] Pellet in S.	
		R.	IOh' S:ON SEN T:ED	
			OTHER (2)	
		(1)	Palmer (SED 459).	1.37
		(2)*	Eaglen (B907).	1.30
343	Hh	O.	hENRICVS REX III. [ ]	
		R.	IOh S.ON SEN T·ED Pellet or colon(?) after first S.	
			OTHER (1)	

		(1)*	Palmer (SED 777).	1.23
			Class Vh (central fleur of three pellets)	
344	Aa	O.	hENRICVS REX III'	
		R.	IOh S[ ] SEN TED	
			Inner circle of eight pellets per segment.	
			OTHER (2)	
		(1)	Palmer (SED 546).	1.38
		(2)*	Eaglen (B586). Glendining, 7 Oct. 1986, 1867 (1/3). Pierced and chipped.	[1.19]
345	Bb	O.	]ENRICVS RE[	
		R.	IOh SON SE[ ] TED	
			Inner circle of seven pellets per segment.	
			OTHER (1)	
		(1)*	BM. Steppingley hoard (1912). Ex Lawrence collection.	1.30
346	Cc	O.	hENRICVS REX III'	
		R.	IOh' SON SEI TED	
			Pelleted 'S's on O. and R.	
			OTHER (2)	
		(1)*	Palmer (SED 430).	1.36
		(2)	*SCBI* Scottish Museums (Glasgow) 686.	1.25
347	Dd	O.	hENRICVS REX III'	
		R.	IOH ON·S EI[H] TED	
			OTHER (1)	
		(1)*	Palmer (SED 416).	1.46
			Class Vi (crude version of Vh)	
348	Aa	O.	hENRICVS REX III[	
			Reading uncertain.	
			ION S.ON S[ ] [ ]D	
			OTHER (1)	
		(1)*	Eaglen (B110). Ex Lawrence 441 (illustrated).	1.14

HENRY III/EDWARD I

Class VI (realistic curls; Lombardic 'N's)

349 Aa O. hENRICVS REX III'·
R. IOH ONS EIh TED

COL (1916 coins)

* Illustration: Eaglen (B251). 1.41

OTHER (1)

(1) BM. Ex Lawrence collection. 1.34

EDWARD I (1272–1307)

Class VII (realistic face and curls)

350 Aa O. hENRICVS R[ ] III'
R. IOh' O[N]S ENT EDM

OTHER (2)

(1)* Palmer (SED 602). 1.44

(2) BM. Ex Lawrence collection. 1.31

351 Bb O.]VS REX III'
R.]EDM
The attribution to 'IOhS' is not beyond doubt.

OTHER (1)

(1)* BM. Mrs A. N. Mann gift (1930). 1.32

Ioce

352 Aa O. hENRICVS REX III'
R. IOCE ONS ENT [EDM]

OTHER (1)

(1)* BM. Ex Lawrence collection. 1.35

353 Bb O. hENRICVS REX III'
R. IOCE ONS E[I]T EDM

OTHER (2)

(1) Palmer (SED 532). 1.34

(2)* Eaglen (B731). Baldwin (1988). 1.08

BIBLIOGRAPHY

A. Primary sources (manuscript)

Bodleian Library, Oxford
Bodley MS 240
Bodley MS 297
British Library, London
BL Add. MS 14847 (White Register)
BL Add. MS 14848 (Curtey's Register I)
BL Cotton MS Julius Ai
BL Hargrave MS 313
BL Harl. MS 447
BL Harl. MS 638 (Werketone Register)
BL Harl. MS 645 (Kempe Register)
BL Harl. MS 743 (Lakenheath Register)
BL Harl. MS 1005 (White Book)
BL Harl. MS 3977
Cambridge, University Library
MS Ff ii. 29 (Red Vestry Register)
MS Ff ii. 33 (Register Sacristarum/Sacrist's Register)
MS Mm iv.19 (Feudal Book of Abbot Baldwin)
Vatican MS Reg. Lat. 12

B. Primary sources (printed)

Anecdota Oxoniensa, ed. J. R. H. Weaver (Oxford, 1908).

Anglo-Saxon Chronicle. A Collaborative Edition (ed. D. Dumville and S. Keynes); III. *MS A*, ed. J. M. Bately (Woodbridge, 1986).

The Anglo-Saxon Chronicle, ed. and trans. G. H. Garmonsway, 2nd edn (London, 1955).

Anglo-Saxon Wills, ed D. Whitelock (Cambridge, 1930).

Anglo-Saxon Writs, ed. F. E. Harmer (Manchester, 1952).

Bede, *Historia Ecclesiastica Gentis Anglorum*, ed. B. Colgrave and R. A. B. Mynors (Oxford, 1969).

Calendar of Liberate Rolls.

Calendar of Patent Rolls.

Chronica Johannis de Oxenedes, ed. H. Ellis (RS 13, 1859).

The Chronicle of Æthelweard, ed. and trans. A. Campbell (London, 1962).

The Chronicle of Bury St Edmunds 1212–1301, ed. and trans. A. Gransden (London, 1964).
The Chronicle of the Election of Hugh Abbot of Bury St. Edmunds and later Bishop of Ely, ed. and trans. R. M. Thomson (Oxford, 1974).
Corolla Sancti Eadmundi, The Garland of St Edmund, ed. F. Hervey (London, 1907).
Close Rolls of the Reign of Henry III Preserved in the Public Record Office.
Curia Regis Rolls of the Reigns of Richard I and John Preserved in the Public Record Office, ed. C. T. Flower, 7 vols (London, 1923–35).
The Customary of the Benedictine Abbey of Bury St. Edmunds in Suffolk, ed. A. Gransden, Henry Bradshaw Society 99 (London, 1973).
The De Moneta of Nicholas Oresme and English Mint Documents, ed. and trans. C. Johnson (London, 1956).
Dialogus de Scaccario. De Necessariis Observantiis Scaccarii Dialogus, qui vulgo dicitur Dialogus de Scaccario, ed. and trans. C. Johnson, revised edn with corrections by F. E. L. Carter and D. E. Greenway (Oxford, 1983).
Domesday Book: Huntingdonshire, ed. J. Morris and S. Harvey (Chichester, 1975).
Domesday Book: Suffolk, ed. A. Rumble, 2 vols (Chichester, 1986).
The Early Charters of Eastern England, ed. C. R. Hart (Leicester, 1966).
English Historical Documents I *c. 500–1042*, ed. D. Whitelock, 2nd edn (London and New York, 1979).
English Historical Documents II *1042–1189*, ed. D. C. Douglas and G. W. Greenaway, 2nd edn (London, 1981).
Feudal Documents from the Abbey of Bury St Edmunds, ed. D. C. Douglas (London, 1932).
Gervase of Canterbury, *Opera Historica*, ed. W. Stubbs, 2 vols (RS 73, 1879–80).
Gesta Regis Henrici Secundi Benedicti Abbatis, ed. W. Stubbs, 2 vols (RS 49, 1867).
Gesta Stephani, ed. K. R. Potter and R. H. C. Davis (Oxford, 1976).
The Great Roll of the Pipe for the Seventh Year of the Reign of King John Michaelmas 1205, ed. S. Smith, Pipe Roll Society new series 19 (London, 1941).
The Great Roll of the Pipe for the Third and Fourth Years of the Reign of King Richard the First Mich. 1191 and Mich. 1192 (Pipe Rolls 37 and 38), ed. D. M. Stenton, Pipe Roll Society new series 2 (1926).
The History of King Eadmund the Martyr [Corpus Christi College, Oxford, MS 197], ed. F. Hervey (Oxford, 1929).
Jocelin of Brakelond, *The Chronicle of Jocelin of Brakelond*, ed. and trans. H. E. Butler (London, 1949).
The Kalendar of Abbot Samson of Bury St Edmunds and Related Documents, ed. R. H. C. Davis, Camden Society 3rd series 84 (London, 1954).
Liber Eliensis, ed. E. O. Blake, Camden Society 3rd series 92 (London, 1962).
Matthew Paris, *Chronica Majora*, ed. H. R. Luard, 7 vols (RS 57, 1872–83).
Memorials of St Edmund's Abbey, ed. T. Arnold, 3 vols (RS 96, 1890–6).
The Peterborough Chronicle 1070–1154, ed. C. Clark, 2nd edn (Oxford, 1970).
The Pinchbeck Register, ed. F. Hervey, 2 vols (Brighton, 1925).
Ralph of Diceto, *Radulfi de Diceto Decani Lundoniensis Opera Historica*, ed. W. Stubbs, 2 vols (RS 68, 1876).
Reading Abbey Cartularies I, ed. B. R. Kemp, Camden Society 4th series 31 (London, 1986).

The Red Book of the Exchequer, ed. H. Hall, 3 vols (RS 99, 1896).

Regesta Regum Anglo-Normannorum I *1066–1100*, ed. H. W. C. Davis and R. J. Whitwell (Oxford, 1913).

Regesta Regum Anglo-Normannorum II *1100–1135*, ed. C. Johnson and H. W. C. Davis (Oxford, 1956).

Regesta Regum Anglo-Normannorum III *1135–1154*, ed. H. A. Cronne and R. H. C. Davis (Oxford, 1968).

Robert of Torigny, *Chronica Roberti de Torigneio, Abbatis Monasterii Sancti Michaelis in Periculo Maris*, ed. R. Howlett, *Chronicles of the Reigns of Stephen, Henry II and Richard I*, 4 vols (RS 82, 1884–90), IV, pp. 81–315.

Roger of Howden, *Chronica Magistri Rogeri de Houedene*, ed. W. Stubbs, 4 vols (RS 51, 1868–71).

Roger of Wendover, *Rogeri de Wendover Chronica sive Flores Historiarum*, ed. H. O. Coxe, 5 vols (London, 1841–4).

Rotuli Chartarum in Turri Londinensi Asservati, 1199–1216, ed. T. D. Hardy (London, 1837).

Rotuli Litterarum Clausarum in Turri Londinensi Asservati, 1204–1227, ed. T. D. Hardy, 2 vols (London, 1833–44).

Rotuli Litterarum Patentum in Turri Londinensi Asservati, 1201–1216, ed. T. D. Hardy (London, 1835).

Thomas Rymer, *Foedera, Conventiones, Litterae et cuiuscunque Generis Acta Publica*, ed. A. Clarke and F. Holbrooke, 7 vols (London, 1816–19).

William Dugdale, *Monasticon Anglicanum*, ed. J. Caley, H. Ellis and B. Bandinel, 7 vols (London, 1817–30).

William of Jumièges, *Gesta Normannorum Ducum*, ed. J. Marx (Rouen, 1914).

William of Malmesbury, *De Gestis Pontificum Anglorum*, ed. N. E. S. A. Hamilton (RS 52, 1870).

William of Malmesbury, *De Gestis Regum Anglorum libri quinque*, ed. W. Stubbs, 2 vols (RS 90, 1887–9).

William of Malmesbury, *Historia Novella*, ed. and trans. K. R. Potter (London, 1967).

William of Newburgh, *Historia Rerum Anglicarum*, ed. R. Howlett, in *Chronicles of the Reigns of Stephen, Henry II and Richard I*, 4 vols (RS 82, London, 1884–90), I, pp. 1–408; II, pp. 409–53.

William Thorne, *William Thorne's Chronicles of St Augustine's Abbey Canterbury*, ed. and trans. A. H. Davis (Oxford, 1934).

C. Secondary sources

Allen, D. (F.), 1938–41. 'Treasure Trove, 1933–9. 2. Hornchurch, Essex, 1938', *BNJ* 23 (1938–41), pp. 274–80.

—— 1951. *A Catalogue of English Coins in the British Museum. The Cross-and-Crosslets ('Tealby') Type of Henry II* (London, 1951).

Allen, M. (R.), 1979. 'The Carlisle and Durham mints in the Short Cross period', *BNJ* 49 (1979), pp. 42–55.

—— 1989. 'The provision and use of Short Cross V dies', *BNJ* 59 (1989), pp. 46–76.
—— 1994. 'The Durham mint before Boldon Book', *Anglo-Norman Durham*, ed. D. Rollason, M. Harvey and M. Prestwich (Woodbridge, 1994), pp. 381–98.
—— 1995. 'The date of King John's conference of moneyers', *BNJ* 65 (1995), pp. 223–4.
—— 1999a. 'Documentary evidence for the output, profits and expenditure of the Bury St Edmunds mint', *BNJ* 69 (1999), pp. 210–13.
—— 1999b. 'Mint output in the English recoinage of 1247–1250', *BNJ* 69 (1999), pp. 207–10.
—— 2001a. 'The chronology, mints and moneyers of the English coinage, 1180–1247', in J. P. Mass, *The J. P. Mass Collection: English Short Cross Coins, 1180–1247*, *SCBI* 56 (London, 2001), pp. 1–12.
—— 2001b. 'Ecclesiastical mints in thirteenth-century England', in *Thirteenth Century England VIII: Proceedings of the Durham Conference 1999*, ed. M. Prestwich, R. Britnell and R. Frame (Woodbridge, 2001), pp. 113–22.
—— 2001c. 'Hoards and the circulation of the Short Cross coinage', in J. P. Mass, *The J.P. Mass Collection*, pp. 112–30.
—— 2001d. 'The volume of the English currency, 1158–1470', *EcHR*[2] 54 (2001), pp. 595–611.
—— 2002. 'English coin hoards, 1158–1544', *BNJ* 72 (2002), pp. 24–84.
—— 2003. *The Durham Mint*, BNS Special Publication 4 (London, 2003).
—— 2004a. 'The archbishop of York's mint after the Norman Conquest', *Northern History* 41 (2004), pp. 21–34.
—— 2004b. 'Medieval English die-output', *BNJ* 74 (2004), pp. 39–49.
Alliss, G. and Seaby, P. J., 1984. 'King Stephen's mint of 'Eie'', *SCMB* 791/2 (July-Aug. 1984), pp. 182–4.
Andrew, W. J., 1901. 'A numismatic history of the reign of Henry I', *NC*[4] 1 (1901), pp. 1–502.
—— 1903–4. 'Buried treasure: some traditions, records and facts', *BNJ* 1 (1903–4), pp. 9–59.
—— 1913. 'A numismatic history of the reign of Stephen, A.D. 1135–1154 [part 2]', *BNJ* 10 (1913), pp. 43–67.
Appleby, J. T., 1965. *England without Richard 1189–1199* (London, 1965).
Archibald, M. M., 1984. 'Coins', *English Romanesque Art, 1066–1200*, ed. G. Zarneki *et al.* (London, 1984), pp. 320–41.
—— 1991. 'Dating Stephen's first type', *BNJ* 61 (1991), pp. 9–21.
—— 2004. 'The German connection: German influences on the late Anglo-Saxon and Norman coinages in their English context', *Fundamenta Historiae: Geschichte im Spiegel der Numismatik und ihrer Nachbarwissenschaften; Festschrift für Niklot Klüssendorf zum 60. Geburtstag am 10. Februar 2004*, ed. R. Cunz with R. Polley and A. Röpcke (Hanover, 2004), pp. 131–50.
Archibald, M. M. and Cook, B. J., 2001. *English Medieval Coin Hoards. I: Cross and Crosslets, Short Cross and Long Cross Hoards*, British Museum Occasional Paper 87 (London, 2001).
Ballard, A., 1904. *The Domesday Boroughs* (Oxford, 1904).

Barlow, F., 1979. *The English Church, 1066–1154* (London and New York, 1979).
—— 1997. *Edward the Confessor,* rev. edn (New Haven and London, 1997).
—— 2000. *William Rufus,* 2nd edn (New Haven and London, 2000).
Battely, J., 1745. *Antiquitates Sancti Edmundi Burgi ad annum MCCLXXII* (Oxford, 1745).
Biddle, M., ed., 1976. *Winchester in the Early Middle Ages. An Edition and Discussion of the Winton Domesday,* Winchester Studies 1 (Oxford, 1976).
Blackburn, M. (A. S.), 1987. 'The Anglo-Norman coins in the Fitzwilliam Museum', *BNJ* 57 (1987), pp. 108–13.
—— 1989. 'The Ashdown (Essex) hoard and the currency of the Southern Danelaw in the late ninth century', *BNJ* 59 (1989), pp. 13–38.
—— 1990. 'Coinage and currency under Henry I: a review', *Anglo-Norman Studies* 13 (1990), pp. 49–81.
—— 1994. 'Coinage and currency', *The Anarchy of King Stephen's Reign,* ed. E. King (Oxford, 1994), pp. 145–205.
—— 2000. '*Metheltun* not *Medeshamstede*: an Anglo-Saxon mint at Melton Mowbray rather than Peterborough Abbey', *BNJ* 70 (2000), pp. 143–5.
Blackburn, M. and Pagan, H., 2003. 'The St Edmund Coinage in the light of a parcel from a hoard of St Edmund pennies', *BNJ* 72 (2003), pp. 1–14.
Blair, P. H., 1977. *An Introduction to Anglo-Saxon England,* 2nd edn (Cambridge, 1977).
—— 1985. 'Secular minster churches in Domesday Book', in *Domesday Book. A Reassessment,* ed. P. Sawyer (London, 1985), pp. 104–43.
Blunt, C. E., 1960. 'Ecclesiastical coinage in England (Part 1. To the Norman Conquest)', *NC*^{6} 20 (1960), pp. i-xvii.
—— 1961. 'Ecclesiastical coinage in England (Part 2. After the Norman Conquest)', *NC*^{7} 1 (1961), pp. i-xviii.
—— 1967–9. 'The St Edmund Memorial coinage', *PSIA* 31 (1967–9), pp. 234–55.
—— 1971. 'The Crowned Bust coinage of Edmund, 939–946', *BNJ* 40 (1971), pp. 17– 21.
—— 1972. 'The origins of the mints of Hertford and Maldon', *BNJ* 41 (1972), pp. 21–6.
—— 1974. 'The coinage of Athelstan, 924–939: a survey', *BNJ* 42 (1974), pp. 35–158.
Blunt, C. E. and Brand, J. D., 1970. 'Mint output of Henry III', *BNJ* 39 (1970), pp. 61–6.
Blunt, C. E. and Dolley, R. H. M., 1952–4. 'The Chester (1950) hoard', *BNJ* 27 (1952–4), pp. 125–60.
Blunt, C. E., Stewart, B. H. I. H. and Lyon, C. S. S., 1989. *Coinage in Tenth-Century England from Edward the Elder to Edgar's Reform* (Oxford, 1989).
Boon, G. C., 1986. *Welsh Hoards 1979–1981* (Cardiff, 1986).
—— 1988. *Coins of the Anarchy, 1135–54* (Cardiff, 1988).
Brand, J. D., 1964. 'Some Short Cross questions', *BNJ* 33 (1964), pp. 57–69.
—— 1971. 'The Shrewsbury mint, 1249–1250', *Mints, Dies and Currency: Essays Dedicated to the Memory of Albert Baldwin,* ed. R. A. G. Carson (London, 1971), pp. 129–50.

—— 1984. *Periodic Change of Type in the Anglo-Saxon and Norman periods* (Rochester, 1984).

—— 1994. *The English Coinage, 1180–1247: Money, Mints and Exchanges*, BNS Special Publication 1 (London, 1994).

Brand, J. D. and Dolley, R. H. M., 1963. 'Two 'new' Yorkshire hoards of Short Cross pennies', *BNJ* 32 (1963), pp. 94–6.

Brand, J. D. and Duplessy, J., 1977. 'A parcel from the Montpellier (1934) hoard', *BNJ* 47 (1977), pp. 77–91.

Brand, J. D. and Elmore Jones, F., 1966. 'The emergency mint of Wilton in 1180', *BNJ* 35 (1966), pp. 116–19.

Brett, M., 1975. *The English Church under Henry I* (Oxford, 1975).

Brooke, G. C., 1914. 'A find of Long Cross pennies at Slype (West Flanders)', *NC*[4] 14 (1914), pp. 256–9.

—— 1916. *A Catalogue of English Coins in the British Museum. The Norman Kings*, 2 vols (London, 1916).

—— 1927. 'The first coinage, or "Tealby" Type, of Henry II', *NC*[5] 7 (1927), pp. 313–41.

—— 1950. *English Coins*, 3rd edn (London, 1950)

Brown, I. D., 1997. 'Active mints and the survival of Norman coins', *BNJ* 67 (1997), pp. 1–10.

Cam, H. M., 1963. *Liberties and Communities in Medieval England*, rev. edn (London, 1963).

Campbell, J., 1975. 'Observations on English government from the tenth to twelfth centuries', *TRHS*[5] 25 (1975), pp. 39–54.

—— 1982. *The Anglo-Saxons*, ed. J. Campbell (Oxford, 1982).

Carlyon-Britton, P. W. P., 1905. 'Edward the Confessor and his coins', *NC*[4] 5 (1905), pp. 179–205.

—— 1912. 'A numismatic history of the reigns of William I and II (1066–1100) [part 2]', *BNJ* 9 (1912), pp. 129–43.

—— 1927–8. 'Some coins of Henry I', *BNJ* 19 (1927–8), pp. 93–107.

Carson, R. A. G., 1947., 'The Clifton (Lancashire) find of Short-Cross pennies', *NC*[6] 7 (1947), pp. 80–2.

Carter, A., 1978. 'The Anglo-Saxon origins of Norwich', *ASE* 7 (1978), pp. 175–204.

Challis, C. E. (ed.), 1992. *A New History of the Royal Mint* (Cambridge, 1992).

Chew, H. M., 1932. *The English Ecclesiastical Tenants-in-Chief and Knight Service* (Oxford, 1932).

Chibnall, M., 1986. *Anglo-Norman England 1066–1166* (Oxford, 1986).

Clarke, D. T.- D., *et al.*, 1974. 'The 1969 Colchester hoard', *BNJ* 44 (1974), pp. 39–61.

Clarke, R. R., 1960. *East Anglia* (London, 1960).

Conte, W. J. and Archibald, M. M., 1990. 'Five round halfpennies of Henry I: a further case for reappraisal of the chronology of types', *NCirc* 98 (1990), pp. 232–6.

Corbett, W. J. (ed.), 1926. *The Cambridge Medieval History*. V (Cambridge, 1926).

Craig, J., 1953. *The Mint* (Cambridge, 1953).

Crafter, T. C. R., 1998. 'A re-examination of the classification and chronology of the *Cross-and-Crosslets* type of Henry II', *BNJ* 68 (1998), pp. 47–63.

Cribb, J. (ed.), 1986. *Money from Cowrie Shells to Credit Cards* (London, 1986).
Cronne, H. A., 1970. *The Reign of Stephen, 1135–54: Anarchy in England* (London, 1970).
Crump, C. G. and Johnson, C., 1913. 'Tables of bullion coined under Edward I, II and III', *NC*[4] 13 (1913), pp. 200–45.
Danson, E. W., 1968. 'The Nottingham find of 1880: a Stephen hoard re-examined', *BNJ* 37 (1968), pp. 43–64.
Darby, H. C., 1971. *The Domesday Geography of England. Eastern England*, 3rd edn (Cambridge, 1971).
—— 1977. *Domesday England* (Cambridge, 1977).
Darby, H. C. and Campbell, E. M. J. (eds), 1962. *The Domesday Geography of England. South-East England*, (Cambridge, 1962)
Darby, H. C. and Maxwell, I. S. (eds), 1962. *The Domesday Geography of England. Northern England* (Cambridge, 1962)
Darby, H. C. and Terrett, I. B. (eds), 1971. *The Domesday Geography of England. Midland England*, 2nd edn (Cambridge, 1971).
Darby, H. C. and Finn, R. W. (eds), 1967. *The Domesday Geography of England. South-West England* (Cambridge, 1967).
Davis, H. W. C., 1909. 'The Liberties of Bury St. Edmunds', *EHR* 24 (1909), pp. 417–31.
Davis, R. H. C., 1967. *King Stephen, 1135–1154* (London, 1967).
Davis, R. L., 1977. 'Class II coins of the Long Cross coinage, 1247–1248', *BNJ* 47 (1977), pp. 138–41.
Dawson, A. and Mayhew, N., 1987. 'A Continental find including Tealby pennies', *BNJ* 57 (1987), pp. 113–18.
Dolley, (R. H.) M., 1955–7a. 'A note on the mints of Sudbury and Southwark at the end of the reign of Æthelred II', *BNJ* 28 (1955–7), pp. 264–9.
—— 1955–7b. 'The Stockbridge Down find of Anglo-Saxon coins', *BNJ* 28 (1955–7), pp. 283–7.
—— 1961. *Anglo-Saxon Coins. Studies presented to F. M. Stenton*, ed. R. H. M. Dolley (London, 1961).
—— 1964. *Anglo-Saxon Pennies* (British Museum, 1964).
—— 1966. *The Norman Conquest and the English Coinage* (London, 1966).
—— 1968. 'The Anglo-Norman coins in the Uppsala Cabinet', *BNJ* 37 (1968), pp. 29–34.
Dolley, R. H. M. and Elmore Jones, F., 1958–9. 'A parcel of Cross-and-Crosslets pence from the Tealby find', *BNJ* 29 (1958–9), pp. 82–6.
Dolley, R. H. M. and Metcalf, D. M., 1961. 'The reform of the English Coinage under Eadgar', *Anglo-Saxon Coins. Studies presented to F. M. Stenton*, ed. R. H. M. Dolley (London, 1961), pp. 136–68.
Douglas, D. C., 1999. *William the Conqueror*, rev. edn (New Haven and London, 1999).
Dumas, F. and Brand, J. D., 1971. 'The British coins in the Gisors (1970) hoard', *BNJ* 40 (1971), pp. 22–43.
Dunger, G. T., 1999. 'A First Hand penny of Æthelred II from the Abbey mint of Medehamstede, Peterborough', *NCirc* 107 (1999), p. 209.

Eaglen, R. J., 1998. 'The mint at Bury St Edmunds', *Medieval Art, Architecture, Archaeology and Economy at Bury St Edmunds*, ed. A. Gransden, British Archaeological Association Conference Transactions 20 (Leeds, 1998), pp. 111–21.

—— 1999. 'The mint of Huntingdon', *BNJ* 69 (1999), pp. 47–145.

—— 2001a. 'How rare is the Pyramid type of Edward the Confessor?', *NCirc* 109 (2001), pp. 309–10.

—— 2001b. 'The ranking of mints under Edward the Confessor by monetypes', *NCirc* 109 (2001), pp. 361–2.

—— 2003. 'Choice of mints for the Tealby issue', *NCirc* 111(2003), pp. 5–6.

Eaglen, R. J. and Grayburn, R., 2000. 'Gouged reverse dies in the Quatrefoil issue of Cnut', *BNJ* 70 (2000), pp. 12–37.

Eaglen, R. J., Mitchell, P. D. and Pagan, H. E., 2001. 'Coin tickets in the British Hammered series', *BNJ* 71 (2001), pp. 136–57.

Ekwall, E., 1960. *The Concise Oxford Dictionary of Place-Names*, 4th edn (Oxford, 1960).

Ellis, H., 1833. *General Introduction to Domesday Book* II (London, 1833).

Elmore Jones, F., 1945–8. 'The last Short-Cross issue of Henry III (class 8)', *BNJ* 25 (1945–8), pp. 286–90.

—— 1955–7. 'Stephen type VII', *BNJ* 28 (1955–7), pp. 537–54.

—— 1966a. 'A parcel of 'Tealby' type pennies from France', *NCirc* 74 (1966), pp. 125–6.

—— 1966b. 'A suspicious looking penny of Stephen type VII', *NCirc* 74 (1966), p. 204.

—— 1975. 'Two suspect coins of Stephen', *SCMB* 681 (May 1975), pp. 151–3.

Elmore Jones, F. and Blunt, C. E., 1967. 'A remarkable parcel of Norman pennies in Moscow', *BNJ* 36 (1967), pp. 86–92.

Evans, J. 1869. 'On a hoard of coins found on Tower Hill', *NC*[2] 9 (1869), pp. 247–56.

Fernie, E. C., 1998. 'The Romanesque Church of Bury St Edmunds Abbey', *Medieval Art, Architecture, Archaeology and Economy at Bury St Edmunds*, ed. A. Gransden, British Archaeological Association Conference Transactions 20 (Leeds, 1998), pp. 1–15.

Finn, R. W., 1967. *Domesday Studies. The Eastern Counties* (London, 1967).

Forbes, J. S. and Dalladay, D. B., 1960–1. 'Composition of English silver coins (870–1300)', *BNJ* 30 (1960–1), pp. 82–7.

Fox, H. B. E. and Fox, S., 1909. 'Numismatic history of the reigns of Edward I, II and III [part 1]', *BNJ* 6 (1909), pp. 197–212.

—— 1910. 'Numismatic history of the reigns of Edward I, II and III [part 2]', *BNJ* 7 (1910), pp. 91–142.

Fox, H. B. E. and Shirley-Fox, J. S., 'Numismatic history of the reigns of Edward I, II, and III [part 5]', *BNJ* 10 (1913), pp. 95–123.

Freeman, A., 1985. *The Moneyer and the Mint in the Reign of Edward the Confessor, 1042–1066*, 2 vols, BAR 145 (Oxford, 1985).

Freeman, E. A., 1870–6. *The History of the Norman Conquest of England*, 2nd edn, 6 vols, (Oxford, 1870–6).

—— 1882. *The Reign of William Rufus and the Accession of Henry I*, 2 vols (Oxford, 1882).

Fryde, E. B., Greenaway, D. E., Porter, S. and Roy, I., 1986. *Handbook of British Chronology* (London, 1986).

Gage, J., 1838. *The History and Antiquities of Suffolk. Thingoe Hundred* (London, 1838).

Galbraith, V. H., 1925. 'The East Anglian See and the Abbey of Bury St Edmunds', *EHR* 40 (1925), pp. 222–8.

—— 1961. *The Making of Domesday Book* (London, 1961).

Garnett, G., 1986. 'Coronation and propaganda: some implications of the Norman claim to the throne of England in 1066', *TRHS*[5] 36 (1986), pp. 91–116.

Gauthiez, B., 1998. 'The planning of the town of Bury St Edmunds: a probable Norman origin', *Medieval Art, Architecture, Archaeology and Economy at Bury St Edmunds*, ed. A. Gransden, British Archaeological Association Conference Transactions 20 (Leeds, 1998), pp. 81–97.

Gittoes, G. P. and Mayhew, N. J., 1983. 'Short Cross sterlings from the Rotenfels hoard', *BNJ* 53 (1983), pp. 19–28.

Golding, C., 1868. *The Coinage of Suffolk* (London, 1868).

Gomm, J. D., 1985a. 'Henry I chronology: the case for reappraisal', *SCMB* 799 (April 1985), p.105–7.

—— 1985b. [Letter to the Editor], *SCMB* 805 (Nov. 1985), p. 365.

Gottfried, R. S., 1982. *Bury St Edmunds and the Urban Crisis: 1290–1539* (Princeton, 1982).

Gransden, A., 1974. *Historical Writing in England c. 550 to c. 1307* (London, 1974).

—— 1975. 'The Democratic Movement in the Abbey of Bury St Edmunds in the late twelfth and early thirteenth centuries', *Journal of Ecclesiastical History* 26 (1975), pp. 25–39.

—— 1981. 'Baldwin, abbot of Bury St Edmunds, 1065–1097', *Proceedings of the Battle Conference on Anglo-Norman Studies* 4 (1981) pp. 65–76, 187–95.

—— 1985. 'The legends and traditions concerning the origins of the Abbey of Bury St Edmunds', *EHR* 100 (1985), pp. 1–24.

—— 1991a. 'The Abbey of Bury St Edmunds and national politics', *Monastic Studies*, II, *Proceedings of the 1990 Bangor Conference on Monastic Studies*, ed. J. Loades (Bangor, 1991), pp. 67–86.

—— 1991b. 'The question of the consecration of St Edmund's Church', *Church and Chronicle in the Middle Ages. Essays presented to John Taylor*, ed. I. Wood and G. A. Loud (London, 1991), pp. 59–86.

—— 1994. 'The alleged incorruption of the body of St Edmund, king and martyr', *Antiquaries Journal* 74 (1994), pp. 135–68.

—— 1995. 'The composition and authority of the *De Miraculis Sancti Eadmundi* attributed to 'Hermann the Archdeacon'', *Journal of Medieval Latin* 5 (1995), pp. 1–52.

Green, J. A., 1986. *The Government of England under Henry I* (Cambridge, 1986).

Grierson, P., 1961. 'Sterling', *Anglo-Saxon Coins. Studies presented to F. M. Stenton*, ed. R. H. M. Dolley (London, 1961), pp. 266–83.

—— 1985. 'Domesday Book, the geld *de moneta* and *monetagium*: a forgotten minting reform', *BNJ* 55 (1985), pp. 84–94.

—— 1987. 'The monetary system under William I', *Domesday Book: Studies* (London, 1987), pp. 75–9.

Grierson, P. and Blackburn, M., 1986. *Medieval European Coinage, with a catalogue of the coins in the Fitzwilliam Museum, Cambridge*, I (Cambridge, 1986).

Grinsell, L. V., 1973. *The Bath Mint: An Historical Outline* (London, 1973).

Grueber, H. A., 1903. 'A find of silver coins at Colchester', *NC*[4] (1903), pp. 111–76.

—— 1912. 'Palmer's Green hoard', *NC*[4] (1912) pp. 70–97.

Harris, E. J., 1962. 'Debasement of the coinage', *SCMB* 524 (Jan. 1962), pp. 5–7.

—— 1983–8. 'The moneyers of the Norman kings and the types they are known to have struck', *SCMB* 773 (Jan. 1983), pp. 9–11; 774 (Feb. 1983), pp. 33–5; 778 (June 1983), pp. 149–52; 781 (Sept. 1983), pp. 228–30; 784 (Dec. 1983), pp. 314–16; 785 (Jan. 1984), pp. 4–6; 787 (March 1984), pp. 68–70; 794 (Oct. 1984), pp. 246–8; 796 (Dec. 1984), pp. 314–16; 797 (Jan.- Feb. 1985), pp. 15–17; 796 (March 1985), pp. 61–3; 800 (May 1985), pp. 149–52; 803 (Sept. 1985), pp. 280–2; 806 (Dec. 1985), pp. 409–12; 807 (Jan.- Feb. 1986), pp. 7–9; 808 (April 1986), pp. 99–100; 811 (June 1986), pp. 168–70; 814 (Oct. 1986), pp. 293–4; 816 (Dec. 1986), pp. 372–5; 817 (Jan.- Feb. 1987), pp. 5–7; 819 (April 1987), pp. 88–91; 822 (July–Aug. 1987), pp. 188–90; 824 (Oct. 1987), pp. 270–2; 825 (Nov. 1987), pp. 306–8; 826 (Dec. 1987), pp. 342–5; 828 (March 1988), pp. 38–41.

Harvey, S., 1967. 'Royal revenue and Domesday terminology', *EcHR*[2] 20 (1967), pp. 221–8.

Hawkins, E., 1842–3. 'An account of coins and treasure found in Cuerdale', *NC*[1] 5 (1842–3), pp. 1–48.

—— 1887. *The Silver Coins of England*, 3rd edn, revised by R. L. Kenyon (London, 1887).

Heywood, N., 1903–4. 'The first coinage of Henry II', *BNJ* 1 (1903–4), pp. 97–111.

Hildebrand, B. E., 1881. *Anglosachsiska mynt i Svenska Kongliga Myntkabinettet funna i Sveriges jord*, 2nd edn (Stockholm, 1881).

Hill, D., 1981. *An Atlas of Anglo-Saxon England* (Oxford, 1981).

Hollister, C. W., 2001. *Henry I* (New Haven and London, 2001).

Houghton, B., 1970. *Saint Edmund – King and Martyr* (Lavenham, 1970).

Howell, M., 1962. *Regalian Right in Medieval England* (London, 1962).

—— 1982. 'Abbatial vacancies in the divided *mensa* in medieval England', *Journal of Ecclesiastical History* 33 (1982), pp. 173–92.

Hurnard, N. D., 1949. 'The Anglo-Norman franchises', *EHR* 64 (1949), pp. 289–327.

James, M. R., 1895. *On the Abbey of S. Edmund at Bury* (Cambridge, 1895).

—— 1930. *Suffolk and Norfolk* (London, 1930).

Jonsson, K., 1975–6. 'Fyndet från Smiss i Tingstäde Sn på Gotland', *Nordisk Numismatisk Årsskrift* 1975–6, pp. 66–82.

—— 1987. *The New Era. The Reformation of the Late Anglo-Saxon Coinage*, Commentationes de Nummis Saeculorum IX–XI in Suecia Repertis, new series 1 (Stockholm and London, 1987).

Keary, C. F., 1887–93. *A Catalogue of English Coins in the British Museum. Anglo-Saxon Series*, 2 vols (London, 1887–93).

Kenny, M., 1989–90. 'The Kilmaine hoard: silver pennies, mainly English Short Cross of Henry III, deposited c.1240', *Journal of the Galway Archaeological and Historical Society* 42 (1989–90), pp. 87–113.

Keynes, S., 1978. 'An interpretation of the Pacs, Pax and Paxs pennies', *ASE* 7 (1978), pp. 165–73.

Knowles, D., 1948. *The Religious Orders in England* (Cambridge, 1948).

—— 1966. *The Monastic Order in England. A History of its Development from the times of St Dunstan to the Fourth Lateran Council, 940–1216*, 2nd edn (Cambridge, 1966).

Knowles, D., Brooke, C. N. L. and London, V. C. M., 2001. *The Heads of Religious Houses: England and Wales, 940–1216*, 2nd edn (Cambridge, 2001).

Lawrence, L. A., 1897, 'On a hoard of Short-Cross pennies', *NC*[3] 17 (1897), pp. 235–8.

—— 1912. 'The Long-Cross coinage of Henry III and Edward I [part 1]', *BNJ* 9 (1912), pp. 145–79.

—— 1913. 'The Long-Cross coinage of Henry III and Edward I [part 2]'; *BNJ* 10 (1913), pp. 69–93.

—— 1915a. 'The Long-Cross coinage of Henry III and Edward I [part 3]'; *BNJ* 11 (1915), pp. 101–19.

—— 1915b. 'The Short-Cross Coinage, 1180 to 1247', *BNJ* 11 (1915), pp. 59–100.

—— 1918. 'On the first coinage of Henry II', *BNJ* 14 (1918), pp. 13–37.

—— 1922. 'On a hoard of coins chiefly of King Stephen', *NC*[5] 2 (1922), pp. 49–90.

Lawrence, L. A. and Brooke, G. C., 1914. 'The Steppingley find of English coins', *NC*[4] 14 (1914), pp. 60–76.

Lawson, M. K., 1982. 'Edward the Confessor's England', *The Anglo-Saxons*, ed. J. Campbell (Oxford, 1982) pp. 226–7.

Lewis, J. M., 1970. 'A Short Cross hoard from Wrexham', *BNJ* 39 (1970), pp. 19–23.

Lindsay, J., 1842. *A View of the Coinage of the Heptarchy* (London, 1842).

Lobel, M. D., 1935. *The Borough of Bury St. Edmunds* (Oxford, 1935).

Loyn, H. R., 1961. 'Boroughs and mints, A.D. 900–1066', *Anglo-Saxon Coins. Studies presented to F. M. Stenton*, ed. R. H. M. Dolley (London, 1961), pp. 122–35.

—— 1984. *The Governance of Anglo-Saxon England, 500–1087* (London, 1984).

Lyon, (C.) S. (S.), 1971. 'Variations in currency in Late Anglo-Saxon England', *Mints, Dies and Currency: Essays Dedicated to the Memory of Albert Baldwin*, ed. R. A. G. Carson (London, 1971), pp. 101–20.

—— 1976. 'Some problems in interpreting Anglo-Saxon Coinage', *ASE* 5 (1976), pp. 173–224.

—— 1989. 'Die estimation: some experiments with simulated samples of coinage', *BNJ* 59 (1989), pp. 1–12.

—— 1998. 'The 'Expanding Cross' type of Edward the Confessor and the Appledore (1997) hoard', *NCirc* 106 (1998), pp. 426–8.

Mack, R. P., 1966. 'Stephen and the Anarchy, 1135–1154', *BNJ* 35 (1966), pp. 38–112.

Madox, T., 1711. *History and Antiquities of the Exchequer of the Kings of England* (London, 1711).

Maitland, F. W., 1897. *Domesday Book and Beyond* (Cambridge, 1897).

Manville, H. E. and Robertson, T. J., 1986. *British Numismatic Auction Catalogues*, Encyclopædia of British Numismatics, I (London, 1986).

Martin, E., Pendleton, C. and Plouviez, J., 1997–9. 'Archaeology in Suffolk 1997' *PSIA* 39 (1997–9), pp. 209–45.

Mason, E., 1999. 'William Rufus and the Benedictine Order', *Anglo-Norman Studies* 21 (1999), pp. 113–44.

Mass, J. P., 2001. *The J. P. Mass Collection: English Short Cross Coins, 1180–1247*, *SCBI* 56 (London, 2001).

Mate, M., 1969. 'Coin dies under Edward I and II', *NC*[7] 9 (1969), pp. 207–18.

Metcalf, D. M., 1977. 'A survey of research into the pennies of the first three Edwards (1279–1344) and their continental imitations', in *Edwardian Monetary Affairs (1279–1344). A Symposium held in Oxford, August 1976*, ed. N. J. Mayhew, BAR 36 (Oxford, 1977), pp. 1–31.

—— 1981. 'Continuity and change in English monetary history *c.* 973–1086. Part 2', *BNJ* 51 (1981), pp. 52–90.

—— 1987. 'The taxation of moneyers under Edward the Confessor', *Domesday Studies: Papers Read at the Novocentenary Conference, Winchester, 1986*, ed. J. C. Holt (Woodbridge, 1987), pp. 279–93.

—— 1988. 'Notes on the PAXS type of William I', *Yorkshire Numismatist* 1 (1988), pp. 13–26.

Metcalf, D. M. and Northover, P., 2002. 'Sporadic debasement in the English coinage *c.*1009–1052', *NC* 162 (2002), pp. 217–36.

Moore, E. W., 1985. *The Fairs of Medieval England. An Introductory Study*, Pontifical Institute of Medieval Studies and Texts 72 (Toronto, 1985).

Mossop, H. R., 1970. *The Lincoln Mint c. 890–1279* (Newcastle upon Tyne, 1970).

Norgate, K., 1887. *England under the Angevin Kings*, 2 vols (London, 1887).

—— 1902. *John Lackland* (London, 1902).

—— 1912. *The Minority of Henry III* (London, 1912).

North, J. J., 1980. *English Hammered Coinage* I. *Early Anglo-Saxon to Henry III c.600–1272*, 2nd edn (London, 1980).

—— 1988. 'A re-examination of classes 7 and 8 of the Short Cross coinage', *BNJ* 58 (1988), pp. 25–39.

—— 1991. *English Hammered Coinage* II. *Edward I to Charles II, 1272–1662*, 3rd edn (London, 1991).

—— 1994. *English Hammered Coinage* I. *Early Anglo-Saxon to Henry III c.600–1272*, 3rd edn (London, 1994).

—— 1995. 'Some imitations and forgeries of the English and Irish Long Cross pence of Henry III', *BNJ* 65 (1995), pp. 83 -119.

Oman, C., 1931. *The Coinage of England* (Oxford, 1931).

Owles, E., 1970–2. 'Archaeology in Suffolk, 1972', *PSIA* 32 (1970–2), pp. 282–91.

Packe, A. E., 1893. 'The coinage of the Norman Kings', *NC*[3] 13 (1893), pp. 129–45.

Pagan, H. and Farthing, C., 2003. 'Members of the British Numismatic Society, 1903–2003', *BNJ* 73 (2003), pp. 213–67.

Page, W. (ed.), 1907. *The Victoria History of the County of Suffolk. Volume Two* (London, 1907).

Painter, G., 1949. *The Reign of King John* (Baltimore, 1949).

Petersson, H. B. A., 1969. *Anglo-Saxon Currency* (Lund, 1969).

Pevsner, N., 1974. *The Buildings of England. Suffolk*, 2nd edn, revised by E. Radcliffe (Penguin, 1974).

Pollock, F. and Maitland, F. W., 1895. *The History of English Law before the time of Edward I*, 2 vols (Cambridge, 1895).

Poole, A. L., 1955. *From Domesday Book to Magna Carta, 1087–1216*, 2nd edn (Oxford, 1955).

Power, E., 1941. *The Wool Trade in English Medieval History* (Oxford, 1941).

Powicke, M., 1947. *King Henry and the Lord Edward*, 2 vols (Oxford, 1947).

—— 1962. *The Thirteenth Century, 1216–1307*, 2nd edn (Oxford, 1962).

Prestwich, J. O., 1954. 'War and finance in the Anglo-Norman state', *TRHS*[5] 4 (1954), pp. 19–43.

Redstone, V. B., 1908. *Memorials of Old Suffolk* (London, 1908).

Reynolds, S., 1977. *An Introduction to the History of English Medieval Towns* (Oxford, 1977).

Ridyard, S. J., 1988. *The Royal Saints of Anglo-Saxon England* (Cambridge, 1988).

Robertson, A. J., 1939. *Anglo-Saxon Charters* (Cambridge, 1939).

Rollason, D. W., 1978. 'Lists of saints' resting-places in Anglo-Saxon England', *ASE* 7 (1978), pp. 61–93.

Round, J. H., 1895. *Feudal England: Historical Studies on the Eleventh and Twelfth Centuries* (London, 1895).

Ruding, R., 1840. *Annals of the Coinage of Great Britain and its Dependencies*, 3rd edn, 3 vols (London, 1840).

Sainthill, R., 1844. *An Olla Podrida: or, Scraps, Numismatic, Antiquarian, and Literary*, I (London, 1844).

Sawyer, P. H., 1968. *Anglo-Saxon Charters: An Annotated List and Bibliography* (London, 1968).

Sawyer, P. H. (ed.), 1985. *Domesday Book: A Reassessment* (London, 1985).

Seaby, P. J., 1955–7. 'The sequence of Anglo-Saxon coin types, 1030–1050', *BNJ* 28 (1955–7), pp. 111–46.

—— 1980. 'King Stephen and the interdict of 1148', *BNJ* 50 (1980), pp. 50–60.

—— 1984. 'King Stephen's mint of 'EIE'', *SCMB* 791–2 (July–Aug. 1984), pp. 182–4.

—— 1988. 'Henry I coin types: design characteristics and chronology', *Yorkshire Numismatist* 1 (1988), pp. 27–43.

Seaman, R. J., 1978. 'A re-examination of some hoards containing coins of Stephen', *BNJ* 48 (1978), pp. 58–72.

Skeat, W. W., 1913. *The Place-Names of Suffolk* (Cambridge, 1913).

Smart, V., 1985. 'The moneyers of St. Edmund', *hikuin* 11 (1985), pp. 83–90.

Spufford, P., 1988. *Money and its Use in Medieval Europe* (Cambridge, 1988).

Standard Catalogue of British Coins. Coins of England and the United Kingdom, 35th edn (London, 2000).

Statham, M., 1998. 'The medieval town of Bury St Edmunds', *Medieval Art, Architecture, Archaeology and Economy at Bury St Edmunds*, ed. A. Gransden,

British Archaeological Association Conference Transactions 20 (Leeds, 1998), pp. 98–110.

Stenton, F. M., 1971. *Anglo-Saxon England*, 3rd edn (Oxford, 1971).

Stephenson, C., 1933. *Borough and Town. A Study of Urban Origins in England* (Cambridge, 1933).

Stewart, (B. H.) I. (H.), 1955–7. 'The Stamford mint and the connexion with the abbot of Peterborough under Ethelred II', *BNJ* 28 (1955–7), pp. 106–10.

—— 1964. 'Second thoughts on medieval die output', *NC*[7] 4 (1964), pp. 293–303.

—— 1977. 'The Bournemouth find (*c.* 1901) of coins of Henry I', *NC*[7] 17 (1977), pp. 180–3.

—— 1979a. 'English coinage in the later years of John and the minority of Henry III. Part 1', *BNJ* 49 (1979), pp. 26–41.

—— 1979b. 'A hoard of English sterlings from the Aegean', *Coin Hoards* 5 (1979), pp. 141–4.

—— 1981. 'English coinage in the later years of John and the minority of Henry III. Part 2', *BNJ* 51 (1981), pp. 91–106.

—— 1986. 'A new mint for type VII of William I', *NCirc* 94 (1986), pp. 78–9.

—— 1989. 'King John's recoinage and the conference of moneyers in 1208', *BNJ* 59 (1989), pp. 39–45.

—— 1991. ' Moneyers in the 1130 pipe roll', *BNJ* 61 (1991), pp. 1–8.

Stewart, B. H . I. H. and Brand, J. D., 1971. 'A second find of English sterlings from Ribe (1958)', *Nordisk Numismatisk Årsskrift* 1971, pp. 38–59.

Stewartby, Lord, 1993. 'English Short-Cross coins from the Eccles hoard', *NC* 153 (1993), pp. 137–51.

—— 1994. 'The "Naxos" hoard of thirteenth-century sterlings', *NC* 154 (1994), pp. 147–66.

Sturman, C., 1989. 'Sir Joseph Banks and the Tealby Hoard', *Lincolnshire History and Archaeology* 24 (1989), pp. 51–2.

Suffolk County Council Planning Department, 1975. *East Anglian Archaeology Report No. 1. Suffolk* (1975).

Tait, J., 1936. *The Medieval English Borough* (Manchester, 1936).

Temple, E., 1976. *Anglo-Saxon Manuscripts, 900–1066* (London, 1976).

Thompson, J. D. A., 1956. *Inventory of British Coin Hoards, A.D. 600–1500*, Royal Numismatic Society Special Publication 1 (London, 1956).

Thompson, R. M. (ed.), 1980. *The Archives of the Abbey of Bury St Edmunds* (Woodbridge, 1980).

—— 1981–4. 'Obedientiaries of St Edmund's Abbey', *PSIA* 35 (1981–4), pp. 91–103.

Tibbo, G. K., 1954. 'The Organisation of the Currency, 1180–1250', unpublished MA dissertation, University of Reading, 1954.

Tout, T. F., 1905. *The History of England from the Accession of Henry III to the Death of Edward III (1216–1377)* (London, 1905).

Tymms, S., 1891. *A Handbook of Bury St. Edmunds*, 6th edn, with additions by J. R. Thompson (Bury St Edmunds and London, 1891).

Vaux, W. S. W., 1865. 'Some notes on the Eccles find of silver coins', *NC*[2] 5 (1865), pp. 219–54.

Vinogradoff, P., 1908. *English Society in the Eleventh Century* (Oxford, 1908).

Wakeford, G., 1883. 'On a hoard of early English coins of Henry I and Stephen, 1135–40', *NC*[3] 3 (1883), pp. 108–16.

Walker, D., 1984. 'A possible monetary crisis in the early 1130's', *SCMB* 795 (Nov. 1984), pp. 284–6.

—— 1985. 'Christmas 1124: end of Henry I type XIV?', *SCMB* 802 (July–Aug. 1985), pp. 232–3.

Warren, W. L., 1973. *Henry II* (London, 1973).

—— 1978. *King John,* 2nd edn (London, 1978).

—— 1984. 'The myth of Norman administrative efficiency', *THRS*[5] 34 (1984), pp. 113–32.

—— 1987. *The Governance of Norman and Angevin England, 1086–1272* (London, 1987).

Wells, W. C., 1934–7a. 'Notes on the Long Cross Coinage of Henry III, 1247–1250', *BNJ* 22 (1934), pp. 79–107.

—— 1934–7b. 'The Stamford and Peterborough mints', *BNJ* 22 (1934–7), pp. 35–77.

West, S. E., 1970–2. 'The excavation of the town defences at Tayfen Road, Bury St. Edmunds, 1968', *PSIA* 32 (1970–2), pp. 17–24.

—— 1981–4. 'A new site for the martyrdom of St. Edmund?', *PSIA* 35 (1981–4), pp. 223–5.

Whitelock, D., 1967–9. 'Fact and fiction in the legend of St Edmund', *PSIA* 31 (1967–9), pp. 217–33.

Whittingham, A. B., 1952. 'Bury St. Edmunds Abbey: the plan, design and development of the church and monastic buildings', *Archaeological Journal* 108 (1952), pp. 168–87.

—— 1971. *Bury St Edmund's Abbey* (London, 1971).

Williams, G., 1998. 'A hoard of Expanding Cross pennies from Appledore: preliminary report', *NCirc* 106 (1998), pp. 152–3.

Yates, W., 1805. *An Illustration of the Monastic History and Antiquities of the Town and Abbey of St. Edmund's Bury* (London, 1805).

York Powell, F., 1896. 'Review of English coins in the British Museum. Anglo-Saxon, I and II', *EHR* 11 (1896), pp. 759–61.

INDEX

Edward the Confessor: Morcere

BMC ii — *BMC* v — *BMC* vii — *BMC* ix — *BMC* xi

1 2 3 4 5 6

William I: Godinc

BMC xiii — *BMC* III (Canopy)

7 7A 8

Henry I

——— (Godric) (Wulfstan) Godric (Odd)o

BMC VII — *BMC* X — *BMC* XI — *BMC* XIII

9 BM (1973) Ashmolean 10 11 12

EDWARD THE CONFESSOR – HENRY I

Henry I (*cont.*): Godric
BMC XIV

Oddo

A – – A B C

a – – a b c

13 *BMC* 111 BM (1973) 14 15 16

Gilebert
BMC XV

D A B C D E

d a b c d e

17 18 19 20 21 22

Stephen: Gilebert
BMC I (Watford)

F A B C C

f a b b c

23 24 25 26 27

Stephen: Gilebert (*cont.*)
BMC 1 (Watford) (*cont.*)

D E F G H I

d e f g h i

28 29 30 31 32 [33]

Acelin — — Hunfrei Henri Oddo ?

A B C A A –

a b c a a –

[34] 35 [36] 37 38 SED 611

——— Acelin Hunfrei Acelin Hunfrei ——ric

BMC II (Cross Voided) *BMC* V1 (Cross and Piles)

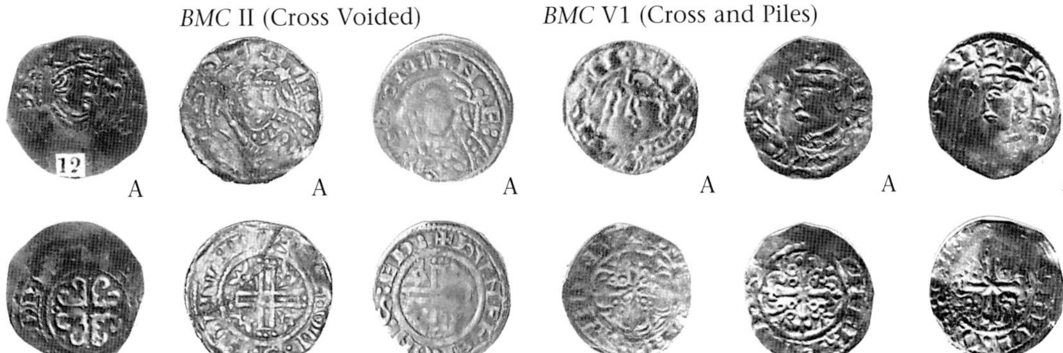

A A A A A A

a a a a a a

[39] 40 41 42 43 44

STEPHEN (cont.)

Stephen (*cont.*)

—— Acelin

BMC VI (*cont.*) *BMC* VII (Awbridge) (Gilebe?)rt Willem

A A1 A2 A3 A A

a a a a a a

45 46A 46B 46C 47 48

Henry II (Tealby): Willem

A1 A2

B A B C D

b a b b d

49 50 51 52 53

Henri

C1 C1 C2

E F F F I J

e f g h i j

54 55 56 57 58 59

STEPHEN (cont.) – HENRY II (TEALBY)

Henry II (Tealby): Henri (*cont.*)

B1 D1 D1? D3 D3?

K L M N1 N2 O

k l m m m o

60 61 62 63 63 64

Raul

E2–3 F1

P Q1 Q1 Q2 R S

p q r r r s

65 66 67 67 68 69

F2

T T V W X Y

t u v w x y

70 71 72 73 74 75

HENRY II (TEALBY) (cont.)

Henry II (Tealby): Raul (*cont.*)

F..

76 77 78 [79]

Short Cross (John): Fulke

Vb1 Vb2/1 Vb2

80 81 82 83 84 85

86 87 88 89 90 91

HENRY II (TEALBY) (cont.) – SHORT CROSS Vb2

Short Cross (John): Fulke (*cont.*)

Vb2 (*cont.*) Vc

X X X E E E

f g i f i j

92 93 94 95 96 97

Rauf

VIc1 VIc1–2 transitional/VIc2

A A B B B B

a b c d e f

98 99 100 101 102 103

VIc2

C C D D E E

g h i j k l

104 105 106 107 108 109

SHORT CROSS Vb2–VIc2

Short Cross (John): Rauf (*cont.*)
VIc2 (*cont.*)

Henry III (?): Rauf
VIc2/3

F F G E F G

m n o p q r

110 111 112 113 114 115

VIc3 VIc3/2 VIc3

G H H I I I

s s t u v w

116 117 118 119 120 121

Henry III: Rauf
VId VIIaA VIIaB

Willem
VIIaB-C1

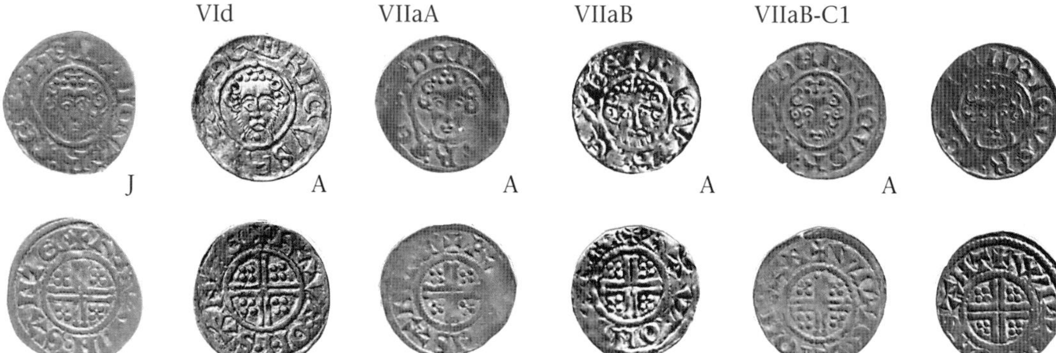

J A A A A B

x a a a a b

122 123 124 125 126 127

SHORT CROSS VIc2–VIIaB–C1

Henry III: Willem (*cont.*)
VIIaB–C1 (*cont.*) VIIaB–C2

Norman
VIIaC

128 129 130 131 132 133

134 135 136 137 138 139

140 141 142 143 144 145

SHORT CROSS VIIaB–C1–VIIaC

Henry III: Norman (*cont.*)
VIIaC (*cont.*) VIIaD

L M N O P Q

l m n o p q

146 147 148 149 150 151

VIIbA VIIbB1 Simund VIIbBx VIIbB1 (*cont.*)

R A A A B A

r a a a b a

152 153 154 155 156 157

B C D E F G

b c d e f g

158 159 160 161 162 163

SHORT CROSS VIIaC–VIIbB1

Henry III: Simund (*cont.*)

VIIbB2

A B C D E F

a b c d e f

164 165 166 167 168 169

VIIbB3

G H I J A B

g h i j a b

170 171 172 173 174 175

VIIbC

C D A B C D

c d a b c d

176 177 178 179 180 181

Henry III: Simund (*cont.*)
VIIbC (*cont.*)

182 183 184 185 186 187

VIIbD

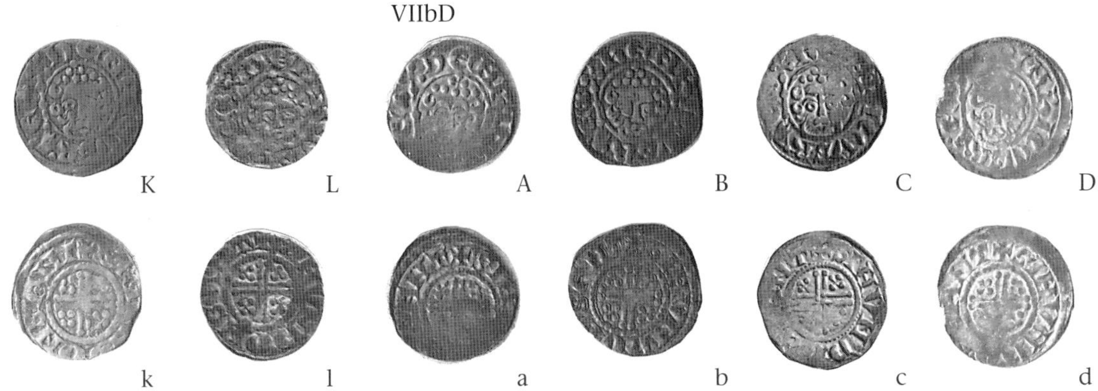

188 189 190 191 192 193

194 195 196 197 198 199

Henry III: Simund (*cont.*)

VIIbD (*cont.*) VIIcA

200 201 202 202A 203 204

VIIcB

Ioan
VIIcB (*cont.*)

205 206 206A 207 208 209

210 211 212 213 214 215

Henry III: Ioan (*cont.*)
VIIcB (*cont.*)

 H  I  J  K  L  M

 h  i  j  k  l  m

216 217 218 219 220 221

VIIcC | VIIIb1 | Ioan (as Iohan) VIIIb2

 A  B  C  A  A  B

 a  b  c  a  a  b

222 223 224 225 226 227

 C  D  E  F  G  H

 c  d  e  f  g  h

228 229 230 231 232 233

Henry III: Iohan (*cont.*)
VIIIb2 (*cont.*)

234 235 236 237 238 239

VIIIb3

240 241 242 243 244 245

246 247 248 249

SHORT CROSS VIIIb2–VIIIb3

Henry III:

—— Ion

Ib IIa IIb

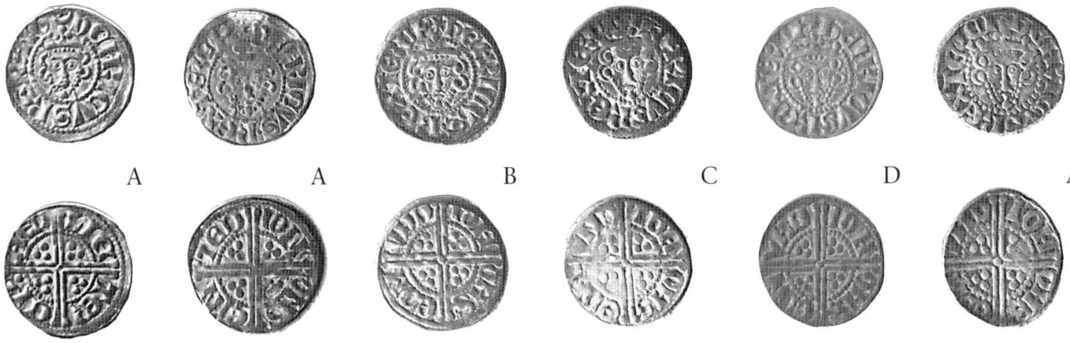

A A B C D A

a a b c d a

250 251 252 253 254 255

IIIa IIIab1

A B C D E A

a b c d e a

256 257 258 259 260 261

IIIab2 IIIac IIIb

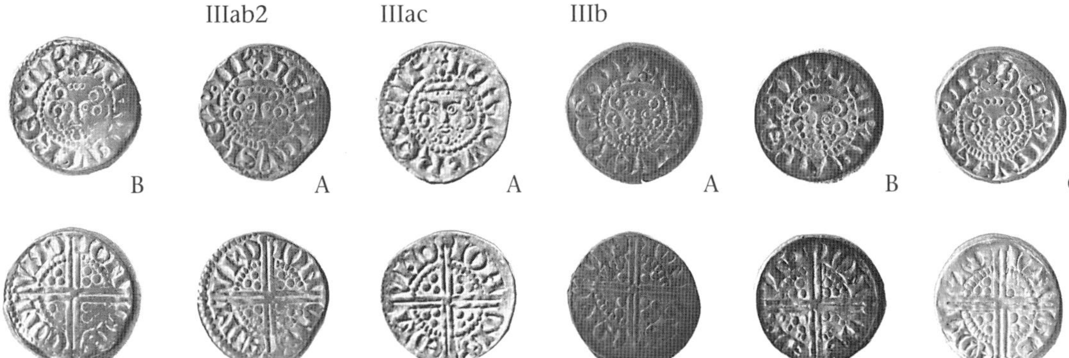

B A A A B C

b a a a b c

262 263 264 265 266 267

LONG CROSS Ib–IIIb

Henry III: Ion (*cont.*)

IIIbc IIIc

268 269 270 271 272 273

274 275 276 277 278 279

280 281 282 283 284 285

LONG CROSS IIIbc–IIIc

Henry III: Ion (*cont.*)

IIIc (*cont.*) IVab Va2

Q A A B C D

q a a b c d

286 287 288 289 290 291

Va3

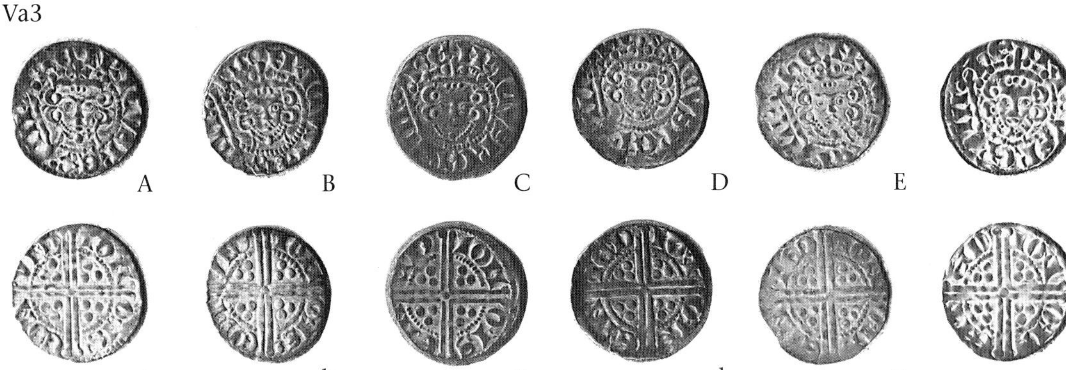

A B C D E F

a b c d e f

292 293 294 295 296 297

G H I J K L

g h i j k l

298 299 300 301 302 [303]

Henry III: Ion (*cont.*) Randulf

Va3 (*cont.*) Vb2/Va3 Vb2

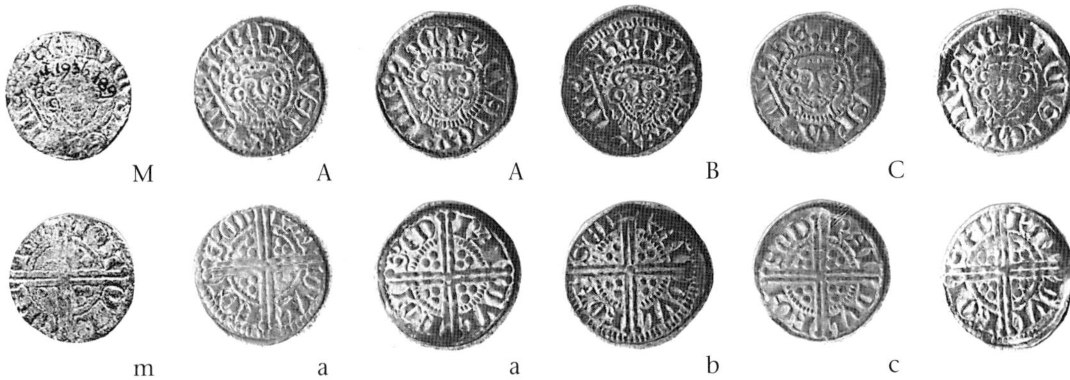

304 305 306 307 308 309

310 311 312 313 314 315

Vc Vc(x)

316 317 318 319 320 321

Henry III: Randulf (*cont.*)

Vd

A a 322

Vf

A a 323

B b 324

Renaud

Vg

A a 325

B b 326

C c 327

D d 328

E e 329

F f 330

Stephane

Vg (*cont.*)

A a 331

B b 332

C c 333

D d 334

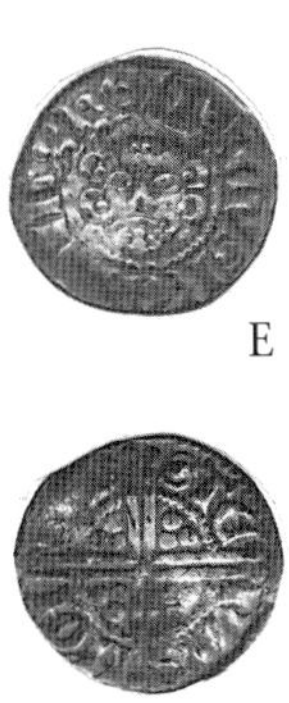

E e 335

Ion (Iohs)

Vg (*cont.*)

A a 336

B b 337

C c 338

D d 339

Henry III: Ion (Iohs) (*cont.*)

Vg | Vh

E F G H A B

e f g h a b

340 341 342 343 344 345

Henry III/ Edward 1 | Edward I

Vi | VI | VII

C D A A A B

c d a a a b

346 347 348 349 350 351

Ioce

VII (*cont.*)

A B

a b

352 353